I0831630

VOICES OF NEGRITUDE IN MODERNIST PRINT

Modernist Latitudes

MODERNIST LATITUDES

Jessica Berman and Paul Saint-Amour, Editors

Modernist Latitudes aims to capture the energy and ferment of modernist studies by continuing to open up the range of forms, locations, temporalities, and theoretical approaches encompassed by the field. The series celebrates the growing latitude ("scope for freedom of action or thought") that this broadening affords scholars of modernism, whether they are investigating little-known works or revisiting canonical ones. Modernist Latitudes will pay particular attention to the texts and contexts of those latitudes (Africa, Latin America, Australia, Asia, Southern Europe, and even the rural United States) that have long been misrecognized as ancillary to the canonical modernisms of the global North.

Barry McCrea,
In the Company of Strangers: Family and Narrative in Dickens, Conan Doyle, Joyce, and Proust, 2011

Jessica Berman,
Modernist Commitments: Ethics, Politics, and Transnational Modernism, 2011

Jennifer Scappettone,
Killing the Moonlight: Modernism in Venice, 2014

Nico Israel,
Spirals: The Whirled Image in Twentieth-Century Literature and Art, 2015

VOICES OF NEGRITUDE IN MODERNIST PRINT

Aesthetic Subjectivity, Diaspora, and the Lyric Regime

Carrie Noland

Columbia University Press New York

Columbia University Press
Publishers Since 1893
New York Chichester, West Sussex

Columbia University Press gratefully acknowledges permission to reprint the following:

Extracts from "Le temps des noyaux," "Tentative de description d'un dîner de têtes à Paris-France," and "La grasse matinée" in *Paroles* by Jacques Prévert appear by permission from Éditions Gallimard.

"Cubes" from *The Collected Poems of Langston Hughes* by Langston Hughes, edited by Arnold Rampersad with David Roessel, associate editor, copyright © 1994 by the Estate of Langston Hughes. Used by permission of Alfred A. Knopf, an imprint of Knopf Doubleday Publishing Group, a division of Random House LLC. All rights reserved. Other rights by permission of Harold Ober Associates Incorporated.

Aimé Césaire, *Cahier d'un retour au pays natal* © Présence Africaine Editions, 1956.

Léon-Gontran Damas, *Pigments-Névralgies* © Présence Africaine Editions, 1972.

The Collected Poetry by Aimé Césaire, translated by Clayton Eshleman and Annette J. Smith, © 1983 by the Regents of the University of California. Published by the University of California Press.

Excerpts of chapter 1 were previously published in Gail Hart and Anke S. Biendarra, eds., *Visions of Europe: Interdisciplinary Contributions to Contemporary Cultural Debates* (Frankfurt/M.: Peter Lang, 2014). Chapter 5 appeared in an earlier version as "Red Front / Black Front: Aimé Césaire and the Affaire Aragon," Copyright © 2006 Johns Hopkins University Press. This article was first published in *Diacritics* 36, no. 1 (Spring 2006): 64–84. Reprinted with permission by Johns Hopkins University Press. The author thanks both publishers for granting permission to reprint her work.

Library of Congress Cataloging-in-Publication Data

Noland, Carrie, 1958–

Voices of Negritude in Modernist Print: Aesthetic Subjectivity, Diaspora, and the Lyric Regime / Carrie Noland.

pages cm

Includes bibliographical references and index.

ISBN 978-0-231-16704-8 (cloth: alk. paper) —ISBN 978-0-231-53864-0 (ebook)

1. French poetry—Foreign countries—History and criticism. 2. French poetry—Black authors—History and criticism. 3. Negritude (Literary movement). 4. African diaspora in literature. 5. Book industries and trade—France—History—20th century. 6. Literature—Aesthetics. 7. Blacks in literature. 8. Modernism (Aesthetics)—France. I. Title.

PQ3897.N65 2014
840.9'896—dc23 2014013368

Mais je suis fondamentalement un poète,
quelqu'un qui se cherche et se trouve dans et par le langage.
—Aimé Césaire, Interview with Jean Pierre Salgas,
Jeune Afrique, no. 1142 (Paris, November 24, 1982), 72

Figure 0.1: Léon-Gontran Damas and Aimé Césaire at a book signing celebrating the twenty-fifth anniversary of their early work, in Martinique, 1972. Photographer unknown. Photographs and Prints Division, Schomburg Center for Research in Black Culture, The New York Public Library, Astor, Lenox, and Tilden Foundations.

CONTENTS

ACKNOWLEDGMENTS

I would like to express my gratitude to several granting agencies that made it possible for me to finish this book: the American Council of Learned Societies and the National Endowment for the Humanities jointly accorded me an ACLS/SSRC/NEH International and Area Studies Fellowship that released me from teaching during the academic year 2011–2012; the International Center for Writing and Translation and the Council of Research, Computing and Library Resources at the University of California, Irvine, supported my research trip to Martinique in 2009.

I would also like to thank the librarians and curators who helped me find the materials I needed: Diana Lachatanere and Mary Yearwood at the Schomburg Center for Research in Black Culture; Dominique Taffin at the Archives Départementales in Fort-de-France; Dominique Ozonne at the Bibliothèque Schoelcher in Fort-de-France; and a devoted librarian at the Archives d'outre-mer in Aix-en-Provence. A website is asssociated with this book where readers may find images that these librarians helped me locate: http://faculty.sites.uci.edu/aestheticsubjectivity/. Cecile Gry shared her warm home with me when I was conducting research in the South of France; Brent Hayes Edwards facilitated my research on Léon-Gontran Damas at the Schomburg Center in New York; and Vanessa Agard-Jones provided valuable information for my stay in Fort-de-France.

In Martinique, I was fortunate to befriend Alise Meuris, who took me with her on hikes through the jungle and taught me to identify some of the region's plants. Christian Lapoussinière was generous with his time. Richard and Sally Price offered me a wonderful meal in their beautiful home. I will always be grateful for their welcome and advice.

Back in the States, I gained inspiration from the musicological research of Julian Gerstin, who turned out to be a neighbor. Professor Edward Ahearn, my former teacher and mentor at Brown University, offered timely words of encouragement. A. James Arnold provided a model of scholarly generosity when he allowed me to read the edited files of his genetic edition of Aimé Césaire, *Poésie, théâtre, essais et discours* months before it was published (Éditions CNRS, 2013). Alex Gil also went out of his way to provide me with documents he had discovered during his own research trips. The conference that he organized with Kaiama Glover, Brent Edwards, and David Scott, "'The Work of Man Has Only Just Begun': Legacies of Aimé Césaire" (Columbia University, December 5–6, 2013), will remain for me an exemplary instance of democratic, open-source scholarly collaboration. Thanks as well to Jonathan Blake Fine for his translations from German of documents pertaining to performances of Césaire's *Et les chiens se taisaient.*

I have learned a great deal about poetry—and collegiality—from my longtime friends Jean-Pierre Bobillot, Barrett Watten, Carla Harryman, Richard Terdiman, Jean-Jacques Thomas, Aldon Nielsen, and Michael Davidson. I need to make a special shout-out to Roland Greene for inviting me to speak about this project during its early stages at Stanford University; the conversations I had during that visit with him, Johanna Drucker, and Peggy Phelan would prove to be extremely generative. I think Peggy, especially, will recognize how important she has been to me as she reads through these chapters. She, Ngũgĩ wa Thiong'o, and Fred Moten all gave seminars at UC Irvine that were seminal for my thinking. During my many years at Irvine, Ngũgĩ has consistently been a generous colleague and a source of much-appreciated spontaneous hugs. Fred has also shared his work and thoughts with me, for which I hope he knows I am grateful. Nick Nesbitt was a supportive reader whose work remains a touchstone for my own. Finally, a critical reader for the manuscript provided a necessary shove in the right direction. I thank him/her for exemplary honesty and circumspection.

The most wonderful part about academic life is that sometimes the people one admires become valued and faithful friends. This has certainly been the case for me. Outside and on the fringes of academic life I have enjoyed the company and support of Sally Ann Ness, Amelia Jones, Mark Franko,

Kathy Ragsdale, Michael Fuller, Victoria Bernal, Tekele Wolde-Michael, Marjorie Beale, Ève Morisi, Ann Walthall, Simon Penny, Susan Klein, and Joe McKenna. During the course of writing this book I also had the privilege of joining a new department where I established fruitful working relationships with new colleagues. Herschel Farbman gave me a really good tip at an important moment. David Pan and John Smith engaged me in fascinating conversations on Adorno and helped me to translate passages of his texts from the original German. And Gail Hart, my new Chair—well, Gail is just sensational. Thanks, also, to Jane Newman for her unflagging support. While finishing the copyediting for this book, I learned of the passing of my former colleague and Chair, the distinguished Renaissance scholar Richard Regosin. Richard's wisdom, kindness, and sense of balance sustained me through many difficult times and I will always be grateful to him.

The short-lived "Poetry and Theory Group" at UC Irvine, led by Sean Nelson, exposed me to some inspiring readings, and my last graduate seminar in French with Evan Foster, Sokrat Postoli, and Kristin Anthony was a true delight. Philip Leventhal at Columbia University Press has been a terrific editor, offering sage advice and sustained encouragement. Ron Harris and Audrey Smith were patient and considerate during the production process.

To my husband, Chris Beach, I extend my deepest love and gratitude; without you, Julian, and Francesca, the path of scholarship would be a lonely one indeed.

VOICES OF NEGRITUDE IN MODERNIST PRINT

INTRODUCTION

This book is a study of Negritude as an experimental, text-based poetic movement developed by diasporic authors of African descent during the interwar period in France through the means of modernist print culture. Each term in this description matters—"experimental," "poetic," "diasporic," and "modernist"—but perhaps none more than "text-based," since this is the aspect of Negritude that has been most frequently neglected and misunderstood. By "text-based" I mean a writing practice embedded in and determined by both the formal conditions of the print medium (spatial and typographic) and the practical entailments of modernist print media (selecting, editing, and publishing for a largely French audience). The Negritude poets—Léon-Gontran Damas (from French Guiana), Aimé Césaire (from Martinique), and Léopold Sédar Senghor (from Senegal)—deliberately wrote poems that explore the possibilities inherent to the printed textual support. The genres they chose to write in, the modes of address they employed, the rhythmic structures they adapted, and even the lexicon they enlarged were givens of the "typosphere," that uniquely modern (post-Gutenberg) world in which paper and typeface are the matter of words.[1] While several critics have read Negritude poetry as dramatizing a "crisis of the subject" torn by the negativity of a historical predicament, none has sufficiently explored the part of that crisis caused by the act of writing for print.[2]

This is not to say that Damas, Césaire, and Senghor merely inherited traditional French poetic conventions or extended preexisting avant-garde strategies; far from it. The poets of Negritude intervened in the history of written poetry in original and generative ways, some of which, as I hope to show, should revise our approach to that history. Yet by the very act of circulating their works first in "*tapuscript*" (the typescript submitted to editors), then on the pages of small reviews, and later in published collections, these poets submitted to a set of conditions identical to those that reign over all authors of published poems. The Negritude poets would be read by readers of many varieties and tendencies, some of whom might not constitute the public they sought to address. Further, their poems would be interpreted by generations of professional critics according to a host of evolving paradigms that might in turn lyricize, historicize, decontextualize, depersonalize, universalize, or racialize the speaker (as well as the author) of the poem. In short, poets of Negritude are subjects of an "aesthetic regime" in Jacques Rancière's sense: they are born into a culture that threatens to bury the living author under the disembodied architecture of his printed words.[3]

Accordingly, Negritude poets are just as concerned as other poets of the modernist period with the textual instantiation of their subjective "voice"—perhaps even more so, since they are attempting to address and bolster a diasporic community by textual means. Deeply invested in communicating a shared empirical experience, these writers find that the question of mediation—how expression is modified by textuality, how voice is performatively produced in print—cannot be avoided. Indeed, in their work, the question of mediation assumes particular urgency. Although Damas claims to have destroyed his early verses inspired by Stéphane Mallarmé in order to compose the fiercely direct *Pigments* (1937), Mallarméan concerns with the typographic instantiation of his poems are never far away from his own compositional and editorial practices. Césaire also experiments with *mise en page*, versification, and typography in ways that have hardly been assessed. Even Senghor, a less daring poet than the other two, sometimes takes on a typographical tone that evokes the experimental verse structures of Guillaume Apollinaire. All three understand the writing subject—as embodied in modernist print culture—to be far more than a mere inscription, yet something *other* than an author who directly and unproblematically speaks his own mind.

Insofar as the poets of Negritude are published writers, they express themselves neither in uniquely oral forms nor—despite what many critics have said—through the rhythms of musical genres. They participate in—

and alter—a very specific literary culture, that of the European print lyric, and this culture constitutes an evolving field of rhetorical, generic, and technological possibilities that impose historically specific demands on writers of poetry.[4] These demands transform a personal voice into a hybrid entity, a set of marks on the page that can be phenomenalized, given sensual and cognitive form in the mouth and mind of a reader. Theodor Adorno named this peculiarly textual entity an "aesthetic subjectivity," a creation of craft that is neither entirely coincident with the poet's empirical self nor an overdetermined result of the medium.[5] An "aesthetic subjectivity" is necessarily disembodied (or, rather, it is embodied as print); it is the source from which the poem seems to be emitted, a subjectivity "suspended, lyrically, in place and time."[6] No matter how closely readers and critics may identify this aesthetic subjectivity, or lyric "I," with the empirical person of the author (and such an identification has characterized readings of Negritude poetry for many years), it is not logically coherent to treat a poem circulated by the means of modernist print culture as if it were unconditioned by a history of typographic, prosodic, and generic conventions that necessarily modify, even as they transmit, the expressive impulses of the author concerned. Negritude writers as well as their readers operate within what might be called a "lyric regime," a historical epoch dating from the Romantic period onward during which printed poems with first-person speakers generate peculiar problems for reception and interpretation.

As I will argue in greater detail throughout this book, Negritude writers present a challenge to both form-based (deconstructive) theories and identity-based theories of poetic representation. On the one hand, they insist on the "blackness" of their writing—that is, they express a desire for their poems to be identified by readers as having been written by black writers (although "black" is defined differently by each).[7] To this extent, they affirm the continuity of the author with the poem's speaker. Yet, on the other, they develop a highly idiosyncratic style nurtured not only by regional or native languages but also by the combinatory possibilities of modernist print, a historically specific written idiom that they share with other text-based poets, most of whom have no direct link to Africa or the Caribbean. Césaire may claim, for instance, that he racializes written French ("I have always striven to create a new language, one capable of communicating the African heritage"[8]), but it remains the case that the medium he used is a disembodied one, and that, accordingly, his blackness must be conveyed through textual rhythms, rhetorical figures, and a subject position that is performative as well as constative, animated by a reader (of whatever color, age, gender, or class) while reflective of a concrete historical being. Although it is often taken for granted that Césaire "speaks" in his poems, this speaking takes place in the form of marks in space, a circumstance of which the Martiniquan poet is well aware and to which he repeatedly draws our attention.[9] Negritude poets in general tend to thematize the mediation of writing, most likely because mediation, or distance from one's public or one's fellow citizens, is a source of anguish and regret.

Studying the reception conditions of nineteenth-century French—rather than twentieth-century francophone—poetry, Jacques Rancière has maintained that the disembodiment resulting from typographical remediation has the effect in general of attenuating the author's connection to a living public.[10] By virtue of the fact that Césaire, Senghor, and Damas are writers (members of the typosphere, and thus by definition "modernist"), they risk losing a connection to the very community they claim to speak for or long to represent. They are unable to enjoy, in other words, what Rancière calls "the immediacy of the ethical regime," a state of total communion between audience and speaker putatively available to preliterate communities in which "all bodies directly embody the sense of the common."[11] Rancière's allusion to embodiment ("all bodies directly embody the sense of the common") is highly pertinent to the case of Negritude poetry in which references to the body—as well as communion—abound. (One need merely recall the Noël episode in the *Cahier d'un retour au pays natal*; or "Solde," Damas's famous poem on mimicry and embodiment; or Senghor's evocation of shared song in "Que m'accompagnent kôras et balafong.") In the Western imaginary that Rancière evokes, communion is associated with the presence of multiple bodies in a single space while embodied expressive practices such as dancing and chanting are the forms in which such communion takes place. Not surprisingly, dancing and chanting are also the figures Negritude poets evoke as analogies for their own writing, while the speaker's body is the site upon which the drama of communion is played out. It is no accident that each of the three major poets of Negritude gravitates toward a performance genre as a model for poetic practice: Césaire hesitates between lyric and dramatic forms; Damas shapes his lines around calypso and the blues; and Senghor imagines live instrumental accompaniment for the recitation of his verses. Paradoxically, though, live performance is often associated in their works with performing—that is, with stylizing the self for an audience or even impersonating what one is not.

The more skeptical among us may suspect that the state of ethical communion, the mass embodiment of a shared understanding, that Rancière describes (and to which, at moments, our poets seem to aspire) never actually existed or could exist. The fantasy of a perfect Greek demos, or a homogeneous ritual community, is, after all, a topos of the French and German philosophical tradition.[12] Still, Rancière's distinction between typosphere and orasphere—or a modern print society and a premodernist oral one—does bear some weight. As Édouard Glissant observes in *L'intention poétique*, the physical proximity created by a circle of spectators grouped around an oral poet produces a unique experience of intimacy, one that is not available to readers of the printed word (who enjoy a different variety of intimacy, as we shall see). According to Glissant, the organ of print produces an alternative "orality," one in which a displaced "voice" is "multiplied throughout the world."[13] This voice is animated by readers far beyond the range of the writer's own vocal apparatus; it is thus primarily the eye that sounds what Rancière eloquently terms a "*parole muette*." And yet it is important to note that the link between reading and hearing, the poet's body and that of his reader, is not entirely severed despite the intervention of print. The reading eye is connected to a sonorous body, just as the print on the page bears testimony to the embodied existence of a writer in time. Recalling that embodiment, even if—or more strongly, *because*—it has been remediated—is an important element of the practice of reading as cognition, or at least an important element for our purposes insofar as it is one upon which Negritude writers implicitly rely. Much of their innovative practice is born of a desire to render printed words percussive and palpable, to make the text into a cavity that resonates where the author's voice cannot. While this is true to some extent for all poets, the desire to make the text resonate with a physical presence takes on a particular pathos—and political valence—in the case of Negritude.

Negritude poets struggle with the demands of their time—to speak for and produce solidarity among the silenced peoples of African descent, to represent the singularity of their own region, and to testify to the peculiarities of their individual lived experience as *assimilés*. Their struggle takes place in the field of modernist print culture, that is, in an equally time-bound, modernist way. Similar to other poets of the modernist generation, Negritude poets follow a pattern of modernist publication: they publish first in ephemeral (and often politically contestatory) reviews, then in more conventional literary reviews with a larger circulation, then in anthologies and translations, and finally in single-author volumes, or "*recueils*." Césaire, Damas, and Senghor are all sensitive to the ironies of a situation in which writing and publishing engage them in the very networks of distribution that threaten to contain the radicality of their intervention (if only because such networks confine them to a reading public of a particular kind). Desiring at once to be writers who speak *through* a craft and subjects who speak *for* a "race," Negritude poets confront the problems inherent to a specific medium that can never be an unambiguous or direct conduit for self-expression or political change. As Melvin Dixon has observed, they publish poems "for intercultural consumption."[14] The publication venues they found—or created—provided a field in which to explore the relationship between a personal crisis and a shared historical condition, self-expression and the rules of a craft, a deeply felt connection to what Senghor called "Black values" and an equally strong identification with other poets as poets *tout court*.[15] It should be acknowledged, then, that the challenges posed by writing for print—indeed, by aesthetic practice in general—are by no means incidental to diasporic experience. Because Negritude poets explore the constructive process of subjectivation in writing (as well as the alienation from collective experience that writing entails), their poetry remains a rich resource for thinking through the antinomies of being a diasporic artist in an age of mechanical reproduction.

Negritude may be seen to stand at the cusp, then, between two distinct moments in the evolution of poetics, exemplifying for some the depersonalization and disembodiment that occurs in an "aesthetic regime" while ushering in for others a new valuation of the author and his or her presence in the text. To a large extent, the way in which printed words are received by readers is a function of the history of criticism (as well as the history of technology): different reading communities construct the author–text relation in different ways. As a result of the many challenges to deconstructive reading practices that have emerged in the past few decades (challenges launched by feminism, ethnic studies, queer studies, postcolonial theory, and the "new phenomenology"), there now exist a number of ways to understand the threat of disembodiment posed by the printed "I"—as a slight but inevitable depersonalization that merely stylizes the identifiable voice of an empirical person, or, at the other extreme, as a significant deconstruction of subjective agency (even of the coherence of the subject itself) integral to and coincident with the act of writing.

The first understanding is shared by lyric theorists invested in the possibility—no matter how slim—of subjective expression, those who believe that a real voice, real emotions, and real intentions lie behind and can be discerned in the words on the page. In the field of comparative poetics, Susan Stewart has offered the most recent and, I believe, most compelling case for considering the lyric poem as at once an act of intersubjective communication and a highly formal affair.[16] Similar to other theorists who have reacted against the hypostatization of literary language (or the "personification" of the text), Stewart reinvokes "voice" as a salient category, arguing that the lyric relation—in which an embodied reader confronts an alphabetic "I"—should be treated as a "face-to-face encounter" and that poetry (hardly a "mute word") may be "encountered with and through our entire sensuous being."[17] Likewise, Jahan Ramazani, in *A Transnational Poetics*, keeps "one eye on poetry's luminous singularities and the other on global flows and circuits" with the presumption that the poem conveys the ("transnational") experience of a situated author to a reader able to feel between the lines.[18]

In France a parallel development has occurred in the area of poetry criticism. The linguistic-deconstructive turn of the 1960s and 1970s perhaps inevitably ushered in a "return" to the "lyric," a genre that represented to many poets and poetry scholars something other than a failed or diverted communication (or a field of unauthored signifying play). Over the past thirty years, French poetry studies has become an immensely rich field (although it remains practically unknown to poetry scholars in the American academy and receives scant attention from scholars of francophone literature). Rather than attempt to summarize that field here, I will instead evoke a few relevant points concerning the nature of the first-person, subject-centered poem that have been made in the course of what might be called "the lyric wars" of the past decades. Defining the "lyric" in ways that should resonate with the qualities of the poetry we will be studying in this book, proponents of the *nouveau lyrisme* identify the lyric genre with a specific form of enunciation (the first person); a specific way of organizing words on a page (in verses or *versets* of whatever length); and a specific type of rhetorical content (most often comparison, metaphor, and prosopopeia). The French critic Laurent Jenny, much like Stewart, has suggested in his rehearsal of recent debates in France that the lyric poem is consistently defined as "an act of communication between the poet and his reader."[19] But the assumption here—not just that the "poet" is male but also that "he" speaks in the lyric poem—may be understood in a variety of ways. The "I" in the poem may be read as the "autobiographical I," the "figure of the empirical author"; as the poet engaged in articulating the self's "alterity," its difference from that empirical identity; or as a universal or general subject, a "nous inclusif" (an inclusive we).[20] Reluctant to jettison the cogent critique of authorial intention (and lyric expressivity) advanced in the latter half of the twentieth century, proponents of the *nouveau lyrisme* nonetheless tend to cling to the notion of "voice." Extending a voice in print represents for these critics an ethical gesture; print promises phatic contact. To write "I," then, is implicitly to search for relation, even across the barrier of the page.

Approaching the issue of authorial voice from a different angle, recent work in francophone postcolonial studies has also tended to reject the most extreme of deconstruction's formulations (the "death of the author"), indicating instead the ways in which the poem's speaker remains proximate to an empirical person or, in some cases, an ethnic collective, regional population, or language group. Scholars focusing on the francophone world have accomplished a good deal: they have opened up the canon; questioned the putative universality of "theory"; and shifted the frame from national literatures to regional networks. However, one thing they have *not* done is present a compelling poetics, a theory and method for reading poems. (Conversely, French poetry criticism has neglected to provide a poetics of the *raced* lyric subject.) What remains to be explored is the impact of racial identification on lyric production and the impact of modernist textuality on the representation of race.[21] Negritude authors demand that we attend to many contexts at once (colonialism *and* modernism; the Black Atlantic *and* the Parisian avant-garde; racial identity *and* the lyric construction of the self) while never letting our eyes stray from the page. To do their work justice, we must integrate a wide variety of approaches, some of which might seem incompatible at first. As Simon Gikandi has cogently argued, Caribbean writers respond to conditions utterly different from those encountered by their Anglo-European modernist peers, practicing a "contramodernity" that forces us to redefine what modernity in literature might be.[22] Yet it is also clear that Caribbean writers are full-fledged members of the typosphere, and that, accordingly, they confront as a primary condition of authorship their engagement in a print culture shared—in real material terms—with their Anglo-European modernist peers. By placing critics of the lyric in conversation with theorists of the Black Atlantic, and by juxtaposing scholarship on transnational (or "global") modernism with scholarship on French poetry, I hope to contribute to a more robust account of how poetics and politics, word craft and representation, intertwine.

Negritude poets wrote and published in French, and this fact allowed them to participate in a print culture that arguably dominated all others throughout the Western world. As Pascale Casanova has pointed out, "each author is ineluctably situated first in the global field of literary production according to the position that that author's own national literary space occupies within it"—and for Casanova, a national literary space, like a nation, is based on a common national language.[23] "That is why," she continues, "when we seek to characterize a writer, we must situate him twice over: according to the position his national literature holds within the global literary universe, and according to the position which the author occupies within that national literature."[24] Casanova's observation suggests that by writing in French, the Negritude poets were immediately able to assume a prominent place in the global literary field of their time—simply by virtue of writing in French—even if their status within their own national literature was precarious. This is not to say that they chose French solely in order to propel themselves into the literary limelight (although professional preoccupations would naturally play a part in any writer's decision). Rather, given their choice of métier, writing in French would have presented itself as inevitable since French was the language (among those available to them) with the most developed tradition of poetry in print.

All this seems fairly logical, and yet the choice of French was also ideologically charged in a way that Casanova's treatment tends to neglect. It may have been clear to Césaire, Damas, and Senghor that to write for print necessitated that one write in French, but that has not stopped them from being the target of reproach. The allegation that Negritude poets failed their people by writing in French has plagued their reception for decades; consequently, it is worth spending a moment on this prickly but fundamental issue before moving on. Why, indeed, did Negritude poets choose to write not just in French but in an impeccable French? Although they attacked French colonialism and its policy of cultural assimilation, they did not fundamentally deform the language of colonial rule.[25] Despite Césaire's claim to have "inflected" French (or to have "cannibalized" it), his poetry exhibits both a respect for and a mastery over the most complex grammatical forms and erudite vocabularies imaginable.[26] Not only Césaire but also Senghor, Damas, and Negritude's successor, Édouard Glissant, all write in an impeccably elegant French only occasionally enriched by Creole words or Serer-inspired turns of phrase. As opposed to writers such as the Kenyan novelist Ngũgĩ wa Thiong'o or, closer to home, the Martiniquan poet and novelist Raphaël Confiant, the Negritude poets never—even at the end of their careers—published works in the languages exclusive to their respective regions.

Arguably, the first great work of literature to emerge from a French colony (or an overseas department) could have been written in Creole; it could have advocated for a national (rather than a racial) identity; and it could have focused on regional themes. Instead, the first great work was in French; it advanced a Pan-African black ("nègre") identity; and it focused on transcontinental connections. Césaire's *Cahier d'un retour au pays natal* defines its "original geography" as "*la carte du monde*" (the map of the world); it measures solidarity "*au compas de la souffrance*" (with the compass of suffering); and it unfolds its complex imagery in a beautifully modulated lyric language. In a lucid rendering, F. Abiole Irele indicates why this might have been so:

> The dispersal of millions of Africans over a period of some three hundred years all over America, without regard to their primary ties and dispositions, had the effect of creating black communities in the New World. Separated as they were from the mother continent, their ethnic and in some respects cultural peculiarities took on in the general consciousness a significance that was related in an immediate way to the fact of race, and became directly associated with Africa. . . . We owe the unified concept of Africa to these communities who collectively form what has come to be known as the "Black Diaspora."[27]

As Irele points out, the idea of Africa as a unifying concept was an invention of the diaspora belying the fact that, over those three hundred years, both Africa and the populations displaced from Africa had undergone further creolization and individuation, bringing into being communities as diverse (and culturally rich) as they were similar (rooted in a shared past of slavery and colonial rule).[28] However, the post–World War I generation—the first to gain access to the resources of modernist print culture—clearly needed to privilege general affinities (rather than underscore regional particularities) for political reasons. Recent studies by Brent Hayes Edwards and Gary Wilder have confirmed that the dominant preoccupation of francophone and anglophone blacks during the interwar period (and until well into the mid-1960s) was coalition building, the weaving together of diverse orientations as opposed to the aggressive furthering of a single one.[29] Among diasporic and African blacks, a cultural politics—that is, the belief that cultural practices can have political consequences—very decidedly existed, giving birth to numerous reviews, presses, and colloquia that changed the face of modernism and modernity (and that continue to inform the existential conditions of millions today).[30] Negritude authors understood clearly that the most lasting impact they could have was to follow the path forged by Sterling Brown, Langston Hughes, and Jacques Roumain, respected diasporic writers who published in English or French in an attempt to reach out to a Pan-African (rather than regional) audience.[31] Indifferent to this context, the Créolistes famously accused Césaire, in particular, of having failed to contribute to the creation of a "littérature créole d'expression créole."[32] It is true, he did not (and neither did Damas); but the accusation should strike one as anachronistic, given that the only author publishing poetry in Martiniquan Creole at the time (before it was called "Kreyol"), Gilbert Gratiant, was obliged to invent a written form to address regional themes, a practice that was hardly congruent with either the Pan-African political agenda or the aesthetic project of Negritude writers.[33]

As aspiring writers, the choice of French was clear. The question remains, however, why they chose to *write* at all—that is, why they elected to bend their verbal skills to the production of literature rather than orature. The answer, of course, has a great deal to do with the educational policy of the French colonial administration and the conviction that educators sought to impress upon colonial subjects (as well as the black citizens of the four Communes of Senegal) that literacy was, as Frantz Fanon put it, "the key able to open doors which, fifty years earlier, forbade access."[34] As is well known, the elementary and middle schools in the French Antilles and French Africa promulgated a hierarchy that valued writing over oral performance; French over local languages; and—last but not least—poetry over prose. This hierarchy would have inevitably predisposed the Negritude poets to make the choices they made. It might even be an exaggeration to call these "choices," given that obtaining social distinction (and therefore the power to determine one's own life) depended largely on accepting the terms of this cultural hierarchy as they were imposed from without.

In *Decolonising the Mind: The Politics of Language in African Literature*, Ngũgĩ wa Thiong'o has provided a sensitive account of colonial educational conditions as they existed in British-controlled Kenya. Although Ngũgĩ writes with the British colonial system in view, his description illuminates the situation of French colonial subjects quite well. Ngũgĩ makes several points pertinent to the cases of Césaire, Damas, and Senghor.[35] He observes, for instance, that in the colonial environment, language choice takes on a highly charged symbolic significance. Mastery of the local language—or even of several local languages—does not count as symbolic capital, whereas an ability to manipulate the language of the colonizer is a mark of superior cognitive skills, promising successful assimilation into the imposed culture.[36] As Ngũgĩ notes, the colonial language policy is part of a larger campaign to belittle the local/regional culture and thus to discourage resistance: "The biggest weapon wielded and actually daily unleashed by imperialism against that collective defiance (of the oppressed and exploited) is the cultural bomb," he writes. "The effect of a cultural bomb is to annihilate a people's belief in their names, in their languages, in their environment, in their heritage of struggle, in their unity, in their capacities and ultimately in themselves."[37] What makes it so difficult to eradicate this campaign against the indigenous culture, he adds, is that the colonial administration mobilizes the intellectual class to perpetuate the "annihilation" of the people's belief in themselves. Convinced that English (or French) is the superior, more literary language, indigenous writers publish in that language and thus implicitly fortify its symbolic value, enriching the tradition of the colonial culture and impoverishing their own.

Léopold Senghor could be accused of falling into precisely the trap Ngũgĩ describes. Famously, the Senegalese poet privileged French over Serer and Wolof, circulating the notion that African languages were not up to the task of articulating complex concepts: "Emotion is Negro [*nègre*], as reason is Greek [*hellène*]," his motto goes.[38] When asked point blank in 1954 why he wrote in French, he formulated this response:

> "Why do you write in French?" . . . Because if we feel as Negros [*nègres*], we nonetheless express ourselves in French, because French is a universal language [*une langue à vocation universelle*] and we address our message to the French of France as well as other men, because French is 'a language of gentility and candor' [*une langue 'de gentillesse et d'honnêteté'*]. . . . French is a great organ that lends itself to all timbres, all effects, from the most subtle sweetnesses to the thundering of the storm. French can be flute, oboe, trumpet, tom-tom, and even canon fire. And then French has also given us the gift of its abstract words—so rare in our maternal languages—where tears are transformed into precious stones. In our [maternal] languages, words are naturally surrounded by a halo of sap and blood.[39]

What is surprising here is not so much that Senghor considers French the language of diplomacy and good citizenship ("*de gentillesse et d'honnêteté*"), or even that he disparages maternal languages for lacking abstract, philosophical terms. These are sentiments typical of the time. Rather, the odd thing is that Senghor seems to believe the French language capable of articulating *everything*, not just the timbre of the organ but also the beat of the "tom-tom." However, this is not a position Senghor maintained earlier. In "Le problème culturel en A.O.F.," a speech given in 1937, the year Damas's *Pigments* was published, Senghor states that French is in fact *not* capable of communicating all the soundscapes and experiences to which a colonial subject is exposed: "There is a certain flavor, a certain scent, accent, and dark timbre [*timbre noir*] inexpressible by means of European instruments."[40] Anticipating Ngũgĩ, he advocates the composition of poems, "*contes*," and dramas in the indigenous African languages but stops short of according orature the same status as the written word.

Senghor's attitude in 1937 was, for the most part, shared by Césaire and Damas. That is, the young Senghor, only a few years after his arrival from Dakar, still experienced conflicts between his African upbringing and his Parisian education, the "dark timbre" of Serer and the "great organ" of French. If we are to credit the sentiments his persona expresses in early poems such as "In Memoriam," "Neige sur Paris" (Snow in Paris), "Aux tirailleurs Sénégalais morts pour la France" (To the Senegalese soldiers who died for France), and "Je suis seul" (I am alone), the young Senghor felt both anger and alienation as he tried to come to terms with French culture and his place within it. "Seigneur," he writes in "Neige sur Paris," "je ne sortirai pas ma réserve de haine, je le sais, pour les diplomates qui montrent leurs canines longues / Et qui demain troqueront la chair noire" (Lord, I know I'll never release this reserve of hatred / For diplomats who show their long canine teeth / And tomorrow trade in black flesh).[41] His later embrace of universalism, as well as his association of French with that universalism (due to its supposedly superior capacity to express all "timbres"), appears somewhat at odds with his frequently stated desire to "baign[er] dans une présence africaine" (bathe in an African presence) (in his poem "Intérieur").[42] In fact, at times Senghor could be very clear that unique aspects of his homeland could not be seized by the French language. For instance, he added a "*lexique*," or glossary, to the Seuil edition of his *Oeuvre poétique*, noting that African words appeared in his poems not to "faire de l'exotisme pour l'exotisme" (to be exotic for the sake of being exotic) but rather to be accurate: the African words simply could not be replaced by French ones. "I will add that I write, first of all, for my people. And my people know that a *kôra* is not a harp any more than a balafon is a piano."[43] Senghor's own practice thus contradicts the statements he made (perhaps for a largely French audience) in 1954; indeed, of all Negritude poets, Senghor had the most reason to distrust the claim that French is a "universal" language, having been raised, like Ngũgĩ, in a community rich with local customs, religions, and languages possessing highly developed vehicles of artistic expression.

More than thirty years before the publication of *Decolonising the Mind*—but in the context of a different colonial history—Frantz Fanon had already pointed out that the acquisition of the colonizer's language could have pathological consequences. In the first chapter of *Peau noire, masques blancs*, titled "Le Noir et le langage," Fanon maintains that speaking the language of the colonizer entails far more than mastering a different grammar; it entails "assuming a culture, bearing the weight of a civilization."[44] Not only the black Antillean, he says, but "all colonized peoples" suffer from a kind of "entombment" of their original culture—"la mise au tombeau de l'originalité culturelle locale."[45] Yet the case of the black Antillean is somewhat different from that of the African, Fanon nuances; whereas the African who speaks Wolof or Peuhl may acknowledge the existence of "works" ("de véritables ouvrages")[46]—and Fanon does not specify whether these "works" are oral or written, musical or verbal—in these native languages, the Antillean is taught to believe that nothing substantial has ever been created in Creole, that the "patois" belongs to no culture (and certainly no civilization). For Fanon, this is a more severe version of the colonial pathology Ngũgĩ describes, involving as it does a denial of the existence (rather than a subordination) of any creative activity not conducted in French.

If Fanon is representing in "Le Noir et le langage" a general attitude, one shared by the educated elite of Césaire's and Damas's generation, then it is easy to see why their meeting with Senghor was so critical to the development of Negritude. At the very least, as a Sénégalais, Senghor had access to "works" other than those written in French; he could share with the Antilleans his pride in things African even if he could not turn them toward the culture they—as Antilleans—already had. It is no wonder, then, given Fanon's account, that the two diasporic writers sought legitimation in African roots rather than an Antillean past, for this past provided (they thought) no previous examples of "works" in the medium they valued.[47]

There is perhaps no need to belabor the point, for Césaire has repeatedly made it himself. Yet there is one last element of the situation worth recalling. In his diagnosis of the blacks' relation to language, Fanon alludes to the tendency of colonial writers to write in an exaggeratedly elaborate French: "We often find that Antillians, when entering the upper echelons we've been describing, tend to search out linguistic subtleties, rare words [*des subtilités, des raretés du langage*]; these are so many ways of proving themselves adequate."[48] Fanon is obviously thinking of Césaire here, a poet whose attraction to *le mot rare* has been noted by many. Jean-Jacques Thomas, for instance, has suggested along the same lines that recourse to an erudite vocabulary was Césaire's way to prove himself a better master of the French language than the French master himself. I believe, however, that there is a good deal more involved. All the explanations that have been offered for the adoption of French—from Senghor's contention that French offers "abstractions" where "maternal" languages do not, to Ngũgĩ's and Fanon's contention that using French is a symptom of colonial oppression—implicitly define the indigenous, maternal, or Creole language as a more immediate, accurate, and intimate vehicle for lived experience. For Senghor, the indigenous languages of Africa have a "halo of sap and blood"; they are languages consecrated by flesh, capable of relaying embodied experience. Likewise, for Fanon, the Martiniquan "*Umwelt*" is more readily accessible when shared in Creole.[49] From their perspective, the search for "des subtilités, des raretés du langage" can have nothing to do with the expressive potential of these "raretés."[50] Rather, for them, an author's verbal pyrotechnics must be a sign of his colonial subjection, his desire to prove that he is "adequate" to the foreign culture he bears.

But what if the "raretés du langage" introduced by the poet are valued precisely because they are *not* part of the everyday, supposedly more immediate discourse? Without displacing Ngũgĩ's and Fanon's accounts—which clearly possess explanatory power and historical pertinence—I still hope to qualify them, for it seems to me that the dichotomy they maintain between original and imposed, immediate and alienating, may not be entirely adequate to the writer's experience of colonial bilingualism. It is with this in mind that I want to return to Ngũgĩ's biographical narrative of language acquisition in Kenya—and to his general claims concerning the native language—before moving on to the case of Césaire in particular.

Although describing different contexts, Fanon and Ngũgĩ both provide insight into the psychic schism created by early exposure to two linguistic lifeworlds. Fanon is relatively silent on the issue of childhood and maternal language acquisition, but Ngũgĩ makes clear that the division between the two linguistic spheres corresponds to the division between two spaces: the domestic and the institutional. So strict are the boundaries between linguistic worlds that each one becomes a distinct epistemology, a way of knowing, a conduit to—and an index of—a specific order of psychic experience. In an autobiographical moment, Ngũgĩ describes this epistemological predicament, one brought on by the system of imposed (and hierarchical) bilingualism. I summarize his account below because it illustrates perfectly an assumption shared by many critics and writers, namely, that a colonial subject's apprehension of the world is not only divided between two languages but also between two levels of mediation. According to this account, the first language (the "maternal" language) is the concrete, sensual language in immediate contact with lived experience (full of "sap"), while the other (the language of the colonizer) is abstract and cerebral, forever divorced from the deepest, most visceral content of psychic existence. Ngũgĩ's example concerns his introduction to the subject of anatomy and reveals in succinct form the dichotomies between immediate and mediated, sensual and cerebral, oral and written that I would like to address.

At grammar school, Ngũgĩ recounts, he learned about anatomy by studying the organs of large mammals in science class and reading the English names for each one in a book. Around the same age, he also became acquainted with animal anatomy by observing the slaughter and dissection of sacrificial goats in preparation for a seasonal ritual. Here he heard the Gikuyu names as he handled the animal's liver, kidneys, and intestines; thus, these names were fused with tactile, olfactory, and visual sensations rendered sharper and more memorable by their novelty. In contrast, the understanding he gained in school was schematic and disembodied; the substantives he memorized were abstract, each one referring to entire categories of phenomena rather than specific, sensually experienced organs of a still warm body. In the first case, words were embedded in a stream of personal existence; in the second, they were introduced as written signs.[51]

Ngũgĩ's description of a doubled experience of reality, a kind of psycholinguistic schism, has been treated at length by Maghrebian writers as well; in fact, the crisis caused by colonial bilingualism is a theme frequently found in the works of Abdelkebir Khatibi, Assia Djebar, and others. What stands out in Ngũgĩ's account—and what makes the African and Caribbean diasporic experience somewhat different from the North African—is that, during the period with which we are concerned, neither Gikuyu nor Martiniquan Creole possessed a stable scribal form.[52] In contrast, the Arabic language has a textual tradition reaching back to at least the seventh century. This point goes a long way toward explaining the supposed "choice" of the Negritude writer (although there were several more factors involved). For black writers of sub-Saharan Africa and the Antilles, it must have seemed as though the language of the colonizer were the only one that offered a script (not to mention an entire *dispositif* of editors, presses, reviews, and readerships) with which to indulge their love of writing. In interviews, whenever Césaire was asked why he chose French over Creole, he would reply that the absence of a formalized writing system for the Creole language was, for him, decisive. In a famous interview with Jacqueline Leiner in 1978, for instance, he explains again—with no small measure of exasperation—that for him, writing equals French. Writing in Creole was simply never an option:

> But neither Ménil nor I would have been capable of writing in Creole. I already mentioned the Martiniquan cultural lag; that's precisely what I'm talking about, a kind of cultural lag at the level of language. Creole was extremely *low* [*bas*], if you will. It remains—and this was even more the case back then—at the level of immediacy; it is incapable of rising to the level of abstraction? [*sic*] That's why I wonder

> if such a work [as the *Cahier*] would have been conceivable in Creole. . . . Creole was uniquely a spoken language [*une langue orale*], which, by the way, still remains to be fixed in written form. . . . If we had written in Creole, nobody would have understood a word.
>
> . . . French is the language in which I have always *written* [*écrit*]; I never imagined, even for a second, that I could have written in any other language, that's all!"[53]

To a certain extent, Césaire's comments simply invert the terms of Ngũgĩ's account. For Ngũgĩ, the putative immediacy of the "*langue maternelle*" makes it an appropriate vehicle for the expression of authentic, grounded experience; for Césaire that same immediacy makes it "incapable of rising to the level of abstraction" (an idea he probably borrowed from Senghor). In both cases the "indigenous" language represents immediacy; the colonial language, mediation. Yet two points distinguish one author from the other. First of all, Césaire embraces what he believes to be the nonimmediacy, or "abstraction," of French. For reasons not unlike those motivating Khatibi (or Samuel Beckett, for that matter) Césaire cherishes the distance that writing—and writing in French—affords. That is, he seems to seek a different relationship to the language in which he writes, one that results in a heightened sensitivity to language *as object*, as aural, graphemic, and rhetorical phenomenon, rather than language as transparent vehicle, capable of "properly reflect[ing] or imitat[ing] the real life of this community."[54] If Césaire uses an unusual number of what Fanon calls "des raretés du langage," it is not simply to impress upon others his erudition but also—and, I believe, more symptomatically—to sound the full range of his instrument. For Ngũgĩ (and increasingly for Fanon), contributing to a national literature is paramount, for such a literature might function as a form of political representation in the cultural realm. For Césaire, in contrast, representation is not necessarily the goal. In fact, whenever he feels called upon to serve as a representative for others, Césaire expresses a good deal of ambivalence by raising the specter of an ineradicable gulf between the life of the people—"à côté de son cri"—and the experience of the poet, similarly alienated but *assimilé*.

Such a note of ambivalence is clearly sounded in a preface Césaire wrote to the 1996 reprint of Gilbert Gratiant's *Fables créoles et autres écrits*, a work explicitly concerned with the poet's role as representative or spokesperson for "the folk." At first, Gratiant earns Césaire's praise. As the first poet to create a scribal complement for Creole, he is to be commended for his effort to capture the spirit of Creole, for communing with its "Stimmung," its "génie," its "*sève*" (sap—Senghor's word).[55] But then Césaire intimates that this Heideggerian Stimmung may be in part an invention, a fantasy projected by the intellectual, who knows the "*petit peuple*" from a distance and therefore cannot, despite his good intentions, become one with a community he has left behind: "Curious, in truth, is the relation between Gilbert Gratiant and the Creole language. Gilbert Gratiant," Césaire clarifies, "was certainly not a Creole-speaker as one might imagine. Actually, he had little occasion to use it." Finally, Césaire adds (somewhat impishly) that Gratiant, having left Martinique at the age of ten to study in Vendôme, spoke Creole "à la française, and yet, he wrote it superbly. . . . Gratiant was less a Creole user than a Creole inventor."[56]

What Césaire suggests here is worth underscoring, for it introduces a distinction that will be crucial to his work. Gratiant *writes* Creole, he does not speak it, and writing Creole places him in a category all his own—somewhere between being a writer (and belonging to a community of writers) and being a Martiniquan (belonging to a community exposed to Creole). Gratiant's position, as Césaire recognizes, is a somewhat perverse one, for while claiming to capture the Creole Stimmung, he ends up isolating himself completely, writing a language that he alone knows how to read and write. This is what Césaire means by a "curious" relation to Creole, a relation that he obviously does not emulate. Without saying so directly, Césaire intimates that Gratiant was laboring under an illusion when he imagined the possibility of maintaining complete harmony with "the people," just as it was impossible, as Fanon himself recognized, for any *assimilé* to deassimilate himself (or herself). Not only had years of advanced education removed Gratiant and the Negritude writers from the *Umwelt* of their birthplace, but the act of writing itself would have introduced a new way of being toward and with the community. The fact that writing is a unique way of being in the world is true to some extent for any writer, but it is even more so for a diasporic writer whose original community—or at least many members of it—cannot read the words he places on the page. This brings us to the second point that differentiates Ngũgĩ from the Negritude poets. Whereas Ngũgĩ learned to write in Gikuyu at an early age and a readership for books in Gikuyu (at least the Christian Bible) existed when he began writing, the parallel case cannot be made for the French Caribbean. Césaire and Damas did not learn to write Creole in school. During their most fertile years, no consistent scribal form of Creole existed, and the illiteracy rate in the region was roughly 90 percent. In the 1978 interview with Leiner, Césaire underscores that a work written in Creole in 1939 would not have been any more accessible to the Martiniquan people than a work written in French: "If we had written in Creole, nobody would have understood a word."[57]

Reviewing the decision Césaire (and many others) made, Édouard Glissant has suggested that a distinction be established between a "*poétique naturelle*" and a "*poétique forcée*," a means of expression in which there is no tension between content and language and a means of expression in which that tension is implicit and unavoidable.[58] In *Le discours antillais* of 1981, Glissant posits the existence of a "*poétique naturelle*" based on an uninterrupted continuity between the (practical) language in which local debates are carried out within a single community and the (aesthetic) language that a subgroup of that community uses for poetic creation. His comments bear a resemblance to those offered by Fanon insofar as both presuppose that Caribbean writers labor under a sense of lack: they are "forced" to choose the language of the colonizer because their own language is presumed to be insufficient or—quite simply—not a language at all. Glissant argues that the francophone Caribbean writer senses the need "to forge a path" through French in order to arrive at a more intimate language not internal to French's "*logique*."[59] A "forced poetic" is born from "the awareness of an opposition between the language one uses (*dont on se sert*) and the language one needs (*dont on a besoin*)." While Glissant's point may be granted, especially since it is so often thematized in Negritude poetry itself, it should also be noted that most writers sense a disconnect between the language they use and the language they need, whether they are colonial subjects or not. There is a difference, of course, between the alienation one feels toward language (or the Symbolic) in general and the alienation one feels toward the language of the colonizer in particular. And certainly Negritude writers understood their objective to include "forging a path," adapting French in such a way that it could be bent to new uses. Yet it is by no means clear that the actual experience of writing in French inspired feelings of loss alone. That is, although the choice to write in French was overdetermined by a colonial dogma that destroyed the author's faith in the powers of the indigenous or Creole language, the imposed language could be approached by the author as entailing both loss *and gain*. Alex Gil has astutely observed that there were practical advantages to using French—and, especially, to using print: "Césaire wrote most of his life on a typewriter or with a pen. His art was destined for the printed page, with the occasional stage or spoken word. Why didn't he restrict himself to the oral traditions of the Africa and Caribbean he loved and channeled?" asks Gil: "Why didn't he write in Creole? I say he wanted to leave a mark on the present. . . . The book and the French language were tools of Empire, but Césaire would make miracles out of these weapons, transmuting them beyond their ordinary, yet toxic uses."[60] It is worth pointing out, in the same vein, that "making miracles out of these weapons"—the book and the French language—was a practice that allowed not only Césaire but Negritude writers in general to familiarize themselves with a singular materiality: that of the printed word. As I hope to show, the materiality of the printed word would prove to possess sensual and expressive potentials all its own.

Césaire's decision to write in French has been placed under even greater scrutiny as a result of the 1989 publication of Jean Bernabé, Patrick Chamoiseau, and Raphaël Confiant's *Éloge de la créolité*. The pressure on Césaire—as an exemplary Caribbean writer—to justify his choice has only increased since 1993, when Confiant turned to attack him less mercifully in *Aimé Césaire: Une traversée paradoxale du siècle*.[61] Sensitive to the accusation that he had ignored or belittled the Creole language (and Creole culture in general), Césaire returned to the issue in a seldom-quoted interview with Jean-Michel Djian published in 2005. Here he reiterates the same points made earlier—that during the years of his maturation "in Martinique, one only read French," and that, as a consequence, the act of writing would have been inextricably linked to the French language. However, he adds to his earlier response an important clarification: not only did he love French, he loved *written* French. The disembodied signs of the French language exercised a unique seduction upon him precisely because they were inscriptions: "I read all the writers. Already, at a very young age, my father introduced me to Alexandre Dumas, whom he adored. I then plunged headfirst into Corneille, Racine, Hugo, Pascal, the writers of the eighteenth century. I loved them. I loved their words. [*J'aimais leurs mots*]."[62]

This testimony indicates that Césaire, as opposed to Ngũgĩ, learned the language of the colonizer at home as well as in school; further, the passage tells us that although Césaire's first apprenticeship in French was oral and intimate, his infatuation only increased as he began to read for himself. The school and the library were thus an extension of his experience of family intimacy, not a violation of it. It could be argued, then, that Césaire's contact with the French language was different from Ngũgĩ's contact with the English language. However, I can't help believing that Ngũgĩ, too, must have felt seduced by the *written-ness* of English. Indeed, a passion for the written text is characteristic of writers in general—whether this text is in the maternal tongue or not; whether it is first introduced aurally or not. As children or adolescents, authors often experience the written word as somehow *more* intimate—rather than less—than the speech they hear around them. The words on the page seem directed toward them personally and thus offer an escape from a collective daily reality at times experienced as banal or repetitive in comparison. In the 2005 interview with Djian, Césaire insists—twice, in fact—that he loves French writers; he loves their written words. This is an extremely significant distinction often ignored by writers and critics of the post-Negritude generation, who tend to think of language—French or Creole—as a homogeneous entity. But it must be recalled that writers love writing, they love the orthography of words, the choice of fonts, the meaningful space of the page, and even the uncommon or unpronounceable terms to which literary texts lend a stage, and not necessarily "language," or "French," in general. Some writers appreciate spoken language, dialect, lyrics, and slang as much as, if not more than, the discourses of canonical literature. (This may have been the case for Langston Hughes and, to a lesser extent, his admirer, Léon Damas.) But it is clear that in the case of other writers—and Césaire is exemplary in this regard—the language of the *written word* is experienced as a separate, highly charged verbal phenomenon, a medium in its own right.

If we take this into account, it is easier to see why a writer such as Césaire would embrace a highly literary form of the French language as his medium. The "highly literary" is not necessarily abstract and "cerebral." *It is entirely possible to have a visceral experience of the written word.* A second language—even if it is that of the colonizer—can be experienced with the senses of the body, experienced even as an erotic object, a point made overtly in the works of Khatibi (and celebrated by his critics) that has not been sufficiently noted (or celebrated) in the works of Negritude. To deny the salience of this visceral experience to the poets of Negritude is at once to exclude them from the modernist moment (when a sensual investment in the grapheme was paramount) and to condemn them to playing only one role in culture, that of the griot (oral poet) or *conteur* (storyteller). We might wish to acknowledge that there is something Mallarméan in every poet insofar as he or she not ony speaks in the service of a present audience but also writes in the service of a readership yet to come.[63] To insist that a Césaire or Damas be closer to a *conteur* than a Symbolist is implicitly to prescribe what kind of an artist a black colonial or postcolonial subject can be.[64]

The Antillean writer is, inevitably and perhaps *à contre-coeur*, what Patrick Chamoiseau has called a "*marqueur de paroles*," someone who, by marking, inscribes the self into a graphic tradition with a history of its own.[65] Writing is a practice that many contemporary Caribbean authors associate with colonial domination, and thus it is approached with suspicion; yet writing also offers a unique chance. Despite the attacks Césaire has received, he in fact approaches the acquisition of writing as a complex negotiation, anticipating and nuancing the portrait of colonial subjectivation through literacy offered in works such as Chamoiseau's *Écrire en pays dominé*. For instance, in the *Cahier*, Césaire presents a scene of instruction, a portrait of a typical colonial classroom, in which a young schoolboy's voice ("*la voix*" of "*un négrillon*") is reduced to silence as the catechism—and with it the entire machinery of the book—is drummed into his brain.[66] "Et ni l'instituteur dans sa classe, ni le prêtre au catéchisme ne pourront tirer un mot de ce négrillon somnolent, malgré leur manière si énergique à tous deux de tambouriner son crâne tondu, car c'est dans les marais de la faim que s'est enlisée sa voix d'inanition" (And neither the teacher in his classroom, nor the priest at catechism will be able to get a word out of this sleepy little nigger, no matter how energetically they drum on his shorn skull, for starvation has quicksanded his voice into the swamp of hunger).[67] Here the subject's voice is reduced to silence by poverty ("les marais de la faim") as well as by the rhythm of the colonizer's drums ("à tous deux de tambouriner"). An interesting reversal thus takes place in which the colonizer's words appear as repetitive, drum-like sound (*un-mot-un-seul-mot*)—and drumming is associated with the colonizer and negatively valorized—while the voice that has been buried in the swamp—"*sa voix . . . s'est enlisée*"—reemerges in the words we read on the page. The reflexive verb "*s'enliser*" resonates with the conjugated forms of the verb "to read," "*lire*," suggesting through phonic association that the voice that goes underground also emerges into legibility, into graphic form. (The present participle of "*lire*" is "*lisant*," while the conjugated forms in the present tense are "*je lis*," "*tu lis*, . . . *ils lisent*," etc.) In other words, Césaire makes the disappearance of voice *into an occasion for reading*. He does so not to deny the coercive nature of instruction and the insidious neutralization of "les expressions les plus intimes des peuples dominés,"[68] but rather to enact, poetically, the work of resistant transformation required.[69] Out of the swamp in which the subject is buried, there may spring forth a subjectivity suppressed but not eliminated, a voice submerged (*enlisée*) yet rendered legible (*en-lisait*) in the form of marks.[70] Never innocent, never untainted by the conditions of its apprenticeship, writing nonetheless does not belong to the "*instituteur*" or the "*prêtre*" who first introduces it. Writing is not the sole possession of the colonizer for the same reason that it fails to transmit, unproblematically, "the most intimate expression" of a dominated people. Writing belongs to those who read; the voice submerged in marks is altered as it is relayed.

In the chapters that follow, I will examine the poetry of Negritude with respect to the ways in which it balances an attention to the chosen medium—French lyric in print—against an attempt to convey an experience that medium has never been charged with conveying before. Chapter 1, "'Seeing with the Eyes of the Work' (Adorno): Césaire's *Cahier* and Modernist Print Culture," examines the reception conditions of Negritude's inaugural masterpiece, *Cahier d'un retour au pays natal* (Notebook of a return to the native land), by situating the 1939 version in its original context of publication. Césaire experienced difficulties finding a publisher for the *Cahier* but then gained a hearing from the editorial board of *Volontés*, a review affiliated with the high modernist aesthetics of Eugène Jolas, the publisher of James Joyce's *Work in Progress* (*Finnegans Wake*). Chapter 1 explores this little-known publication history, demonstrating that while the *Cahier* conformed to the high modernist demand for verbal craft, the poem also advanced this craft by forcing it to accommodate a deeply traumatic empirical predicament. I juxtapose Césaire's diasporic modernism, which insists upon the connection between the "lyric I" and the author, with Theodor Adorno's paradigm of modernist construction, which separates the "aesthetic subjectivity" of the text from the empirical person of the writer and his intentions. The case of Césaire puts pressure on Adorno's understanding of what constitutes an aesthetic subject in lyric poetry, for the Negritude author is not exactly a modernist lyric subject in Adorno's sense. Chapter 1 initiates a line of questioning that is pursued throughout the book: What, or who, is the empirical subject that enters the crucible of writing? How must we revise Adorno's theory when the "aesthetic subject" concerned is associated with a human being urgently attempting to convey the experience of his own racial subjectivation under colonial rule?

Chapter 2, "The Empirical Subject in Question: A Drama of Voices in Aimé Césaire's *Et les chiens se taisaient*," approaches the curiously multidimensional and non-self-identical nature of the human being, or empirical subject, as depicted by Césaire in *Et les chiens se taisaient* (And the dogs fell silent). Césaire's first drama, rewritten over a span of fifteen years (approximately 1941–1956), testifies to the difficulty he experienced both as a poet called on to represent a shared experience of suffering and as a statesman required to play the role of leader. Whereas Adorno's paradigm of lyric creation presents the "aesthetic subject" as a fabrication of words and the "empirical subject" as a nondiscursive entity, Césaire's play encourages us to see the empirical subject—and thus the author himself—as a complex amalgam of conflicting voices. *Et les chiens se taisaient*, first performed as a radio play in 1956, allows us to reflect on the relation between performing roles (drama) and expressing subjectivity (lyric). Lyric, I argue, is more like drama (and subjectivity more like a set of roles) than we might suppose. Examining the production context of *Et les chiens se taisaient* through documents that have just come to light, I suggest that the ambiguous status of Césaire's "lyric oratorio" points to the hybrid nature of the aesthetic subject caught between literature and performance, text and voice.

The next two chapters explore the relation between performance and literature, voice and text, in the work of the other great diasporic poet of Negritude, Léon-Gontran Damas. Chapter 3, "Poetry and the Typosphere in Léon-Gontran Damas," is concerned with analyzing the graphemic features of Negritude's first poetic volume, *Pigments*, and the way these features call for their own phenomenalization through the voice of the reader. In 1937 *Pigments* was published by Guy Lévis Mano, an editor of artist books patronized by the surrealists whose attention to the print support—typeface and layout—was unrivaled at the time. Chapter 4, "Léon-Gontran Damas: Writing Rhythm in the Interwar Period," questions the critical assumption that Damas's poetry is based on the musical rhythms of diasporic or African forms. I define "rhythm" via the work of Henri Meschonnic as an ever-renewed "*ré-énonciation*." Against the grain of current scholarship on Damas, I argue that the rhythm of a poetic line can only partially be dictated by a written text, and thus the "soundscape" of the author must be conceived as textual sound created through textual means.[71] Each reading (or *ré-énonciation*) differs slightly from every other, just as each performance of a score finds new stress patterns and possibilities for syncopation. Prior to 1937 Damas published his poems in small socialist reviews circulated at strikes and union meetings. Although his rhythmic structures have suggested to later critics the polyrhythms of African drumming, Cuban calypso, *biguine*, or African American blues, study of the archive suggests that they were modeled on techniques of lineation present in contemporaneous works by Jacques Prévert, Robert Desnos, and Louis Aragon. Bringing to bear performance theory as well as theories of the lyric voice, I study Damas's poems as the site where the empirical author produces an aesthetic subjectivity within a specific rhetorical field.

The chapters on Damas attempt to situate his early poetry in a number of poetic and political contexts; likewise, chapter 5, "Red Front / Black Front: Aimé Césaire and the Affaire Aragon," returns to Césaire's work to analyze the poetic choices he made during the interwar period. I examine the tension between the competing exigencies to which the Negritude author was subjected. On the one hand, Césaire felt the need to satisfy poetic demands: he wanted to live up to and advance the technical and rhetorical standards of the twentieth-century print lyric. On the other, he was committed to political change; his recourse to journalistic discourse suggests that he was responding to an ethical imperative to testify for a shared experience of oppression. Césaire's *Cahier* weaves together both referential (journalistic) discourses and self-referential (lyric) discourses, attempting to be situated and to transcend situation at the very same time. The tension between political relevance and poetic transcendence was also at the heart of the Affaire Aragon, a debate between Aragon's communism and André Breton's surrealism that leaves its mark on Césaire's approach to writing the *Cahier*. This chapter examines more closely the critical reception of Negritude, arguing that the *Cahier*—from the perspective of the 1930s—raises some of the same questions animating postcolonial theory today. What kinds of hermeneutic and ethical limits does a committed poem impose on formalist reading practices? Conversely, what pressures does a formally experimental poem place on content-oriented approaches?

And finally, what kind of aesthetic subjectivity might emerge from a heterogeneous, aggressively intertextual poem?

The final chapter of the book moves forward in history to address the poetry produced as the Pan-African solidarity of the modernist period waned and a specifically Caribbean consciousness emerged. In chapter 6, "To Inhabit a Wound: A Turn to Language in Martinique," I propose that, paradoxically, the written (rather than the spoken) word becomes a means for Césaire to return to the Caribbean landscape. During a period when numerous critics were insisting that Creole constitutes the only language in which an authentic connection to Martiniquan history and experience can be achieved, Césaire elected to write in a profoundly literary French. Instead of gravitating toward the rhythms and idioms of speech, he works to develop an even more rarified poetic vocabulary, purposefully selecting arcane terms found only in books and technical manuals. In "Calendrier lagunaire" (Lagoonal calendar), a late poem from the collection *moi, laminaire* (1982), Césaire incorporates geographical, zoological, and botanical lexicons that turn out to possess roots in languages ranging from Arawak to Greek. Thus, instead of obscuring the specificity of Martinique through a language supposedly foreign to it, Césaire reveals the hybrid origins of the languages used to designate a specific site. The poet, so frequently criticized for writing in French, shows through ingenious lexical means that in fact he does *not* write in French—not because he writes in Creole but because French is not French.

In his own way, then, Césaire anticipates the thesis of *créolisation*, namely, that no language is originary, self-identical, or pure. His revelation of an imperial history embedded in toponyms, geographical terms, and botanical nomenclatures buttresses Édouard Glissant's contention that, in a land without written history, history is inscribed in the land and its names.[72] Critics who have sharply opposed Negritude to later movements, such as Antillanité and Créolité, have missed the opportunity to identify within Césaire's work a strong resistance to essentialism.[73] Far from exhibiting a "preoccupation with *enracinement*, filiation, and a foundational poetics," the poet inscribes within his work—by means of his very diction—a history characterized by the layering, intermingling, and creolization of cultures.[74] All three major poets of Negritude are aware of and celebrate the process of creolization to which they owe their poetic voice, their "aesthetic subjectivity," even as they seek to redress the suppression of Africa and recall specific conditions of suffering. My conclusion points to ways in which we might consider Negritude to be a modernist movement precisely because it performs that work of retrieval and recall. The poems of Negritude tell an imperial tale of diaspora and creolization, albeit through indirect, poetic, and exclusively textual means.

1

"SEEING WITH THE EYES OF THE WORK" (ADORNO)

Césaire's *Cahier* and Modernist Print Culture

MODERNIST NEOLOGISMS AND THE PLEASURES OF THE TONGUE

In "Césaire's *Notebook* as Palimpsest," A. James Arnold carefully separates out the layers of Césaire's *Cahier d'un retour au pays natal*, demonstrating how, with each successive edition, the poet built on—and altered—its initial articulation in print.[1] That initial articulation appeared in a small review titled *Volontés* in August of 1939; it was followed by seven more versions, the last few labeled by the publisher "definitive" (from 1956 on).[2] Arnold points out that the first publication of the *Cahier* as a separate volume was in a Cuban translation by Lydia Cabrera, prefaced by Benjamin Péret and brought out in Havana during World War II. This fact suggests what Arnold calls "the Caribbean vocation of Césaire's poetry at this time [1943]" and reveals "the role of the surrealist group in its diffusion."[3] In effect, Arnold reads the poem through the nature of its later reception, claiming that, because the Cuban surrealists were the first to publish the *Cahier* under separate cover, the poem must have had a "Caribbean vocation . . . at this time." While Arnold's observation holds some weight, it is not clear that the 1939 version was intended primarily for a Caribbean audience. Who were Césaire's first readers? How might they have shaped the *Cahier*'s first appearance in print?

Cabrera, a Cuban poet with an interest in diasporic religious syncretism, and Péret, an ex-surrealist studying pre-Columbian culture in Mexico, may indeed have felt an affinity with Césaire's work. I believe it would be a mistake, however, to take Cabrera's gesture of appropriation for a grasp of the poem's essence. Of course, a different appropriation, interpretation, or framing (mine, for instance) would also overdetermine the nature of what we find in the poem. The site where we choose to begin the story—in Havana or Paris or Martinique—has an impact on the reading we produce. My argument, though, is that the claim for a "Caribbean vocation" of the poem, as popular as it currently is, obscures another equally important but less fashionable reading. Without wishing to create a hierarchy of interpretations, I suggest that our understanding of Césaire's *Cahier* and of its place in transnational modernism is incomplete if we do not study the circumstances in which the 1939 pre-Cuban version arrived on the French literary scene.

It is clear that the surrealists were instrumental in bringing Césaire's writing to the attention of publishers, and we should never forget the subsequent influence they exerted on the development of both the *Cahier* and Césaire's entire career.[4] However, the "vocation" of the original 1939 poem was neither Caribbean nor surrealist alone, if what we mean by "vocation" is the direction intended, the public first addressed.[5] This is not to say that Césaire had no Caribbean readership in mind but rather that, given his situation as a black *assimilé* living in Paris yet identifying increasingly with the Africans he met there, he had to envision (and accommodate) several reading publics with differing orientations at the same time. We know that the original publication of the *Cahier* was facilitated by one of Césaire's professors at the Rue d'Ulm, Pierre Petitbon. Curiously, Arnold insists that this 1939 edition is *not* the original edition but rather the "pre-original" edition. "We must abandon the maddening habit [*la fâcheuse habitude*] of returning to the first edition of the *Cahier*," he asserts; "The text of August 1939, published in the Paris review *Volontés*, constitutes a pre-original."[6]

Arnold's stated reason for neglecting the *Volontés* version—despite the fact that it contains more than three quarters of the "definitive" version—is that it flew beneath the critical radar: "Nobody commented on it before the war and thus its public history [*son rapport à l'Histoire*] only begins in 1947."[7] This is a strange way of understanding "History," even literary history. The publication history of a poem comprises not only the readership it gains but also the milieu in which it is first appreciated, even *before* it reaches publication. If we "abandon" the "maddening habit" of consulting the *Volontés* edition, we neglect the fact that Césaire's very first readers were not Caribbean surrealists but rather the cosmopolitan globe-hoppers of high modernism.[8] To be sure, Césaire's immediate milieu was not that of the *Volontés* editorial board (or readership). During the same period he was composing the *Cahier*, he was engaged in publishing articles in the student review *L'Étudiant Noir*. These articles remain important intertexts, just as his collaborations with other students from Africa and the Caribbean constitute the background of his affective and political engagements. Yet the fact that *Volontés* was produced by an odd assortment of French and American modernists—unaffiliated with any of the movements with which Césaire is usually associated—should not prevent us from asking why it was *these* modernists who chose to publish him early on. What was it, precisely, about his style that persuaded them to devote twenty-eight pages of their penultimate issue to his work? Why would a distinguished scholar like Arnold opt to neglect this inaugural reception of the poem in print? Why would attention paid to the earliest ("pre-original") edition distort our understanding of the work—its contents and "vocation"?

Paradoxically, Arnold has done much to advance Césaire as a modernist in *Negritude and Modernism*, his monograph of 1981, in which he demonstrates the influence of modernist writers and anthropologists on the development of Césaire's style and concerns.[9] His demotion of the *Volontés* edition to a "pre-original"—and thus his relative lack of interest in the conditions of the *Cahier*'s initial publication—may have something to do with the shift in critical orientation that has occurred since Arnold first published his ground-breaking book; the effort to establish a properly Caribbean literature, with a properly "Caribbean vocation," has accelerated ever since Césaire's review, *Tropiques*, was reprinted in 1978. It is understandable that Arnold might not want to recall an earlier time before the notion of Antillanité (not to mention Créolité) had time to change the very way we regionalize (and thus read) literatures of the Atlantic. Be that as it may, there is no historical reason to neglect the productive conditions that led to the *Cahier*'s first publication. On the contrary, an examination of these conditions offers insight into the way in which even an engaged text, one that employs heavily charged referential language, responds to discrepant demands. The grandeur of an author's oeuvre is by no means diminished when we acknowledge that the conditions of its production and reception inevitably exerted pressure on the form the text could take. Negritude poets obviously felt inspired (or compelled) to address a variety of editors and audiences, and their expectations left marks on the texts we now read.[10]

I suggest, then, that it is worth rehearsing the particular conditions that led to the appearance of the first edition—the original print edition—of the *Cahier*, if only to understand better how the print medium and the mediological register of the small review affected the creative process of a major Negritude writer. It has been established in biographical accounts that after the manuscript was rejected by the first review Césaire sent it to, his professor put him in touch with Georges Pelorson, the editor of *Volontés*.[11] Despite considerable archival research, I have been unable to ascertain which review rejected the *Cahier*, but I suspect it was one of several that his close friend Léon Damas was publishing in at the time: between 1934 and 1936, Damas placed poems in *Charpentes* and *Cahiers du Sud* (soft rather than hardcore surrealist reviews of southern France), *Esprit* (a leftist Catholic review run by Emmanuel Mounier) and, most interestingly, *Soutes*, a socialist pamphlet in which Jacques Prévert and Louis Aragon were also publishing at the time. (We will get back to these venues in chapter 3.) The *Cahier* did not fit the mold of the directly militant Damas (or Prévert) poem, nor does the *Cahier* appear to have received a warm welcome from the more mainstream French reviews of the period. However, his work did find a sympathetic audience in the milieu of *Volontés*, as did Senghor's first published works.[12]

Volontés promoted a very specific wing of the avant-garde—not surrealist, not militantly socialist or communist, but rather high modernist international. There were several important French contributors—Raymond Queneau, quite frequently, and Jean Follain, Michel Leiris, Roger Caillois, and Le Corbusier, sporadically—but most consistent was the participation of Henry Miller, whose work appears in almost every issue.[13] Miller was in fact a member of the editorial *équipe*, along with Pelorson and—most significantly for our purposes—Eugène Jolas, a founding member. This is the same Eugène Jolas who created *transition* in 1927, the English-language journal in which James Joyce's "Work in Progress"—or *Finnegans Wake*—first appeared. *Transition* existed from 1927 to 1939, overlapping with *Volontés* by one year. In a sense, *Volontés* served as *transition*'s Franco-American *relais*; during the first year of its monthly run, *Volontés* consistently ended with an advertisement for *transition* announcing the imminent publication of a French translation of Joyce's "L'oeuvre en cours."[14] *Transition*, however, was decidedly a more international, multilingual modernist review than *Volontés*, which promoted a heterogeneous set of writers whose only shared tendency, as far as I can discern, was a resistance to the Freudism of the surrealist movement and a preference for vaguely Nietzschean theories of will and self-determination (*d'où le titre: Volontés*). Aside from Jolas, the most interesting collaborator was Raymond Queneau, who could have been the reviewer for the *Cahier* and thus would have left his own small mark on the history of Negritude.[15]

It is hard to detect a connection between Queneau's style and Césaire's, but the affinity between Césaire and Jolas is clear. Jolas's particular contribution to the poetics of *Volontés* was an emphasis on multilingual experimentation fostered by the poet's lived, almost ethnographic experience of modernity (rather than the poet's surrealist quest for unconscious truths). Multilingual experimentation was, as we know, the tenor of the time: Ezra Pound's "linguistic flexibility" was showcased in his review, *Exile*, where several of the *Cantos* were first published in the late 20s;[16] T. S. Eliot's shored, multilingual ruins appeared as *The Waste Land* (in *The Criterion*) in 1922; and Jolas began publishing Joyce's "polysynthetic" *Work in Progress* in 1927.[17] I believe that one of "Jolas's multilingual legacies" (to evoke Marjorie Perloff's terms) was in fact Césaire's *Cahier d'un retour au pays natal* (although it has never been recognized as such). Jolas's name on the masthead set a tone for *Volontés* that made it uniquely hospitable to the kind of work on language that Césaire was engaged in—the very work on language that makes him at once an iconoclastic experimentalist in the context of Caribbean poetry and a crafter of words conforming surprisingly well to the cosmopolitan, modernist poetics of both *transition* and *Volontés*.

Jolas writes in his memoir, *Man from Babel*, that during the interwar period he sought "an enrichment of language, new words, millions of words."[18] Significantly, in "Revolution of the Word," *transition*'s manifesto of 1929, he associates this linguistic enrichment and innovation with the creation of neologisms.[19] Jolas courted neologisms, both in his own verse and in the verse of the writers he published—Joyce, to be sure, but also Léon-Paul Fargue, Henri Michaux, and Césaire.[20] In the 1929 issue of *transition*, Jolas presents his foremost aesthetic axiom as the "right" of the "literary creator . . . to use words of his own fashioning"; he vows to promote writers who "disintegrate the primal matter of words imposed . . . by text-books and dictionaries . . . the writer expresses: he does not communicate," Jolas concludes: "the plain reader be damned."[21] Of course, Jolas was thinking of modernists like Joyce, not Césaire, when he penned these words, but they nonetheless indicate the aesthetics of the literary milieu to which Jolas belonged, the same milieu that first introduced Césaire's variety of writing onto the literary scene. I suspect that Césaire would have published anywhere he could have, and the fact that he ended up in *Volontés* does not necessarily reflect his intentions or his own sense of his place in the mid-1930s field of literary production. But the *Cahier*'s first publication venue does tell us something about the nature of his earliest reception; it indicates how his poem appeared to members of a sophisticated, cosmopolitan modernist elite distanced from specific schools; and it helps us to discern aspects of the *Cahier* that have not yet received sufficient attention. Before André Breton marveled over the richly figurative passages printed in *Tropiques*, another public had already found in Césaire an experimental impetus consistent with modernism's most adventurous word-crafters. Ostensibly, Césaire was published by *Volontés* because the editors judged him to be an experimental writer, able to invent, as Jolas put it, "words of his own fashioning." A glance at the leftist literary journals of the time, however, reveals that other, less literary factors were involved. *Soutes* regularly published poems by someone named "Nigg" (one titled "Lynch" in 1936), and we read in a 1939 issue of *Charpentes* that the editors are actively seeking the contribution of "voices from the colonies."[22] Césaire's was certainly a voice from the (former) colonies, but he also offered much more. With his modernist sensibilities and his overt positioning as "nègre," he fit a unique bill.

Let us recall another relevant aspect of Jolas's poetics. Increasingly during the interwar period, the modernist editor and poet came to associate linguistic innovation not only with multilingualism but also with "racial and ethnic equality."[23] In "Logos," an essay published in *transition* in 1929, he celebrates what we would now call "*créolisation*": "In modern history we have the example of the deformations which English, French and Spanish words underwent in America, as in the case of Creole French on Mauritius, Guyana, Martinique, Hayti [*sic*], Louisiana, and Colonial Spanish."[24] Despite his use of the word "deformations," it is clear from the context that Jolas is applauding the intermingling of languages as a form of cultural renewal. In fact, the salient difference between *transition* and *Volontés*, or the Jolas of the 1920s and the Jolas of the 1930s, is the accent placed on the role of black expressive practices and the phenomenon of diaspora in the salutary revision of Western languages and cultures. In 1933 Jolas returned to New

York (he was born in the United States but moved to Europe as a child) and, as he tells us in *Man from Babel*, walked the streets in thrall to the melodies of new idioms, dialects, inflections, and—most important to Jolas—individual words. In the two poems he published in *Volontés* (in issues immediately prior to the one that contains the *Cahier*), his persona relates sentiments familiar to readers of Césaire in an anaphoric manner that Brent Hayes Edwards has attributed specifically to black American writing of the interwar period.[25] From "Frontière" (no. 1, 1938) we read:

Je suis venu de loin
J'ai quitté un continent de scories
Je suis seul
Dans une rue de songes

I came from afar
I left a continent of slag/discarded cinders
I am alone
On a street of dreams

From "Lettre transatlantique" (no. 16, April 1939):

Je suis revenu à la terre des ancêtres
Je suis revenu de loin
J'ai parcouru les Amériques
. . .
J'apportais avec moi les mots d'innombrables races

I returned to the earth of the ancestors
I returned from afar
I crossed the Americas
. . .
I brought with me the words of innumerable races[26]

Granted, Jolas's "retour" was quite different from Césaire's, but on the thematic level, the two correspond to a similar editorial interest. *Volontés* was obviously receptive to the theme of diaspora, the politics of race consciousness, and the prosodic forms of African American poetry. Jolas had already created an atmosphere in which both neologistic practices and diasporic themes were welcome. In *Mots-déluge* of 1933, Jolas produced a kind of template for the creation of neologisms that, surprisingly, anticipate Césaire's own. Consider, for instance, these two lines from "Le troisième oeil":

> La terre m'aveugle je tombe dans la *présentade*
> L'éveil des *millionitudes* est plein de fièvre
>
> The earth blinds me I fall into the presentness
> The awakening of millionitudes is full of fever[27]

Note the use of the suffixes "-ade" and "-itude" to make abstract states of the nouns "présent" and "million." This is a fairly consistent technique in the first section of *Mots-déluge*, where a suffix like "-imanes" produces "*rulimanes*" (13) and "-ards" yields "*nuitards*." In addition, Jolas ends the collection with a stream of invective that very easily could have inspired the opening passage of the *Cahier* added for the first time to the Bordas editon in 1947:

> Je ne vous entends plus
> Crétinards des isolations grammaticales . . . Vos mots de philistins
> Vos mots de curés vos mots de fumistes
>
> I don't hear you any more,
> idiots of grammatical segregation . . . Your philistine words
> Your little priest words your crackpot words (203)[28]

While we have no direct evidence that Césaire read *Mots-déluge*, it is hard to believe that all these resemblances are merely coincidental. Even the name of the publishing house that produced Jolas's volume, Éditions des Cahiers Libres, resonates uncannily with the title Césaire chose for a poem he submitted to a journal that sported Jolas's name on its masthead. If recent scholarship is to be trusted, Césaire employed the neologism "*négritude*" as early as 1935 in an article titled "Nègreries: Conscience raciale et révolution," published in the third issue of *L'Étudiant Noir*; he was clearly attracted to neologisms before contacting *Volontés*.[29] The point is not to prove that Césaire read *Mots-déluge*, or, more broadly, that he developed neologisms like "*négritude*" and "*verrition*" as a result of the influence of Jolas *et compagnie*, but rather that he belongs to a generation of writers invested in word creation as both art and act.

A "VERTIGINOUS" ENDING

Jolas's poetics evolved as a result of his contact with the interracial syncretism of New York: so, too, Césaire's *Cahier* evolved as a result of his contact with the poetics and editorial policies of *Volontés*. The famous ending, which has remained unchanged throughout all subsequent editions, was in fact not part of the original manuscript that Césaire submitted to his *Volontés* editor. We know from a letter dated April 29, 1939, that it was Pelorson who requested a new ending, and that in response to that request, Césaire supplied three final pages—"plus vertigineuse et plus finale, je crois" (more vertiginous and final, I believe), as he wrote in his letter to Pelorson. These final pages include the famous passage on the "langue maléfique de la nuit" and its "immobile verrition."[30]

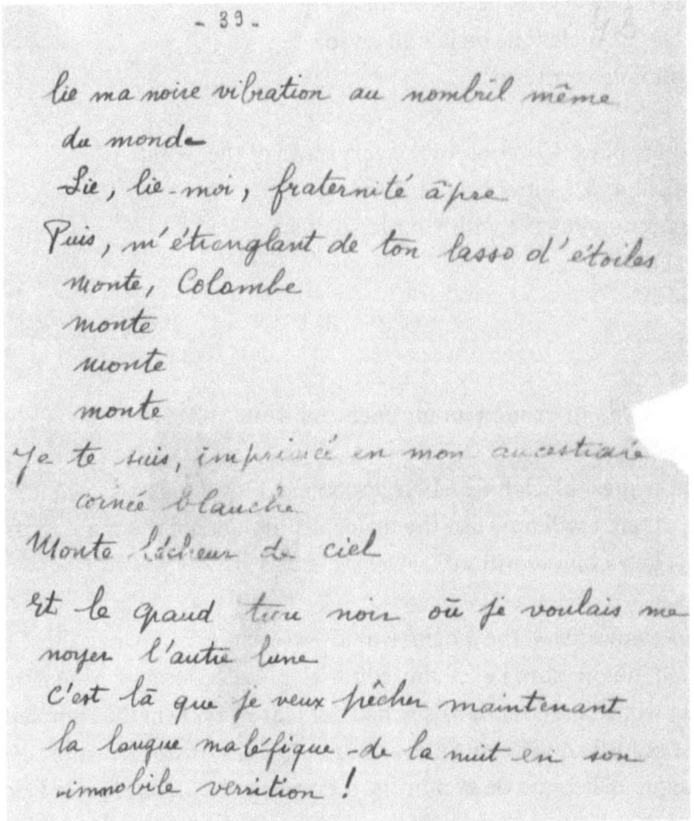

- 39 -

lie ma noire vibration au nombril même
du monde
Lie, lie-moi, fraternité âpre
Puis, m'étranglant de ton lasso d'étoiles
monte, Colombe
monte
monte
monte
Je te suis, imprimée en mon ancestrale
cornée blanche
Monte lécheur de ciel
et le grand trou noir où je voulais me
noyer l'autre lune
C'est là que je veux pêcher maintenant
la langue maléfique de la nuit en son
immobile verrition !

Figure 1.1: Aimé Césaire, "tapuscrit" of *Cahier d'un retour au pays natal*, 1939, final page. Reproduced courtesy of the Bibliothèque de l'Assemblée nationale, Paris, France.

lie ma noire vibration au nombril même
    du monde
    lie, lie-moi fraternité âpre
Puis, m'étranglant de ton lasso d'étoiles
    monte, Colombe
     monte
      monte
       monte
Je te suis, imprimée en mon ancestrale
    cornée blanche
Monte lécheur de ciel
Et le grand trou noir où je voulais me
  noyer l'autre lune
  c'est là que je veux pêcher maintenant
  la langue maléfique de la nuit en son
  immobile verrition![31]

bind my black vibration to the very navel of the world
 bind, bind me, bitter brotherhood
 then, strangling me with your lasso of stars
rise, Dove
 rise
  rise
   rise
I follow you imprinted on my ancestral white cornea
rise sky licker
and the great black hole where a moon ago I wanted to drown it is
        there I will now fish the malevolent tongue of the night in its
        immobile veerition![32]

Who knows how the poem would have ended, or what the *Cahier*'s reception might now be, if the editorial predilections of *Volontés*, if its peculiar word-based modernism, had not played a role in the completion of the first published version. Surely Césaire had his own reasons for evoking the "langue maléfique de la nuit" in the passage he submitted to Pelorson; however, it is likely that the editors (and the readership) of *Volontés* would have heard in Césaire's French phrase an echo of Joyce's "language of the night," the famous description he gives of his *Work in Progress*, printed on the pages of *transition* from 1927 to 1938 and published as *Finnegans Wake* the same year that the *Cahier* appeared, 1939. The phrase obviously had a great deal of resonance at the time: imitating Joyce, Jolas authored a slim volume titled *The Language of the Night* in 1932. We cannot know whether Césaire read Jolas's pamphlet, which reiterates many of the points made in "Revolution of the Word" while stressing the poet's "visionary faculty."[33] But the resemblance should give us pause. Is it possible that Césaire understood his own efforts to correspond in some way with those of the transnational writers grouped around Jolas? Is it possible that his choice of the word "verrition" was motivated—at least in part—by his adoption of the poetics *Volontés* promoted? Is it a mere coincidence that the only neologism in the *Cahier*—other than the crucial word "*négritude*"—appears in the finale written specifically under the tutelage of *Volontés*?

I do not mean to imply that Césaire was simply following the mandate of his publisher. On the contrary: if we look closely at the poem, we note how carefully the word "verrition"—the neologism that concludes the last stanza of the *Cahier*—has been anticipated by the sonic landscape of the entire poem. (This is not the place to enter into a thorough analysis of that sonic landscape—I do so later in chapter 5.) Obviously, poetic decisions are informed by more than one consideration alone. Césaire might have wanted to end the poem with a neologism—or something resembling one—because his poem had finally found a public who celebrated, even expected them. Or, alternatively, "verrition" might have blossomed from its root in "*vertere*," to turn, for semantic reasons; Césaire needed a word that could suggest the action of spinning, but "*tourbillonnement*" (used previously) didn't fit the rhythmic bill. Or, a further possibility (the one I find most convincing) is that the choice of the word "verrition" presented itself as a morpho-phonemic inevitability, given the startling number of words with the morpheme "vers" already contained in the poem. There were clearly many reasons why Césaire chose to end his poem with the word "verrition," but the atmosphere around *Volontés*, which was favorable to neologisms, arguably contributed to his decision.

It is important to note, however, that "verrition" may not even have been a neologism—or at least, not a creation of Césaire's—although most readers experience it as such. Countering the popular belief that Césaire invented the term himself, René Hénane claims to have discovered the word "verrition" in a work by Jean Anthelme Brillat-Savarin titled *Physiologie du goût*, which he located—on Césaire's suggestion—in the library of the École Normale Supérieure at the Rue d'Ulm.[34] If we consult Brillat-Savarin's work, we indeed find the word "verrition," which in context serves to designate an action of the tongue, one of several movements of mastication that Brillat-Savarin distinguishes during the course of an investigation into man's "superior" taste buds.[35] "Verrition" is the name Brillat-Savarin gives to the action "when the tongue, curling itself around, dislodges portions of food remaining in the semi-circular canal formed by the lips and gums."[36] What Hénane does not underscore is that Brillat-Savarin himself invented the technical term. It is one of several neologisms that the annotator of the second edition—none other than Roland Barthes—identifies as original to the author. In his preface to *Physiologie du goût*, Barthes indirectly suggests why the word might have been so compelling to Césaire—both as a gesture of word creation and as a bridge between two understandings of the "tongue." The metaphor, "la langue maléfique de la nuit," takes on new significance when we consider it in light of this source. "La langue" referred quite directly to Brillat-Savarin's meaning ("langue" as tongue) while opening onto the field of language ("langue") as a site of enchantment and transformation.

It is Barthes who underscores in his preface the continuity between the tongue as an organ of mastication and the tongue as an organ of speech, characterizing Brillat-Savarin as a writer who savors the nuances of language in the same manner as he savors the flavors of food. The author of *Physiologie du goût*, Barthes observes, "is clearly bound to language—as he was to food—by a love relationship: *he desires words, in their very materiality*."[37] This tendency to enjoy words as though they were full of flavor and texture, as though they were a material substance, is a trait Brillat-Savarin shares with the modernists in the circle of *Volontés* (not to mention Barthes himself). The lingual pleasure taken in using the tongue (either to pronounce words or to taste food) is described by Barthes as a "*double jouissance*," a figure thoroughly consistent with the verbal erotics of James Joyce and the "*gourmandise*" of Césaire. Of course Césaire could not have read Barthes' preface since it was published in 1975; however, he might very well have read Brillat-Savarin's own. Here the author indulges in a veritable hymn to the neologism (worthy of Jolas) in which word invention is associated with the sensual pleasures of speech. The relation between the tongue (*la langue*) as language and the tongue (*la langue*) as the organ of taste is exploited in Césaire's own ending, where the speaker calls for the invention of a language that moves, a performative language able to touch the cosmos, like the "Colombe" who, not incidentally, "licks the sky" (*lecheur du ciel*). For Césaire, words are clearly a form of nourishment; they lend strength to the project of emancipation. It makes sense, then, that he would call in the *Cahier* for a "pays restitué à ma gourmandise" (a country restored to my gourmandise) (V, 27; PA, 14). The poet is hungry not simply for the milk of the "*gros téton*" of the "*morne*" (large breast of the hill) but also for the rich, succulent words whose pronunciation provides sensual satiation (like the "*goutte de lait*"—drops of milk—that gush out near the end of the poem). Given the poem's insistence throughout on the physical pleasures of word formation, Césaire must have been delighted when he struck upon the neologism "verrition" in *Physiologie du goût*. Not only does it extend beautifully the resonant alliterative technique of the poem (echoing all the instances of the morpheme "vers" scattered throughout), but it also encapsulates the thematic bond between word craft and physical nourishment that Césaire established even before composing the new ending for his editor at *Volontés*.

THE LINGUISTIC HABITUS OF THE RARE WORD

What comes more fully to light when we resituate the *Cahier* in the context of its first publication is that the word craft Césaire develops is by no means uniquely oral in nature, as critics have so often insisted. Rather, this word craft is fully implicated in the Gutenberg revolution, drawing on the inventions peculiar to print—in this case, Brillat-Savarin's scholarly, Latinate neologisms.[38] One of the most interesting features of poetic neologisms—and this is true as well of neologisms introduced in scientific (or pseudo-scientific) texts like Brillat-Savarin's—is that they exist as writing before they exist as speech. Few of Césaire's readers, if any, would have heard the word "verrition" pronounced before they saw it typographically produced. (Césaire himself had probably never heard the word uttered before adding it to his poem.) Such a prioritization of writing over speech is not inconsistent with Césaire's lexical choices in general. In fact, "verrition" strikes the reader of the *Cahier* in the same way that many other unfamiliar words do, words that are not neologisms but rather obsolete, rare, or erudite terms known only to a small group of specialists. Césaire is particularly prone to saturating his texts with words so consistently indecipherable (at least without a set of specialized dictionaries) that he enforces a kind of silent reading on the part of the reader, a "subvocalization" of the written word.[39] The *written-ness* of the *Cahier* is thus what leaps into view when it is considered in the company of *transition* and *Volontés*. In addition, the tight relation between writing and the body becomes palpable as a result of this recontextualization of Césaire's work.

Césaire's claim, then, that his writing is performative, similar to the propulsive gestures of the body, merits our attention. Contemporary cognitive science has recently buttressed with empirical evidence the notion that reading is a process involving activation of the organs of speech. Stanislas Dehaene, for instance, has argued that confrontation with the rare or unknown word *in particular* is likely to stimulate the silent miming of pronunciation.[40] If Dehaene is correct, then Césaire's poems actually make our tongues move. We can understand the *Cahier* as a performative work, then, not because it imitates the beating of the drum (*pace* Martin Munro) or the sorcerer's incantation (*pace* Lilian Pestre de Almeida) but because it encourages through lexical means the transformation of marks into vibration, into sound.[41] Césaire's interest in written language as a medium in and of itself—an interest he shares with modernist poets in general—merges with his unique political project of self-affirmation, forcing phrases never before uttered into the reader's mouth.

Césaire takes much of his lexicon not from spoken language but rather from the grapholect, that curious vocabulary that Walter Ong associates specifically with book learning and the invention of print.[42] The bookish nature of his poetry is thrown into even greater relief when one places it next to contemporaneous works by Langston Hughes, for instance, a poet who uses a fairly colloquial vocabulary when discussing features of diasporic experience. In contrast, Césaire's poetry appears practically clotted with erudite terms drawn from treatises on botany, anatomy, zoology, geology, pathology, ornithology, mineralogy, and archaic Latin, producing a unique texture we easily recognize as his own. Hénane lists over six hundred entries in his *Glossaire des termes rares dans l'oeuvre d'Aimé Césaire*, terms like "*noctiluque*," "*cyathée*," "*érésipèle*," and "*squasme*" that at first appear to the reader as obdurately opaque and thing-like.[43] They belong to no previously existing poetic (or even literary) idiom, although their use might recall the precision of discrimination and the breadth of technical know-how we associate with a William Shakespeare or a Herman Melville (or a James Joyce, for that matter). There is indeed in Césaire a kind of encyclopedic conceit; the "Cahier," as a genre, could be read as a massive set of notes integrating all that the poet has ever heard or found in books. And this last point is crucial: Césaire insists on terms found *only* in books, and he does so with a frequency that is striking. These print-generated words—not just neologisms but technical terms and obsolete words from Medieval Latin—draw attention to themselves first and foremost as clusters of letters on a page. They resemble the units of a dead language whose individual phonetic elements one can discern even though one has never before heard them pronounced. For the average reader, these rare words appear to the eye as virtual sonic phenomena ("acoustic images," in Ferdinand de Saussure's terms) lacking, at first, a conceptual content. The experience of reading a line such as "ma reine des squasmes et des chloasmes"—closed as it is to immediate comprehension—resembles closely the experience early readers first have of written words, an experience of the visual opacity and the aural viscosity of language. Whereas for some, confrontation with the materially present but conceptually void letter cluster is frustrating and disenfranchising, for others—that is, for lovers of the written word—this confrontation constitutes a variety of the sublime.

It is plausible, then, that Césaire (whether consciously or not) sought in poetry a way to recall for his reader the primal experience of literacy acquisition, that strange and magical act by which letters of the alphabet morph into sounds. Césaire's poetry obliges the reader to extrapolate from the known (the recognizable phonemes of French) the pronunciation of the unknown (a word that uses these phonemes in a new way). In a sense, Césaire denaturalizes the process of reading, reminding us of the *techne* required. He renders French strange, making it into a written language we need to learn to read—phoneme by phoneme—all over again. Ever since the famous interview with Jacqueline Leiner in which Césaire describes his desire to "inflect French" (*infléchir le français*), the critical tendency has been to associate his neologisms and rare words not with the modernist enterprise to renew language in general but, more specifically, with an active resistance against colonial power as it is incarnated in the French language.[44] Ultimately, however, it is not clear that Césaire's lexical strategy was motivated by a desire to "cannibalize" French, as scholars later claimed.[45] Certainly he practiced a variety of appropriation (or "piratage") that directs a quotation or strategy toward new ends.[46] But much of his work on language remains an extension of his lifelong obsession with marks on the page as generators of sound. It is no accident that the young Césaire, who listened for hours to the books his father read to him out loud (books that contained words he would never hear in his daily life) ended up becoming a student of the classical "dead" languages, Latin and Greek. These languages share roots, prefixes, and suffixes with French—they share its phonemic palette—yet they demand many long hours in the company of dictionaries and a willingness to confront opacity as a fundamental aspect of the verbal world.

Thus, instead of "cannibalizing" French, I would speculate that Césaire was developing—even globalizing—its morphological and lexical possibilities. Along with Latin and Greek terms, Césaire incorporates into his poems words specific to Martiniquan experience—"*morne*," "*marigot*," "*balisier*," "*piton*," "*fer de lance*," "*cassave*," and many more—in effect creolizing the text as well as the mouth that pronounces it.[47] His poetry makes as full a use as possible within French orthography of the entire grapho-phonemic repertoire of his Creole/French/Greek/Latin larynx, registering creolizations, regionalisms, expletives, and erudite vocabularies in order to increase the physical, gesticular, and choreographic range of the poem's potential actualizations. His expansive diction could be seen as an effort to break through the boundaries of French phonetics in order to express a body afforded more than one linguistic habitus. There is indeed something violent in his expansiveness, as if he wanted to explode the limits of French not to do damage to French per se, or exorcise it from his mouth, but rather to realize the full multiplicity of lingual movements available to his Franco-Creole-Greco-Latin tongue.

CEDING CESAIRE'S INITIATIVE TO WORDS

It should be clear by now that the text-based nature of Césaire's linguistic strategies by no means hinders him from generating effects on the ear. Like Joyce, who jump-started the career of *Finnegans Wake* by reading sections in public, or Mallarmé, who enjoyed reciting his works at gatherings, Césaire also experimented with the potential of his written work to generate, rather than reflect, sound patterns by reciting the *Cahier* to Léon Damas before it went to press. In the previous sections I emphasized the multiple influences that contributed to producing the unique quality of the *Cahier*'s "tongue," including the aesthetic preferences of the editorial team at *Volontés*. Here, I want to suggest that the *Cahier* may be considered to participate in a broader modernism consistent with that described by Adorno in *Aesthetic Theory*—but with a significant twist. If the sources for Césaire's poetic diction are highly varied (from botanical manuals and a treatise by Brillat-Savarin to

Martiniquan Creole and the *vaudou* religion of Haiti), in contrast, the compositional technique responsible for the arrangement of Césaire's phonemes recalls procedures for linking sound values developed by Arthur Rimbaud and Mallarmé, procedures that Adorno refers to as belonging to the poetics of "construction." An essential term of analysis in *Aesthetic Theory*, "construction" refers in its first incarnation to the variety of letter and sound patterning available only in writing, a patterning that in high modernism ends up informing to a greater degree what the lyric subject will say.[48]

The lexical strategy pursued by Césaire in the *Cahier* (his use of neologisms and rare terms) is thus only one of several modernist techniques that he adapted for his own use. Generations of scholars have followed Jean-Paul Sartre in identifying Césaire's style with the surrealist "rapprochement" or the technique of the "*métaphore filée*"—and to be sure, hypotaxis and an unusual combination of lexemes à la Lautréamont are marked elements of his approach. Yet Césaire perfected another text-based technique that has hardly received the attention it deserves: the technique of grapho-phonemic and syllabic repetition he first encountered in Rimbaud. Mallarmé is also an important role model for the word craft of the *Cahier*; however, it is Rimbaud who figures most prominently in Césaire's unpublished lectures on poetry, the "Notes de classe" from his preparatory classes at the Lycée Schoelcher only recently donated to the Archives Départementales of Martinique.[49] I want to close this chapter by attending to these "Notes de classe" and the huge influence of Rimbaud on the *Cahier* that they reveal.

Although it is well known that Césaire was an avid reader of Rimbaud, until now it has not been possible to pinpoint exactly which compositional techniques Césaire borrowed from the nineteenth-century poet. As early as 1947 André Breton associated Césaire directly with Rimbaud; in "Un grand poète noir" (first published in *Hémisphères* in 1943, reprinted in *Tropiques* in 1944 and then again in the Bordas edition of the *Cahier* in 1947), Breton mentions that during his brief sojourn in Martinique Césaire was in the process of conducting preparatory classes on Rimbaud at the Lycée Schoelcher.[50] The "Notes de classe," transcribed by two of Césaire's pupils, indicate precisely what Césaire's technical preoccupations were, not only during the 1940s, when he was teaching Rimbaud, but also earlier, when he was studying literature at the École Normale Supérieure and ostensibly collecting the materials he would later present to his students in Martinique. These "Notes de classe" tell us that in the course of a lesson devoted to the concluding passage of *Une saison en enfer*, Césaire brought in a copy of Jacques Rivière's 1914 essay on Rimbaud in order to explicate his use of alliteration and assonance. "Le choix de syllabes est calculé" (the choice of syllables is calculated) we read in the handwriting of Michael Yang-Ting, who meticulously copied down the words from Rivière that Césaire must have quoted or circulated in class.[51] "There is a composition of sonorities, an arrangement of vowels and diphthongs according to the most subtle but premeditated laws."[52]

Césaire's decision to quote (or assign) these lines was not an arbitrary one. As any reader of the *Cahier* knows, an attention to the "arrangement" of sound values is a marked feature of the work. In fact, if we open up the *Cahier* at almost any point we find that tremendous care has been exerted to produce the same intricate sound effects that Rivière attributes to Rimbaud. Consider the following passage, chosen at random but typical of the *Cahier* as a whole:

> Ce qui est à moi, ces quelques milliers de mortiférés qui tournent en rond dans la calebasse d'une île et ce qui est à moi aussi, l'archipel arqué comme le désir inquiet de se nier, on dirait une anxiété maternelle pour protéger la ténuité plus délicate qui sépare l'une de l'autre Amérique . . . (*Cahier*, V, 32/ PA, 24)

> What is mine, these few thousand deathbearers who mill in the calabash of an island and mine too, the archipelago arched with an anguished desire to negate itself, as if from maternal anxiety to protect this impossibly delicate tenuity separating one America from another . . .[53]

We should observe right away the insistent "-ier" diphthong ("millier," "nier," "inquiet") as well as the repetitive glottal attack of the velar /k/ in "qui," "quelque," "arqué," "inquiet," and "Amérique." (The /k/ returns at the end of the stanza in "Afri*que*," "gigantes*que*ment," and "hispani*que*.") In addition, a closer look at the phonemic content reveals the careful reprise of a controlled number of sounds: the refrain "ce qui est à moi" provides the consonantal structure—the gutteral /k/, the sibilant /s/, and the nasal "m"—that will generate "millier" (which echoes in turn "île") as well as the "est," which, arched slightly, generates "désir," "anxiété," "protéger," "ténuité," "séparer," and "délicate." The double sibilant in "aussi" and "calebasse" is also an important phonic tool in the *Cahier*, entering like the double "l" in "maternelle" as a soothing, counterbalancing element, opposed affectively to the sharp dentals, glottals, and edgy "-ier" diphthong /j/, associatively bound in the passage to the verb "nier"—to negate or deny—and, on a larger scale, to the title *Cah-ier* itself.

While it is true that persistent reprisal of the same or similar sounds is possible in speech as well as writing, it is harder to sustain phonemic and syllabic echoes over a very long period—the two and a half hours it takes to read the *Cahier* out loud, for instance, or the fifty-eight pages of the current Présence Africaine edition. Writing has a much longer memory than speaking, and these kinds of effects result, as Albert Lord has shown, from the technical possibilities open to *written*, not oral, forms.[54] Césaire extends such paronomastic soundplay over a vast number of stanzas. According to Rivière, this is also the strategy employed by Rimbaud: both poets distribute "les sonorités dominantes" over a large space of text, creating an underlying "vibration" that replaces the rhythms vouchsafed formerly by metrics.[55] "I regulated the form and movement of every consonant" (*Je réglai la forme et le mouvement de chaque consonne*), wrote Rimbaud, to which Rivière replies: "he knew how to make use of consonants, how to exploit their natural inclinations [*leurs dispositions naturelles*] as means of expression. In effect, he harnesses all that can be suggestive: the noise they make once pronounced . . . the 'movement' they impress on the lips or the tongue."[56]

While it is not clear what the "natural inclination" of a consonant would be, we can surmise that Rivière is referring to the way in which verbal sounds can take on affective meanings in context, both through their cross-modal connotations (the /k/ as a hard or sharp sound, for instance) and through the differential values they develop in the given poem (e.g., dentals as sharp when contrasted with labials as smooth or liquid). Rivière makes another important observation that applies to Césaire as well, namely, that the sound effects he is analyzing in Rimbaud are produced through the modality of the "letter." "It is impossible not to see here," he writes with reference to "Nocturne Vulgaire," "the use of the letter *o*, taken by turns in all its sonorous variations."[57] For Rivière, the letter "o" is at the root of the soundplay in Rimbaud's poem. That is, a *letter*—not a particular phoneme—returns repeatedly, registered differently each time by the internal voice according to its placement among other letters: as nasalized in the case of "songe," for instance, or long and perfectly round in the case of "Sodomes," or yet again swallowed in the /wa/ of "envoyer." Rivière points to—without theorizing—a crucial element of the acoustics of written poetry, an acoustics that so many poets exploit: the fact that the marks on the page we call "letters" (abstract and arbitrary atomizations of the full spectrum of verbal sound) possess a wide range of potential phenomenalizations. The return and methodical variation of these letters *as letters* can become the object of patterning, creating one rhythm that is visual and another that is aural at the very same time.[58]

The poetic innovations introduced during the period Rivière studies are in fact predicated on the existence of a textual voice, that is, on the existence of an order of sonic phenomenality that is unique to the medium, not thoroughly identical to any preexisting authorial voice or utterance. Rimbaud and Mallarmé both evince an awareness that the text is performative in just this way—that it may generate rather than imitate patterns of sound. The repetitions of a letter might produce various or identical phonemes, but in each case it is a graphemic patterning that is governing an aural experience. While Rivière merely gestures in the direction of Mallarmé in his essays on Rimbaud, it is clear that his reading of Rimbaud's "composition of sonorities," his "arrangement of vowels and diphthongs according to the most subtle but premeditated laws," is richly informed by his familiarity with "Crise de vers." What Mallarmé knows as surely as the scholars of sound writing today is that, ever since poets began committing their words to a durable support, there has emerged a soundplay unique to the printed text. A specific "acoustics of textuality," as Garrett Stewart puts it, animates our readings of the printed poem.[59] "That the letter signified for Mallarmé the principle of rhythmic expansion *in the space proper to literature* is one of the essential aspects of his poetics," Roger Dragonetti also reminds us.[60] And this "space proper to literature" is, for Mallarmé, not the handwritten manuscript but "The Book." If the metered musicality of orature relies to a far greater extent on accentual organization (beats), syllabic counting, and phonic rhyme, the written poem—extended by the printed book—sets up an oscillation between patterns addressed to the ear and patterns addressed to the eye. In this regard, the book-length publication of the *Cahier* takes on particular relevance. As opposed to Damas and Senghor, who began their careers with short lyrics, Césaire enters the literary scene with a poem that calls out to be printed in codexical form. The lineation of the final passage achieves its effect largely through contrast with the earlier nonlineated stanzas that accumulate over the previous pages. The format (twenty-eight pages in the *Volontés* version; fifty-eight pages in the Présence Africaine version) offers an immense canvas upon which visual and sonic networks may be elaborately extended. On the thematic level, the length of the *Cahier* permits for epic development; on the sonic level, the length encourages an arrangement based on the reprisal of letters and syllables—another structure, or "Structure, une autre," in the words of Mallarmé.[61] In the sequence just parsed, rich chains of sound glitter in print—" l'archipel arqué comme le désir inquiet"—recalling "une virtuelle traînée de feux sur des pierreries" (a virtual swooping of fire across precious stones).[62] In what Adorno calls the "constructivist writing" of Mallarmé, "words, through the clash of their ordered inequalities . . . light each other up." The poet "cedes the initiative" to these patterns, which come to "replac[e] the primacy of the perceptible rhythm of respiration or the classic lyric breath, or the personal feeling driving the sentences."[63]

This last allusion to Mallarmé's famous synesthesic metaphor is far from gratuitous: the Rimbaud that Césaire presents to his students (via Rivière) is the Mallarméan Rimbaud, the poet concerned with the relation between words and other words, not the relation between words and the world beyond them. The turn toward what Rimbaud calls an "objective poetry" is exaggerated in Mallarmé to the point where "personal feeling" no longer dictates what the poem says.[64] It might seem perverse to emphasize Césaire's commitment to a tradition of "objective" or "constructivist" poetry when the contents of the *Cahier* are so explicitly personal in nature, so tied by concrete references to the conditions of life and struggle in the colonized Caribbean. But time and again Césaire reveals himself to be wedded to a poetry that is capable of offering "to the ear or to the eye an unexpected but ineluctable body of vibrations" that he himself associates with Mallarmé.[65] Time and again he expresses his preference for "textual acoustics" over what he calls "the primitive" rhythms of African music derived from "the basest order of humanity, its nervous system" (his words), even if his goal is also to reflect subaltern experience.[66] In this context, it should be recalled that his main reservation concerning the African American poets he studied, translated, and admired was specifically that they failed to provide—to "a strictly lettered mind" ("un esprit strictement lettré"), as he puts it—the treasured Mallarméan "vibration."[67] Such remarks indicate that Césaire was fully a member of the modernist generation—and that he could not have been otherwise. Having grown up with the written rhythms of Victor Hugo ringing in his ears, Césaire might have found the textual vibrations of French poetry to be as visceral to him as the Creole rhythms he heard around him and the "black" rhythms he chose to study later in life. Of course, it is important to consider the attraction African American writing exerted on him—and this influence has received attention.[68] Further, we should take into account the role that black writing from many regions—including Haiti and Senegal—played in complicating his relation to the white French Symbolist tradition.[69] But during the first part of his career, Césaire was as influenced by the textual acoustics of Mallarmé and Rimbaud as he was by the verses he translated by Sterling Brown and the prose he admired by Claude McKay. It makes some sense, then, to place Césaire in the lineage of the French lyricists insofar as he, too, sought to "hear what is transpiring within the material, to see with the work's own eyes."[70] Pursuing what Adorno terms the "constructivist" impulse in modernist practice, Césaire yielded to the letter some of the initiative usually retained by constraints either prosodic (metrical, formal, generic) or expressive (representational, descriptive, declarative) in nature.

It is important to note, however, that listening to the relations among words, seeing their unfolding from the perspective of form, is significantly different from charging language with the task of revealing the true self. To be sure, "listening" to the medium ("*elle*," "*la langue*") is something the surrealists believed they were doing as well. We read in the *Manifesto of Surrealism* that the surrealist writer does nothing more than record an inner voice with an "*appareil enregistreur*." At least since Sartre's appraisal in 1947, Césaire has been read in the context of surrealism as if he, too, engaged in a variety of "automatic writing" for the purpose of divulging a true black unconscious. But it is specifically this image, inherited from generations of Césaire scholarship, that I wish to question here. In "Orphée noir," Sartre first depicts Césaire as a surrealist, casting him as the eponymous figure who descends "the royal road of his soul . . . to reach its limits and awaken the immemorial potentialities of desire."[71] The advantage of an account such as Adorno's (or Mallarmé's, or Rimbaud's, for that matter) is that it portrays writing as a much more complicated business, one having to do less with the revelation of some personal, or even collective unconscious than with a dialogue between a situated subject and equally situated means.[72] These means arguably expose an aspect of subjectivity—the writer's inscription in a particular field of cultural production—that cannot be equated with the writer's identity—understood either as his ethnic affiliation (his politics) or his unique psychological being. As Adorno observes in *Aesthetic Theory*, "technique," while instantiating "the extended arm of the subject, also leads away from that subject."[73] Exercising an aesthetic "sensibility," that singular "capacity to hear what is transpiring within the material, to see with the work's own eyes," involves activating another part of the self, a receptive, affective self that Adorno associates with attending to the internal relations among words.[74]

Of course, the craft of poetry writing in general requires that the poet "learn to be affected," as William James once put it.[75] The poet must develop an "ear" for the sounds that letters can make as well as an eye for the patterns that graphemes and words form on a page. All poets learn to be affected in this way. However, Adorno's point is that some (his canon of constructivists) privilege that affectual responsiveness, the mind's submission to language as thing, even at the expense of the communicative or referential function of language. Césaire's participation in this tradition is a matter of degree; every poet could be placed along a spectrum leading from one pole (the declarative, constative, referential, expressive) to the other (the metaphorical, alliterative, "constructive," "objective"). Although Césaire might not have been able to acknowledge it at the time, the African American poets he discusses in his "Introduction à la poésie nègre américaine" of 1941 are—as poets—also practicing a cultivated sensitivity to language; they are also "listening" through the "ears" of the work and "seeing" through its "eyes." But what distinguishes Césaire—and what makes his poetry so unique—is that he makes the page a site of friction between constructivist and expressivist modes. To a greater degree than most black poets of his time, Césaire "cedes the initiative to words," thereby relinquishing the insularity of the empirical self in an effort to discover a deeper "Self" registered in textual effects. In an interview accorded to Jacqueline Leiner published in 1978, Césaire associates these textual effects specifically with the constructivist conceit. In his words: "Influenced as I was by Mallarmé, I believe that the word has its own music, color, form, and force. I also believe that the word is PREHENSILE. The word allows me to grasp my Self. I only grasp myself through *a word*, through *the word*."[76] Or, in Adorno's rendering: "It is as labor, and not as communication, that the subject in art comes into its own."[77]

What is the relation between Césaire's contention—that "the word" grasps the "Self"—and Adorno's formulation—that labor on language reveals "the subject in art"? To begin with, one might want to register the difference between a "Self" with a capital "S," hypothetically a truer, deeper version of the subject, and "the subject *in art*," that is, a subject constituted only in the art object and existing nowhere else. Yet, on reflection, Césaire's "Self" and Adorno's "subject in art" do not appear so far apart. Adorno is stating that, while labor on language constructs an aesthetic subjectivity that is not identical to the empirical author, this labor nonetheless reveals important truths about that author (his or her implication in a set of productive conditions) that would otherwise remain foreclosed. In that regard, the "subject in art" provides a truer, more authentic account of the "I" than the author could consciously render without the mediation of a technique ("labor" on language).

Similarly, Césaire seems to be indicating that the mediation of writing is required to disclose aspects of his being that colloquial language use, or a less aestheticized approach, could not disclose. In both cases, it is forms of alienation (ideological constructions embedded in ordinary language) that obscure the truths that writing reveals. Writing—as mediation, not "communication"—works against these forms of alienation, allowing another order of discernment, another grasp on the world, to emerge. We might conclude, as does Sartre, that Césaire is pointing to the necessity of using writing—more precisely, automatic writing—to penetrate the carapace of identity that assimilation into French culture has imposed. But Césaire is not talking here (in his interview with Jacqueline Leiner) about automatic writing. He is not referring to the surrealist practice by which one putatively allows words to flow forth from the unconscious to reveal a deeper, un-alienated Self. Instead, Césaire is referencing Mallarmé's belief in what we might call the personality of words, his belief that "the word has its own music, color, form, and force"; Césaire then conjoins this belief to his own: "I also believe that the word is PREHENSILE." "Prehensile," we should note, is a zoological term meaning the faculty of being able to seize, to grasp, "with the hand or the mouth."[78] The craft that consists in relying upon one's syllabic intelligence to compose sonorities, to hear with the ears of the work, thus lends the word a kind of body (a "hand" or "mouth"—as well as "ears" and "eyes"). The paradox here is that a high level of craftsmanship (and thus agency) is needed to abandon volition (or agency); that is, a Mallarméen sensitivity to the "music, color, form, and force" of words is required to by-pass reified forms of expression (to derail the "direction personnelle enthousiaste de la phrase"), thereby allowing a "locus of authenticity" *other than the personal* to appear. Cultivating impersonality becomes a way of bursting open the confines of a congealed identity. Or, put differently, the act of fusing with the body of the text (refusing the author/medium, or subject/object, divide) is a way to avoid reiterating the stereotyped images of subjectivity that have been imposed on the raced, classed, and gendered self.

It is an attention to the letter that reveals a world of unpredictable images to Césaire. It is this same attention to the letter that draws Césaire closer to the high modernist craftsmen he admires. In response to the question I raised earlier—Why would some scholars wish to overlook Césaire's strong attachment to a text-centered modernism?—I would thus offer the following. By privileging Césaire's relation to Rimbaud and Mallarmé (as well as to Jolas and Joyce), we do indeed risk neglecting the African "soundscape" to which he might have been exposed.[79] To situate Césaire in the European modernist canon could indeed distort both the provenance and the purpose of his poetic experimentation. Yet by admitting that several orders of language—both written and oral, European and Afro-Caribbean—braid together to form his unique voice in writing, we facilitate a more complex account of diasporic literary production. Further, by resituating Césaire in the context of interwar modernist discourse, we discover the opportunity that an emphasis on textual experimentation can provide to re-think the very category of the self. Adorno's "subject in art," or aesthetic subjectivity, represents an alternative to more fixed notions of identity insofar as this aesthetic subjectivity will always escape definitive form. An aesthetic subjectivity rendered in letters will be sounded (phenomenalized) and interpreted in a limitless variety of ways as the text receives new readings. Such readings complicate the image of a self-identical subject, productively releasing the "I" from the hold of prefabricated representations while placing that "I " within the "grasp" of the circulating written word.

THE INDIVIDUAL SPHERE

One should be wary, however, of applying Adorno's understanding of the lyric project directly to Césaire without qualification. Adorno's comments on the lyric are written from the perspective of a European intellectual whose capacity to maintain the position of individual subject has been well established. Similarly, a Mallarmé or a Rimbaud has the luxury of "ceding" the initiative to words because that initiative is an unquestioned prerogative of the white author. In contrast, Césaire writes from a position that is far less secure; his right to be an author—indeed, his very ontology as a subject—is, among certain circles, still in question. My purpose is thus not to insist that Césaire is a modernist like any other, or that he adopts preforged techniques to produce what Adorno calls a "monadic" self-reflexive poem, a poem single-mindedly focused on its own internal dynamic. To a certain extent, Césaire is similar to his modernist contemporaries insofar as he, too, values a word-based craft (Jolas's "revolution of the word" and the invention of neologisms); he also resembles his symbolist predecessors insofar as he approaches words as modular, composed of letters and syllables that can enter into paronomastic and graphemic play. At the same time, though, he is committed to an expressive project of political emancipation. He thus mediates these high modernist practices through a lived situation that contains racial determinations forced on the collectivity to which he belongs, not to mention psychobiographical determinations all his own.

The subject who writes, the aesthetic subject or the "subject in art," clearly gives up something of his empirical, biographical substance. The act of writing lifts him out of the sphere of what Sartre would call his "situation" and allows him to engage in an imaginative performance guided by conventions, lexicons, and possibilities of technical innovation unique to a given métier.[80] In a sense, then, writing lends the empirical subject a new body, an affective subjectivity with textual eyes and textual ears. As Sartre writes in *Qu'est-ce que la littérature?*, writing offers freedom from facticity, transcendence from all determinations except those of the "prehensile" word.[81] Yet it must be stressed that the writing subject, as an empirical living being, also *mediates the medium*, bringing to bear an equally urgent set of communicative and expressive objectives that focus the project of "listening to" and "seeing" language in singular ways.[82]

Thus an important question remains, one that is particularly pressing in the case of Césaire: What happens when the modernist writer's charge is not only to "see with the eyes of the work" but also, and equally importantly, to convey a historical experience of trauma, to speak for a collective whose voice also demands to be inscribed? Adorno's own answer to that question is to insist that trauma as empirical fact can either silence language entirely ("after" Auschwitz) or, alternatively, reveal itself in negative form, as the cancellation of whatever remains of the subjective voice. Any attempt to forward the individual voice is complicit with a capitalist regime that has hypostatized (and marked) the "individual" as the ultimate end in itself. If art must go on, he concludes, the only viable ("authentic") artistic response to subjection ("total administration") is mimesis: the author mimes within the realm of language his abdication to powers beyond his control. A "ceding" of the initiative to language in the nineteenth century becomes, in the twentieth, a complete absorption into the linguistic machine, and lyric registers this state of total alienation by making the "linguistic quality" of the poem its "veritable subject."[83] In Adorno's most extreme articulation, that which speaks in the poem is a "latent I immanently constituted in the work *through the action of the work's language* [*durch dem Akt von dessen Sprache*]."[84] If the "latent I" or "poetic subjectivity" that "speaks in the poem" is "on no account identical" with the "empirical I"—if the "part played by the empirical I is not, as the topos of sincerity would have it, the locus of authenticity"—then the voice in the poem is nothing other than a kind of performative residue of the text, as Adorno's use of the German "*Akt*" (as in "speech act," or *Sprechakt*) implies.[85]

But is the work's "linguistic quality" the veritable subject of Césaire's poem? Is it the case that the "I" of the *Cahier* is "immanently constituted," that it is simply a linguistic object generated through internal textual play? Can we reduce the voice we read in the text entirely to the "action [*Akt*]" of the work's language? Or does Césaire's poem transmit something more, something other, than the driving agency of language alone?

Several problems derive from a strictly Adornian reading of the *Cahier*, a work written by a colonial subject racialized as black and only just beginning to emerge from colonial isolation in 1931. The first problem, of course, is that Adorno's theory is based on his reading of a European tradition of art and aesthetic thought, and that the *Cahier* fits only partially into this tradition.[86] Adorno is "not readily portable," as Deepika Bahri has observed, even if the conditions he analyzed—those of increasing global capitalization—underlie aesthetic epiphenomena throughout the colonized world.[87] As many critics now acknowledge, geographical distance and uneven histories of modernization create alternative temporalities of modernity and modern writing in the marginalized spaces of the colony (and postcolony). A second problem thus presents itself as a corollary of the first: If Beckett is the logical twentieth-century result of a nineteenth-century gesture (the abdication of authorial initiative to language), the question still remains why Césaire differs so strikingly from Beckett, why the "I" in the *Cahier* cannot—even for the sake of argument—be reduced to a "speech act" of language, witnessing and commenting on its own effects. The temporality of Césaire's modernism is obviously quite different from the modernist temporality (not to mention the modernist geography) of the canonical authors Adorno invokes.

And yet the possibility that an aesthetic subject might be constituted by a conflict between two equally strong forces—here, a need to communicate a shared condition of oppression (and establish a space for subjectivity) versus a desire to explore textual acoustics—is not foreign to Adorno's understanding. To be sure, similar to many Marxists of his generation (with the equivocal exception of Sartre), Adorno neglects the category of race as a distinctive case of alienation; for that reason alone his theory of the lyric voice fails to account for the singular positioning of the black author with respect to European culture and its implication in centuries of slavery and exploitation. Nevertheless, a reading of the Adornian corpus through the *Cahier* ends up shedding light on precisely those moments in his work when he returns to the empirical subject—not simply a "diminished" subject to be subsumed in textual dynamics, or "abdicated" in order to reflect the oppressive conditions of "total administration," but rather the empirical subject as a site of difference that exerts an agency all its own. In *Negative Dialectics*, a work that is clearly critical of the category of the "individual" as a twentieth-century commodied form, Adorno paradoxically states that the "sphere" of the individual is in fact the space that must be preserved if any freedom is to be won: "In this age of universal social repression, the picture of freedom against society lives in the crushed, abused individual's features alone."[88] And in *Minima Moralia*, Adorno's more sustained hymn to the contingencies of empirical subjectivity, he avers that "in the period of his decay, the individual's experience of himself and what he encounters contributes to knowledge. . . . In the face of the totalitarian unison with which the eradication of difference is proclaimed as a purpose in itself, even part of the social force of liberation may have temporarily withdrawn to the individual sphere. If critical theory lingers there, it is not only with a bad conscience."[89]

Ultimately, then, Adorno seems to be saying that the specific perspective the individual brings to poetic composition (gleaned from "the individual's experience of himself and what he encounters") is what determines the positionality—and provides the elocutionary energy—of resistance. What is not articulated in Adorno's text—but what rings clear in the writings of Negritude—is that confirming the individual may be a way of confirming the subjecthood, the political interiority, of the entire community to which the individual belongs. Bringing their trauma to expression via the individual allows that trauma to be heard, albeit in a mediated—but not necessarily reified—way. If it is true that "part of the social force of liberation may have temporarily withdrawn to the individual sphere," then a work that hopes to advance "liberation" must draw its force, at least in part, from that "individual sphere." Some of the resistant (and innovative) quality of the text—and thus its expressiveness—must derive from the lived experience of the author who composes it. Although Adorno is clear (sometimes to the point of blind insistence) that the writer's "subjectivity is on no account identical with the I that speaks in the poem"—and that the "part played by the empirical I is not, as the topos of sincerity would have it, the locus of authenticity"[90]—it is impossible to maintain the strictness of this assertion in the face of his equally urgent retrieval of "the crushed, abused individual's features" as "alone" the site of resistance to reification.[91] The empirical "I" of the author, his "experience of himself and what he encounters," contributes to the formation of the aesthetic subjectivity manifested in the poem in ways that must be examined in turn.[92]

Césaire's fascination with the French lyric tradition and his various modes of identification with that tradition's most celebrated figures have been well documented.[93] So, too, have his affinities with African American, Martiniquan Kreyol, Haitian Creole, and African expressive practices.[94] But Césaire did not merely absorb the influence of the latter (the African-inflected traditions), nor did he merely "cannibalize" the former (the French tradition). Instead, he worked to balance a sophisticated constructivist poetics inherited from Mallarmé and Rimbaud (leading "away from the [empirical] subject") with an expressive poetics developed alongside other members of minority and subaltern communities. As a black *poet*, he engaged in the modernist project to advance the most sophisticated textual techniques of his era. Yet as a *black* poet, he employed these techniques to represent a particular psychobiography informed by a particular collective experience—and of course representing the particular always involves developing yet another set of tools.

Césaire was "*absolument moderne*," then, in at least two senses. He lived a modern life, deeply involved in the twentieth-century vicissitudes of world war and decolonization; these vicissitudes left an imprint, as scholars have observed, on the various editions of a poem he felt compelled to rewrite again and again.[95] He also lived a modern *poet's* life, exposed early on to the printed word, educated to carry forward the flag of the Western canon, and enmeshed in the most progressive literary circles of interwar Paris. Thus, instead of writing a dated Parnassian poetry in the vein of Emmanuel-Flavia Léopold and Daniel Thaly, and instead of emulating the rhythms of dialect or composing oral epics associated with Africa or African-derived peoples, Césaire reworked the textual techniques he admired to produce effects I will call "oral*isms*"—innovative solutions to the pressures of both a biographical dilemma and "un esprit strictement lettré." These oralisms include most prominently the numerous refrains (e.g., "Au bout du petit matin"; "Ce qui est à moi"), modeled after what Albert Lord has called the "formulaic" nature and repetitive syntactic structure of oral epic; the rhetoric and anaphoric pattern of chant (e.g., "Eia pour . . ." [PA 47]; "voom rooh oh" [PA 30–31]); the repetition of single words in an enumeration intended to evoke for the eye (as well as the ear) the rhythmic pulse of the drum (e.g., "debout à la barre/ debout à la boussole / debout à la carte/ debout sous les étoiles" [PA 62]); and finally, the exploitation of the page itself to direct the reader's subvocalization. The ending of the *Cahier*, for instance, employs the "vers en escalier" (staircase verse)

debout
  et
  libre

to suggest an insistent beat—or the beat of insistence—by means of a typically modernist mode of lineation. As the following chapters demonstrate, Césaire and all the poets of Negritude mobilized the means of print—capitalization, indentation, punctuation, and the white of the page—to draw our attention to individual words or phrases, to produce (not necessarily to transcribe) modulations of pitch, tempo, and volume associated with the oral world.

Finally, the most pertinent (and symptomatic) oralism in the *Cahier* may be found in the multiplicity of its editions, the restless rewritings that characterize the history of its evolution (and presentation to the public) over the course of Césaire's entire lifetime. Just as oral epics change over time, so too the *Cahier* evolved, integrating fragments of stories, myths, and belief systems that the poet came across as he traveled and read. Critics who stress Césaire's debt to orature are correct insofar as oral forms also assimilate new events (or "encounters") into the narrative fabric. An oral poem is not fixed for all time on the page but rather is allowed to develop in ways not dictated by the letter. The newly integrated passages stand as marks of the empirical experience of the author, marks that may introduce inconsistencies on the level of graphemic and phonic patterning, symbolic structure, and narrative flow, endangering even the coherence of the perspective offered by the poem's "I." Such inconsistencies produce the sensation of the poem's restlessness or mobility. Lilian Pestre de Almeida relates this mobility of the *Cahier* to the oral aspirations of its author: "We discern in these constant revisions a visceral refusal of a *ne varietur* version," she writes; "it seems that this moving text [*ce texte mouvant*] is so because the author is most deeply attached to the *word*, not the *letter* [*il se rattache à la* parole *et non pas à la* lettre]."[96] Pestre de Almeida is right to underscore the sensation we have of the text as a moving object. However, I would attribute the restlessness, the numerous revisions and additions that transform the *Cahier* over time, to Césaire's simultaneous frustration with *and deep attachment to* the letter. If he had not maintained a respect for the letter's possibilities, then why would he have continued to write? Encounters with the letter and encounters beyond the text exerted equal pressure on Césaire, producing the unique quality of an aesthetic subjectivity that knows no rest.

We might think of the movement of the *Cahier* as a kind of nonidentity politics in the realm of writing, a refusal to treat the poem as a reified thing, just as Césaire's theory of Negritude refuses to treat "black" identity as congealed and defined for all time. While never relinquishing a commitment to context, Césaire proposes a model of writing as a process of perpetual unfolding that can also serve as a model of selfhood in general and Negritude in particular. His repeated attempts to revise the *Cahier* evince a desire to stage Negritude again and again, as a politics of identity *and* a politics of nonidentity—it had to be both at once. The *Cahier*'s failure to integrate all its multiple fragments, to massage its conflicting impulses into a seamless and stable whole, should thus be seen as its success. Only as an inconsistent and evolving aesthetic subjectivity—only as a text incorporating the aesthetic values of high modernism as well as the existential challenges of diasporic experience—could Césaire testify fully as a writer—not as a person but *as a writer*—for his time and place.

Through the action of the work's language, then, the *Cahier* speaks for a medium (the printed word). Yet simultaneously, through the pressure of the subject's history on the work's language, the *Cahier* speaks for a racialized experience. To evoke the terms provided by Nathaniel Mackey in *Discrepant Engagements*, a text that remains fully pertinent twenty years after its publication, we might say that Césaire explored to the fullest extent his commitment to two "discrepant," potentially incompatible programs. By advancing procedures associated with the avant-garde—for example, foregrounding the agency of the written support—Césaire ended up inflecting his racial identity, displaying an affinity that might have appeared "discrepant" at the time with respect to his political and racial affinities.[97] Conversely, Césaire also developed an experimental practice that is in turn inflected by his other "engagement," his commitment to a specific political agenda. To quote Mackey, he engaged "the discrepancy between [the] presumed norms [of modernist textuality] and qualities of experience that such norms fail to accommodate."[98] The many versions of the *Cahier* and the fact that Césaire found himself incapable of finishing it suggest that the historically situated subject continued to exert significant pressure, to push back against what Adorno calls the purely "linguistic quality" of the work. In this sense, the *Cahier* really is a work of "immobile verrition," in constant movement even as it remains fixed on the page. Challenging the autonomy of the text, Césaire maintains a constant dialectic between the empirical "I" constituted by facticity and the lyric "I" constituted "immanently through the action of the work's language" such that the law of this dialectic, its circular advancing rhythm, becomes the law of the work itself.

2

THE EMPIRICAL SUBJECT IN QUESTION

A Drama of Voices in Aimé Césaire's *Et les chiens se taisaient*

Je viendrais à ce pays mien et je lui dirais: "Embrassez-moi sans crainte . . . Et si je ne sais que parler, c'est pour vous que je parlerai."
Et je lui dirais encore: "Ma bouche sera la bouche des malheurs qui n'ont point de bouche, ma voix, la liberté de celles qui s'affaissent au cachot du désespoir."
Et venant je me dirais à moi-même: "Et surtout mon corps aussi bien que mon âme, gardez-vous de vous croiser les bras en l'attitude stérile du spectateur, car la vie n'est pas un spectacle, car une mer de douleurs n'est pas un proscenium, car un homme qui crie n'est pas un ours qui danse."[1]

I would go to this land of mine and I would say to it: "Embrace me without fear . . . And if all I can do is speak, it is for you I shall speak."
And again I would say: "My mouth shall be the mouth of those calamities that have no mouth, my voice the freedom of those who break down in the solitary confinement of despair."

> And on the way I would say to myself: "And above all, my body as well as my soul, beware of assuming the sterile attitude of a spectator, for life is not a spectacle, a sea of miseries is not a proscenium, a man who cries out is not a dancing bear."[2]

It is often hard, when teaching the *Cahier d'un retour au pays natal*, to draw my students' attention to the quotation marks surrounding the triptych of dramatic, declarative statements that serve as an epigraph to this chapter. My students—and, I suspect, readers in general—simply do not want to see them.[3] Overwhelmed by the relentless humiliations described in the opening pages of the *Cahier*, the reader yearns to believe that in this passage the poetic persona has at last achieved an apotheosis, that he has discovered his vocation and is now assuming that vocation in a performative gesture of almost oracular authority. And indeed, the images are potent: "the sterile attitude of a spectator"; "a sea of miseries"; "a dancing bear." Further, the triple negation in the last paragraph and the thrice repeated "I would say" are rhetorically powerful, constructed along the lines of classical oratory and fortified with the imperative "beware."[4] Césaire demonstrates his command of precisely the kind of speech his poetic persona dreams of performing. To take control of language in this way—and thereby to take control of a people's destiny—is an act that would transform mere speaking ("if all I can do is speak") into an event with material consequences. Such a speech act would strike down the "proscenium" and lift the masks off the actors, revealing them—their complaints and sufferings but also their gestures toward emancipation—to be real. Given the litany of sufferings and degradations that precede this passage, it is no wonder that readers long for the passage to be historical rather than rhetorical, and for the persona, the speaking "I," to rise fully to his elevated station, bearing the torch of resistance forward toward the dawn.

However, we must note that Césaire undercuts this moment of imagined apotheosis in several ways. First of all, the passage (entirely in the conditional and the future tenses) is followed immediately by the defeated, sarcastic exclamation in the present: "Et voici que je suis venu!" (And behold here I am!). We learn in the next line that all has returned to status quo: "De nouveau cette vie clopinante devant moi" (Once again this life hobbling before me). If we have read this far, we know that the victory has proved illusory and the grand gesture merely theatrical. We might notice, in addition, the persistent parabasis, the rhetorical act in which the actor—

dramatically—steps away from his dramatic role. The fact that "I would say" is followed by quotation marks signals that we are in the genre of soliloquy, privy to an interior monologue addressed to an absent "pays mien" ("my country," then "my people"). Although we might long for the speaker to assume his heroic role, we are obliged to acknowledge that he is merely quoting himself. He is rehearsing a speech he would like to make. In the guise of an authentic, inaugural intervention in history, the speaker is actually performing a theatrical act. In sum, the speaker repudiates performance ("a man who cries out *is not a dancing bear*") even as he indulges in performance, rendering his own gestures ambiguous, increasingly similar to an elaborate rhetorical act.

What, then, is the status of his warning: "beware of assuming the sterile attitude" of spectatorship? Against what, precisely, does the speaker need to guard himself? Why must his "body" and "soul" beware of spectating, of taking a safe distance from the "sea of miseries" that marches by before him like a parade across a stage? Is the warning (not to be a distanced spectator) precisely the kind of warning a leader, a speaker for "his people," must heed? Is the temptation of distance, of rhetoric, really so great? Finally, does it matter that the words "body" and "soul" have an intertextual ring ("above all, *my body* as well as *my soul*, beware"), that they conjure up the final lines of Rimbaud's *Une saison en enfer* in which the poet promises himself that "il me sera loisible de posséder la vérité dans une âme et un corps" ("I will be able to possess truth in *one soul* and *one body*")?[5] Is the danger of spectatorship linked somehow to the danger of allegory, to the fear that even when speaking to oneself, one is really quoting another, and that even when speaking for the other, one is reciting (white) lines? Or is the true danger of the dramatic situation that it highlights the possibility that one is *not* able to "possess truth" in "one" soul and "one" body? Could it be that truth distributes itself across many voices that inhabit (but are not exclusive to) a single self?

What would happen if these questions were brought to the stage, if the promise—"My mouth shall be the mouth of those calamities that have no mouth"—were spoken out loud? What if the warning—"beware of assuming the sterile attitude of a spectator"—were addressed to a group of live spectators watching a play? Or, alternatively, how would it feel to play the role of leader off the stage and beyond the text, to lend one's "voice" to "those who break down in the solitary confinement of despair" *for real*? And what if, in doing so, in acting out an ideal in the empirical world, one discovered that playing roles is in fact coextensive with being a leader who makes speeches? That is, what if the "empirical subject" were in some ways (which ways?) an aestheticized being?

THE PERFORMANCE WORLD VIEW

These may have been the very questions that Césaire was asking himself upon his return to Fort-de-France in 1939 and during the period of his confinement on an island controlled by Vichy until the summer of 1943. We now know that while teaching literature at the Lycée Schoelcher, Césaire was also developing two other careers, one as a dramatist (critics believe that he began his first play, *Et les chiens se taisaient*, in 1941[6]) and one as a politician (he won his first election in 1945). Both would require a good deal of stagecraft; both would test his ability to cross the line between imagination and reality; and both would cause him to interrogate the distinction between playing a role on stage and playing a role in history.

In the previous chapter, I followed Adorno in maintaining a distinction between the "aesthetic subject" and the "empirical subject"; in this chapter I begin to trouble the boundary between the two through a close reading of Césaire's first play, *Et les chiens se taisaient*. Adorno elaborates on the notion of the "aesthetic subject" that he inherits from the German aesthetic tradition in sections of *Aesthetic Theory* where he treats the "lyric I." He neglects, however, to develop a clear account of the *other* of the "lyric I," what he calls the "I" of "empirical existence," the "private person" of the author, or the "historical subject."[7] From the citations I have provided, it would be easy to conclude that the "aesthetic subject" is highly mediated whereas the "empirical subject" is not. After all, Adorno tells us that the living writer "constantly admit[s] into the production of his work an element of negativity toward his own immediacy," implying in this way that such an "immediacy" could exist.[8] Yet, clearly, Adorno never considers the human subject unmediated or fully coincident with himself. He indicates, to be sure, that the heightened mediation of aesthetic expression provides a greater scope for self-invention than the pressures of lived conditions would allow; even so, no subject functioning in the realm of everyday lived reality could remain consistently wedded to one essential identity or one "authentic" role. Adorno's critique of "the jargon of authenticity" and his treatment of the individual in *Negative Dialectics* and *Minima Moralia* is enough to dissuade any reader from erecting an Adornian "empirical subject" that would be consistently self-identical and transcendent of relational constraints. Still, Adorno's corpus is arguably not the place to look for a theory of the empirical subject as citational, or as defined by a series of different roles.

Instead, I turn to a text that I believe contains Césaire's own incipient theory of the "empirical subject" as a creation of performance, *Et les chiens se taisaient*. The model Césaire implicitly offers in this play resonates well, I hope to show, with the model of subjectivity advanced by scholars in the field of performance studies, one of the main contributions of which has been to put pressure on the distinction between performance and authenticity and thus to complicate our notion of what constitutes a person in "real life." Peggy Phelan has stated the matter succinctly: "It takes more than one person to be who you are."[9] From this perspective—which Phelan calls "the performance world view"—the question to ask is not "Which is the authentic self?" but rather "What are the *many* voices that inhabit and constitute the self?"[10] To do justice to a text as complex and enigmatic as *Et les chiens se taisaient*—an early work that has inspired surprisingly few critical readings—we need to bring Negritude studies into conversation with performance studies, a field that interrogates the very dichotomy between authentic and inauthentic on which many scholars of Negritude rely.

It is relatively easy to find Negritude texts in which the distinction between role-playing and sincerity, contingent identity and fundamental essence, serves as the rhetorical undergirding. For instance, in Damas's "Solde," the image of the inauthentic self-conscious *évolué* is contrasted with the fully revealed black body. Damas captures the speaker's fragile construction of identity through colonial mimicry in the following lines: "J'ai l'impression d'être ridicule / dans leurs salons / dans leurs manières / dans leur courbettes / dans leur multiple besoin de singeries" (I feel ridiculous / in their *salons* / with their manners / their bowing and scraping / their insatiable need for pretense).[11] Damas's conceit appears to be that if only the assimilated black could be liberated from his confining costume (the "smoking," "plastron," and "faux col"), the authentic African would finally burst out. Such a conceit, at least, is suggested by the engraving supplied by Frans Masereel that formed the frontispiece of the original 1937 version of *Pigments*.[12]

We might locate in Césaire's work evidence of a similarly dichotomous understanding of the subject (as either authentic African or inauthentic *assimilé*). For instance, in the earliest piece of writing by Césaire that scholars possess, "Nègreries: Jeunesse noire et assimilation," the author, like Damas, places "acting" on the side of assimilation (colonial mimicry) and authenticity on the side of "being oneself": "Mais pour vivre vraiment, il faut rester soi" (To truly live, one must remain oneself). "L'acteur," he writes in his contribution to the first issue of *L'Étudiant Noir* (March 1935), "est l'homme qui ne vit pas vraiment: il fait vivre une multitude d'hommes—affaire de rôles—mais il ne se fait pas vivre. La jeunesse Noire ne veut jouer aucun rôle; elle veut être soi" (The actor is the man who doesn't truly live: he brings alive a multitude of different men—really, a multitude of different roles—but he doesn't really bring himself to life. Black youth do not want to play any role whatsoever; they want to be themselves).[13]

The article's opposition of "être" (being) and "paraître" (seeming) is stark indeed; however, it is worth noting the arresting nuance introduced by the epigraph that Césaire draws from Jules Michelet: "Le difficile n'est pas de monter, mais en montant de rester soi" (What's difficult is not to rise in the world, but in doing so, to remain oneself).[14] By adding this epigraph, Césaire suggests that it is not only the black *évolué* who alone fears losing himself in the roles he is obliged to play; rather, social ascension entails self-alienation *in general*.[15] Césaire's intention is clearly not to conflate colonial mimicry with the congealment of personality that comes from assuming any representational function whatsoever; yet he demonstrates an awareness that role-playing is part of every public life—and increasingly so as one rises ("monter") in standing. Michelet's verbs ("monter" and "rester") tell the full story in gestural terms, the very same gestural terms that Césaire will evoke in "Nègreries," the *Cahier*, and throughout *Les chiens*: the problem is how to be consistant and stay in place ("rester") and yet evolve ("monter"), how to advance upward ("debout") and remain anchored ("lie-moi")—both at the same time.

Whereas much scholarship on Negritude has portrayed Césaire as the famous "nègre fondamental," highlighting the passages in which he seeks an originary African identity in the face of colonial subjectivation, I argue here that there exists another Césaire, one who refuses the rhetoric of identity and shows himself to be "multiple et difficile" (as the Rebel describes himself in *Les chiens*).[16] In Nick Nesbitt's probing terms, Césaire's works present "something more than the unambiguous affirmation of a self-identical black subject."[17] *Les chiens* is central to developing an alternative reading of Césaire that interrogates the rigid dichotomy between identity and performance, "être" and "paraître," for not only is *Les chiens* a play, and thus intrinsically concerned with the question of staging authenticity, it is also a sustained reflection on what it means to become a leader, to "monter" while struggling to "rester soi." The question *Les chiens* implicitly raises is whether identity is in fact inherently theatrical and citational. Can the "empirical subject"—the actor in history—"rester soi" (remain himself)? Isn't being a subject of any kind already a matter of negotiating various selves, voicing heterogeneous impulses, performing roles?

"THE OBSCURE SOURCE"

Until recently scholars believed that the first version of *Les chiens* was the one published in the 1946 volume, *Armes miraculeuses* (subtitled "Tragédie"), and that subsequently this version was transformed into a radio play, then a stage drama in 1955–1956 with the help of the German Africanist (and actor) Janheinz Jahn. In 2008, however, Alex Gil discovered what he calls the "Ur-text" of the play in the archive of Yvan Goll, the Alsatian poet responsible for translating and publishing Césaire's work while in New York during World War II.[18] Apparently, Césaire sent a copy of this "Ur-text" (subtitled "Drame") to André Breton during the war in order to keep it in safe hands; subsequently, Breton conveyed the manuscript to Goll, perhaps to be published. But Césaire did not want the manuscript to be published; on this point he is adamant in his letters to Breton. His comments (as well as Gil's own account of the manuscript) reveal to what a great extent the first version was attached to "circumstances." It related specific historical events, including the revolt and imprisonment of its historical hero, Toussaint Louverture. The reason Césaire gave for not wanting this version published was that "la part de l'histoire, ou de l'historicité" (the quotient of history, or historicity) was too great and would have to be "éliminé à peu près complètement" (eliminated more or less completely) in the versions to come.[19] Between the time Césaire began writing the play—which may have been as early as 1941—and the moment when he judged it complete—the play's publication by Présence Africaine in 1956 (subtitled "Arrangement théâtral")—he did indeed eliminate almost all traces of "historicité." The figure named Toussaint Louverture becomes the generic "Rebelle," and the scenes of a slave revolt in Haiti enacted in the first version on center stage become figments of the Rebel's imagination, "frescos" presented as memories or hallucinations occurring in an unspecified place and time.[20] In the first version, only the third act shows the hero imprisoned in a cell; in the final version, the entire play takes place in "solitary confinement," an echo chamber peopled by voices and figures produced in the delirium of the Rebel's last hours on earth.

As far as scholars have been able to ascertain, *Et les chiens se taisaient* was performed only a handful of times—as a radio play on January 16, 1956 (Radio Frankfurt, directed by H. O. Müller),[21] and at least four times as a staged performance (in Paris, for the Premier Congrès des Écrivains et Artistes Noirs in 1956; in Basil in 1960; in Hanover in 1963; and in Haiti in February 1993).[22] For this reason, the text is often considered a "texte-charnière," a "hinge" or transition text, located somewhere between the page and the stage.[23] Césaire himself designated *Les chiens* a "lyric oratorio," a genre that stages the voice in a very particular way. As a lyric, the text would focus on the internal drama of a single speaker, but as an "oratorio," the act of speaking would be drawn closer to collective spoken performance, presumably with little or no action realized on the stage. The voice in a lyric oratorio (as in a musical oratorio) bears the full burden of bringing all the action alive either through episodes of narration and description or, alternatively, through reenactments of scenes that hover somewhere between the imagined and the real. The fact that the text wavers ambiguously between genres is worth pointing out in itself. The generic ambiguity of *Les chiens* indexes an ontological problem at the heart not only of the play but of Césaire's work as a whole. *Les chiens* asks us where to draw the line between poetry and drama, drama and reality—or, to put it in Adorno's terms, the creation of an "aesthetic subjectivity" in writing and the action of the empirical person in history. More, it asks us to define what an "empirical person in history" *is*. The play, in other words, refuses to take for granted the nature of a living being, and it uses textual means—the poetry of the written word—to explore that nature on a page that is always, potentially, a stage.

Césaire stated in a 1969 interview that *Les chiens* was the obscure source—or "*nébuleuse*" (diffuse nebula)—from which all his other plays were generated.[24] He also admitted elsewhere that it bore the scars of the "problems" he was experiencing in his own life at the time.[25] These two statements taken together strongly suggest that *Les chiens* was the crucible in which he worked through many of the tensions fundamental to his creative and political lives. As A. James Arnold has written, "The problematic relationship of a heroic persona, lyric or dramatic, to the mass of colonized people is at the heart of the question."[26] If we return to the passage from the *Cahier* cited at the beginning of this chapter, we can see a pattern emerging: in both the poetic and theatricalized versions of the dilemma (that is, in both the *Cahier* and *Les chiens*), we meet a hero who yearns to speak for others, to lend his voice so that their words may be heard ("Ma bouche sera la bouche des malheurs qui n'ont point de bouche, ma voix, la liberté de celles qui s'affaissent au cachot du désespoir"). Yet this same hero worries about spectacularizing himself; that is, he worries that in the act of lending his voice to others, rising onto the stage of history, he might himself become a spectacle, an actor playing a role and thus false and inauthentic in his own eyes. In *Les chiens*, Césaire underscores even more clearly his fear that in representing others, one risks acting against one's own inner convictions, betraying one's own moral truths—which may be plural rather than singular, conflicting rather than univocal. How to lend one's voice to others without losing one's integrity is the moral problem staged, appropriately, in the form of a play of voices (not actions). "Integrity," this play of voices suggests, may consist not in the self's consistency, that is, not in the reduction of the self to a single objective or impulse; rather, "integrity" may entail a resistence to univocity, an admission of self-difference and internal contradiction. If the function of leader demands the performance of only *one* role, is assuming that role the accomplishment of authenticity, or is it instead a betrayal of being?

Many aspects of the play indicate that "the voice" ("la voix") is Césaire's central figure for the selfhood that he wishes to interrogate on stage. For instance, the very first stage directions of the play indicate that *Les chiens* will provide a *sound*scape, not a landscape; the curtain does rise, but it reveals an aural rather than a visual world: "Pendant que lentement se lève le Rideau on entend l'écho" (7) (While the curtain is slowly rising, the Echo is heard [3]). One *hears* the "echo"—and that aural phenomenon is the very essence of the character named "Echo." Indeed, one could argue that the Césairean character is, at bottom, a sonic entity, one that echoes, rather than produces, words. Beyond the main character of the play, "Le Rebelle" (the Rebel), we hear no fewer than forty-nine other voices, some of which receive names explicitly referring to their purely aural function, such as "Le Récitant" and "La Récitante" ("Reciters," male and female); the "Orateur"; "La Voix Céleste" (Celestial Voice); "La Voix souterraine" (Underground Voice); "Écho"; "Chantre" (Cantor); or simply "Voix." Many of these characters (or

"Voix") speak only once in the play, and few receive more than one line. Césaire in fact added to the number of "Voix" on stage every time he revised the play, complicating in this way the sonic environment more and more. Speeches uttered by one character in the earliest version were splintered into clusters of lines and distributed among an ever-increasing number of individual speakers in the later versions. It is as though the author had chosen to separate out and personify—to incarnate in a set of differently textured voices—the multiple and contradictory impulses that had originally been collected together and accorded to a single role.

For this reason, perhaps, *Les chiens* has proven difficult to stage, requiring as it does a large cast of characters lacking individuation (and whose means of entrance or egress are never indicated). The play is also a somewhat intimidating read, for it combines the metaphorical density of the *Cahier* with stage directions that, as textual and gestural elements, also deserve attention. Carried over from the *Cahier* we find the image of revolt as a volcanic force, of voyage as a path toward self-affirmation, of flora and fauna as figures both for the island's disease and its potential rebirth. Recent scholarship on the play has indicated that the passages the author introduced over time—from the initial draft, to the *Armes miraculeuses* edition of 1946, to the stage version of 1956—all move the plot toward a "mise en valeur de la problématique coloniale" (a privileging of the colonial problem).[27] Césaire indeed clarified the stakes of the play by adding the figures of the "Administrator" and the "Promotor," unidimensional straw dogs that parody the arguments of Empire in lines like: "Et nous leur aurions volé cette terre? . . . Dieu nous l'a donné" (10) (And they say we have stolen this land from them? . . . God gave it to us [5]).

While the author obviously wishes to emphasize the general attack he is making on colonialism (in terms consistent with his *Discours sur le colonialisme* of 1950), and while the change in the hero's name from Toussaint Louverture to "le Rebelle" also generalizes the action, there are reasons to believe that, over time, the figure of the Rebel was actually rendered more—not less—specific. This specificity derives not from any precise association with a given historical character but rather from the author's efforts, through revision, to place in the Rebel's mouth questions that reflect his own quandaries of the time. Following his visit to Haiti from May to December of 1944, Césaire ran on the Communist Party ticket and on May 27, 1945, was elected mayor of Fort-de-France and a few months later, on November 4, representative ("député") of Martinique at the Assemblée Nationale in Paris.[28] In the immediate postwar period, after suffering the isolation imposed on the island by the Vichy regime, Césaire was able to experience renewed and enriched contact not only with France but with many different regions of the world. The composition of the 1946 version coincides with the period during which Césaire prepared and successfully argued for the "Loi de départimentalisation" of Martinique, Guadeloupe, French Guyana, and La Réunion (ratified March 19, 1946). Also during the late 1940s, he deepened his affiliation with the French Communist Party and published the first version of *Discours sur le colonialisme* in a Parisian communist review, *Réclame*, on June 7, 1950. The first Congrès International des Écrivains et Artistes Noirs held at the Sorbonne September 19–22, 1956, brought him into contact with the African American writers Richard Wright and James Baldwin. Further, the Pan-African sentiments that had motivated his collaborative journalism while studying at the Rue d'Ulm were confirmed and nourished by his friendship with the Senegalese teacher, writer, and senator Alioune Diop, with whom he cofounded the review *Présence Africaine* in 1947. The third version of *Les chiens* was written during the years 1955–1956, a period that coincides with his growing dissatisfaction with and final departure from the French Communist Party and the publication on October 24, 1956, of his *Lettre à Maurice Thorez.*

In sum, it is hard to imagine a time of greater political turmoil in Césaire's life than this one. As critics have observed, the underlying narrative of most of Césaire's works is the "problematic relationship" between private and public, or individual and crowd; but in *Les chiens*, the author's struggle with this relationship is reflected in the fundamentally unstable generic identity of the work, the way it borrows conventions from tragic, historical, mythic, and lyric modes.[29] First a "*drame*," then a poem, then an "oratorio," then a "*tragédie*," *Les chiens* offers us a main character whose identity cannot be exhausted by a single genre (with its genre-based understanding of the subject). No posture Césaire could assume, no image he could fabricate, could entirely resolve the issues with which he was faced. In a language heightened by dense metaphor, scored as symphonic arrangement, and accompanied by physical gestures of great dramatic resonance (the Rebel lies prone in the form of a cross; he wanders blindly through a sea of corpses), the play eludes representation while drawing communicative force from a plethora of genres and intertexts. The Rebel is at once a tragic hero, a mythic demigod, a historical figure, and a vulnerable subject. To serve as the vessel through which Césaire could project his own dilemmas, questionings, reversals, and transformations, the Rebel had to be all at once.

A THEATER OF INTERIORITY

As one might expect, a study of the text reveals that the scenes added to the 1956 revision tend to underscore the Rebel's complexity, his many facets as a human being, even as the basic plot line is maintained. This plot line unfolds as follows: A slave (le Rebelle) who has killed his master is placed in a cell to await execution; during a long night, he relives in a kind of dream state scenes from the history of slavery and colonialization, imagining the arrival of the whites ("Les Blancs débarquent!"), evoking a lost African past, and describing the historical conditions of enslavement. Intermittently, he also rehearses personal travails: in scenes that could be played as occurring in real time or as hallucinations (depending upon the choice of the director), he hears but denies the pleas of his mother, who wants him to renounce his role as leader, and he fends off the seductions of the Lover (L'Amante), who reminds him of his responsibilities to his son. For the dramatic version of 1956, Césaire enlarged the role of the Lover, suggesting the greater pull on him of carnal and domestic needs. In addition, Césaire inserted two long and important monologues to the second and third acts, monologues that lend the hero a depth of self-reflection we tend to associate with the speaker of the *Cahier*. The inserted passages challenge what is otherwise a continuous momentum leading us from the early scenes in which the Rebel refuses intimacy with the important figures in his life (the Lover and the Mother), to the culminating scene in which he fuses with an anonymous cry of revolt, the "*cri farouche*" that gives voice to "trois siècles de nuit amère conjurés contre nous" (61) (three centuries of bitter night conspiring against us [35]).

One of the major themes of the play is that of solitude, understood both as a physical condition (the "solitary confinement" of Toussaint in his cell) and a metaphysical condition (the loneliness of the martyr who chooses transcendence over implication in the prosaically human). The Rebel's exchanges with the other characters suggest that he must break all personal ties that identify him as a unique individual in order to serve single-mindedly his people and his cause. First the Lover comes to visit him in his cell, then the Mother; both scenes end with the Rebel's rejection of the compromise they offer. Here Césaire is employing the topos of the epic hero who must choose solitude over intimacy in order to perform his duty to a greater (and anonymous) collective. Given that a similar scene takes place in *La tragédie du Roi Christophe* between Christophe and his wife (the scene between Aeneas and Dido in Virgil's *Aeneid* is probably the intertext for both plays), it is easy to assume that Césaire also understood his own dilemma (as a young father and husband) in this way. To represent a people, to be "la bouche de ceux qui n'ont point de bouche," a leader must shut his ears to the voices of libidinal desire and filial affection calling out to him. Appropriately, then, in *Les chiens* the Rebel's quest for metaphysical solitude is figured as a series of *vocal* dispossessions (and, at times, repossessions). Abjuring all earthly temptations, he longs to become the vessel of only one cry—the authentic cry of revolt. In one of the most compelling scenes of the play (in act 2 in the 1956 edition), the Rebel puts this desire into words:

> Le Rebelle (tâchant de se relever): Et laissez-moi, laissez-moi crier à ma suffisance le bon cri saoul de la révolte, je veux être seul dans ma peau,
> je ne reconnais à personne le droit de m'habiter,
> est-ce que je n'ai pas le droit d'être seul entre la paroi de mes os?
> et je proteste et je ne veux pas d'hôte, c'est terrible
> je ne peux faire un pas sans que je sois agrippé.
> Du ravin, de la montagne, du bayahonde, mâchant de la canne, suçant des cirouelles . . .
> La statue que nous sommes en train d'ériger, camarades, la plus belle des statues. C'est pour les coeurs absolus avec sur les bras notre très grand désespoir à force de frémir, dans l'air lourd et dégagé d'oiseaux, la plus belle des statues, la seule où ne pousse pas l'ortie: la solitude. (50)

> And let me shout [*crier*], let me shout out the good drunk shout [*cri*] of revolt to
> My heart's content, I want to be alone in my skin,
> I do not grant anyone the right to inhabit me,
> haven't I the right to be alone between the walls of my bones?
> and I protest and I don't want a guest—it's awful—

I can't take a step without being seized.
In the ravine, on the mounain, in the bayahonde, chewing on
  sugarcane,
sucking on ciruelas . . .
The statue that we are erecting, comrades, the most beautiful
  of statues. It is for absolute hearts, across its arms our
  terrible despair from so much trembling, in an air heavy and
  emptied of birds, the most beautiful of statues, the only one from
  which nettles do not sprout: solitude. (29; translation modified)

Ultimately the Rebel will accomplish his goal: he will be left alone ("laissez-moi") to cry out as loudly as he wishes ("crier à ma suffisance") a singular cry: "le bon cri saoul de la révolte"—or the "cri d'animal pris au piège" (78) (cry of a trapped animal [45]). Yet in doing so, in achieving the solitude of the singular cry, he also succumbs to death. Rodney Harris reads this speech as announcing the hero's "mission," which is to "liberate himself from all obstacles, those that he finds within himself and those posed by others."[30] Harris's reading makes a good deal of sense, for the Lover and the Mother are indeed obstacles to the Rebel's quest, voices of desire that remind him of the voices of desire within himself. Throughout the play, seductions both domestic and political are figured as voices that threaten to "inhabit" the "the walls" of the self: "la paroi de mes os." Pure solitude, the imagery suggests, would transform the Rebel into a kind of architectural edifice, a monument ("la statue") not to the self but to an anonymous "we."

After the Lover leaves the scene (but before the Mother arrives), two potentially more dangerous temptations assail him, both represented as "voices." The "Première Voix Tentatrice" (First Voice of Temptation) seems to do nothing more than echo the Rebel's own fears, namely, that he cannot maintain a steady course because he has no guide, no ancestry, and no future. In the Rebel's words: "j'ai beau aiguiser ma voix / tout déserte tout . . . ma voix tangue dans le cornet des brumes sans carrefour / et je n'ai pas de mère/ et je n'ai pas de fils" (36) (no matter how I sharpen my voice / all deserts me . . . my voice pitches in the foghorn of mists without crossroad / and I have no mother / and I have no sons [20]). These sentiments are repeated by the First Voice of Temptation, who echoes: "je n'ai pas de mère je n'ai pas de passé" (39) (I have no mother I have no past [22]). Specifically why total forgetting ("oubli") should be a temptation is not clear, but we might surmise, given other indications in the play, that reconnection with the past is an arduous task, one the Rebel would at times prefer to abandon. This path is denied not just by the whites in the play but also by his fellow slaves who, speaking in the guise of the "Choeur," consistently urge the Rebel to choose compromise over vengeance, a connection with the living over a connection with the dead, and therefore forgetting over remembering.

The Second Voice of Temptation sounds yet another note of hopelessness; near the close of act 1, this "Voice" exclaims that there is no more justice in the world: "l'action de la justice est éteinte" (40) (judicial function is finished [22]). Apparently, in the "Ur-text" of *Les chiens*, the speech delivered by the Second Voice of Temptation was originally part of the Rebel's own monologue; in revising his play, Césaire transferred what were the Rebel's own words into the mouth of an external character.[31] The fact that the Rebel's thoughts and observations could be assigned to other characters suggests that many of the voices we hear in the play are actually vessels for the Rebel's own inner voices. That is, those who contradict, tempt, or echo him may be stage incarnations of parts of his own psyche. These stage incarnations, these multiple voices of consciousness, are highly seductive, as continuous allusions in the play to the sensual texture of the speaking voice confirm: "Ma voix froisse des mots de soie," states the First Voice of Temptation (84) (My voice rustles with silken words [48]). Again, it is the character's "voice" that seduces, not the character's appearance or actions. The voice, as a conveyor of words, bears the threat of dissuading the Rebel from his course.

The two Voices of Temptation that we first encounter in act 1 reappear later in the play as well. This time their function is clearer: they are there to encourage the Rebel to assume yet another role he will ultimately decline, the role of King. These Voices of Temptation are joined by the "Récitant" who also insists upon the royal nature of the Rebel: "il habite en toi un être royal" (84) (I say that there lives in you a regal being [48]). The First Voice of Temptation then follows up with a more insidious form of seduction: "veux-tu de l'argent? des titres? de la terre? Roi? . . . c'est ça . . . tu seras roi" (85) (is it money you want? Titles? Land? King . . . that's it . . . you will be king [49]), to which the Second Voice of Temptation adds: "c'est vrai qu'il y a quelque chose en toi qui n'a jamais pu se soumettre" (85) (it's true, there's something in you that could never submit [49]). We find articulated here the same temptation that the speaker in the *Cahier* also encounters, then rejects:

"Je refuse de me donner mes boursouflures comme d'authentiques gloires. . . . Non, nous n'avons jamais été amazones du roi du Dahomey . . . " (I refuse to view my sick swellings as true glory. . . . No, we have never been amazons of Dahomey's king [PA 38]). In both poem and play, the hero insists upon refusing all roles other than that of the incorrigeable rebel, rising up against historical injustice. To the chorus's "Tu n'échapperas pas à ta loi qui est une loi de domination" (86) (You will not escape your own law, which is the law of domination [50]), the Rebel responds that his law is, conversely, to efface himself, to become the pure voice of revolt: "Ma loi est que je courre d'une chaîne sans cassure jusqu'au confluent de feu qui me volatilise qui m'épure et m'incendie de mon prisme d'or amalgamé"(87).[32] Ultimately, what he seeks is to be transformed from a human being (lover, son, father, king), traversed by all sorts of desires, voices, and imperatives, into a hollow vessel, something "intact" and "nu" but also emptied of life: "Eh, bien, je périrai. Mais nu. Intact" (87) (So, I will perish. But naked. Intact [50]); "je suis nu / je suis nu dans les pierres / je veux mourir" (88) ("I am naked / I am naked in the stones / I want to die" [51]). The Rebel's "law," he states, is not to consolidate an identity but rather to advance ever further toward the dispersal of that impure amalgam that is the self: "my prism of amalgated gold" (50). Finally, in a scene in which a messenger arrives to announce an offer of clemency, even the act of hearing or acknowledging the voice of the other is associated with the betrayal of a singular "law" or mission. The Messenger, at first unheard, repeats his greeting, "J'ai dit salut" (I said, hail), to which the Rebel responds: "qui m'appelle? J'écoute je n'écoute pas . . . / ravale ton message / je veux mourir ici/ seul" (78–80) (Who calls me? I listen I don't listen . . . / Swallow your message / I want to die here/ alone" [45–46]).

As the play draws to a close, the Rebel pulls himself up one last time to announce his radical solitude, only now that solitude is the precondition for an even greater fusion with the larger community of the suffering, also represented as "voices" that penetrate the self. He has been badly beaten by his two jailors (both a woman and a man) and now feels his entire body rupturing and breaking apart: "des mains coupées . . . de la cervelle giclante" (108) (Severed hands . . . spurting brain" [61]). With all temptations now in the past, he assumes the role he always wanted to play, that of a disembodied mouth, channeling the voices of the dead. He begins his final monologue by invoking the gods of the "en bas" (as opposed to some distant, celestial divine), then alludes to his injured "gueule," an animal mouth or muzzle, and designates it a vessel for the sounds of anonymous beings: "Dieux d'en bas, dieux bons / j'emporte dans ma gueule délabrée / le bourdonnement d'une chair vivante/ me voici" (116) (Gods below, benevolent gods / I bear within my broken muzzle / the buzz of a living flesh/ here I am[33]). The deictic, "me voici," which the Rebel repeats again and again, could almost be read as a confirmation of his reduction to pure voice—"me *voix*-ci," for his person has been reduced to a ruined mouth, a "gueule délabrée." What follows is a long incantation in which he imagines other sounds, not simply the "bourdonnement" of his flesh but also "une rumeur de châines" (a rumble of chains) from the depths of the sea, "un gargouillement de noyés" (a gurgling of the drowned), "un claquement de fouet" (the cracking of a whip), and finally, "des cris d'assassinés" (cries of the murdered) (116; 67). By hollowing himself out, by refusing to allow others to "inhabit" the "paroi" of his bones, the Rebel has recreated the self as a cavity within which the voices of the past may now resonate. The imagery suggests that an entire ship of drowned slaves has reached the surface via the vessel that is his throat. He thus imagines himself speaking not for himself, nor even for the crowd, but rather for an entire people, including generations of ancestors carried over the Middle Passage, as in the *Cahier*'s final passage: "la négraille assise / inattendument debout . . . debout et non point pauvre folle dans sa liberté et son dénument maritimes" (PA 61–62); "je te livre mes paroles abrupte . . . embrasse-moi jusqu'au nous furieux / embrasse, embrasse NOUS" (PA 64).

In the final climactic scene the Rebel's broken body welcomes the voices of the dead—"Obstacle donc salut!"—as though they were his salvation (the alternate meaning of "salut"). The "gargouillement des noyés" and the "cris d'assassinés" mingle with voices emerging from the local landscape: "Oh le cri," he exclaims, "toujours ce cri fusant des mornes . . . et le rut des tambours" (117) (oh the cry . . . always this cry bursting from the mornes . . . and the rutting of the drums" [67; translation modified]). However, in the final moments, even these sonic presences are drowned out by the beating of the drums. The stage directions indicate that all voices on stage have been overwhelmed by one sound alone: first that of the barking dogs, then that of the tom-toms: "Le Rebelle s'affaisse, les bras étendus la face contre terre, à ce moment des tams-tams éclatent, frénétiques, couvrant les voix (117) (The Rebel collapses, his arms outstretched, his face against the ground; at that moment a frenetic burst of tom-toms blocks out the voices" [68]). "Aboyez tams-tams / Aboyez chiens" (Bark tom-toms / Bark dogs), the Rebel implores. It seems that the ultimate battle between forces is finally to take place. As "secrets enfermés sous un tour de gorge montent dans le clocher du sang" (119) (secrets choked back by a twist of the gullet ascend to the steeple of the blood" [69; translation modified]), the barking of the dogs and the beating of the drums rise up to meet them.[34] The entire soundscape is saturated with a cacophony that gradually fades out as the last human presences, the Récitant and the Récitante, also die. We are left, then, not with the sound of human voices, and not even with the barking of dogs or the beating of drums, but with a soundless tableau of an unpeopled world. The final stage directions of the play depict a purified but mute "Vision"; "Vision de la Caraïbe, bleue semée d'îles d'or et d'argent dans la scintillation de l'aube" (120) (Vision of the blue Caribbean spangled with gold and silver islands in the scintillation of the dawn [70]). If the play is, as I have been arguing, a theatricalization of consciousness through the multiplication of voices, then why does it end with silence, all sound replaced by a singular Vision? What does it mean when the cacophony of a conflicted consciousness fades into the muteness of the seen?

FROM "SAVAGE CRY" TO WORD

At this point, we might want to recall that before being performed live on a stage, *Et les chiens se taisaient* existed as a radio play. Césaire's first revisions to the 1946 text (as a result of Janheinz Jahn's prodding) were thus completed with the goal of producing a set of radiophonic voices. Douglas Kahn and Gregory Whitehead have observed that the radiophonic voice tends to establish a curious (and media-specific) type of intimacy between the speaker and the listener.[35] Radio, although a nonimmediate form of communication, nonetheless produces the fantasy of a unique address; the listener, often secluded in a room rather than outside in public, feels as though the voice coming over the airwaves were destined for her ears alone. In contrast, the staged drama presupposes a numerous spectatorship; it draws on both the aural and the visual senses, offering at once the proximity implied by hearing and the distance ensured by the faculty of vision. By choosing to end his drama with a "Vision"—afforded by the silencing of the dogs—Césaire underscores the visual dimension of the theater, the way in which it approximates (and partakes of) pure spectacle. (There can be no "Vision" in a radio play; silence can only be described by yet another voice.) As in the *Cahier*, where "spectacle" is associated with oppression, indifference, and the denial of suffering ("car la vie n'est pas un spectacle . . . un homme qui crie n'est pas un ours qui danse"), so too in *Les chiens* pure visual spectacle may be associated with domination, with the stamping out of the "cry" and the silencing of all rebellion and critique. Such an association is established in a speech the Rebel delivers to the Lover, the mother of his son: "Dis-lui que je n'ai pas voulu que ce pays fût seulement une pâture pour l'oeil, la grossière nourriture du spectacle" (61) (Tell him that I did not want this country to be nothing more / than fodder for the eye, the crude stuff of spectacle [35]). In a sense, these lines provide an explanation for the Rebel's actions: he has raised his voice (uttered the "cri" and proferred the "Parole") specifically so that the "pays" will not be reduced to an empty spectacle ("une pâture pour l'oeil"). If one keeps Césaire's symbology of the visual in mind (his association of spectacle with suppression), then one cannot help wondering whether the final "Vision" at the end of the play might represent not merely the death of the Rebel but also the death of subjectivity, the total silencing and suppression of consciousness understood as a lively contest of voices.

In *The Ritual Theater of Aimé Césaire*, Marianne Wichmann Bailey reads the ending in more positive terms than I have offered here. She sees in the final "Vision" an "apocalyptic scenario" in which "forces of obliteration" clean the slate (clear the stage) so that a new, purer world may emerge. The barking dogs, she contends, represent "heralds of the Apocalypse, messengers of the fruitful death."[36] There is much to be said for a mythic interpretation of *Les chiens*; as Bailey observes, the dramatic arc of the play follows the classical trajectory in which a hero passes through the land of the dead (the Rebel channels the voices of drowned slaves) in order to rise up again and die—spectacularly—in an act of cathartic self-immolation that purifies the world. Femi Ojo-Ade, however, has also questioned the positive reading of *Les chien*'s conclusion as hearkening a new day. In *Aimé Césaire's African Theater: Of Poets, Prophets, & Politicians*, Ojo-Ade contends that the play ends inconclusively with a Rebel who has become tragically disconnected from his people.[37] The supposed leader suffers from an inability to reconcile his craving for solitude—which Ojo-Ade finds "cynically" expressed in the line "One does feel better alone"—with his desire for "total brotherhood." What remains unexplained in these two insightful, if incompatible, readings is the symbology of the voices, which is not exhausted by recourse to a mythic subtext.

Why, for instance, would the Rebel's mouth, finally sheltering voices of the past, become a "gueule," a dog's muzzle, emitting the "cri d'animal pris au piège" (78)? Why would the retrieval of the past, the painful recall of human suffering, require a protest that has lost its human tone?

Bailey surmises that animality constitutes the appropriate response to the savagery of Empire: "Unbearable atrocity mounts to its apex" at the end of the play, she writes, "and invokes its own culmination." The land, "despoiled and plunged into bestiality, finds again its primitive, barbarous face, its monstrous animal powers."[38] But if Césaire ever believed that showing a "barbarous face" was the appropriate way in which to confront the barbarity of colonialism, he did not consistently aver that this should be so. When he published the play a second time in 1956 as an independent volume, he added two significant passages that address the difference between human voices and animal sounds, and the difference between a reasoned response to violence and bloodthirsty revenge. It is now time to turn to those revisions and examine the way in which they complicate the kind of mythic reading Bailey offers. The revisions also provide further evidence that the author was by no means convinced that a complex and conflicted interiority (the variety of human voices that constitute the self) could be replaced by a single, authentic identity. Indeed, the added passages, like the dramatic ending of the play, suggest instead that the alternative to polyvocal heterogeneity is not authenticity but rather the spectacularization (and silencing) of the self.

Already in 1946 the author had made significant revisions to the play, replacing vivid scenes of action with heroic monologues in which that action is recalled or hallucinated (played out in the background). For instance, the slave revolt that initially occurred in act 1 in the 1944 version became a pantomime two years later. We read in the stage directions of the 1946 version:[39] "Loin, très loin, dans un lointain historique le choeur mimant une scène de révolution nègre . . . " (27) (Far, very far, in a historical distance—while the chorus mimes a scene of black rebellion . . . [15]). The hero also describes the murderous revolt, presumably so that, if the text were read or performed as a radio play, listeners could still imagine what had taken place. He tells us that a group of slaves (which the stage directions call "énergumènes," suggesting that they are possessed, like followers of Dionysios) shouted out the refrain "Mort aux Blancs. Mort aux Blancs" (28) (Death to the whites, death to the whites [15]). The 1956 version distances the action even further, for here, in the added scene, the Rebel explicitly repudiates his earlier participation in the revolt: "pourquoi ai-je dit 'mort aux Blancs'?" he asks himself; "est-ce qu'ils croient me faire plaisir avec ce cri farouche?" (55) (Why did I say 'Death to the whites? / Do they think this savage cry pleases me? [32]). Perhaps overhearing the cry "Mort aux Blancs" coming from the crowd outside the jail, the Rebel now winces at the reminder of his own unleashed fury.

The 1956 addition suggests that, at least at this moment in the (revised) play, the Rebel no longer identifies completely with the animal-like ("farouche") cry he embraces at the play's end. Césaire chose to leave the ending of the play unchanged, yet the passage added in 1956 suggests an equivocation:

> Le Rebelle: (Il réfléchit.)
> . . .
> *Ressentiment*? non; je ressens l'injustice, mais
> je ne voudrais pour rien au monde troquer
> ma place contre celle du bourreau et lui ren-
> dre en billon la monnaie de sa pièce sanglante
>
> Rancune? Non. Haïr c'est encore dépendre
> Qu'est-ce que la haine, sinon la bonne pièce de bois attachée au cou
>   de l'esclave
>   et qui l'empêtre
> ou l'énorme aboiement du chien qui vous prend à la gorge
> et j'ai, une fois pour toutes, refusé, moi d'être esclave
> Oh! rien de tout cela n'est simple. Ce cri de 'Mort aux Blancs,' si on ne
>   le crie pas
> C'est vrai on accepte la puante stérilité d'une glèbe usée, mais ha!
> si on crie pas: 'Mort" à ce cri de 'Mort aux Blancs,' c'est d'une autres
>   pauvreté
>   qu'il s'agit.
>   Pour moi,
> je ne l'accepte ce cri que comme la chimie de l'engrais
> qui ne vaut que s'il meurt
> à faire renaître une terre sans pestilence, riche, délectable, fleurant
>   non l'engrais

Mais l'herbe toujours nouvelle
Comment débrouiller tout cela? (55–56)

The Rebel: (He reflects.)
. . .
Resentment? No. I resent the injustice, but under no circumstances would I trade my place for that of the executioner and give him small change for his bloody coin.

Rancor? No. To hate is to still be dependent.
What is hatred, if not the wood collar tied to the slave's neck and that hampers him
or the awesome barking of the dog that sinks its teeth into his throat
and I, I have refused, once and for all, to be a slave.
Oh! none of this is simple. This cry of 'Death to the whites,' not screaming it,
it is true, means accepting the fetid sterility of worn-out soil, but ha!
But crying 'Death' to this cry of 'Death to the whites' involves another poverty. For me,
I accept this cry only as the chemical in the fertilizer
whose sole worth is in that dying
that regenerates a land without pestilence, rich, delectable, smelling not of fertilizer
But of ceaselessly fresh grass.
How to disentangle all that? (32)

We might speculate that Césaire added this expression of remorse to the 1956 version in order to remind his audience that rebellion against enslavement does not have to become an incitement to murder. Césaire might have been sensitive to the accusation that Negritude could become a racist anti-racism, a movement as inhumane as the inhumanity it protests.[40] The addition appears to reflect a growing suspicion on the part of the author that violence and hate are morally unacceptable—and perhaps even ultimately ineffectual—ways to end the violence inflicted by colonialism itself. It is not incidental that during the 1950s Albert Camus was also reflecting on the problem of violence, particularly the violence incited by injustice and thus potentially legimized as a form of resistance. In 1951 Albert Camus published *L'homme révolté*, a philosophical-political text that considers killing another human being, even in a rebellion against injustice, to be morally repugnant. Césaire may very well have been influenced by this work as well as by the post-Occupation debates around the "*épuration*," the Nuremburg trials, and the growing tensions in French intellectual circles caused by the behavior exhibited by Stalin's Soviet Union, not to mention the rising turmoil in Algeria that would erupt into war in 1954.

It is clear from literary and extraliterary evidence that all throughout the era immediately prior to the decolonization of Africa and the establishment of independent African states, Césaire was battling within himself to reconcile his yearning for change with a fundamental mistrust of violence. For instance, in the essay "L'homme de culture et ses responsabilités" (The man of culture and his responsibilites), the text he presented at the Second Congrès des Écrivains et Artistes Noirs in April 1959, he supports armed resistence as an inevitable facet of revolution; yet later he chose to suppress the text from publication in the 1976 Désormeaux edition of his *Oeuvres complètes*.[41] Perhaps he considered lines such as the emphatic "*l'impérialisme aura été militairement vaincu*" (imperialism will have been vanquished by military means) and "*la décolonisation vraie sera révolutionnaire ou ne sera pas*" (true decolonization will be revolutionary or not at all) too incendiary to be preserved for posterity.[42] The tensions that arose between Césaire and Fanon between 1956 and 1959 (or, the First and the Second Congrès des Écrivains et Artistes Noirs) were caused by what the latter perceived as the older statesman's reticence with regard to militant action. Although Césaire expressed several times his admiration for Fanon's involvement in Algeria's resistence movement, the Front de Libération Nationale, he maintained a distance from armed struggle all his life.[43]

In short, the role of violence was a problem for Césaire, and it is a problem for the Rebel as well. Although "rien de tout cela n'est simple," as the Rebel states, the play makes it clear that the violence of reprisal—the violence that counters violence—is generated by the contagion of colonialism itself. Thus, by saying "no" to "Resentment" and "Rancor," the Rebel is indicating that he does not want to have his actions determined by the actions of the colonizers. Stated figuratively, the Rebel does not want his body to be burdened by taking on the weight of the hate that the white colonizers have generated: "Qu'est-ce la haine, sinon la bonne pièce de bois / attachée au cou de l'esclave." Perceiving that a reaction-formation is at the root of the slaves' cry "Mort aux blancs!" he challenges himself not to make that cry, to step outside the relentless cycle of retribution, to cry "death!" to the "cri de 'Mort aux Blancs'" itself. Of course, there is some irony in Césaire's recycling of the same terms ("death" to "death"), yet calling for the death of a deathwish is not the same thing as calling for the death of a human being. The latter, the call to murder, is a "cri farouche," a savage cry that makes men into dogs. "Hatred" is the "awesome barking of the dog that sinks its teeth into his throat," we read in the passage inserted in 1956. To utter the cry of hatred is, in effect, to become a dog, to allow one's throat to be transformed into a dog's "gueule."[44]

The last lines of the 1956 addition intimate that there might be an alternative to the cycle of violence, an alternative to identifying with this "cri farouche . . . qui vous prend à la gorge." Instead of repeating the cry "Mort aux Blancs," that is, one might imagine a world in which the howling of dogs—and the shouting of cries ("Mort aux Blancs")—would cease. This world, depicted by the Rebel in the passage cited below, resembles one we have already seen in the *Cahier*. As in the earlier poem in which the speaker claims that there is sufficient room "pour tous au rendez-vous de la conquête" (PA, 57–58), in the play the Rebel envisions a world in which diverse races (figured here as diverse species of trees) might grow together and flourish:

> Je suppose que le monde soit une forêt. Bon!
> Il y a des baobabs, du chêne vif, des sapins noirs, du noyer blanc;
> je veux qu'ils poussent tous, bien fermes et drus,
> différents de bois, de port, de couleur,
> mais pareillement pleins de sève et sans que l'un empiète sur l'autre
> différents à leur base
> mais oh! (56)

> Let's suppose the world is a forest. Fine!
> There are baobabs, some live oaks, black firs, white walnut tree;
> I want all of them to grow, nicely firm and dense,
> different in wood, in bearing, in color,
> but equally rich in sap and without one encroaching upon another,
> different at their bases
> but . . . oh! (33)

At this high point of affective transcendence, when the human world is figured metaphorically as a harmonious landscape, the stage directions indicate that the actor playing the Rebel should exhibit "ecstacy"; he is "Extatique" as the dawn breaks ("O douceur, et voici Aurore"; 56–57). (Note that this utopian resolution looks quite different from the "Vision" at the end of the play.) Arguably the most important point in the added scene, however, is not the ecstatic end but rather its quiet beginning. The stage directions read "Il réfléchit," suggesting that the scene is to be played as a soliloquy, an internal dialogue of self-questioning. Significantly, at no other point in the play are these stage directions, "Il réfléchit," repeated. What is accomplished in this moment of solitude, or rather, in this moment in which the self communes with the self? Why would Césaire have felt compelled to insert it here?

The scene is important because it shows through an astute and subtle manipulation of pronouns how a strong emotion—here, the emotion of hate—can be separated from the subjectivity of the speaker (and perhaps from the enslaved masses) through an act of reflection. That is, it shows that "bestiality" is not the only "face" the Rebel can display. As the passage opens, the Rebel acknowledges that refusing violence leaves one with few weapons indeed: "si on ne le crie pas / c'est vrai on accepte la puante stérilité d'une glèbe usée." Therefore violence, even though it manifests "une autre pauvreté," may be at times necessary. (It is "la chimie" in the fertilizer that encourages new growth.) Next, the Rebel proposes that the vengeful violence of retribution might be acceptable only if "*it* dies" in the battle for a new world: "je ne l'accepte pas ce cri que comme la chimie de l'engrais / qui ne vaut que *s'il* meurt / à faire renaître une terre sans pestilence" (56; added emphasis). The personification of the cry of hatred in the added passage ("il meurt") suggests that neither the Rebel nor the slaves he leads need to identify themselves entirely with that cry, for it may be only one of the many voices that "inhabit" the self. In other words, the suggestion is that hatred is neither the self's essence nor the full identity of the individuals who make up the crowd. Rather, hatred is a burden they bear and a tool they can use. It is important to note, however, that although the Rebel reflects upon his hatred (and personifies it with the pronoun "il"), the Rebel's hatred does not disappear. At the beginning of act 2 the Rebel announces his hate once again: "Et ma haine ne mourra pas" (77) (And my hatred will not die [44]).

In terms of the plot, the inserted scene serves to interrupt without reversing the momentum of the play, a momentum that leads from the first scenes in which the Rebel describes himself as "coupé" and "vaincu," to the end, when he dies with his "cri intact," "Intact et nu" (78). "O mes membres de mur bousillé," the Rebel addresses his ruined state, "vous n'étiendrez pas de fatigue et de froid / mon cri fumant mon cri *intact* d'animal pris au piège" (78; added emphasis) (O my limbs of smashed walls / you will not extinguish my fatigue and my cold / my smoking cry my intact cry of a trapped animal [45]). Yet the scene of reflection in which the Rebel disassociates himself from the bestiality of an instinctual response produces interesting ripples throughout the play that build up to the second monologue Césaire added in 1956, the monologue the Rebel recites just before he expires in act 3. It is clear that Césaire wrote both insertions with the same themes in mind. We find again the motif of the "cri farouche," the image of building an edifice or statue, and even the image of the "glèbe usée," the abused, sterile soil of inaction from which nothing may grow. Just as the earlier addition to act 2 included a scene in which the Rebel complicates—and interrogates—an initial instinctual response, so too the addition to act 3 proposes an alternative to the naked howl of vengeance, the "cri d'animal pris au piège" (78), namely, a "Parole" (Word), or "nom" (name):

> Le Rebelle: Est-ce qu'il croient m'avoir comme la laie et le marcassin?
> m'extirper comme une racine sans suite? [Here begins the 1956 addition:] Parole,
> entre les hautes rives de sel, entre les gorges, tu sinues, je te hèle, ramenant de très loin ton butin de choses patientes raclées aux profondeurs, tu sinues.
> Toi, bouche, fais face,
> nom assourdi de la blessure énorme!
> (*Pause*)
> . . . Oh! mes pauvres héros.
> Ceux qui du Dahomey venaient, n'ayant emporté, trésor,
> que leur bouche fermée sur quelques simples formules
> . . .
> Ceux qui pour venir avaient traversé de hautes forêts, de larges déserts, surtout
> La mer immense
> . . .
> et me voici tout soudain nul la bouche amère seul vraiment vous-même

et me voici au milieu de la route
. . .
car ce qui ouvre la route
c'est tout aussi le cri puisé au creux boueux de l'attentif gisement fidèle.
. . .
je bâtirai ce nom au creux vif du courant (113–14)

Rebel: Do they expect to have me as if I was a wild boar and her young?
To extirpate me like a root without descendants? [1956 addition begins here:] Words
between high salt banks, between gorges, you wind your way, I hail you, dragging up
Your booty of things patiently scraped from the great depths, you wind your Way.
You, mouth, be poised,
muted name of the enormous wound!
(A pause.)
. . . O! my pitiful heroes.
Those who come from Dahomey, having brought along a treasure, only their lips shut on some elemental formulas
. . .
Those who in order to come had crossed high forests, vast deserts, above all an
endless sea,
. . .
and here I stand suddenly null mouth embittered alone truly yourself
here I stand in the middle of the road
. . .
for what opens the way
is equally the scream [*cri*] sprung from the muddy hollow of the faithful attentive
lode. (64–65)

The Rebel's call for a "Parole" at the very beginning of the inserted passage implies that he desires more from the resurfacing "noyés" than a "gargouillement," more from his throat than an "aboiement," and more from the soundscape of the play than the sound of tom-toms that die out at the end. He hails, or calls out for, a name with which to designate the "blessure énorme" that is his past, his present, and his own torn corporeal being. The shut mouths of those who have been lost—"Ceux qui du Dahomey venaient, n'ayant emporté, trésor / que leur bouche fermée"—must find their silenced cries vocalized once again in the Rebel's mouth. In one of the most curious lines in the play, the Rebel states: "me voici tout soudain nul la bouche amère seul vraiment vous-même" (114). It is as though he had achieved, by the end of the play, a force of negativity so great ("me voici tout soudain nul") that it allows him, alone ("seul"), to speak for others ("vous-même") with his mother-less mouth ("bouche a-mère"). As in the concluding lines of the *Cahier*, the Rebel seems to wish for a purification, a scrubbing clean of the self (one sense of "verrition") that would leave him empty and thus able to perform the function of resonating cavity. But in the passage Césaire added in 1956, what the Rebel desires, what he "hails," is not a "cri farouche" or even a "cri d'assassins," but a "nom assourdi," a sign that has been silenced and that must be made audible again.

Many reprisals in the passage indicate that the author wished to suture the additions of the 1956 version to the 1946 version rather than make an entirely new play.[45] Still, the 1946 version never fully succeeds in associating the "cri" of suffering and ferocity with a verbal sign, even though the Rebel claims (in that version) that the word is his only offering: "je n'ai pour moi que ma parole," he states; "ma parole puissance de feu . . . ma parole qu'aucune chimie ne sauraient apprivoiser ni ceindre" (46) (All I have is my word . . . my word the power of fire . . . my word that no chemistry could ever tame or encompass" [27; translation modified]). The suggestion here is that the "parole" is itself wild, untameable; as in *Une saison en Congo*, the hero considers his word a "weapon." Lumumba: "J'ai n'ai pour arme que ma parole" (My only arm is my word). But a fissure has opened up between the hero and his people, between a reflexive, reasoning (verbal) character and a chorus composed, as in the original Greek drama, "of satyrs: wild, primitive creatures, half animal, half human."[46] The Rebel prides himself, in fact, on having brought his people to a higher state of self-consciousness: "J'avais amené ce pays à la connaissance de lui-même" (36) (I had brought this land to the knowledge of itself [19]), he explains to the chorus (who demands, instead, a king, someone who will "sing" for them) (31). Yet this self-consciousness, which awakens the people to revolt, does not bring them to language, which remains the sole possession of the Rebel. He (much like Césaire himself) has both the gift of oratory and the gift of analytical recursiveness, that is, he has the ability to reflect upon, to consider from a distance procured by the Symbolic ("la Parole"), his own instinctual reactions. Ultimately, the dilemma of the Leader is that he can see himself *as* Leader, he can step away, momentarily, from his role. It is this *seeing as*, this aspectual consciousness or parabasis, that distinguishes him from those whose anger, understandably, compels them toward acts of "Rancune" and "Ressentiment."

Césaire was obviously not comfortable with this distinction between (reflective) Leader and (impulsive) crowd, for he returned to it incessantly in his poetry and plays.[47] Perhaps this is why his 1956 additions work so hard to reunite the reflective Leader (with his privileged access to the "Parole") with the crowd and their impulsive "cri." In the 1956 version, the Rebel's task is to bring the Word into line with the energies of revolt, or, to evoke the imagery of the *Cahier*, to lead "un peuple à côté de son cri" back to a "cri" that has been rendered verbal in the speaker's "mouth." This verbal, *legible* cry would allow the "cri farouche" to be heard—in Jacques Rancière's terms—as speech. Césaire's 1956 additions seem to have been forged precisely to prefigure this reconciliation, to harmonize the "cry" and the "Word," or, conversely, to animate that which is frequently described pejoratively as "mere words" (34) with a force as strong as the river's "current" (66). The "cri" provides a directional force, a pull that the Word must obey.[48] Both are required: the energy of righteous anger and the gravitas of reflection. The cry of suffering must be sounded again, but not necessarily through the "gueule" of a dog.

In the end, of course, the Rebel's reasoning voice is overwhelmed by the beating of the drums and the barking of the dogs. Nonetheless, the significance of the reflective moment in act 2 should not be underestimated, given that it was intentionally added to the edition that Césaire considered the most definitive version of the work. The moment of self-reflection introduces a crucial structural element that is often present in a heroic narrative (the hero doubts his own resolve, or regrets the means he must use to obtain his goal) but rarely commented on in the case of *Les chiens*.[49] When Césaire personifies the cry "Mort aux Blancs" (with the pronoun "il"), he suggests that the cry, or the instinctive recourse to violence, only intermittently inhabits the self, just as all the other voices—of love, desire, ambition, despair—circulate like moods within the Rebel's being. In the full version of the play we witness the Rebel undergo a complete identification with the "cri farouche"; the will to revenge, to seek justice, is not expressed in a voice like any other but rather subsumes him completely. However, in the reflection scene, we are invited to imagine the possibility of a hero who could step away, momentarily, from the role he feels called on to play. This slight hint of parabasis opens up the potential for an alternative reading, one that would stress the heterogeneous and performative rather than singular and essential nature of the empirical self. In performance terms, we might say that the two monologues Césaire added to the 1956 version allow the Rebel to acknowledge that he is indeed "inhabited" by a number of different impulses, none of which may be his alone. The role of murderer filled with "rancune" and "ressentiment" is not the only role available for him to play. Neither, however, does he have to renounce that role entirely since such renunciation might lead to passivity and inaction. The act of reflection thus entails neither total identification with, nor complete eradiction of, the other ("il"), the "cry" that "inhabits" the self.

The added scene suggests, finally, that the true accomplishment of reflection is not the acceptance of violence as an inevitable part of the fight against injustice—although that may be the conclusion at which the Rebel arrives. Rather, the true accomplishment of reflection is the recognition that the self is internally conflicted, possessed by more voice than one.[50] On the one hand, the passage Césaire inserted into the 1956 edition could be seen as introducing a new theme, or a new mode of staged action (reflection) to a host of other actions already admitted to the blocking of the play (such as "Il s'arrête," "Il s'incline," and so on).[51] On the other, the staged reflection seems consistent with the play's overall structure: the scene in which the Rebel expresses one thought, then a conflicting thought, then yet another could be seen, that is, as a microcosm of the entire play as itself an act of reflection. Just as the Rebel's self-reflection reveals not a single self or consistent identity but instead a complex self who raises questions ("Comment débrouiller tout ça?"), expresses contradiction ("mais oh!"), refuses participation ("Non"), advances speculations ("je suppose que . . ."), promotes violence ("Mort aux Blancs"), and condemns violence ("mort au cri 'Mort aux Blancs'"), so too the play points to an authorial presence, an "empirical subject," that is splintered into multiple voices distributed into distinct roles and even distinct versions of the same play.

EN GUISE DE CONCLUSION

I wrote at the beginning of this chapter that the Rebel worries about "spectacularizing himself"; he fears that while lending his voice to others, "he might himself become a spectacle, an actor playing a role." My evidence for this claim is drawn from one more scene Césaire added to the 1956 version, and it is with a reading of this scene that I will conclude. In the 1946 version, the Lover dies near the close of act 1. As previously stated, Césaire chose to bring her back in 1956, inserting a rather long dialogue between her and the Rebel in act 2. Critics have interpreted her return as furthering the seduction plot: she holds out the promise of a fulfilling domestic and romantic life. What has not been noted, however, is her role as accuser: she does not merely tempt the Rebel; she also draws from him the most succinct, even mechanical rearticulation of his mission, revealing the possibility that his motives might be less than pure:

> Le Rebelle: je veux bâtir le monument sans oiseaux du Refus.
>
> L'Amante: . . . des mots! Ce sont des mots que tu dis là!
> Avoue, tu joues à te sculpter une belle mort . . .
> . . .
> tu feins! (58–60)
>
> Rebel: . . . I want to carve a birdless monument of Refusal . . .
>
> Lover: Words! Those are mere words!
> Confess, you're playing at carving a beautiful death for yourself . . .
> . . .
> You're pretending! (34)

Césaire has chosen his words with great care, making sure to integrate the imagery from the 1956 additions into the imagery of the earlier version. For instance, the expressions "sculpter une belle mort" and "bâtir un monument" echo the Rebel's earlier allusion to his desire to erect a "statue" ("La statue que nous sommes en train d'ériger, camarades, la plus belle des statues" [50]). What is most interesting, though, is that Césaire adds the verbs "jouer" and "feindre" to the Lover's characterization of his behavior, thereby underscoring the theatricality of the Rebel's persona, the danger he runs (at least according to the Lover) of losing touch with reality as he gains rhetorical power and dramatic force. The accusation that the Rebel may be playing a role, that he may be aestheticizing his task ("sculpter une belle mort"), cannot be contained once it has been uttered; in fact, such an accusation reverberates throughout Césaire's entire dramatic oeuvre, where heroes often acknowledge (and regret) their self-aggrandizing motives.[52] We need only think of King Christophe's desire, at the end of *La tragédie du Roi Christophe*, to exit the "formidable spectacle" he creates in his "théâtre d'ombres" to see that for Césaire, leadership involves a kind of theatrics.[53] Leadership of the people always threatens detachment from the people ("gardez-vous de vous croiser les bras en l'attitude stérile du spectateur" the speaker of the *Cahier* warns himself)—and it also threatens detachment from the self. To return to the epigraph by Michelet cited by Césaire in "Nègreries: Jeunesse noire et assimilation," "to rise up" ("monter") and "to remain oneself" ("rester soi") are gestures that may be deeply incompatible.[54] Yet the problem is even more serious than that, for to "rester soi" may be to stand still, to congeal into a figure, or, worse, to be nothing at all. What posture can the Rebel assume that is not, in some sense, a role? To what voice can he listen without becoming, to some extent, a ventriloquist? What does an authentic voice sound like if not a fusion ("amalgam") of voices, each of which represents some contingent aspect of the self?

And what are we to make of the "monument sans oiseaux" that the Rebel evokes in the passage quoted earlier? If, as the speaker announces in the *Cahier*, "ma négritude n'est ni une tour ni une cathédrale" (47), then why does the Rebel insist upon envisioning self-affirmation as erecting a "statue" or building a "monument"? Could it be that a lifeless monument ("sans oiseaux") is ultimately not the best affirmation of black identity? Could it be that the "négritude" the speaker evokes in the *Cahier* requires instead an unfolding, ever changing, ever self-revising text (not a monument), a malleable document (not a statue) that can be cut into, altered, shifted around, and revised—that is, precisely the kind of text that Césaire provides? Could it be that textual revision, the process in which Césaire engaged during almost his entire lifetime, is the literary equivalent of a racial identity that cannot be congealed into any single "definitive" form?

If self-consciousness entails self-questioning, and if acting requires parabasis, then performance cannot be entirely repudiated or treated as a falsification of the self. After all, representing the self (or others) is an operation that must draw on conventional verbal and gestural languages, otherwise, the representation would not be recognizable to others as the exterior face of an internal state.[55] There is, of course, an important distinction to be made between a play-acting, or a "feigning," that falsifies in an intentional manner and the quotidian role-playing in which any individual engages throughout his life. Césaire is clearly concerned with policing the boundary between the two. That boundary, however, may be difficult to discern.

A performance world view does not neglect that boundary, however. It suggests neither that all affect is acting nor that all persons are "personas" (although, as Marcel Mauss has shown, the two are etymologically linked).[56] Rather, a performance world view locates identity in a subject formation "structured through multiple and sometimes conflicting sites of identification."[57] The model of the empirical subject that emerges in *Les chiens* is close to a performance studies model insofar as it depicts the subject as "inhabited" by a variety of voices, identifying and disidentifying (through acts of reflection) with a number of roles. The orchestration of those roles constitutes the subject at any given point in time. The self depicted in *Les chiens*—at least the versions from 1946 on—is thus the self of a lyric oratorio, an interwoven fabric of melodies and refrains that together constitute the *persons* one is. Although the Rebel never abandons his mission (and to that extent he remains faithful to an impulse he has at the start), to complete that mission he must echo, he must quote; that is, he must verbalize the "silenced" speech of the Dahomey that rises up in his throat in act 3. By citing, he finds aural support for urges sincerely felt. Sincerity, then, can be seen to require, not repudiate citation. How to tell the difference between the speech imposed upon us by others (colonial mimicry, or the interpellations of authority) and the speech we seek to retrieve (ancestral voices we recognize as continuous with our own, and thus the interpellations of a community we accept)—such is the problem the play seeks to resolve. Césaire suggests that reflection is the act that might potentially allow us to differentiate between the two: feigning an identity that is not ours versus locating identity in a variety of roles. Like parabasis, reflection encourages us to examine the source of the voices that inhabit us, to step away momentarily from our (their) words.

While it would be a stretch to consider Césaire a poststructuralist, wedded to the notion that the subject is a discursive construction, it is arguable that there exist proto-poststructuralist moments in his work. That this would be the case seems both logically consistent and historically inevitable, given that he matured during the period when Alexandre Kojève's version of Hegel was circulating in Paris, the same version that would inform the work of Michel Foucault, Georges Bataille, Jacques Derrida, and Judith Butler.[58] Further, Césaire was alive, well, and traveling regularly to Paris during the 1960s and 1970s, a time when many intellectuals were attempting to balance a theory of the subject "whose access to itself is opaque and is not self-grounding" with an ethics of agency.[59] It is not clear to me that these intellectuals—Césaire included—would have believed that moments of parabasis, or even "permanent parabasis," are necessarily at odds with ethical action.[60] Thus, I am not convinced that Césaire would have found a "performance world view"—according to which we are composed of heterogeneous voices—inconsistent with a sincere commitment to any one of those voices at a given moment in time.[61] We can always interpret *Les chiens* as a play that offers implacable resistance to colonial authority—indeed, it does. But the way in which it does so may be less obvious than we first assume. The resistance against colonial authority that Césaire depicts may include moments when resistance to the dominant narrative of selfhood is imperative as well.

As readers, we hope for a victorious ending. We look to Negritude for the articulation of a clear political message, the indication of a straight path. Magisterial works such as *Le discours sur le colonialisme* and "L'homme de culture et ses responsabilités" provide precisely that. But I am not convinced that a work like *Les chiens* is, as Roger Toumson and Simonne Henry-Valmore maintain, "une oeuvre de combat, un pamphlet politique. . . ."[62] Neither do I believe that *Les chiens* (or the *Cahier*, for that matter) constructs a frozen image of authentic blackness, as other critics have asserted, one that is blind to internal hybridity or self-difference. To both groups who, for different reasons, seek in Césaire a single message, I would reply that, on the contrary, the author creates heroes whose search for authenticity is at once relentless and frustrated, celebrated and ironized. We never really know whether Césaire's protagonists embody their authentic identity because they find or escape an image of themselves.

It is a premise of genetic criticism that various versions of a work reflect the evolving perspective of an author as he returns to the same issues over time. Taken together, the various versions constitute the textual record of an empirical subject's diachronic unfolding. Certainly, this premise may be applied to the author of *Et les chiens se taisaient*: Césaire was maturing during the decade between 1946 and 1956, and, as scholars have averred, the changes he made to the play testify to the dilemmas he was facing during a tumultuous period both in history and in his own life. What is less obvious is that the text—even one version of it—may reflect the empirical subject's *synchronic* identity (or rather, his non-self-identity), the complexly layered and self-contradictory impulses of a self that is authentic not because it is consistent but because it is *not*. Even the 1946 version of *Les chiens* already contains contradictory voices; indeed the difference between the *Cahier* and *Les chiens* is not that one presents a consistent, coherent subjectivity and the other does not but rather that in the play the supposedly unified utterances of the *Cahier*'s lyric subject have been broken up and distributed among a large cast of characters, or "Voix."

The genre of the lyric oratorio was the ideal medium for Césaire to depict his own conflicting impulses, for he could realize (that is, attribute to diverse speakers) the many voices inhabiting him without having to identify thoroughly with any single one. We would be mistaken, though, to believe that the lyric oratorio, as a genre, is substantively different from a lyric poem. To be sure, the lyric poem, with its pretense of a singular aesthetic subjectivity, or lyric "I," suggests that all utterances in the poem emanate from one source. But the lyric oratorio may simply reveal what has always been true about the lyric poem, namely, that it is composed of a heteroglossic fabric of harmonizing and dissonant voices, performing in succession or overlapping, in dialogic interaction or drowning each other out. It is precisely because a lyric poem *is*, ultimately, an oratorio—and a lyric subject *is*, ultimately, a cast of characters—that we may legitimately interpret an aesthetic subject as a reflection of the empirical subject, or author. Since both author and aesthetic subject are internally heterogeneous, they can stand for each other in this regard. However, whereas the empirical subject continues to evolve through, as Adorno puts it, the "experience of himself and what he encounters," in contrast, the aesthetic subject evolves only through the revisions the author makes, the readings the poem receives, or the stagings the drama inspires.[63] And here, finally, is where the significance of Césaire's tendency to revise (and republish) appears in its true light: Modernist textuality—the medium but also the media of small reviews, pamphlets, small presses, and grand maisons d'éditions—allowed Césaire, the empirical author, to treat his texts as if they were performances, to interpret and reinterpret his reasons for writing them again and again. Césaire shows that the printed text lends itself not just to a reading but to a rewriting, that is, to a reincarnation in multiple forms. Far from being opposed to performance as the stationary is to the mobile, the fixed to the fleeting, the printed text is impermanent, provisional, only one incarnation of itself. Ever since Montaigne (at least), print culture has offered authors the opportunity to rearrange, excise, and add passages, to produce multiple editions, reprintings in different formats (with changes of title or subtitle), new versions on the page, the airwaves, or the stage. Modernist print culture in particular, with its invention of the "work in progress" genre, made it possible for authors to circulate mobile texts, to publish in *transition*—or *Volontés*—works that could, like their empirical authors, evolve and change under the public eye. To ask "Which is the 'definitive' text?" is thus like asking "Who is the authentic subject?" There is no answer except that provided by a reading, which in turn is an act of ventriloquism that animates the text with being.

3

POETRY AND THE TYPOSPHERE IN LÉON-GONTRAN DAMAS

Ceux qui n'ont inventé ni la poudre ni la boussole
Ceux qui n'ont jamais su dompter la vapeur ni l'électricité
Ceux qui n'ont exploré ni les mers ni le ciel
mais ils savent en ses moindres recoins le pays de souffrance[1]

Those who invented neither powder nor compass
those who could harness neither steam nor electricity
those who explored neither the seas nor the sky
but who know in its most minute corners the land of suffering[2]

These lines by the poet laureate of Negritude present what might very well contain the most powerful, most harmful, and most ubiquitous stereotype of black subjectivity to inhabit the French imaginary of the twentieth century. Caribbeans, Africans, and black Americans living in Paris between the two world wars would have been exposed to this image: the black man "indifferent to conquering" ("insoucieux de dompter"), lacking initiative ("who could harness neither steam nor electricity"), in continuity with the very matter of the world ("flesh of the world's flesh").[3] Not surprisingly, we find almost the same words penned by Léon-Gontran Damas a few years earlier: "De n'avoir jusqu'ici rien fait / détruit bâti / osé" ("Never, until now, to have done anything / destroyed built / dared anything"), he laments in his 1934 poem "Réalité." Marcel Cohen, a professor of linguistics at the Institut d'Ethnographie where Damas was a student, taught that African peoples were "sans écriture" (without writing); their societies were poor in technologies of all kinds.[4] Clearly, in the 1930s the black subject of the diaspora would have had to combat the racial stereotype—one among many—according to which possessing African ancestry means suffering an attenuated relation to all advanced technologies, including writing. Writing, the story goes, is an acquisition belonging to the mediosphere of modern Western man alone.

Ironically, however, before setting foot in France in 1926, Damas would have thought of himself as a full, card-carrying member of the modern mediosphere of writing and the printing press.[5] Born in 1912 in French Guiana, Damas was an exemplary product of the assimilation policies imposed by the French. He followed almost the same trajectory as Césaire (they even attended the same English class), having left Guiana in 1924 to attend the Lycée Schoelcher in Fort-de-France. He arrived in France in 1926 to complete his secondary studies at the Collège de Meaux, then attended classes on law and finally ethnography at the Institut d'Ethnographie. The recipient of an education "très français français," as Damas would say, he had every reason to believe that writing—and thus print culture—belonged to him just as much as it did to all the other offspring of "nos ancêtres les gaulois." The overseas colonial institutions of France promoted the basic principle that black schoolchildren (and certainly mulattos, or *métis*) could learn to read and write and that eventually they would be able to intervene productively in the administrative, political, and professional arenas of French life. (Of course, in reality, this principle was not always applied, and equal opportunities were rarely meted out to all.[6])

It was thus upon disembarking in France that Damas confronted a blanket policy of discrimination that no longer distinguished between educated *assimilés* and low-class *nègres* but instead bundled them all together, either in the embrace of "*negrophilia*" or in the chains of disgrace.[7] This far less subtle racial hierarchy associated even the mulatto *assimilé* more closely with black Africa and its mediosphere (supposedly "without writing") than with the advanced scriptural mediosphere of the industrialized West. According to the view that would have dominated at the time, the young Guyanese belonged not to a cultural elite but rather to a Negro race having never "done anything / destroyed built / dared anything." Damas and his fellow Caribbeans suddenly found themselves deprived—in the eyes of their white compatriots—of any scriptural tradition whatsoever. Césaire and the students associated with the review *L'Étudiant Noir* quickly realized that this state of affairs left them with only two ways to respond: either they could deny their own cultural specificity (a mélange of Amer-Indian, East Indian, African, and European influences) and strive to express themselves in an impeccable "français français," or—a much riskier venture—they could choose to explore their cultural specificity by reaching out to cultural traditions that were only imaginatively their own (such as African American music or African religious beliefs). Césaire and Damas forged a third route. While responding to Étienne Léro's call in *Légitime Défense* of 1932 to reject the mimicry of "white culture, white education and white prejudices," they set out to further a singularly Caribbean agenda that includes embracing the means and techniques of Western print.[8]

Benedict Anderson has argued persuasively in *Imagined Communities* that print culture played a major role in the development of modern Europe and thus, by corollary, in the construction of the colonial assimilationist project. A circulating print culture was the condition of possibility for the emergence not only of the political structures we call the nation but also of the sentiment of belonging to a collectivity defining itself primarily as a linguistic readership rather than a racial or even geographical body. It would be hard to overestimate the importance of print culture as a distribution system across regional and national boundaries; it contributed, according to Anderson, to the inception of the modern subject and defined this subject's place in the public sphere.[9] Building on Anderson's work, Brent Hayes Edwards has demonstrated in *The Practice of Diaspora* that the social and aesthetic formation we call Negritude would never have seen the light of day without the mediating potential of print culture, its modes of distribution and material supports. The print network connecting Africans, African Americans, and Caribbeans, created by the transatlantic circulation of multiple reviews and translations, was absolutely indispensable to the production of a Pan-African solidarity—particularly the solidarity that characterizes Negritude as an engaged poetics. As Edwards avers, "the periodical print cultures of black internationalism were robust and extremely diverse on all sides of the Atlantic," and translation of texts from English to French—and vice versa—was at the heart of the movement that revolutionized literature on both sides of the ocean.[10] From *Les Continents* and *La Voix des Nègres* to *L'Etudiant Noir* and *Présence Africaine*, it was the mediosphere of writing technologies that permitted black affirmation movements to formulate a collective imaginary, one shared by peoples widely dispersed but drawn together by a common project articulated in print.

It was thus through means furnished above all by what Jean-Pierre Bobillot has called the "typosphere" that black writers and militants found it possible to explore their racial and cultural bonds. In this regard, it is worth noting that francophone black writers living in Paris, despite their familiarity with a varied and animated black popular culture, tended to associate their cultural project more closely with political and literary print matter than with jazz or the Bal Nègre. Damas and Senghor were admirers of African American jazz (and, with varying familiarity, Caribbean *biguine* and Serer drumming), but their respective styles reflect more consistently either the elevated diction of modern French poetry (from Baudelaire to Saint-John Perse), or the discourse forged by the militant black press (*Le Cri des Nègres* and *La Race Nègre*). In short, with few exceptions, it was the typosphere that afforded the tools with which Senghor, Césaire, and Damas interrogated and defined what they understood to be their racial voice and cultural values.

However, each writer of Negritude envisioned his task in a slightly different fashion. As I argued in chapter 1, Césaire sought to explore all the resources of the French language as it resonated in his local environment, which included a reading environment. His project involved bending ("infléchir" is his verb) the French language such that it could accommodate (while constituting in print form) "ce moi, ce moi-nègre, ce moi-créole, ce moi-martiniquais, ce moi-antillais."[11] Senghor, in contrast, desired to produce poems that would lend themselves to a musical scansion; he claims to have modeled his poetic meters on rhythms that were African in origin. (We will come back to this point later.) Finally, for Damas, the task of the poet consisted in forging a written language capable of incarnating visually as well as through text-produced sound the "stutter" ("bégaiement") or "hiccup" ("hoquet") that he associates with the profoundly negative experience of assimilation. According to Damas, assimilation could produce nothing other than a man out of step ("en syncope") with his own essence, nothing other than a voice trapped in repetitious behaviors that could only be made expressive through their formal exaggeration.[12] He turned to the medium of modernist print to capture what Frantz Fanon would later call the *Leib noir* of the *assimilé*, according great expressive power to the typographic support.[13] Exploring experimental techniques for lineation and layout, Damas transformed the page itself into a site where a lack of essence, a negative ontology of the self, could be graphically staged and realized as a sonic positivity by the reader.

Damas was not alone in emphasizing the value of print culture for black self-expression and resistance. Despite the enormous interest the Negritude poets expressed in African and African-inspired traditions, they do not seem to have aspired to practice orality in some putatively pure, pretextual form. That is, although Negritude poets often drew attention to the rhythms of incantation, the refrain of the blues, or the narrative structure of the griot tale (either thematically or through verbal mime), they did not choose to produce or reproduce oral genres. It is indeed striking that during the interwar period not a single Negritude author developed a poetics of orality that was actualized in an exclusively oral form. The primary gesture toward orature remained that of the ethnographer: in 1943 Damas published a collection of Guyanese tales titled *Veillées noires* and, in 1948, *Poèmes nègres sur des airs africains*, a volume of African poems translated into French. Even if oral recitation was a widespread practice, and the orality of the griot or the musicality of the blues won unanimous praise, poets in general declined to produce verbal works that could not also play a significant role in the typosphere of modernity.[14]

The poets of Negritude may have stated that forms of orature, music, or dance were more authentically African, less corrupted by the colonial or diasporic experience, but they were decidedly writers invested in publishing texts. In fact, even when Damas collected African poems and published them under the title *Poèmes nègres sur des airs africains*, he did not present these "airs" as reconstitutions of some pre-lapserian ideal African world untouched by print culture.[15] In contrast to Blaise Cendrars's *Anthologie nègre* of 1921, Damas's collection clearly registers the signs of European intervention. References to current events underscore the topical and evolving nature of supposedly "traditional" genres; whites are mentioned frequently, as in "Jamais Plus" and "Chants Funèbre"; and the page layout of the "airs" (as well as their verse structure) is modeled on European textual conventions. Similarly, although Senghor expresses admiration for the instruments of his native Senegal, and although he indicates at the head of each poem of *Éthiopiques* which instrument(s) should accompany which poem (the *khalam*, a tetracord guitar; the *tabala*, a war drum; the harp-like *kôras*; or the xylophone *balafong*), the poem still exists as a textual and not sonic entity in its first circulated form. In his preface to the poetic volume *Éthiopiques*, Senghor explicitly emphasizes that "reciting" is not "singing"; his poetry is a "mixed" form ("forme métissée"), he states, exposing a marked bias for "French" and French in print as singularly appropriate to the "expression" of what is nonetheless felt "en nègres."[16]

Ostensibly, then, the preferred medium of Negritude was print, the preferred mediasphere—or organ of commercial distribution—the "revue," the philosophical meditation, and the ethnographic tome, and—most importantly—the collection of poems. However, at the same time, and somewhat paradoxically, the poets of Negritude charged print (and French) with the responsibility of translating sound phenomena into written words. Text-based poetry now had to preserve the rhythm of the tom-tom (Senghor), the phrasing of blues and the melopoeia of song (Damas and Senghor), and the repetitive structure of chant (Césaire). A fact that has rarely been observed is that the poetry of this period constitutes one of the most rigorous, ambitious, and persistent attempts to generate graphic and graphemic equivalents for phenomena claimed to be of a fundamentally aural kind. If critics have often drawn attention to the "musicality" of a verse by Senghor or the calypso-like rhythm of a stanza by Damas, they have not yet fully inventoried the ways in which efforts to actualize sound in print influenced the evolution of the French lyric itself. The original practices that Damas in particular developed over the course of the mid-twentieth century opened up new possibilities for using typography and *mise en page* to represent but also produce sound. That is, Damas's experimentation in the typosphere gave birth not to copies of verbal performance but to purely graphic means for symbolizing patterns that might have had no prior equivalent in the sonic realm.

Of course, the project of securing visual equivalents for aural phenomena is intrinsic to the poetics of the printed poem in general. However, it is also true that this project was taken up with renewed enthusiasm both by poets of the Harlem Renaissance and in the diasporic milieux of early twentieth-century Paris. As this project of remediation evolved, it began to grow the seeds of its own inversion. In other words, once the poet was able to create effective graphic means of evoking sound, the affective charge of enunciation could be transferred to the act of reading, thereby eliminating the need to recite. Ironically, then, the poet most concerned with aurality might also turn out to be the poet most distant from, least similar to, an oral poet. His technical understanding of the printed page distinguishes him from the griot and the *dyâli*; the printed poem that results from such technical understanding functions according to different strategies and conventions than a poem composed in the mouth and intended to be chanted out loud. Of course, nothing would prevent Negritude poets (and their readers) from reading a poem out loud, but such a reading would no longer be necessary, innovations in print having already visually incarnated the rhythms to the point where the verbal form could exist entirely without vocalization. Lesley Wheeler has argued persuasively that even silent reading (or "subvocalization") engages the vocal cords in an active way, a point that I discussed in chapter 1 and that we will explore more thoroughly in the next chapter.[17] But if subvocalization occurs during the silent reading of a poem by, say, Damas, this reading effectively transforms the reading body into the originary source of sound (here an imagined rather than actualized sound), a sequence produced on the page and thus subject to variation. Instead of being a transcription of a rhythm heard, the Negritude poem is a text from which performances may spring. In the hands (or mouths) of readers, the poem produces what Henri Meschonnic calls "ré-énonciations," instantiations driven by the directives woven into the poem.[18] These directives—line breaks, spatialization of words, font size and weight, diacritical marks—orient the initiated reader of print to vocalize (or subvocalize) a piece of printed matter in a particular way (although variations always occur). The printed poem can actually engender (and not simply convey) experience, producing in the reader a variant sensation of the *Leib noir* as an epiphenomenon of transmission. This is emphatically not to say that experience is "constructed" by its reenunciation but rather that it is altered in iteration, animated in performance, in ways that an author cannot entirely control.

"THE GAME OF BLACK AND WHITE"

Among the three poets of Negritude, Damas most clearly understood the possibilities of modern print culture and best exploited its political and aesthetic resources. It was Damas who participated in the first literary reviews dedicated to Pan-African solidarity—*La Revue du Monde Noir*; *Légitime Défense*; and *L'Étudiant Noir*.[19] Again, it was Damas who made use of print (as had René Maran) to disseminate an ethnographic and historical study of a colony eviscerated by administrative abuse (*Retour de Guyane*, 1938). Yet again, it was Damas who produced the first anthology of francophone poetry in 1947 (*Poètes d'expression française d'Afrique noire, Madagascar, Réunion, Guadeloupe, Martinique, Indochine, Guyane 1900–1945*), even before Senghor's more famous anthology appeared in 1948. And finally, it was Damas who published the first volume of poetry written by a man explicitly—and thus politically—*nègre*: *Pigments*, in 1937. If Césaire adopted (and transformed) the syllabic poetics of Rimbaud and the surrealist poetics of rapprochement, and if Senghor based his prosody on the rhythms of a supposedly racial heritage, Damas took hold of the graphic possibilities of the printing press, of spacing and typography, to elaborate a poetics of negativity capable of transmitting the peculiar facticity of the *assimilé*.

From the very beginning of his career, Damas distinguished himself from the Caribbean poets of the past by imitating the verse structure, the style of diction, the tone, and even the syntax of African American writing. Of the three major Negritude poets, Damas was closest to the African American poets living in or passing through Paris; his friendships with Langston Hughes and Countee Cullen probably account for his singular position in the field of Parisian cultural production as well as his greater interest in the possibilities of modernist print. Damas's short, syntactically repetitive, appositive lines evoke in particular those of Langston Hughes, who in turn shared a number of syntactical innovations with Jacques Roumain. It is well established that Roumain, Damas's classmate at the Institut d'Ethnographie, and Hughes, a fellow traveler from 1938 on, were both instrumental in his evolution as a writer.[20] According to biographical accounts, Damas began writing around 1926, a date that coincides with the appearance of *The Weary Blues* of Langston Hughes, not to mention, a few months later, the publication of the first poems by Jacques Roumains in *La Revue Indigène*. Although Damas's experimentation with typography culminated in 1962 (when he published what he called his "définitive" version of *Pigments*), he was already imitating typographic innovations introduced by Roumain and Hughes in the first version of 1934.[21] Unique among the Negritude poets, Damas abandoned traditional verse structures early on in order to take fuller advantage of the printed page, treating it increasingly as a plastic and symbolically charged support.

Yet another connection with African American writers might have influenced the course of his career, awakening in him a greater interest in typographic experiment as a potential form of subversion. Damas's first collection, *Pigments*, was published by the foremost printer of surrealist books, Guy Lévis Mano, who owned Éditions GLM, a publishing house central to the interwar field of modernist production. Lévis Mano, a printer-cum-editor, was known to conceive of his typesetting work as "a typographic 'interpretation' of the text."[22] During the interwar period, Lévis Mano was responsible for publishing the most typographically experimental work by poets and artists of the French avant-garde, from René Char to Joan Miró, Paul Éluard to Man Ray. Damas had perhaps heard news of Lévis Mano through his surrealist friends (most likely Robert Desnos or Jacques Prévert). But it is equally possible that he knew of the printer's work through the African American poets who were also part of his circle. Lévis Mano inherited his printing press in 1935, a Minerva "à pédale," from none other than Nancy Cunard, the heiress and mécène of black writers.[23] The acquisition of this Minerva permitted Lévis Mano to print surrealist works on the press that had produced texts over the previous decade by high modernists such as Samuel Beckett, Ezra Pound, and Laura Riding. The links between anglophone and francophone print culture, between international modernism and the origins of Negritude, were thus material as well as aesthetic. Cunard, Lévis Mano, and the writers they published shared an investment in the expressive potential of typography. Damas, alone among the Negritude poets, joined this company, becoming a member of the cohort that, according to Jerome McGann, "fashioned the bibliographical face of the modernist world."[24]

Clearly, Damas, who published *Pigments* at his own expense, did not choose Éditions GLM at random. He must have selected the printer out of a sense of affinity with the typographical experimentation he witnessed in both surrealist and Harlem Renaissance publications. However, it is likely that Damas was able to interest Lévis Mano in his poems for more than aesthetic reasons. French surrealists as well as expatriot Americans like Cunard nourished a fascination with the exotic, and especially the "primitive" Negro, a fascination that may have worked, in this case, to his advantage. But Damas was by no means adapting to some imposed aesthetic identity manufactured by either milieux. A brief glance at his first published poems reveals that as early as 1934 (even before *Pigments* appeared), Damas was already developing a unique writing style. In "Réalité," for instance, the poem I will take as my first example, Damas has to span the distance between his own experience as a black *assimilé* and the popularized image of the savage, the subject who has never "done" or "built" any lasting thing. Published for the first time in *Esprit* (an organ of the Christian Left run by Emmanuel Mounier), "Réalité" is one of five poems—"Solde" (Sell out), "La complainte du nègre" (The Negro's complaint), "Un clochard m'a demandé dix sous" (A beggar asked me for ten cents), and "Cayenne 1927"—that propelled Damas onto the French literary scene. But before he could accede to the status of high modernist by publishing in the modernist mainstream, Damas had to wage battle against the stereotype of his own incapacity, promoted even in *Esprit*—and this, of course, is one of the ironies of "Réalité":

RÉALITÉ

De n'avoir jusqu'ici rien fait
détruit bâti
osé
à la manière du Juif
du Jaune
pour l'évasion organisée en masse
de l'infériorité
c'est en vain que je cherche
le creux
d'une épaule où
cacher mon visage
ma honte
de la réalité[25]

REALITY

To have never until now done
destroyed built

dared anything
like a Jew
like a Chinaman
for the organized flight en masse
of inferiority
it is in vain that I seek
the hollow
of a shoulder
to hide my face
my shame
from reality[26]

Before taking a closer look at "Réalité," it is worth pausing to consider the way the poem was initially presented by the editors of *Esprit*. A short preface by Marcel Moré frames the five poems contributed by Damas. Titled simply "Poèmes de Léon Damas," Moré's preface tells us how he came to know the poet, as if their encounter—and the presence of Damas's poems in the review—required explanation. Apparently, Moré was inspired to attend the projection of a short film, "Voodoo Magic," upon finishing *L'Afrique fantôme* by Michel Leiris (another classmate of Damas's at the Institut d'Ethnographie). Damas, as it happens, was also at the screening. Afterward Moré and Damas began to converse and decided to cross together the Buttes-Chaumont Park. In a chain of familiar associations, the Buttes-Chaumont Park reminds Moré of Aragon's *Paysan de Paris*, in which the park is surrealistically described. These two allusions—to *L'Afrique fantôme* and *Paysan de Paris*—could not be more loaded, for they situate Damas squarely in a prefabricated context of ethnographic surrealist exoticism.[27] It is not surprising, then, that Moré proceeds to gush over the "nouveauté" ("novelty")—but also the "facilité" ("facility," or "facile nature")—of the poems Damas has contributed. These poems—significantly, for our purposes—appear to Moré to have been "dictated by the rhythm of a tom-tom."[28] Damas is thus framed by a stereotype even before he can begin to be read. He enters the interwar Parisian field of cultural production as the consumate "African," despite his actual birth as a *métissé* in French Guiana (indicated to the readers by the direct allusion to its capital, Cayenne, in the title of one of the poems). The fact that Damas had probably never in his life played a tom-tom, and that he found his avatars not in the African bush but in the

French and American lyric traditions, does not seem to have played the slightest role in his reception by the editors of *Esprit*. Moré's short text efficiently establishes the lens through which Damas would be read by a long line of critics from Senghor to scholars of the present day.[29] As Moré puts it, Damas, "with no political axe to grind . . . yearns only to be 'nègre,'" and "nègres," as everyone knows, play tom-toms and use print merely to evoke tom-toms for their reader's ear.[30]

The poem, however, contradicts each claim Moré makes ("no political axe to grind"?). Right away, in a gesture that will soon be associated with the politics of Césaire's *Cahier d'un retour au pays natal*, Damas identifies the speaker (Moré's "l'être nègre") not with an African body but rather with the "essence" of two other oppressed groups—the "Juif" and the "Jaune" (the Jew and the Chinaman). However, the solidarity among the three groups depends upon a common contingency, not a shared blood. In an important image, Damas tells us that "the manner" of the "Juif," "Jaune," and, by implication, the speaker—that is, their shared "essence" or "way of being"—consists in a tendency to evade ("l'évasion"): "pour l'évasion organisée en masse/de l'infériorité." Looking at this image for the first time, one might be tempted to read "evasion" as eluding responsibility, as running away. And indeed, this form of "evasion" finds its gestural equivalent in the search for a hollow in which to hide ("un creux . . . [où se] cacher"). Yet a second glance suggests that this interpretation is misleading. Damas is, after all, printing these poems in an anticapitalist review. The word "masse" (in "organisée en masse") would clearly evoke a very specific meaning for readers of *Esprit*. In fact, the medialogical context of "Réalité" invites us to read "evasion" in a much stronger sense—"evasion" as "escape from confinement," as uprising, as revolt. From this angle, the verse seems more like a call to insurrection than a description of defection. The shame ("honte") of which the poet speaks is inspired not by some purported "infériorité" but rather by the fact that he has not yet "done" anything "*for*" the evasion: "*pour* une evasion organisée en masse."

The versification of the poem compounds the sense of imminent escape. Damas is careful to draw the reader's eyes neither to the repeated past participles (with the exception of "osé") nor to the agents of the poem in their singular, if repeated, form (the Juif or the Jaune). Instead, the eyes are drawn to the description of the act of evading: "pour l'évasion organisée en masse" is the longest verse of the poem. The other, shorter lines of the poem appear as if they wished to escape toward the spine of the volume; they cling to this spine, collapse into it, with the exception of "pour l'évasion organisée en masse" which extends its length toward the blank space on the right side of the page. Evasion, after all, is an act that takes place in space; it refers to an escape that is at the very same time an assumption of power, a kind of *marronnage*, escaping to the "morne" of Martinique to stage a rebellion, or, at least, to live a different way. Damas's poem may sound to Moré like a tom-tom, but it references the "reality" of an assimilated Guyanese who confronts in turn oppression (described in "Un clochard m'a demandé dix sous"), servitude (described in "La complainte du nègre"), and colonial mimicry (the theme de "Solde").

What the readers of *Esprit* might not have been able comprehend (especially after reading Moré's preface) is that Damas is presenting his "negro being" ("être nègre") as implicated in his specificity as a Caribbean Guyanese. The shame to which he confesses results from inaction, from lack of connection. As the poem implies through synecdoche, his plight as an *assimilé* involves an inability to find solidarity with others, represented here by a comforting—but absent—body: "le creux d'une épaule."[31] His shame ("la honte") might be related to his current passivity and alienation. At the same time, however, to avow this alienation is to rise up, to initiate an eventual "évasion organisée en masse." Damas is presenting here in its most concentrated and concise form the primary poetic mechanism, the tiny but potent rhetorical bomb not only of his own poetry but also of Césaire's. For the *Cahier*, too, is articulated—albeit more gregariously—as a debasement ("la négraille") that simultaneously uplifts. "Réalité" is, in embryonic form, the model of Martiniquan Negritude: it performs the typical Negritude gesture in which a subject repeats an insult ("nègre") until that insult is emptied of its pejorative connotations and produces a neologism—a substantive with no essence—like the word "Negritude." Damas's poem—similar to the neologism "*négritude*"—is a speech act that exposes shame in order to generate revolt. It is a performance in which the speaker removes his mask not to proclaim authenticity but to take up arms.

Whereas Césaire engages in expansive imagery and the build-up of momentum over many pages, Damas employs irony, understatement, and—equally important—the spatial relation among words on one page to establish an equivalence between confession and resistance. That is, Damas carefully uses the paper support to invent what might be called a graphic irony born of an astute manipulation of letters in space. To give just one example from "Réalité," with respect to line 4, we can observe that Damas has taken pains to distance the past participle "osé" ("dared") as far as possible from its auxiliary verb, "avoir": "De n'avoir rien" appears in the first verse, "osé" in the fourth. Damas has expressly isolated "osé" on the page; by doing so, he casts doubt on the meaning of the word itself. "Osé" can be read as a past participle or as an adjective qualifying "Juif" and "Jaune"; in the latter case, the sentence reads, "osé à la manière d'un Juif / d'un Jaune" (daring in the manner of a Jew / of a Chinaman). The distance between the auxiliary infinitive and the past participle is augmented by the versification; the space of the page is working to offer an alternate reading, one that is in conflict with the first. Clearly, Damas is attending to the appearance of his poem (and not just its sonority). This appearance, the way in which the poem offers itself to the eye, permits him to play with the ambiguity of a word, to evoke several ways of understanding an utterance, and thus to trouble the transparent relation between spoken word and written letter presupposed by Moré's preface and its metaphor of "dictation."

Admittedly, these innovations on the level of the *mise en page* are quite modest. It is as though in 1934 Damas were still testing out his muscles, trying to discover what kind of effects he could obtain from small shifts in spacing or different enjambments of the line. In the 1937 GLM edition of *Pigments*, Damas goes much further, resetting verses and sometimes even the letters of poems such as "Réalité." For instance, in "Ils sont venus ce soir" (They came that evening), Damas inaugurates a manner of spacing his words along a kind of invisible descending staircase, an avant-garde typographical procedure he most likely learned from Hughes (and which he applies to the 1962 versions of "Captation," "Le vent," "Limbé," "S.O.S.," and "Shine"). It turns out that the modest strategies Damas develops in 1937 are simply a prelude to a more thorough exploration of the possibilities afforded by the modernist typosphere. One need only consider the resetting of "Réalité" in the 1962 edition to seize immediately how much more "osé" Damas has become.

RÉALITÉ

De n'avoir jusqu'ici rien fait
détruit
bâti
osé

à la manière
du Juif
du Jaune
pour l'évasion organisée en masse
de l'infériorité
C'est en vain que je cherche
le creux d'une épaule
où cacher mon visage
ma honte
de
  la
    Ré
      a
        li
          té

What might have inspired Damas to atomize the syllables of "Réalité" and drop them down the page like staircase steps? Damas's own creativity was considerable; however, it is also clear that between 1934 and 1962 (that is, between the first and the third typesetting of "Réalité") Damas absorbed a good many typographic innovations introduced by, among others, his friend Langston Hughes. It is worth recalling that Hughes first used this "staircase technique" in *The Weary Blues* (1926) in a poem titled "Fantasy in Purple." However, the "staircase technique" or "vers en escalier," as it is known in French, has a long history in French lyric poetry. Mallarmé made the technique famous in "Un Coup de dés jamais n'abolira le hasard" of 1897, but Jules Laforgue had already graduated his lines in a similar way in *L'imitation de notre-dame la lune* of 1885. Guillaume Apollinaire advanced the technique yet further in *Calligrammes* (1918). Perhaps Damas had seen the "vers escalier" in Vladimir Mayakovsky's "Vo ves' golos" (1930), translated by Louis Aragon into French as "À pleine voix" in 1933 (Aragon also translated poems by Langston Hughes). While Damas employs the "vers en escalier" in a rather classical fashion in several of his poems, the typographic reformatting of "Réalité" introduces a new twist. Here it is not complete words that descend the page from left to right (as in Hughes's poem); rather, it is individual letters or letter clusters that float down the page, a practice that strangely disrupts the perceptual norm of reading. Damas often performs this type of syllabic découpage to produce a parodic effect, as we see vividly in the case of "Shine," where the words are cut up as in a dictionary to form sequences of syllables that descend the page:

por-
  no-
    gra-
      phie

In "Shine," the word parts are followed by dashes connecting one to the next, reminiscent of the way lexemes are presented in the dictionary, that archive par excellence of the typosphere. However, in "Réalité," the connective tissue of punctuation has disappeared, leaving only the bare bones of fragments floating in space. At the time, Damas was not the only poet working with such fragments. In 1934, the same year that *Esprit* printed the first version of "Réalité," Hughes published a poem titled "Cubes" in the Marxist review *New Masses*.[32] "Cubes," while not identical to Damas's poem, still suggests a similar intent; Hughes also atomizes the letters of words, but he forms these letters into an undulating wave. Both authors employ a subversive strategy that consists in imitating in exaggerated fashion the perceptual conventions of writing and reading—the letteral regime of inscription—to the point where these very conventions produce the opposite of unimpeded literacy: the left-to-right movement of the eye is mobilized to complicate a clear and unidirectional presentation of meaning. The atomization of sound units facilitated by alphabetic writing ends up working against the unity of the word on the page. Typography, then, becomes a medium in which to expose what Hughes will call the "disease" of civilization, a hyper-rationalization that, when pushed to its extreme, produces a fixation on the grapheme that disrupts the conventional use of textual space. (See the original page of *New Masses* at www.faculty.sites.uci.edu/aestheticsubjectivity/.)

CUBES

In the days of the broken cubes of Picasso
And in the days of the broken songs of the young men
A little too drunk to sing

And the young women
A little too unsure of love to love—
I met on the boulevards of Paris
An African from Senegal

God
Knows why the French
Amuse themselves bringing to Paris
Negroes from Senegal.

It's the old game of the boss and the bossed,
        boss and the bossed,
                amused
                  and
                amusing,
        worked and working,
Behind the cubes of black and white,
                black and white,
        black and white
But since it is the old game,
For fun
They give him the three old prostitutes of
        France—
Liberty, Equality, Fraternity—
And all three of 'em sick
In spite of the tax to the government
And the legal houses
And the doctors
And the *Marseillaise*.

Of course, the young African from Senegal
Carries back from Paris
A little more disease
To spread among the black girls in the palm huts.
He brings them as a gift
        disease—

From light to darkness
                    disease—
From the boss to the bossed
                        disease—
From the game of black and white
        disease
From the city of the broken cubes of Picasso
        d
          i
        s
    e
        a
          s
        e

The historical frame of the poem appears at first to be the arrival of Senegalese soldiers in Paris (the 200,000 *tirailleurs sénégalais* who fought in World War I) and their eventual return to Africa, infected by the European "disease." However, a closer look reveals that there is in fact an even larger frame: the triangular commerce of empire. This commerce included the transport of African objects into France, without which cubism, the movement alluded to in the title, would never have evolved the way it did.[33] The circulation between the two continents of goods and men—and men as goods—is the backdrop against which Hughes stages a trenchant critique of such aesthetics. The poet appears to be making a claim about the relation of modernist aesthetics (cubism in particular) to colonization and imperial rule; he is even suggesting that the typographic experimentation practiced by the cubists (and by the black poets who come after them) ultimately derives from the slave trade as well. On this reading, the "disease" of modernity, here visualized as an almost corporeal fragmentation, attacks the Senegalese soldiers, the cubist artists, and—by implication—the poet too.

Underscoring the image of the "broken cubes of Picasso," Lesley Wheeler has also proposed that the allusion to cubism contains a sharp rebuke. On the one hand, she states, the poem indexes the experimentation of both Picasso and Apollinaire; with typographic sophistication, it investigates (as do cubist works) the difference between the linear temporality of reading and the simultaneity of the gaze, the aural function of poetry and its graphic form.[34] To that extent, "Cubes" is a modernist poem, fully implicated in—and an accomplished example of—the aesthetics of fragmentation that cubism introduced. On the other, Wheeler continues, the allusion to the cubists in the context of imperial power condemns their complicity with a circulation of (human) objects that could only result from European incursion into African space. Picasso and Apollinaire were members of the generation that "discovered" and promoted *l'art nègre*; they drew African tribal (and tourist) objects into the limelight but they also made profitable use of a decontextualized heritage that was not their own. Thus, the fragmentation of the word "disease" in Hughes's "Cubes" serves many purposes at once: it allows Hughes to mime the cubist gesture that accentuates the visual aspect of writing, and it offers an implicit critique of the imperialism that made it possible to do so in the first place. Because the poem ultimately associates experimental techniques (including typographic ones) with "disease"—"the game of black and white" as well as the "broken cubes"—it stands as an acerbic commentary on two incompatible realities: (1) that the poet is an accomplice, insofar as he benefits aesthetically from the same conditions of possibility (imperialism) as do the cubists; and (2) that the poet is a victim, conscious as no white modernist could ever be of the ravages slavery's "disease" has wrought.

In "Cubes," Hughes uses the "staircase" technique repeatedly: the word "disease," for instance, is repeated three times in six lines, appearing each time slightly further to the right. At the same time, he also uses indented words to create shapes, such as the hourglass produced by "amused / and / amusing," which could easily be an allusion to Apollinaire. The irony here is that the critics who have noted the use of patterned lineation in Hughes or Damas have consistently related such patterning to the putative musicality of their poems. Black poets, the story goes, always base the visual rhythms of their writing on the aural rhythms of jazz, the tom-tom, or the calypso; accordingly, a poem written by a black author should be able to be read like a musical score. But Hughes's "Cubes" directly links such scribal experimentation to the attempt on the part of the cubist poets to render poetry more graphic, not the attempt of black poets to render poetry more sonorous. Further, instead of producing a musical score, the typographic layout seems to ask whether it is in fact possible to find a sonic counterpart to the staircase of words—or, for that matter, to the string of letters that ends the poem. How are these sequences to be pronounced? How are we to subvocalize them in our minds or mouths?

Both Damas and Hughes tend, therefore, not to fortify but rather to undermine the supposedly intimate connection between the written and the aural—and, even more surprisingly, between the aural and the African. The mastery displayed in "Cubes," for instance, is clearly a mastery of the printed page, not the musical instrument. The poet places himself on the side of inscription while, on the thematic level at least, the allusion to the *Marseillaise* associates song and music not with the Senegalese but rather with the French. Hughes chooses to place the word "*Marseillaise*" in italics, stressing the convention that allows diacritical decisions to convey information. "Cubes" cultivates our sensitivity to typography as information, and the italics of "*Marseillaise*" prepare us to read other elements of the poem as possessing a graphic identity, such as the repeated *s*'s of "disease" which serve as miniature versions of the undulating, snaking "s" shape of the curling last lines (d / i / s / e / a / s / e). Everything in the poem urges us to look at—not listen to—the figures on the page. An exaggerated use of what the printed text allows ends up shifting our perceptual mode away from reading a text toward contemplating a design. Hughes thus proves himself to be thoroughly in control of the modernist typosphere from which he draws, in large part, his poetic force. Still, as Hughes's irony reinforces, the claim to mastery—"I too am a cubist!"—can turn out to be a case of colonial mimicry rather than postcolonial critique. Demonstrating one's ability to manipulate type might turn out to be just another way of catching the "disease," or "selling out" ("Solde").

THE ASSIMILATION OF NEGATION AS THE POWER TO NEGATE

This cycle of self-affirmation ("I can do what the 'boss' does") and self-implication ("What does that mean that I can do what the 'boss' does?")—or resistance and complicity—is frequently the subtext of Damas's poetry as well. But in at least one sense, Damas manages to go a step further than Hughes does in "Cubes." Damas removes himself from the conflict between "boss and bossed" and "black and white" in order to suggest that prowess with typography—or musicality, for that matter—need not be associated with either one or the other. Perhaps for Hughes the disease of modernity is contagious, and therefore typographic experimentation risks becoming merely another way of showing that he, too, has caught the bug. (He has become "blanchi"—"whitened," as Damas would say.) But for Damas, typographic experimentation can be a powerful weapon, not necessarily a form of colonial mimicry or even a reflection of colloquial speech but rather a means to express the negativity that breaks apart all words, undermines all essences, and weakens all oppositions—including the aural versus the visual, or the black versus the white.

Let us observe again how the fragmentation practiced in "Cubes" differs from its parallel in "Réalité." Immediately, we see that Damas is careful to avoid the association of poetry with an entirely visual exercise. In the closing lines of "Réalité," for instance, the word remains, although splintered, capable of being pronounced. As opposed to "d-i-s-e-a-s-e," the separate letters of which, once pronounced separately, no longer render meaning, "Ré-a-li-té" can be vocalized; it can still produce a recognizable word. However, this word has been blasted, reduced to an assemblage of syllables linked by an eye that must "read" the space of the page in a different way. The systematic rupture of the syllables after the vowel is respectful of the way in which the word would be pronounced (or rendered in a dictionary); yet the fragmenting and "staircasing" of the word manifests a desire to hammer at, even to violate, the word. Damas marries a hyperrespectful approach to textual conventions with a clearly legible destructive intention that is typical of his work as a whole. Such negativity surges up in his poetry in many forms: it is lodged in his sarcasm, palpable in images such as "couper leur sexe aux nègres / pour en faire des bougies pour leurs églises" (cut off the negros' genitals / to make candles for their churches) ("S.O.S."); or "les mains effroyablement rouges / du sang de leur ci-vi-li-sa-tion" (hands frighteningly red from the blood of their ci-vi-li-sa-tion) ("Solde"). We hear it in the insistent repetition of words or phrases, such as "Bientôt" (Soon) in the poem of the same name, or "Moi je leur demande" (I ask them) in "Et caetera." Finally, Damasian negativity resurfaces in the form of a fragmented, constantly interrupted utterance. Damasian negativity is a "stutter" (bégaiement), or "hiccup" (hoquet), a visceral rupture in the skin of the morpheme and the flow of the breath. In "Réalité," as elsewhere, the typographic placement of the letters inspires us to vocalize them, but the exaggerated correctness of this vocalization—"Ré-a-li-té"—transforms the word into a parody of itself. Thus, interruption and fragmentation of the printed word render speech print-like: to vocalize the text we must pronounce the syllables separately, as though reading a spelling manual (or doing a *dictée*). But such interruption and fragmentation also render print speech-like: to make sense of the text we must link the fragments together through their sequential articulation and thus rely on the continuity provided by vocalization in time.

"Hoquet" is a poem that thematizes this experience of rupture while reproducing rupture on the surface of the page in such as way as to produce a series of rhythmic effects singular to scripted sound. (Please see the appendix 1 for an English translation.)

HOQUET

Et j'ai beau avaler sept gorgées d'eau
trois à quatre fois par vingt-quatre heures
me revient mon enfance
dans un hoquet secouant
mon instinct
tel le flic le voyou

Désastre
parlez-moi du désastre
parlez-m'en

Ma mère voulant d'un fils très bonnes manières à table

Les mains sur la table
le pain ne se coupe pas
le pain se rompt
le pain ne se gaspille pas
le pain de Dieu
le pain de la sueur du front de votre Père
le pain du pain
Un os se mange avec mesure et discrétion
un estomac doit être sociable
et tout estomac sociable
se passe de rots
une fourchette n'est pas un cure-dents
défense de se moucher
au su
au vu de tout le monde

et puis tenez-vous droit
un nez bien élevé
ne balaye pas l'assiette

Et puis et puis
et puis au nom du Père
du Fils
du Saint-Esprit
à la fin de chaque repas

Et puis et puis
et puis désastre
parlez-moi du désastre
parlez-m'en

Ma mère voulant d'un fils mémorandum

Si votre leçon d'histoire n'est pas sue
vous n'irez pas à la messe
dimanche
avec vos effets des dimanches

Cet enfant sera la honte de notre nom
cet enfant sera notre nom de Dieu
Taisez-vous
Vous ai-je ou non dit qu'il vous fallait parler français
le français de France
le français du français
le français français

Désastre
parlez-moi du désastre
parlez-m'en

Ma mère voulant d'un fils
fils de sa mère

Vous n'avez pas salué la voisine

encore vos chaussures de sales
et que je vous y reprenne dans la rue
sur l'herbe ou la Savane
à l'ombre du Monument aux Morts
à jouer
à vous ébattre avec Untel
avec Untel qui n'a pas reçu le baptême

Désastre
parlez-moi du désastre
parlez-m'en

Ma Mère voulant d'un fils très do
  très ré
  très mi
  très fa
  très so
  très la
  très si
  très do
  ré-mi-fa
  sol-la-si
    do

Il m'est revenu que vous n'étiez encore pas
à votre leçon de vi-o-lon
Un banjo
vous dîtes un banjo
comment dîtes-vous
un banjo
vous dîtes bien
un banjo
Non monsieur
    vous saurez qu'on ne souffre chez nous
ni ban
ni jo
ni gui
ni tare

les **mûlatres** ne font pas ça
laissez donc ça aux **nègres**

On a first reading, many readers are tempted to associate the eponymous hiccup ("hoquet") with something natural, like the burp ("rot") that surges up from an a-social stomach ("et tout estomac sociable / se passe de rots"). In this case, the hiccup would bring with it "childhood" ("revient mon enfance"), the word "enfance" presumably evoking an innocence and originary authenticity that has been lost. It is conventional, even banal, to speak of the lost innocence of childhood returning suddenly in memory to the jaded adult, but this is not what Damas is saying at all. The initial grammatical parallelism ("tel que") actually links "mon enfance" to "flic" ("cop") and "instinct" to "voyou" ("rascal"). Thus, what returns like a "hiccup"—a convulsive, involuntary eruption—is an "enfance" that has nothing natural or instinctual about it, a childhood characterized by the suppression of the physical body (the "rots"), the memorization of somebody else's history, and the playing of a "vi-o-lon." Considered more closely, the "hiccup" appears to exert a negative power on the subject's ability to utter speech and therefore to vocalize desire. It is a rapid inhalation that cuts speech, an in-pression rather than ex-pression, shaking up the subject ("secouer"), just as a mother might shake the shoulders of an impulsive child.

We should note further that it is not the child ("enfant") who returns with the hiccup but rather the child*hood* ("enfance"), the greatest period of apprenticeship during which the subject learns to adopt the "ci-vi-li-sa-tion" of the colonizer—here, through the conduit of the anxious mother. Because, as Richard Burton has remarked, the "enfance" in question is not only childhood but a childhood of "a peculiarly structured and overdetermined kind," the author encourages us to associate "enfance" with an experience of limitation, not plenitude, of stifling, not self-discovery.[35] As a result, what returns in visceral fashion does not itself belong to the order of an instinct or a positive impulse; rather, what returns is the only thing that can return, the "no" of the repressive mother, anxious for the full integration of her child into a society of culturally elite *métissés*. To be sure, the hiccup belongs to the order of the body, but it is not by the same token emancipatory; it is the visceral, the corporeal turned against itself. Like a reflex, a function of involuntary memory, the hiccup prevents the subject from ever definitively leaving childhood behind; thus, the return of the repressed is the return of repression itself. Even when invited to step onto the stage and assume speech, the subject fails to "parler du désastre" (speak of the disaster) without stuttering, an effect captured in the lines "Et puis et puis / et puis désastre." The repeated "puis" indicates that such speech is not *about* the disaster but is a symptom of disaster itself. The injunctions suffered in childhood return in the form of a hiccup that the adult cannot erase no matter how hard he tries ("J'ai beau avaler sept gorgées d'eau . . ."). The injunctions impose a kind of gag on the adult as well as on the child he once was, practicing on the hapless body of the *assimilé* an internalized form of an oppression imposed initially from without.

This experience of constant negation, of a gag placed on emission, is represented in several ways in the poem. First of all, the repetitive interpellations of the mother create a pattern—the columns of syntactical parallelisms—that proves to be contagious, affecting the way the child performs as well. Thus, the solfège exercises presumably practiced by the child are not occasions for melody but instead enforce a form of delivery that is less like the chant of anaphora than the stuttering of a broken record. Impersonal directives such as "Le pain ne se coupe pas / le pain ne se gaspille pas / le pain de Dieu" eventually resolve into rhythmic nonsense—"le pain du pain"—as a result of the reiteration of syntagmatic units. The repetitive nature of the mother's instructions ends up transforming all utterance into mechanical repetition: the prayer—"et puis au nom du Père / du Fils / du Saint-Esprit"; the lesson—"très ré / très mi / très do"; and even memory's account, the substance of his personal experience, or black *Leib*—"et puis et puis / et puis. . . ." In short, the poem recounts an "enfance" that is nothing but one long stream of repeated injunctions, a sequence of "Taisez-vous"s (Be quiet) spoken in the "vous" form that annihilates the subject through excessive *politesse*. Reduced to a kind of miming monkey, the child can no longer utter much more than rupture itself. This rupture is at the same time an effect and a cause; it is the symptom of a repressive childhood transformed by the poet into a technique productive of visual and sonic patterns. Following the logic of *détournement*, Damas shows here that by assimilating the negativity of a repressive regime he also assimilates the power to negate. And this power to negate turns out to have its own critical force when manipulated as a poetic device.

"Hoquet" is a kind of poetic drama in which three voices—that of the mother, the "je," and perhaps the child—take turns holding the stage. The *mise en page* of the poem underscores the division of voices: the words of the mother (mouth-piece for the colonial system) are indented and placed in a column slightly to the right while the words of the speaker (the "je") are properly lineated on the left. The source of the repeated refrain, "Désastre / parlez-moi du désastre / parlez-m'en," is unclear; these words seem to constitute an interpellation from without, another form of verbal force obliging the child to recount his disastrous childhood. One might argue that the source of the interpellation is the "monsieur" to whom the child—or the mother—responds "non" in the penultimate stanza. Or they could be the call of the adult (the "je" of the beginning) who hopes to make the silenced child deep within him speak. In any case, the refrain punctuates the poem in a regular fashion, encouraging the "je" to tell the story from the point of view of its victim (the child)—that is, to recount a childhood given over to the process of assimilation.

"Assimilation" means, literally, to take in from the outside; the "hiccup" is thus a perfect symbol for assimilation since it cancels speech through the swift, convulsive intake of air. But there is in the poem at least one sign of *ex*-pression, a sign of an intervention into the mother's world that is so disturbing it causes her to respond. "Il m'est revenu," recalls the speaker, addressing the "vous" (presumably the object of all the injunctions), "que vous n'étiez encore pas / à votre leçon de vi-o-lon / Un banjo." This "banjo" appears to have the privilege of temporal priority with respect to the violin lesson.[36] Its eruption into the scene of instruction suggests an alternative lesson that could be learned, an alternative "voice" that could be heard (that could "return": "il m'est revenu"). But "no," the mother interjects quickly: "vous dîtes un banjo / comment dîtes-vous / un banjo / vous dîtes bien / un banjo/ Non monsieur. . . ." Her consternation mingles with astonishment as she begins to repeat her own refusal. However, in repeating herself she inadvertently allows the forbidden word to be pronounced four times in rapid succession, submitting thereby her own words to the hiccupping rhythm, the poetic device, derived mimetically from the force of her injunctions. In a wonderful reversal perhaps available only to written poetry, the text assimilates the mother's logic—the logic of the taboo—and exerts its force on the forbidden words, "banjo" and "guitare," to produce an innovative sequence: "ni ban / ni jo / ni gui / ni tare." In the final passage, the forbidden words are fragmented in space, mutilated by the denial, or "ni," of the mother, thus producing a propulsive rhythm even as the verbal unit is scattered in space. If the child finds himself unable to speak, unable to answer the repeated call to "parlez du désastre," the blame lies with the mother—or more precisely, with the colonial system that encourages her to despise her son. The mother wants a son "très" correct, capable of reciting his *solfège* not for the purpose of making music or of singing but so he can perform his perfect assimilation, his mime of what he has been taught to be. Ironically, however, her quest for perfection, for an exaggerated domestication of his instinctive self, results in nothing more than the mechanical recitation of a list. He can only mutter a scale that is constantly interrupted by the traumatic force of his mother's desire ("*très* ré / *très* mi / *très* do").

What, then, could possibly emerge from the mouth of this thoroughly assimilated, indoctrinated child if not the impulse of denial, the "ni . . . ni" ("neither . . . nor") signifying the double bind of a thoroughly interiorized negativity? What instrument could this child possibly play other than a "vi-o-lon"? The cavity of that violin is rendered almost visible by the typographic characters, the spacing of which evokes the great zero ("-o-") in the middle of the violin, or the hole installed at the heart of this violated "voyou." If the child finally does manage to make some noise, it is due to the hiccup itself, the "hoquet"—the empty "o" added to a "k" ("o-kay") that paradoxically works as a negation. The eruptive hiccup allows him to interrupt the course of what *can* be said, what *can* be done. It sustains the power of the "flic," mobilizing the force of self-denial and repression to forge a writing style. The "hoquet" becomes the vehicle of an aesthetic subjectivity, marking the spaces where the "lyric I" would be. The spasmodic interruption shapes the poem's rhythmic patterns, patterns made both of tones ("ré-mi-fa" or "sol-la-si") and of the silent spaces in which the reader takes (or holds) her breath.

A question the poem seems to raise is whether the child ever manages to express his own rather than his mother's desire. Does the poet—the "monsieur"?—find a way to make this child speak? ("Parlez-moi du désastre.") Another way to ask this question would be: Does the affective experience of a repressive upbringing manage to find expression on the page? Perhaps what the poem illustrates most successfully is the way the disaster of assimilation can be mobilized to organize language—here, into staccato patterns of words constantly ruptured and reruptured as the gag on self-expression is tightened. The hiccup of repression, that gap in speech created by a sudden intake of air, creates a stutter-like rhythm of locution that becomes itself a kind of style, a "stylistique du bégaiement," in Jean-Pierre Bobillot's felicitous phrase.[37] Theorists have written in general terms about stuttering (or "bégaiement") as a style—or, rather, as style itself. We might consider, for instance, Gilles Deleuze's treatment of the stutter as "éminément poétique" in "Bégaya-t-il . . . ," an essay in which he treats the poetry of Gherasim Luca as though it derived from a strategy similar to that at work in "Hoquet": "Every word divides, but divides with itself (*pas-rats, passions-rations*); every word combines, but with itself (*pas-passe-passion*)."[38] Luca's formula, "je t'aime passionément" (I love you passionately), "bursts out [*éclate*] like a cry," writes Deleuze, "after a long series of stutters":[39] "je t'ai je t'aime te / je je jet je t'ai jetez . . . " we finally arrive at "je t'aime" (I love you).[40]

One could see the word "nègres" printed in bold in the very last line of "Hoquet" as a similar moment in which the repressed term of the series is finally blurted out. After all, the one thing one must never say, think, or be, is **black**. For Deleuze, the stutter mechanism, the parsing and parcelling of phonetic packets, constitutes style in general. "Le style," he writes, is "la langue étrangère dans la langue" (style is the foreign language in the language).[41] Similarly, Bobillot understands the "stylistique du bégaiement" to consist in an "effort to find spaces within language where it might be possible to stage a return of the repressed."[42] Both find that a kind of "jouissance" of language is generated not despite but because of repression. The negativity of a law (the "Symbolic") that makes us speak correctly (or hypercorrectly), a law that insists we separate words from noise, ends up producing more noise than words. Out of this noise, the poet creates a verbal universe of fragments that can be organized into new sequences, new patterns, other than those required by conventional syntactical or lexical laws. In other words, not being able to speak produces a verbal style, a qualitatively different sound pattern, and thus a different way of taking up (graphic) space.

UNE MÉDIOSPHÈRE MÉTISSÉE

It is important to signal that both Deleuze and Bobillot consider "le stylistique du bégaiement" to be either a general phenomenon of writing or, alternatively, a phenomenon specific to "grands écrivains" such as Henri Michaux. Further, they both see the stuttering style as an attack not on a particular language (e.g., French) but on the Symbolic, or language in general.[43] In contrast, Fred Moten, writing on the stylistics of African American poetry, has cautioned against equating the resistent practices of African-derived writers with those of writers in general (or experimental writers in particular). He writes astutely that "the tragic in any tradition, especially the black radical tradition, is never wholly abstract."[44] In other words, the attack is not against "the Symbolic" as such but rather is "always in relation to quite particular and material loss."[45] Moten's reminder is crucial, for the problematic Damas confronts in "Hoquet" is specific to the psychic life of the populations named "mûlatres" and "nègres" in the poem. Further, the injunctions voiced by the mother are not exemplary of the "law" of Language, but metonymies for an entire colonial regime. Finally, the subaltern is not just any disenfranchised writer, repressed child, or high modernist practitioner of the "sémiotique" but rather a raced subject struggling with a very concrete set of prohibitions indeed.

Still, the poetic expression of this specificity is not entirely unique to Damas or to black writers as a group. As members of the typosphere, Damas and the Negritude poets draw from a shared set of typographic, alphabetic, and graphemic possibilities for evoking repression on the page. Graphemic–phonemic relations constitute a field of acoustic exploration available to all poets invested in bringing the visceral experience of negative injunctions to the reader's eyes. It may be, as Édouard Glissant has proposed, that the peoples of the Caribbean possess a heightened sensitivity to sound due to the circumstances of their enslavement.[46] For them, sound—not as immediacy but as opacity—bears an almost graphemic heft. But is this not the case for many poets? Of many nationalities, ethnicities, and political orientations? Again, the inflection matters here; the cultural associations with which sound is freighted inform what sound can come to mean. There are historical reasons for the particular attention black cultures have paid to oral and musical forms, and these should be taken into account. Yet it is unlikely that one culture alone has a privileged relation to what Glissant calls the "noise in speech."[47] In his reading of "Hoquet," Richard Burton (echoing a generation of scholars) posits a binary opposition between the "instinctive, lyrical and improvisatory energies expressed in the Afro-creole banjo" and the "hierarchical rigidities and repetitions of the Gregorian scale."[48] Certainly there is a difference between a spontaneous effort and the solfège exercises the child is compelled to recite. But when Burton contrasts "the joyously rebellious rhythms and accents of the colonized" with the "regularized crochets, minims and quavers . . . fixed for all time within the staves, bar-lines and time-signatures of the colonizer" (25) he comes dangerously close to identifying "instinctual" and "joyous" musicality with blacks and the regime of writing ("time-signatures of the colonizer") with whites. Is the acoustic universe so neatly divided?

Brent Hayes Edwards has recently published impressive studies of Duke Ellington and Louis Armstrong *as writers* that place into question what he calls the "compulsion among generations of African American writers"—and, one might add, critics—to associate "black writing" with "the condition of music."[49] By pointing out this "compulsion," Edwards does not mean to "undermine the importance of black music," nor does he wish to deny that black expression pays a heightened attention to sound. But he nonetheless encourages us "to begin to challenge some of our assumptions about the relations among aesthetic media in black culture."[50] To give just one example of how such assumptions might be challenged, Edwards demonstrates that Ellington saw print as a medium that could itself produce rhythm, a medium that could be scored such that words on a page might suggest a phrase or riff. Similarly, I have maintained that Damas by no means abandons the text for either music or noise, nor does he seek a mastery over sounds instead of words. The stuttering sounds of "Hoquet" do not trail off into sonic nonsense but instead produce with ringing clarity (and usher into the lyric tradition) the words "nègres" and "mûlatres," and, elsewhere, "Juif," and "Jaune." In a sense, then, Damas's "stylistique du bégaiement" presents a way out of the trap of colonial mimicry that Hughes points to in "Cubes." For Damas the danger lies not implicating oneself in the master's practice by imitating too closely his techniques; the trap lies instead in assuming those techniques to be owned by one "race" alone. Embracing print as a support, Damas uses the means of print—words, but also spaces, marks of punctuation, and the resources of the written alphabet—to carve out a site of personal expression, something like "le creux d'une épaule" he sought in "Réalité." He manages to convey an experience of alienation that is caused not by the loss of some originary orality but rather by almost complete submission to authority in exaggerated form.

Among all the critics who have glossed "Hoquet"—and there are many—it is perhaps Aimé Césaire who best grasped the import of the poem. In an homage to Damas written soon after his death, Césaire suggests that the Damasian hiccup ("le hoquet damassien") is a version of the Sartian "Nausée": "As there is the Sartian Nausea," he writes, "there is fundamentally the Damasian hiccup, which is disgust, repulsion, attempts never completely fulfilled. . . . [There is] the Damasian stutter ["le bégaiement damassien"] . . . a weakness transformed into strength because it is responsible, ultimately, for creating the Damasian rhythm."[51] As I have argued, the poems of Damas do indeed have rhythm, but it is *his* rhythm, as Césaire states, not the rhythm of Africa resurrected, as Senghor would have us believe. "Hoquet" contains many rhythmic sequences that could easily have been based on, or could produce, a musical recitation, a drum-like beat. Damas was always conscious that he had succeeded in this way. According to witnesses, Damas loved to recite "Hoquet" before his friends; the poem became a sort of poetic signature, a little performance piece that he gave at the conclusion of dinner parties. One could even argue that performance is precisely the theme of "Hoquet"—musical performance as a kind of symbolic capital—not simply a case of colonial mimicry but also, potentially, a source of cultural pride. The poem contains multiple evocations of musical instruments: the violin, the banjo, the guitar, and—implicitly—the drumbeat of syntactical units in apposition, seductive rhythms that are hard to resist. Yet "Hoquet" is also the poem in which Damas refines and systematizes a set of typographical innovations unknown to previous poets of the diaspora: the use of the dash and letters in bold, the placement of phrases, words, and word fragments in vertical columns, and the exploitation of the iconic values of printed characters (as in "vi-o-lon").

Ultimately, Damas does not wish to choose between a sound poetics coded as black and a typosphere coded as white. His best work makes rhythms by shuttling between the graphic entity of the page and the vocalized beating of the syllable. And his most memorable performances are those in which words admit their inability to "Speak of the disaster"—that is, to make repression go away. "Hoquet" deserves its renown—and exerts its influence—not because Damas knew how to imitate the beating of a tom-tom, the strumming of a banjo, or even the tonality of the human voice. The achievement of Damas is to have written a poem, and this poem is neither African nor French, neither black nor white, neither tom-tom nor orchestra but rather a singular phenomenon in print lending itself to actualization on many planes in all the plenitude of a mediosphere *métissée*.

Figure 3.1: Portrait of Léon-Gontran Damas as a youth, about age nine, holding a book, circa 1921. Photographer unknown. Photographs and Prints Division, Schomburg Center for Research in Black Culture, The New York Public Library, Astor, Lenox, and Tilden Foundations.

4

LÉON-GONTRAN DAMAS

Writing Rhythm in the Interwar Period

Le sujet de l'énonciation est un rapport.
—Henri Meschonnic[1]

One of the most compelling theories of poetic writing to emerge in recent years can be found in a work by Jacques Rancière titled *La parole muette: Essai sur les contradictions de la littérature*. Tracing the development of literature in print from roughly 1830 to the end of the nineteenth century, Rancière analyzes the ambiguous status of poems once they have entered the typosphere, or, in his terms, once they circulate under "le régime de l'écriture." Although *La parole muette* is not concerned with engaged literature per se, Rancière's theory indirectly addresses the claim of poetic texts that aspire to represent or advocate a specific politics in poetic form. In *La parole muette* and again in later works, such as *Le partage du sensible* (2000) and *Malaise dans l'esthétique* (2004), Rancière draws a connection between the modern condition of textuality—the way it disengages the author from the audience—and the aporia of the aesthetic in general, its simultaneous desire and inability to affect concrete change. With "the commitment of the word to space," as Walter Ong has put it, the intention of the author becomes irretrievable, her voice lost—or so, at least, the story goes.[2] Therefore, the poem cannot unmediatedly represent either a particular speaker or the community with which the speaker identifies because the tone, pitch, rhythm, and cadence of the voice has been silenced, the meaning of the message "orphaned," detached from the author(ity) that fathered the text. The subjectivity supposedly conveyed by the poem (as "I" or as source of speech) thus loses touch with the empirical writer while the meaning, or message, of the poem is submitted to the vagaries of interpretation over time.

In this chapter I examine more closely the relation between print poem and modern reader, between writing and vocalization, with particular regard to how these relations generate innovations in poetic form. As in the earlier chapter on Césaire and the vicissitudes of performance, I am interested here in the way Negritude writers engage with the print medium and the peculiar conditions of simultaneous distance and heightened intimacy it imposes. In recent years an abundance of new scholarship has turned to the question of voice in poetry, the commerce between letter and sound, not simply from the perspective of the graphic distribution of words on the page but also with respect to the type of subjectivity that might be embodied in the literary text as it is actualized in the mind and mouth of the individual reader. The most systematic treatment of subjectivity in print poetry can be found in the work of Henri Meschonnic; his *Critique du rythme* of 1982 establishes a set of terms that will prove fruitful for approaching specific works of Negritude. In contrast to Rancière, who radicalizes the disconnection between reading and hearing, scholars such as Meschonnic, Rosemarie Waldrop, Jacques Roubaud, Garrett Stewart, Charles Bernstein, Susan Stewart, Lesley Wheeler, Peggy Phelan, and a host of others have sought to rethink what Susan Howe calls "font-voices" and their relation to human subjects.[3] Many of these scholars play a role in what follows. However, as a means to clarify and qualify Rancière's position, I focus on the interventions of Meschonnic and the performance theorist Peggy Phelan in particular. My goal is to explore the tension between presence and distance, performance (oral transmission) and print (written word), as it informs the compositional practices of Léon-Gontran Damas by approaching the poetic text as a site of what Meschonnic calls "ré-énonciations."[4] For Meschonnic, the printed poem is a generator of readings, rhythmic articulations, or *ré-énonciations*, faithful but never identical to the text as utterance. Similarly, in Phelan's words, the text is "haunted" by its past (performances) while also haunting its future ones, reconnecting the human source of utterance and the human source of its reception through what she terms (after Robert Frost) the poem's "oversound." Rancière, Meschonnic, and Phelan, although advancing from different positions, seek alike to understand how poetic textuality implies both repetition and difference. For them, poetry conveys—while betraying—the acoustics and affects linked to an empirical source.

LE RÉGIME DE L'ÉCRITURE

Rancière's work on the aesthetic is now so well known that a full account is not necessary. However, it is worth summarizing his less familiar work on the peculiar conditions of print literature in order to show how he approaches the modernist typosphere to which Negritude writers belong. *La parole muette* is not, strictly speaking, a history of literature, yet it does establish distinct periods of verbal production coincident with successive forms of social organization, or what he calls "regimes." Literature, or "le régime de l'écriture," comes at the end of a long development beginning in oral cultures where epic, ritual, and theatrical forms predominate. The reception conditions of each phase, or "regime," of verbal expression are quite distinct, Rancière explains, and this has an impact on the form and content of verbal forms as they evolve. He imagines that in the "ethical regime" of orature (or what we might call, after Régis Debray, the "aurosphere"), verbal works performed before spectators serve to address and consolidate a homogeneous community. There is no separation, either temporal or situational, between author and audience, and thus no chance—Rancière seems to believe—for misinterpretation, ambiguity, or even exegesis at all; one simply feels what is said in one's bones. Rancière's privileged example is the festival or rite in which "the collective body of a city . . . enacts its own unity through hymns and dances."[5] Such an experience is available to anyone belonging to the collective; it does not require a specialized, formally acquired mode of appreciation (a specialized "sensorium," in Rancière's terms).[6] In *Dissensus*, he calls this pre-Socratic regime "archi-ethical" because the function of art is not to "improve behavior (didactic ethical) through representation"—as in Plato—but to have "*all bodies directly embody the sense of the common*," a point to which we shall have occasion to return.[7] The participants of the festival enjoy an "ethical immediacy" as the words of the epic or orphic poet compel the spectators' bodies to sway to the corresponding rhythm.[8]

This type of performance, Rancière goes on, is differentiated from the modern performances of proscenium theatre, which belong more properly to the second of Rancière's regimes, the "representative regime." A classical theatrical performance (whether in Aristotle's Greece or the Ancien

Régime) functions according to rigid rules that determine the register of speech appropriate to each group of spectators and each occasion. In the "representative regime," subject matter, audience, and artist are all carefully defined entities entering into conventional and regulated relationships with one another. These relationships begin to break down, in Rancière's rendering, as a result of a series of events, including the division introduced by Napoleon between applied arts and beaux arts; the undermining of strict class divisions through the rise of a mercantile bourgeoisie; and the spread of literacy to the working classes (a situation he examines more closely in *La nuit des prolétaires*). Although Rancière is concerned primarily with the case of (white) France, his comments on the mid-nineteenth-century working class are pertinent to the situation of the Caribbean *évolués* who, by the beginning of the twentieth century, also found themselves in a position to take advantage of the colonial administration's first attempts to universalize grade school education.[9] "Militant workers of the 1840s," writes Rancière, "broke out of the circle of domination by reading and writing—not popular and militant but—'high' literature."[10] Of course, the "circle of domination" to which he is referring is class domination; however, a similar phenomenon can be seen to operate decades later in the French West Indies where access to "high literature" accompanied and abetted the social mobility and, eventually, the self-enfranchisement of the nonwhite population. By the same token, however—and this is Rancière's main point—literacy and the new reading habits of "the regime of writing" broke the thread binding the *évolué* to his or her local community. We see Césaire struggling with this same dilemma (the attenuation of the "ethical immediacy" in a regime of writing) in the *Cahier d'un retour au pays natal*; in the section where he aspires to be "la bouche des malheurs qui n'ont pas de bouche" (the mouth of suffering that has no mouth) he finds himself lamentably isolated, abjectly flung back into irrelevance and . . . more writing.[11] The problematic relation of individualized self to atomized community is a constant theme throughout Césaire's oeuvre, and it creates ripples of self-reflexive questioning in the poetry of Damas and Senghor as well.

The conditions of the "regime of writing" are thus emancipatory and duplicitous at the same time, guaranting proximity to the text (democratized education, literacy of the masses) while enforcing distance from the site of its production. In Rancière's terms, the text, although legible, is no longer audible. As a "silenced" ("muette") medium, the text is now divorced from live oratory, live performance, and—if we are to follow Rancière—sound. With the silencing of the text, there is no longer a live author to interrogate, no longer a single "sense" or meaning to determine, and—most importantly for our purposes—no longer an ideal reading capable of (re)animating the text with anything resembling an authorized voice. As opposed to a performance, a text does not speak for itself; it does not occur, so to speak, at any particular point in time before any particular group, nor can it be proven to emanate from any particular source.[12] In short, although theoretically anyone can read the written word, no one can properly perform it. No one can embody its rhythm or distinguish its tone. This, of course, has consequences for poetry, which claims to have greater purchase if not on the author's intention, then at least on the author's distinctive voice, a voice attached to a living body that the rhythmic clusters of syllables, the punctuation, the exclamations, the page layout, and other devices are intended to capture, communicate, and revive.

Now, there are problems, I believe, both with Rancière's sense of what a performance is and with his sense of what a text is. He does not explain precisely what he means by "silenced" or "mute," and the question remains whether all aspects of literature—and all genres—are equally stunted in their ability to evoke an experience in the reader of listening to a distinctive voice. In his study of Mallarmé, *Mallarmé: La politique de la sirène*, Rancière suggests repeatedly that poetry is able, via its "forme sensible," to be "plus que l'écriture"—more than writing.[13] By means of its "musical" qualities—and Rancière does use the word "musical"—the written text doubles its referent ("the thing mimed") with a second phenomenal coat, which he calls a "rhythmic form": "In the musical presentation [la présentation musicale], it is not things [les choses] that are imitated, but the idea itself. The musical fiction [la fiction musicale] depicts the idea in the form of rhythm [sous forme de rythme]."[14] What Rancière (or Mallarmé) might mean by "idée"—and how it differs from "les choses"—need not detain us here. The important point is that Rancière recasts the supposedly "mute word" of textual poetry as something that can appear "in the form of rhythm" even if it is mute. In other words, the "rhythm" or "fiction musicale"—the musicalized unreal—is not necessarily a sound like the sound of a voice on a stage, present before the listener and thereby able to marry audition and gaze. The "rhythm" is in some sense in advance of sound, as Mallarmé intimates in a passage from "Bucolique," which Rancière cites: the poet is "serviteur, par avance, des rythmes."[15] The poet is the "servant of rhythms" that have not yet come to be. Rancière sketches out here (with the help of Mallarmé) a unique temporality of textual sound—or, at the very least, a unique temporality of something belonging to the order of rhythm on a page—and this temporality is anticipatory rather than coincident. As opposed to the actor on the stage, or the epic poet surrounded by his community, the subject of a poem speaks only in the future tense of the reader's reading, and this is a reading that can make noise.

Before we take a closer look at (or lend an ear to) individual poems by Damas, we must begin to redress what Garrett Stewart has called the "phonophobia" of the linguistic turn that Rancière epitomizes.[16] New critical and deconstructive critics have tended to disengage the text not simply from the author's "voice" (as a sign of "authenticity") but also, by implication, from the author's "race."[17] In a poststructuralist world, meter remains a product of tradition, but rhythm is set free from its diagnostic function. In contrast, during the period when Negritude poets first began writing, rhythm was closely associated with a racial or regional identity not simply symbolically but also concretely, as a particular way of placing syllables (or stresses) into patterns. Modernist poets such as Ezra Pound and W. B. Yeats believed that poetry could embody rhythmic features specific to discrete cultures (or "races"); through rhythm, the body of the speaker could be registered, and thus a reader sensitive to these rhythms would feel the impress of this body in the way the words reorganize themselves in her inner ear. Rhythm "scientists" of the early twentieth century "held that a black African person's heartbeats recur at different intervals than those of a Native American, whose heart beats to a different tempo than a white European's—that, ultimately, the difference between a German and a French pulse could be measured and registered—and that hence these different 'peoples' 'naturally' generate and respond to different rhythms."[18] This view was not only held by white Europeans (some of whom were openly eugenicists) but also by many black writers of the time, including Senghor, whose theory of rhythm we will examine more closely in a moment. In short, during the period with which we are concerned, poetry in particular was believed to constitute a "parole rythmique" rather than a "parole muette," a conduit of racialized and regionalized speech patterns rather than an "orphaned" grapheme, and such a belief had a direct influence on the way letters were arranged on the page.

It is instructive to compare the situation of the Negritude poets to that of the African American poets of the Harlem Renaissance publishing work approximately a decade earlier. As Fahamisha Patricia Brown has shown, even while striving "to demonstrate literary competence," African American poets remained in conversation with vernacular traditions associated with diasporic experience, cultural heritage, and racial inheritance, explicitly inventing scribal analogs of speech practices in order to make the word "perform."[19] In contrast, it is not clear that either the folk and popular cultures of the Antilles or the oral and musical forms of Africa were a direct inspiration for Césaire's *Cahier* (although he does make thematic references to drumming in poems like "Batouque," "Tam-tam I," and "Tam-tam II").[20] Césaire occasionally expresses a sense of nostalgia for the performance situation of the "griot," or "conteur" (storyteller), a situation described beautifully by Édouard Glissant in "Une errance enracinée" (A rooted wandering). In Glissant's words, a "conteur" addresses the audience seated at his feet within a "circle defined by the shadows of the night."[21] This charmed circle represents an ideal in which the audience recognizes the words as addressed specifically to them. Such "ethical immediacy" is thematized in Césaire's works, but his high degree of self-consciousness prevents him from laboring under the illusion that the dialogism of the communal recitation could be granted through textual means. In contrast, Senghor and Damas, who identify more closely with the jazz and blues aesthetics of the African American poets, seem to have given credit to the idea that a poem can embody communal values, or a racial Lebenswelt. Senghor, especially, promulgates a view of poetry as "raced," producing essays throughout his lifetime in which he treats writing as capable of transmitting a racialized form of embodiment.[22] It is poetic rhythm that, for him, directly transmits the voice of an individual and, by extension, through the individual, an entire people.

Interestingly, when Senghor discusses Damas in *Négritude et humanisme*, he singles him out as the poet most closely in touch with a race-specific rhythm. Damas's poems, Senghor states, resonate with "un rythme de tam-tam instinctivement retrouvé" (the rhythm of the tom-tom instinctively retrieved).[23] Again, when he presents his selection of Damas's poetry in *Anthologie de la nouvelle poésie nègre et malgache de langue française*, he notes that the poems are "made up of everyday words, noble or vulgar," but that "everything is submitted to the natural rhythm of the tom-tom . . . rhythm, in Damas, is more important than melody."[24] The figure of a poet "submitted" to the "natural rhythm of the tom-tom" returns once more in *Éthiopiques*, when Senghor affirms that "Black poets . . . above all, are 'auditory' [auditifs], they chant"; "They are submitted, tyrannically, to an 'internal music,' first and foremost, to its rhythm."[25]

In their most extreme form, the positions of Senghor and Rancière can be seen as diametrically opposed: for Senghor, the text is never silent but rather resonant with a racial rhythm that the poem conveys directly to the ear, whereas for Rancière the text is mute and can be interpreted—in the sense of vocalized and understood—in any number of different ways. However, neither of these two thinkers is as dogmatic as this rendering would suggest. Rancière, as we have seen, admits the possibility of a poetic "rhythm" in Mallarmé (if not audible then at least "sensible"), and Senghor, as we shall see, reinterprets "rhythm" as something other than a mimetic phenomenon. Navigating a course between them—while drawing from their work—I seek a middle ground between an understanding of rhythm as racial paternity and an understanding of rhythm as "orphaned." The notion of a poetic rhythm that is anticipatory, waiting to be sounded, and thus distinct from a music already heard allows us to thread a path between the two extremes: (1) that poetry by a black writer necessarily contains African rhythms passed through the blood, part of a genetic inheritance that instinctively surges forth in the poetry of writers not born in Africa, yet "submitted tyrannically"—in Senghor's words—to their African essence; and (2) that written poetry bears no rhythmic content whatsoever, or at least no rhythmic content that is on the order of acoustic substance, capable of being sounded as a result of reading the "mute" text.[26] This last account of textuality fails to acknowledge what is a common experience of Damas's readers—and that many readers have of poetry in general—namely, the intimation that a human voice lies behind the words, that some form of embodied presence is at work. While we do not have to—in fact, we shouldn't—accept uncritically Senghor's argument that Negritude poets are "tyrannically subjected" to a primordial rhythm lodged in their racial essence, or that, in the words of Martin Munro, they use rhythm as "a dynamic way of . . . recovering from the depths of time the lost African-ness," we can still ask how Damas's style might convey elements of an experience rooted in historical circumstance and transmitted across the page.[27]

"IL Y A QUELQUE CHOSE QUI PASSE . . . LE COURANT PASSE"

Innovations in poetic form are often linked to a poet's efforts to generate spoken rhythms. Such efforts would be utterly pointless if the phenomenal experience of readers did not confirm that print can indeed produce the illusion of a rhythmed voice generating the text. Inscriptions, however conventionalized, cannot ensure an exact rendering of a voice, rhythm, or melody that may have never preceded the poem in any case. But if an author makes an intentional effort to relate writing to "the world of sound"—as Langston Hughes did when composing "The Weary Blues," or as Paul Laurence Dunbar did in the dramatic monologue "When Dey 'Listed Colored Soldiers"—then the "silenced word" may contain directives and cues that encourage (without guaranteeing) a certain way of performing the text in our heads. In the poetry of Hughes and Dunbar syntax is a clue to accentuation, unconventional spellings impose diphthongs or elongations of vowels, parallelisms evoke the cadences of oratory, and typographic emphases and line breaks tell us when we, as readers, are supposed to pause or imagine heightened volume. In short, the act of reading such poetry contains a performative moment when the text comes into being as "ré-énonciation," if only for the eyes. This "ré-énonciation" is not the authorized copy of the original utterance, dictating and preserving some ideal, accurate, and immutable rendering of the author's own rhythmic phrasing. Instead, the "ré-énonciation" is a kind of spectral retrieval, a form of "twice-behaved behavior," as Richard Schechner famously characterized performance, a repetition that sustains the mirage of a first "behavior." This is precisely where Peggy Phelan's understanding of the written word, an understanding informed by the performance theory of Schechner, can make a valuable contribution to poetry studies. Because her approach assumes neither a "first behavior"—an original enunciation upon which the performance depends—nor a performance untethered from any authorial (vocal or instrumental) directive whatsoever, it can serve as a pivot between the deconstructive poetics of a Rancière and a cultural studies approach à la Munro that, while attentive to the author's identity, fails to observe the transformative intervention of textuality as a medium in its own right.

If Rancière's model for textuality is "the silenced word," Phelan's model for textuality is Robert Frost's oversound, "the thing in the poem that is not simply the result of the specific words or meter, an elusive thing more than the sum of these."[28] Phelan understands Frost's oversound to designate the "tone of meaning," a phrase she borrows from Frost's poem, "Never Again Would Birds' Song Be the Same," in which he claims he hears "the tone of meaning, but without the words." But what would a "tone of meaning" be? And how might we seize such a tone in writing? What use does Phelan make of this notion, and how can it help us understand the communicative potential of the Negritude poem, its "mute word"?

As Phelan presents it, the tone of meaning, or oversound, is an elusive entity indeed. In an earlier attempt to clarify Frost's phrase, Tom Vander Ven has written that the poet understands oversound to be "a voice tone which conveys an attitude and meaning beyond the immediate individual values of the separate words which make up the unit."[29] In fact, Vander Ven continues, Frost believed that the oversound could be read by the ear. It would be like a tone of voice, an affect relayed by the stress, pitch, intonation, and volume of an utterance that ostensibly finds its way into written form. Vander Ven's definition of "oversound" is as suggestive (and vague) as Phelan's, and he too goes about approaching it through a series of negations: "Frost's sound of sense is not individual words, it is not word patterns, it is not metrical rhythm, nor is it context, i.e., a situational reference. Neither is it thought, since there can be sense without sound. What remains is to say what it is, what entity is left when all these elements of communication are stripped from it."[30] In Phelan's rendering: oversound is "the thing not in the words, not in the melody, not in the dance, not in the meter."[31] Importantly, for both, oversound is not music. That is, it is neither melody nor meter. Yet it is nonetheless of the order of the audible, a kind of "tone" that Vander Ven associates with the pathos of a human voice heard from another room when the words are not discernable. Echoing a truism of lyric criticism, that a lyric is an "intimacy overheard," Vander Ven concludes that oversound derives from "the commitment of feeling to sound."[32]

I believe that Vander Ven and Phelan are both angling oversound in the direction of what Senghor refers to as "rhythm" when speaking of Damas. "Rhythm," as an aspect of poetic expression, "is more important than melody," states Senghor. Therefore, rhythm, like oversound, is not melody and it is not words.[33] These critics are trying to get at an aspect of poetry related to but not entirely subsumed by our traditional concepts of rhythm, a kind of "internal music" (Senghor) which, as we shall see, is not exactly music but instead a vocal noise that is only potentially (and inchoately) a communicative sound.[34] One might well ask what is left "when all these elements of communication—words, meter, melody, music—are stripped from the poem" (Vander Ven). Critics have responded in different ways: Henri Meschonnic chooses to name this "entity" with the word "rhythm" itself but heavily alters its meaning; Jed Rasula, twisting T. S. Eliot, offers "voice-over";

and Phelan reworks Frost's term "oversound" to evoke the relational or performance dimension of poetry, its manner of "submitting" us to the sense that, while reading lyric, we are not alone in the room.

Phelan first mentions Frost's "oversound"—albeit cautiously—in a short essay written in response to the Modern Language Association's 2010 call to imagine a "literary criticism for the twenty-first century." In her contribution to the special volume of the *PMLA* titled "'Just Want to Say': Performance and Literature, Jackson and Poirier," Phelan begins by asserting that the textual (formalist-deconstructive) paradigm, so long dominant in literary scholarship, cannot be the privileged paradigm for the next century for a variety of reasons. First and foremost is her sense that a deconstructive rendering (such as Rancière's *La parole muette*) fails to account adequately for an experience we have as readers that something is being sounded, is being given airtime, so to speak, in print. While reflecting on what the next century's paradigm might be, Phelan chooses not to dwell on approaches associated with identity politics, such as the varieties of cultural and postcolonial studies that treat the text as witnessing, confessing, or otherwise transmitting the subjectivity of an identifiable speaker (the identity of the author or the community for whom she stands). Phelan is decidedly not interested in a politics or poetics of self-representation. Neither, however, does she fall back into the deconstructive mode, insisting that any sense we have of relationality, of a presence in the poem, results simply from our seduction by (and blindness to) the figural work accomplished by the letters on the page. Instead she advances a performance studies model for literary studies, sketching out an intriguing but embryonic proposal for renewed attention to that which the text seemingly is not. She enjoins her readers to retrieve "the intimacy of the connection between literature and performance," and thus the possibility, in reading, of a communion with something that haunts the text, something other than ourselves.[35] Similarly, she seems to suggest, performance might be seen to be specular, a presence, or embodiment, taking place in two different temporalities before our eyes. Both literature and performance undermine the "authenticity" of the subject by revealing it to be a reiterated performance; but performance, in turn, is shown to be at the heart of any effort we might make to constitute an authentic "self."

If we neglect or lose sight of "the connection between literature and performance," Phelan warns, "we diminish something vital in and between them."[36] It turns out that this "something vital in and between them" may be captured by Frost's term, "oversound," "the tone of meaning." Finally, "oversound," that "thing not in the words, not in the melody, not in the dance, not in the meter," is a form of what Phelan's teacher, Richard Poirier (to whom the essay is implicitly dedicated) calls "human relatedness."[37] We have traveled a long path here—from a hardly nameable presence in a poem ("not in the words, not in the melody"), to "rhythm" (in a sense we have yet to define), to "human relatedness." But I believe these are all styles of pointing toward the same thing: the elusive nature of sound in a written text (and the elusive nature of inscription in a live performance). To cite Poirier: "The connection between the making of sound and the discovery of human relatedness" may be what poetry, ultimately, is all about.[38] Sound in poetry, Susan Stewart proposes in a similar vein, partakes of the invocatory drive toward recognition by the other; it emerges from a "propulsion to make one's self heard and seen."[39] However, what is "heard" and "seen" is only partially a entailment of that "self"; the link between writing and performing, between recording and constituting, will always trouble the transparency of that "human relatedness," for the presence staged for us in a text bears with it the static, the "grain," of its own "enactment."[40]

The critics whose names I have evoked thus far are obviously not the only ones who struggle with finding a way to define the poetic text as a form of embodiment, a "presence," "subjectivity," "voice," "voice-over," "oversound"—or, at the very least, a "promise" of human relatedness.[41] All of these formulations attempt to capture the sense the reader often has that something has been communicated, across the stage or the page, something that, in Phelan's terms, prevents the text from being cut off entirely from "liveness." Perhaps the best—and the most immediately pertinent—phrasing of this "something" appears in an interview accorded by Aimé Césaire to Jacqueline Leiner in 1978. Prefiguring the debate I will extend in these pages he states:

> [My work] is a matter of sensibility [une affaire de sensibilité], it is a matter of sympathy [une affaire de sympathie], in the strong sense of the term. I believe that my poetry is not hermetic. I've seen that lots of people, perfectly equipped to comprehend my poetry, don't comprehend it at all; and lots of people who have no particular training whatsoever comprehend it quite well. You see, there is definitely communication between my work and them. . . . They don't understand it literally, word for word; that's not what communication is. . . . Is it intuition? Is it due to the rhythm? [Est-ce dû au rythme?] In any case, they feel something [Enfin, ils sentent quelque chose]. . . . There is something that passes . . . the current passes [il y a quelque chose qui passe . . . le courant passe].[42]

Setting aside the metaphor of the "current" (perhaps a hold-over from the surrealist fascination with the discourse of electronics), we can see the resemblance between what Césaire is trying to get at in the interrogative mode—"Est-ce l'intuition? Est-ce dû au rythme?"—and what Phelan means by "oversound." The something vital that "passes" (and that reconnects literature to performance) is not the author's voice in its empirical, everyday existence but rather something created through prolonged interchange with the materials of writing, a special form of embodiment that is not exactly voice, not exactly sound, but oversound. Further, it is crucial to underscore that what "passes" *passes*; that is, Césaire's word is extremely well chosen, for it captures the sense of both a passage, a connection that obtains between text and reader, and a pass*ing*, an ephemeral appearance of something like a human voice that disappears. It is this disappearance of the relationality, of the sound related and the source from whence it came, that characterizes both lyric texts and live performance modes. The oversound is what passes in a written poem when read; it flares up into earshot then quickly desubstantializes when we stop reading, and it flares up differently (because we too have changed, passed) each time we read the poem again. It thus cannot be equated with an individual person, or a fixed identity, or a specific race or culture. It is the sound that identity makes when entering into relation, a sound that has undergone "creolization," necessarily heterogeneous to what it might have been or what it will be in other mouths. The performance element of literature—to take up Phelan's gauntlet once again—can be seen to inhere in this ephemeral presencing of something that cannot be pinned down as a permanent or fixed entity, something that makes noise in our mind.[43] Senghor's term "internal music" is serviceable, but I would distinguish "internal" music from music per se insofar as the former resembles more the noise of the "grapholect," or written words, than a melodic sound in our ears.[44] How might we develop a "more muscular math for calculating oversound," as Phelan prevails upon us to do?[45] Where might we locate the "tone of meaning," or, in Césaire's terms, "le courant qui passe"? What precisely "passes," where is it to be located on the page, and why would calculating it more precisely be relevant to Negritude, a movement so curiously sutured to questions of essence, identity, and the need to communicate subjectivity in language?

"DE RYTHME EN RYTHME"

"They don't understand literally, *mot par mot*," explains Césaire, reflecting on the "tone of meaning" in his texts; "that's not it, communication. . . . Is it intuition? Is it through rhythm?" Césaire's tentative responses, offered, significantly, in the interrogative mode, clearly owe a debt to the poetics of Senghor. It is Senghor who provides Césaire with a vocabulary, a set of (ultimately unsatisfactory) terms for denoting that thing that sounds, that "passes," in the text. Senghor first introduced Césaire to Leo Frobenius, the anthropologist from whom the word "intuition" is borrowed. Senghor is also the source for Césaire's understanding of rhythm as a connection to the past, a potential source for communicating the Black Self. However, "rhythm" is a highly complex term in Senghor's poetics: it serves to evoke the musicality of African cultures, their proximity to bodily awareness, and even their supposed intimacy with the cycles of the earth.[46] In addition, taken literally as a technical component of music, "rhythm," for Senghor, refers to the distribution of stresses in a melodic line. In an interview recorded by RFI (Radio France Internationale) in the late 1970s, Senghor explains that African rhythms in both music and chant consist of "asymmetrical parallelisms," which he contrasts with the "monotonous" twelve syllable line of French prosody.[47] The African line possesses four accents, he explains, but this tetrameter can be filled with diverse and unpredictable groupings of syllables (or notes). Whether symbolic of an intuitive relation to nature or, more technically, a scaffolding for inventive asymmetrical or polyrhythmic play, rhythm is, for Senghor, the very essence of Negritude—by which he means an essence shared by peoples of African descent. Linking the African "race" to African rhythms, he discovers asymmetrical parallelisms in the tattoo of the tom-tom, the Negritude poem, African American blues, and the Caribbean *biguine*.

Senghor's understanding of rhythm is in fact nuanced and inventive. In the postface to *Éthiopiques*, where he associates the poetry of Damas and Césaire with the "rythme du tam-tam," he also associates rhythm itself with anaphora (syntactical parallelism) and, somewhat more paradoxically, with a way of treating imagery. He thus enlarges his notion of rhythm to encompass features of style that have little to do with tetrameter phrasing. With respect to Césaire's *Cahier*, for instance, Senghor writes that the incessant flow of images, the subordinations within subordinations that characterize his clauses, are themselves rhythmic elements, "form[s], among others, of rhythm."[48] He goes on to imply that each poet included in his 1948 *Anthologie de la nouvelle poésie noire et malgache* channels his African rhythmic roots in a totally different—and strictly personal—way. Senghor refers his reader to Sartre's comments on style in "Orphée noir," where the philosopher observes that, whereas Césaire displays his heritage "by pressing his words tightly one against the other" in explosive rage, Étienne Léro composes in a looser, more relaxed style.[49] These differences noted by Sartre cause Senghor to underscore that each poet "uses his pen" to organize his own "danse verbale."[50] Unfortunately, in his short introductory notes to the poets included in his *Anthologie*, he often falls back on a less nuanced understanding of black self-representation in language, insisting, for instance, that the "rythme naturel du tam-tam" is the most raw and unmediated form of expression for a poet who wishes to "sing black" (chanter nègre).[51]

Senghor nonetheless has an intimation of what Henri Meschonnic has more recently developed—namely, a theory that relates rhythm to subjectivity not as it exists prior to the act of writing but rather as it takes form in a collaborative act of writing and recitation that requires the reader to be actualized. As opposed to Senghor and numerous critics in his wake (Keith Q. Warner, Keith L. Walker, Martin Munro, Lilyan Kesteloot, Hubert de Leusse, and Janheinz Jahn, to name just a few), Meschonnic does not associate a poem's rhythm with the (racial) identity of its author—at least not in any fashion that wouldn't be mediated by a host of contingencies such as tradition, geographical location, class, and individual style.[52] Just as "rhythm" turns out to be, for Senghor, a close synonym of "style," so too for Meschonnic the word "rhythm" captures the idiosyncratic nature of a poet's way of making sound on and through the printed page. The advantage of the word "rhythm" over "style," however, is that the former insists on the necessity of actualization, the enunciative or performative element involved in reading a poem. "Rhythm," for Meschonnic, is located neither entirely within the poem (as a type of inscription or score to be phenomenalized as directed) nor entirely beyond the poem (as the free and undirected actualization of an individual reader). Rather, "rhythm" is located at the intersection between that which remains relatively stable in the poem, part of its textual fabric (like punctuation or lineation), and that which changes, the element that is alterable and even unpredictable when performed (aloud or "subvocalized"). As an unstable feature of poetic facture, it can be mobilized to name an equally paradoxical feature of subjectivity, the way in which each performative reiteration, each performance of the self, is both consistent and evolving. Like Césaire, Meschonnic believes that "rhythm" is the word that best denotes "le courant qui passe," the word that comes closest to conveying the force of the poem as perceived by the reader "not in the words, not in the melody, not in the dance, not in the meter." "Rhythm," he states,

> proves that discourse is not made up only of signs. . . . It shows that a theory of language goes beyond a theory of communication [in the sense of communicating a message]. While language includes communication, signs, *it also includes actions, creations, relations between bodies*. . . . There can be no semiotics of rhythm; rhythm demands an anti-semiotics. It shows that the poem isn't made of signs even if, linguistically, it is composed of signs. The poem *passes* through signs [Le poème passe à travers les signes].[53]

Echoing Césaire—only here in the affirmative rather than the interrogative mode—Meschonnic asserts that rhythm is indeed the vehicle through which poetic communication passes. But Meschonnic's definition of what constitutes rhythm is far more capacious than the definition Césaire probably had in mind when he suggested its importance in the interview cited earlier ("Est-ce dû au rythme?"). Césaire might not have added the question mark if he had been able to broaden his notion of rhythm to include the phenomenon to which Meschonnic is gesturing. For Meschonnic, "rythme" refers not simply to the beat of the tom-tom, say, or the swing underlying Louis Armstrong's trumpet riffs; neither is it a primordial pulse in the blood, inherited and specific to one "race" or community. Instead, "rhythm" is a multilayered entity composed of features drawn from the corporeality of the individual who writes the poem; the state of poetic discourses at the point in history when the individual begins to write; the speech rhythms peculiar to the region of the poet; and, most importantly, the transformation that these elements undergo both in the act of writing and in the act of reading the poetic utterance.

Writing during the same years as Kamau Brathwaite, whose *History of the Voice* locates poetic rhythm in the frame of regional discourse, Meschonnic also begins his study in *Critique du rythme* by situating poetry in its historical and geographical context. If, for Brathwaite, there is a "history of the voice," for Meschonnic there is an "anthropology of the voice."[54] Such an anthropology presupposes first and foremost that "the voice, the unique voice, is not wholely an individual voice. The voice has, along with its physiological characteristics, cultural marks that are situated, that situate it."[55] Second, this situatedness informs not only the voice of the author who writes the poem but also the voice of the reader who (sub-)vocalizes it. That is, the voice that reads the poem, even if in silence, brings to the reading of the poem the intonations, accents, and stress patterns specific to that reader's temporality, geographical location, age, gender, class, and so on. These various inflections enter into the meaning of the poem as interpreted by the reader: they "produce a specific semantics, distinct from the lexical sense" of the words.[56] The "tone of meaning, not in the words"—to return to Frost—is thus, for Meschonnic, the result of a collaboration between writer and reader; it is an instance of "human relatedness" (Poirier), a coproduction of two vocal behaviors, each of which is saturated with historical conditioning as well as the vagaries of physiological individuation.

What Meschonnic means by "rhythm," then, is this unique and unrepeatable symbiosis between two situations, two expressive potentials, each of which is guided by written marks and the conventions for interpreting them. The text furnishes a kind of score for this sound, an "organization of marks," but its performative instantiation is not entirely predictable because the voice that reads is not rhythmed in the same way as the voice that writes. Further, while the conventions of poetic recitation affecting the delivery and interpretation of the poem change over time, so too do typographic conventions.[57] It is therefore not possible to determine exactly how a line will be read a century later, just as we cannot know with precision how medieval manuscripts were meant to be recited or how plain chant was meant to be sung. However, this does not prevent writers from attempting to capture local speech patterns as in the case of Paul Laurence Dunbar and Gilbert Gratiant, or, in a different vein, Langston Hughes, who emulates the rhythmic patterns of the blues. On the contrary, these attempts, as Michael North has also noted, are responsible for generating many of the linguistic innovations associated with modernism:[58] "From Wordsworth to Hopkins, on to Pound and Eliot," observes Meschonnic, "poetic novelty in the English tradition has always established a new relation to speech [au parlé], up until the Beats and Charles Olson."[59]

Olson is a particularly good example for Meschonnic to evoke because, as opposed to Senghor, who also posits a relation between poetry and orality, Olson does so with a clear understanding that technologies—in his case, the typewriter—mediate and inform the way a voicing produces text (and vice versa). The attempt to bring the rhythms of everyday speech into poetic diction requires the use—and reinvention—of various *techne*. For Olson, the resources of the phonetic alphabet, the space of the page, and the geometry of the typewriter are all means that contribute to the nonlexical meaning conveyed through rhythm, or what Meschonnic calls the poem's "signifiance."[60] Thus, even if the goal of the poet is to convey the speech patterns of dialect (or the patterns of the breath) through print means, the techniques that he develops to do so can only encourage but not guarantee an "accurate" delivery. This is so not only because readers in the future might not know how to interpret visual cues but also because the techniques themselves create their own static, and this noise is part of the "human relatedness," part of the enactment of vocal presence staged by the poem, a point that will become particularly relevant when we turn to the poetry of Damas.

Before doing so, however, it is worth summarizing Meschonnic's theory of rhythm, for it allows us to treat Damas's work in a more historically informed and technically precise way than it has been treated before. Too many critics in Senghor's wake have taken for granted that Damas's poems choose as their model "the beat and rhythm of the African drums." Senghor believes that Damas's rhythms lead us back to Africa; they are in his blood. There is some justice in construing a poet's rhythmic inheritance in broader terms; we do not know for sure to what degree biological and cultural factors influence the way we move and, thus, the way we rhythm our speech or inflect our phrasing when writing. But we may unwittingly reduce the interest of Damas's rhythmic structures if we attribute them to only one source. As Meschonnic claims in *Critique du rythme*, a poet is exposed to a variety of rhythmic influences. In a first instance, a poem's rhythm may be indebted to an order of sonic phenomena that is cultural and historical rather than personal to the poet (in other words, there is a "history" to the individual "voice"). From an anthropological perspective, the community to which the poet belongs is the one that inflects the individual author's poetic discourse in an incontrovertible way. This communally shared rhythm is what Meschonnic calls "the linguistic rhythm," which he defines as "the way each individual language is pronounced, the rhythm internal to a word, a group of words, or a phrase."[61] We might think of the rhythm of French as instantiated in the pronunciation of the word "café," for instance: neither syllable ("ca-" or "-fé") is accentuated, whereas in the British pronunciation of "café" the accent would fall on the first syllable. The language community into which the poet is born determines the initial level of rhythmic structuring of his or her poetic language. (Regional differences in the pronunciation of French, for instance, would be considered part of a poet's linguistic rhythm as well.[62])

The second level of structuring is imposed by what Meschonnic calls "the rhetorical rhythm": "the particular register or stylization of discourse within the given language."[63] Elements of rhetorical rhythm include genre-specific conventions and the rules governing the manner of delivery appropriate to each rhetorical situation. The final layer of rhythmic structuring emerges from "the organization of a writing [une écriture]" itself; it is this written organization of marks that Meschonnic identifies as poetic rhythm per se.[64] The first two, Meschonnic argues, are "always there"; no linguistic utterance can be formed in which the rhythm is not controlled to some extent by both the accentual and intonational system of the given language and the rules or conventions associated with the particular rhetorical situation. However, the third type of rhythm "only occurs in a work [une oeuvre]," a work of writing.[65] The distinctive technologies of writing add yet another layer to the rhythmic layers (linguistic and rhetorical) already in place. It is important to clarify that poetic conventions of a historical period appear in the second category (that of the rhetorical rhythm) but that these poetic conventions are carried through and reworked on the level of the "poetic rhythm." The pressure of history enters at every level, for a language is not static (modes of pronunciation and accent change over time); generic conventions are transgressed and revised, and a human being responds to these rhythms (as well as others) in various and evolving ways.

It is not out of the question, then, that different sonic patterns (including those of jazz and African or African-derived forms) might have impressed themselves on Damas at various points during his lifetime; however, they would have been mingled with, among others, the rhythms of the French spoken at the Lycée Schoelcher and the rhythms of Mallarmé that so moved Damas when he first started writing. We have no access to Damas's juvenalia, his Mallarmé-inspired efforts, so we must start with his earliest published poems between 1934 and 1937. These poems contain a rich palimpsest of rhythmic influences and reveal the craftsmanship that went into making linguistic and rhetorical rhythms into a "poetic rhythm" in Meschonnic's sense. Let us start with the first poem by Damas that Senghor includes in his anthology, "Ils sont venus ce soir," which Senghor later claimed sounded like an African chant "submitted" to "un rythme de tam-tam instinctivement retrouvé."[66] The poem was originally published in *Soutes* with the title "Fragment" in the July 14, 1936 issue (no. 4), alongside "Save Our Souls" (later titled "S.O.S.") and Jacques Prévert's "La grasse matinée." I reproduce the *Soutes* version here, for it contains lines that were suppressed in the version found in the 1937 *Pigments*, as well as the version Senghor published in 1948.

FRAGMENT

Ils sont venus ce soir où le
tam
tam
roulait de
rythme en
rythme
la frénésie
des yeux
la frénésie des mains
la frénésie
des pieds de statues
DEPUIS
combien de MOI combien de MOI combien de MOI MOI MOI
sont morts
depuis qu'ils sont venus ce soir où le
tam
tam
roulait de
rythme en
rythme
la frénésie
des yeux
la frénésie des mains la frénésie
des pieds de statues

FRAGMENT

They came that night when the
tom
tom
rolled from
rhythm to
rhythm
the frenzy

of eyes
the frenzy of hands the frenzy
of the statues' feet
SINCE THEN
how many ME how many ME how many ME ME ME
have died
since that night they came when the
tom
        tom
                rolled from
                        rhythm to
                                rhythm
                                        the frenzy
of eyes
the frenzy of hands the frenzy
of the statues' feet

It is no coincidence that Damas dedicated "Fragment" to Senghor when it was republished (and renamed) in his *Anthologie*. During their first years in Paris, the Senegal-born *agrégé* represented to both Damas and Césaire their closest link to Africa. In a sense, Senghor was the living embodiment of the "statues" Damas mentions in the middle and final lines. But in reality, Senghor was an ambiguous representative for Africa; in his own "Prière aux masques" (Prayer to masks), for instance, the Senegalese poet describes himself (and his colonized brothers) as "liés par le nombril" (bound at the navel) to Europe.[67] Mirroring grammatically the confusion between past and present emblematized by Senghor's own person, the tenses of "Fragment" shift between the passé composé and the imperfect tense. This oscillation between the two past tenses suggests the difficulty of distinguishing between what is definitively in the past (the many "me"s that are dead—"sont morts"); what is continuous between past and present (the "rolling" rhythm of the drums); and what is occurring only in the present moment of writing (this evening, "ce soir"). The imperfect past tense of the musical action ("le/tam/tam/roulait") represents what was happening when "they" arrived ("Ils sont venus"), some form of "frenzied" dancing. However, the imperfect past tense also evokes the continuity linking all the massacred subjectivities ("MOI MOI MOI"), including that of the author (to whom the word "moi" would seem to refer) and that of the dedicatee, Senghor. That is, among the many "me"s that succumb to the violent invasion (the arrival "this evening") are the metaphorically dead victims of assimilation. Ultimately, the poem establishes no strict divide between that which is alive and that which is inanimate, for the feet of the statues are caught in the same frenzy as the hands and the eyes. As in other Damas poems, the violence of the colonial regime appears to extend beyond the immediate victims to congeal the lives of those who come after, those transformed into statues, or encased ("emmailloté") like mummies in "leur smoking . . . leur plastron" ("Solde"). Although the events recounted in the poem might have occurred centuries earlier, the speaking subject—the "MOI"—appears to join the row of the dead ("Combien de MOI MOI MOI / sont morts"). This exchange of states, or the identification of the living with the dead, resembles what Fred Moten has described as an "inter(in) animation," a bringing to life that requires cocooning death within.[68]

Again, the sense of death in life is evoked in "Limbé," another significant intertext for "Fragment" in which the persona demands the return of his "black dolls" ("mes poupées noires"). Here, it seems as though figurines and statues (or "masks," as in the poem "Position") are more real, more pertinent to the self, than the living beings by which one is surrounded.[69]

Rendez-moi mes poupées noires
  que je joue avec elles
  les jeux naifs de mon instinct
  resté à l'ombre de ses lois
  recouvrés mon courage
  mon audace
  me sentir moi-même
  nouveau moi-même de ce que hier j'étais
  hier
    sans complexité
                hier
quand est venue l'heure du déracinement (*Pigments*).

Bring back to me my black dolls
  so that I can play with them
  those naive games of my instinct
  in the shadow of its laws

covered over with my courage
my audacity
to feel myself
a new me from what I yesterday was
yesterday
  no complexity
    yesterday
when the hour of uprooting arrived

As in "Fragment," the self is doubled, or rather divided into a "me" then ("ce que hier j'étais") and a "me" now ("Rendez-moi"). The plea expressed is that one might return to a time of naiveté and "instinct," that moment before assimilation when the self was truly itself, presented here in the abstract time of the infinitive: "me sentir moi-même." This imaginary moment of self-coincidence would allow yesterday ("hier") to be new ("nouveau") once again. In the line "nouveau moi-même de ce que hier j'étais," Damas carefully reworks the syntax of the French sentence (which would normally produce "de ce que j'étais hier") to produce a pattern in which the word "hier" is always set off from its own repetition by another word or set of words: "que hier j'étais / hier / sans complexité / hier." Thus, the French syntax is indeed "submitted" to a rhythm of theme and variation—consistent word and varying word—that characterizes many poems in Damas's oeuvre. But there is little reason to associate this type of rhythmic repetition with an African drumbeat per se. The poem itself tells us that a rupture with an earlier site (Africa is not explicitly named) has already occurred, thus making the transmission of an original legacy more difficult, if not impossible. We learn that there has been a moment of "déracinement," ostensibly the radical separation from Africa prefigured in "Fragment" as the arrival of the unnamed "Ils." Yet in "Limbé," "hier," the prior moment of simplicity ("sans complexité") seems to be pushed ever further into the distance by the poem's syntax, which extends the time between each reiteration of "hier" (from "j'étais" to "sans complexité") as well as the poem's layout (the *vers en escalier*), which extends the distance between each reiteration of "hier." At the end of the poem, the rhythmic repetition of "noires" reverses the process, such that the distance between reiterations telescopes to the point where "noires" is the only word left, repeating itself insistently with no substantives (only an enjambment) in between:

Rendez-les-moi mes poupées noires
  mes poupées noires
  poupées noires
    noires

Bring me back my black dolls
  my black dolls
  black dolls
    black

Significantly, the plural (feminine) adjective "noires" comes to replace the adverb "hier" as the only lasting element of the past. Meanwhile, the wordplay on "déracinement"—which suggests not only loss of roots ("racines") but also loss of "race"—brings "blackness" into the limelight as that which remains always to be recaptured from the past. However strange it might be for a grown man to call out for his "poupées noires," it seems clear that these substitutes hold the key to some kind of personal renaissance—one that is not, however, without a complexity of its own. Any return to the self appears to require the intermediary of a doll, a statue, a representation. It is entirely possible that the self does in fact return in a mediated form, specifically as play (a playing with dolls). Play—understood as a game of repetition—is in fact the structural principle of the poem, as indicated by the last lines with their B-I-N-G-O structure, their incremental reduction to a single word ("noires"). Yet play, the poem shows us, does not necessarily lead back to a single, authentic self ("sans complexite"). Conversely, here, play is productive of multiple alternative selves: the "jeux naïfs" produce acoustically a set of plural "I"s—"je[s] naifs." Although a straightforward reading might establish that the past is the reserve of the singular, true, authentic self, a reading attentive to wordplay suggests instead that to imagine the past is to play a kind of game, one that is productive of multiple selves, multiple performances of an idealized otherness we call the past (or, alternatively, "instinct"). The notion that play might be a way of bringing back that past, or compensating for its loss, is consistent with the Freudian example of the *fort–da* game in which the child processes the disappearance of the caregiver by repeatedly revealing and taking away a toy from view. Freud argues that the child masters disappearance through a gestural routine, that is, the child comes to terms with the trauma of loss by means of a repeated corporeal practice. In "Limbé," the rhythm of appearance and disappearance structures not only the poet's play with dolls but also his play with words. Damas manages to generate from loss a kind of syncopation—a sonic texture—through processes of rhythmic repetition all his own. As practiced by Damas, rhythmic repetition also has a distinctively corporeal quality, engaging the throat and lips through the conduit of the eye.

If we turn back to "Fragment," we see that repetition is both the theme and the organizing principle of the poem, just as in "Limbé" going backward (to "hier") is a motor of poetic composition. The strategy of reversal in "Limbé" is manifested most vividly in the last lines, which fade out through incremental reduction until they are simply a repetition of the first lines, then just a repetition of themselves: "Rendez-les-moi mes poupées noires / mes poupées noires / poupées noires / noires." Similarly, in "Fragment," the first twelve lines are repeated twice verbatim, once at the beginning of the poem and again at the end, forming a chiasmic structure within which the "MOI MOI MOI" makes its striking appearance. The "break," or middle portion, is introduced by a dramatically capitalized "DEPUIS," which is then followed by two crucial lines:

> combien de MOI combien de MOI combien de MOI MOI MOI
> sont morts

The reiterated "MOI" in the lines above antipates the repeated "noires" of "Limbé" with its similar mouth-opening diphthong /w/ (sometimes coded as a semiconsonant). The "w/w/w"—or "oua oua oua"—is close in texture to the onomatopoeic "oua oua" of the trumpet we hear in Césaire's *Cahier*: "Je sais le tracking, le Lindy-hop et les claquettes. / Pour les bonnes bouches la sourdine de nos plaintes enrobées de *oua-oua*."[70] Damas's "MOI MOI MOI" transmits a similar plangent moan but one that has become deafeningly loud. The capitalized letters ("MOI MOI MOI") indicate typographically just how close to the surface this moan has come. In addition, another version of the insistent "MOI MOI MOI" makes an impression on the reading ear even when it does not appear typographically heightened on the page. The word "me" (as in "*me* sentir moi-même") is visually present in the word "rhyth*me*," which rolls across the entire text. One can choose to pronounce the "-me" of "rythme" in the line "tam-tam roulait de rythme en rythme," or one can make the elision and transform "me" into the nasal moan "m'en," as in "ryth*me‿en* rythme." In any case, there are no metrical rules governing how the lines should be read. Should "rythme en rythme" count as five syllables or four?

One of the most striking features of "Fragment" is the way in which, from the very first line, metrical scansion is placed in tension with rhythmic delivery. The normal French syntax of a poetic line would not sever a definite article from the noun that follows it, but here the unusual enjambment sacrifies normative vocal phrasing to the production of the awkward octosyllable: "Ils sont venus ce soir où le." The rhythm produced by this line, as well as others, is ambiguous, highly dependent upon which feature of poetry the reader wants to stress—syntax, semantics, or spatial organization. For instance, if we were to ride over the enjambment (ignoring the line breaks entirely) we could produce the perfect alexandrine, "Ils sont venus ce soir ou le tam-tam roulait." But it seems as though Damas is intentionally hindering us from basing our rhythmic reading on traditional meters. The tension he produces between verse structure and syntax actually ends up drawing our attention to what can be seen on the page, rather than heard by the ear. For instance, the placement of "le" at the end of the line suggests a rhyme with "de" and the "me" of "rythme" (also placed at the end of lines), even though there is nothing rhythmically compelling in that way of reading. Further, the fragmentation at the level of syntax invites fragmentation at the level of the lexeme. "Tam-tam" is usually thought of as one lexical unit; there is no such thing as a "tam." The argument could be made that by separating the first "tam" from the second, the author is actually using the space of the page to produce continuity, not segmentation; after all, our tendency as readers of French (and all Romance and Germanic languages) is to read continuously from left to right and from top to bottom, so we are not likely to disconnect one "tam" from the next. However, the potential for disconnection, for segmentation, is what poetic rhythm is all about. This is especially true with respect to virtual rhythms on the printed page. We can read words as they are conventionally pronounced, but, as readers, we can also break them up into particles of whatever size. ("Frénésie," for instance, could yield the past participle "né," meaning "born," which would enter into tension, semantically, with the theme of death.) Versification is a way of producing a textual rhythm, a rhythm for the eye that may conflict—as Damas shows well—with how the poem could sound.

Another possible objection to my emphasis on the ambiguity of the rhythm in "Fragment" could be that there is indeed a discernable rhythm: Damas is privileging the kind of syncopation we find in jazz. Indeed, by breaking the alexandrine after the definite article ("le"), Damas invites the reader to pause in the space (in the "break") between lines; if the reader respects this pause, then the syllables "tam-tam" could be actualized as slightly off the metrical beat.

However, my point is not that Damas is *not* basing his poetic choices on jazz syncopations (or African polyrhythms) but rather that what he intended does not—cannot—determine precisely what we as readers do. An author cannot disambiguate entirely the rhythm of a written phrase. It may well be, as Edwin C. Hill Jr. argues, that Damas embeds in his verse structures the "rhythms of popular culture" (say, the *biguine* or the calypso) or, alternatively, that his repetitions echo those of "imperial and colonial beating."[71] But how, in a written text, can we tell one from the other? How do we know when to read a space on the page as suturing lines together or, conversely, keeping them apart? Where do we place our accents when reading a poetic stanza once the poet has left the room?

The most rhythmically clear line of the poem is, of course, "combien de MOI combien de MOI, combien de MOI MOI MOI," which uses typographic emphasis (capitalization) to indicate articulation. Here, the visual and syntactic features of the line are in perfect unison. Curiously, however, after publishing "Fragment" in *Soutes*, Damas chose to excise this passage (the most wonderfully rebellious) from his poem. When he reprinted "Fragment" as "Ils sont venus ce soir" in *Pigments* and in all subsequent editions of the poem, he recast the pertinent lines as follows (with the exception of the 1972 Présence Africaine edition, in which the "MOI" is repeated three times):

> DEPUIS
> combien de MOI
> sont morts

Perhaps Damas later found that the repetition of "combien de MOI" (in "Combien de MOI combien de MOI combien de MOI MOI MOI") overwhelmed the slight "sont morts" that follows it. It is a pity, though, that Damas corrected his first effort, for the original is not only a more powerful expression of the poem's energy, it also exemplifies—and brings to our attention—one of the most idiosyncratic features of Damas's "poetic rhythm." To get a clear picture of what constitutes his poetic rhythm, we must turn for a moment to those features he shares with other poets of his period, the rhetorical rhythm from which his own scribal "voice" is drawn.

"THE PASSING OF THE SUBJECT INTO LANGUAGE"

Although Damas once claimed that his poems "can be danced, they can be sung," it is hard to see how the lines of "Fragment" suggest a musical accompaniment or avatar. On the contrary, they seem to be intentionally composed to ambiguate their rhythmic vocalization. This does not mean that the poem lacks a rhythm, only that we might want to pause a moment before associating that rhythm with the "rythme naturel du tam-tam" (Senghor). Bridget Jones has discerned a Creole-like "duple time with frequent syncopation" in several of his poems;[72] Keith Warner has identified calypso and jazz patterns in his verse structures; and Barthélémy Kotchy has unearthed the structure of popular songs and African polyrhythms in poems like "Obsession."[73] There is nothing to prove these critics wrong. But there are reasons to believe that the very rhythms these critics insist on identifying as "African" (or African-derived) actually belong to the rhetorical rhythm of French interwar poetry while their "linguistic rhythm" is that of Parisian French, not Guianese Creole. To proceed further in our analysis, and to clarify the rhythmic sources from which Damas drew, we need to refer to Meschonnic's tripartite division of rhythm into three categories and inspect each one in turn.

In Damas's case, the first category of rhythm, the "linguistic," would pertain to the way French is spoken by an *évolué* born in French Guyana in the teens. The rhythms of such speech are not fully retrievable, of course, but we can lean on the evidence we have. A recording Damas made of his own poems in 1967, titled *Poésie de la Négritude: Léon Damas Reads Selected Poems from "Pigments, Graffiti, Black Label, and Névralgies,"* suggests just how little his French pronunciation was inflected by the Creole of Cayenne (or the Creole of Fort-de-France, where he spent two high school years). Granted, the recording in the Smithsonian Folkways series supervised by Zora Neale Hurston is a highly artificial affair, made for posterity and thus not an ideal example of either his casual rhythms of speech or even his dramatic mode of delivery in person.[74] Yet we can get a sense of how Damas thought his poems should be recited, how he interpreted the rhythms he himself had written down. On the Folkways Smithsonian recording Damas pronounces each word deliberately, often exaggerating the segmentation of syllables in a staccato manner. His overall style of enunciation is that of the university professor, or official *délégué*. Similarly, Senghor's reading style on his own recording, *Les grandes voix du sud*, is largely independent of musical rhythms; the *kôra* playing in the background while Senghor recites his poems only underscores how spoken (rather than sung) they are. In fact, the speaking voices of Senghor and Damas both evoke the writtenness of the texts they are reading (even if recited by heart).[75] Both are extremely careful to enunciate cleanly each and every consonant, to distinguish each and every vowel, and to avoid elongating a syllable even when stressed. If there is a trace of Serer in Senghor's French (and he admits on the album to speaking Serer "badly" [mal]), it remains indiscernible in his elegant French elocution. Likewise, if Damas's French is governed by Guyanese inflections, they are not apparent to the non-Creole auditor of the Folkways album. An argument could be made that the repetition of words—such as "français français" in "Hoquet"—is characteristic of what Janis Pallister identifies as "Martiniquais speech patterns."[76] This is entirely possible. But Damas's reading strategy on the Folkways album is to produce an impeccably crisp French pronunciation, perhaps to accentuate his staccato rhythms at the expense of more emotive cadences.

Next, to turn to Damas's "rhetorical rhythms," one needs to look no further than the sites of his early publications to find the repertoire from which he draws. Quick study reveals that he has assimilated and subtly transfigured the rhetorical rhythms of a very particular poetic milieu. This is a point worth lingering on before we move on to the third category, "poetic rhythm," for we can distinguish more precisely what is proper to Damas, what characterizes his poetry, if we take the time to understand how other poets of this poetic milieu were writing during the same period. Some of the stylistic features that have been identified with Damas are actually shared with other poets—and here I am not thinking of diasporic poets such as Langston Hughes or Jacques Roumain. In fact, Damas's period style, or rhetorical rhythm, belongs to what we might loosely call the European protest poem. The form of the "vers en escalier," treated in chapter 3, is only one element of this shared period style. Other elements include the repetition of entire grammatical units, as in "Fragment," "En file indienne" and "Hoquet"; the repetition of single lines at regular intervals, as in "Bientôt"; and the repetition of phrases in the form of a chiasmus, as in "Limbé" and "Névralgies," which reverse the order of their opening lines in their concluding stanzas. Most interesting structurally are the poems in which a noun and its modifier appear first together, then sequentially, separated into single-word lines, as in "Nuit blanche," or "Bientôt" and "S.O.S.," where adjectives or verbs employed in earlier phrases are weeded out, accumulated, and listed separately in a tour de force recapitulation at the end. These techniques for using words, phrases, or entire stanzas as rhythmic building blocks to be recombined are techniques that belong to a register of language—the lyric poem—as that register was exercised at a particular moment (the early twentieth century); in a particular place (Paris); and within a particular milieu (the political movements of the artistic left).

We therefore need to resituate Damas's poems in their publication context in order to understand how he was responding—and contributing—to the "period style" of this particular field of production. This publication context has been partially fleshed out by Sandrine Poujols in her postface to the 2005 Présence Africaine edition of *Pigments-Névralgies*. Poujols leads us back to the heady years of the Popular Front when Damas was deeply engaged in the activities of the far-left wing of the PCF (French Communist Party) and the SFIO (Section française de l'Internationale Ouvrière, or the Socialist Party), as well as a regular member of the Rassemblement Colonial.[77] As previously mentioned, the first version of "Ils sont venus ce soir," "Fragment," appeared in *Soutes*, the organ for the left (unionist) wing of Communist sympathizers during the mid thirties. Described on its masthead as "une revue de culture révolutionnaire internationale," *Soutes* was directed by Luc Decaunes, the nephew of Paul Éluard.[78] Although *Soutes* published poetry with a surrealist orientation, its most famous and "faithful" collaborator was a poet (like Damas) on the fringes of the surrealist movement, Jacques Prévert. Prévert published poems in the same issue as Damas (no. 4): "Fragment" and "Save Our Souls" (the first version of "S.O.S.") appeared next to Prévert's "La grasse matinée" (Sleeping late) on July 14, 1936. Another Prévert poem, "Tentative d'une description d'un dîner de têtes à Paris-France" (Attempt to describe a dinner of big-wigs at Paris-France) appeared in the first issue of *Soutes* (December, 1935), while his "Le temps des noyaux" (The time of pits) and Louis Aragon's "Le songe d'une nuit d'été" (Midsummer night's dream) were published in the second issue (February 1936). The "period style" to which Damas contributed was one associated, through *Soutes*, with the avant-garde's effort to reach out to more "popular" audiences. As opposed to *Esprit* and the *Cahiers du Sud*, where Damas also published his poems, *Soutes* targeted the working class; it was sold primarily at outdoor fairs and festivals, meetings of union organizers, and at the sites where strikes were taking place. In the pages of the review, Decaunes announces to his readers that "the poets of *Soutes* write as if delivering blows [*comme on frappe*]. Each poem is a rebellion. . . . [these poems] are beating hearts. They are machine guns."[79]

In the mid-1930s, then, there was nothing particularly black—and nothing particularly African—about a writing style that aspired to approximate the impact of striking or beating ("comme un frappe"). In fact, what drew Damas and the other poets of the journal together stylistically was a similar desire to reproduce the rhythm of insistence, to versify demand. Prévert, Aragon, and Damas were attempting to remain alert to the underlying pulse of political rhetoric. Consider, for example, a few stanzas from Prévert's "Le temps des noyaux":

Soyez prévenus vieillards
soyez prévenus chefs de famille
Le temps où vous donniez vos fils à la patrie
comme on donne du pain aux pigeons
Ce temps-là ne reviendra plus
Prenez-en votre parti
c'est fini
le temps des cerises ne reviendra plus
et le temps des noyaux non plus
. . .
"Descendez-vous la prochaine jeune homme?"
c'est de la guerre dont vous parliez
mais vous ne nous ferez plus le coup du père François
non mon capitaine
non monsieur un tel
non papa
non maman
nous ne descendrons pas à la prochaine[80]

Be warned old men
be warned heads of household
The time when you gave your sons to the homeland
as one gives bread to pigeons
That time won't come round again
Take your sides
it's over
the time of cherries won't come round again
nor the time of cherry pits
. . .
"Will you get down next young man?"
it's the war you're speaking of

but you won't do anymore what father Francis has done
no my captain
no my mister whatever
no papa
no mama
we won't get off at the next stop

In this socialist, antiwar declaration the repetitive syntax and listing produces a momentum building up to the concluding lines, a rhythmic tattoo of "non . . . / non . . . / non . . ." characteristic of strikers' chants as well as hortatory fire-and-brimstone oratory. Parallelism and "incremental repetition" are staples of Prévert's work, and they play a large role in Damas's as well.[81] In "Le temps des noyaux," Prévert contrasts the "temps des cerises" (the time of cherries)—which refers to a song written in honor of the 1871 Paris Commune—with the "temps des noyaux" (the time of cherry pits) leading up to World War II. The latter appears to Prévert to be a bitter farce of the former. In "Tentative de description d'un dîner de têtes à Paris-France," the poem Prévert published in *Soutes* in 1935 (and which Damas very likely read), the butt of Prévert's irony is the jingoistic rhetoric of the French ruling class and their fake and self-important airs, also a favorite target of Damas's scorn. The opening lines read:

Ceux qui pieusement
ceux qui copieusement
ceux qui tricolorent
ceux qui inaugurent
ceux qui croient
ceux qui croient croire
ceux qui croa-croa . . .[82]

Those who piously
those who copiously
those who tricolor
those who inaugurate
those who believe
those who believe they believe
those who baa baa

The poem uses the repeated "ceux qui" to enumerate the various dinner guests, but eventually the insistent /k/ sound of the "qui" enters into a playfully generative relationship with the "croient" and the "croire" of "ceux qui croient croire," producing the "croa-croa" that transforms patriots into croaking fowl. After a long and comical description of the dinner and its guests, Prévert closes with these lines:

ceux qui vieillissent plus vite que les autres
ceux qui ne se sont pas baissés pour ramasser l'épingle
ceux qui crèvent d'ennui le dimanche après-midi
parce qu'ils voient venir le lundi
et le mardi, et le mercredi, et le jeudi, et le vendredi
et le samedi
et le dimanche après-midi.

Those who grow old faster than the rest
those who didn't lean down to pick up the pin
those who die of boredom on a Sunday afternoon
because they see Monday coming
and Tuesday, and Wednesday, and Thursday, and Friday
and Saturday
and Sunday afternoon

Here Prévert exercises the same tight control as Damas does over an idiom that expresses frustration by means of anaphora and enumeration. The mode of lineation and the poetic exploitation of sequencing recall elements of "Hoquet." And anaphora is the guiding structure of "Solde" as well (published for the first time in *Esprit* in 1934):

j'ai l'impression d'être ridicule
dans leurs souliers dans leur smoking
dans leur plastron dans leur faux col
dans leur monocle dans leur melon [. . .][83]

I feel like I'm ridiculous
in their slippers in their robe
in their dickey in their false collar
in their monocle in their bowler

But perhaps the closest link between the two poets is made evident in "La grasse matinée," which Prévert published alongside Damas's poems in *Soutes*. "La grasse matinée" shares with the poems of *Pigments* a number of formal and thematic features that deserve mention. It tells a story about poverty in what would come to be Prévert's signature style, leading from sing-song to shock, from repetition to surprise. "Il est terrible / le petit bruit de l'oeuf dur cassé sur un comptoir d'étain" (It is terrible / the little sound of the hard egg cracked on a tin counter[84]), the poem begins, thereby evoking in one clear image (the sound of an eggshell breaking) the torment of the hungry wanderer as he passes by the café, the "grand magasin," and finally the bakery. Following the footsteps of the famished beggar, Prévert gathers together a bouquet of pungent details, enumerating the many smells, textures, and flavors that torment the hapless beggar and addle his mind. The narration in the first stanza lingers on these details, such as "une tête de veau par exemple / avec une sauce de vinaigre" (the veal's head for instance / with vinegar sauce), or the "pâtés," "conserves," "poissons," and "sardines" seductively arranged in the "protected" vitrines. Near the end of the poem, the poet rehearses these details again in truncated form, creating a list that summarizes contents more fully embroidered upon in previous lines:

l'homme titube
et dans l'intérieur de sa tête
un brouillard de mots
sardines à manger
oeuf dur café crème
café arrosé rhum
o fr. 70
café-crème
café-crème
café-crime
café-crime arrosé sang! . . .

the man reels
and inside his head
a fog of words
sardines to eat
hard egg café crème
café laced with rum

0 francs 70 centimes
café crème
café crème
café crime
café crime laced with blood!

The strategy Prévert uses here of summarizing a poem's contents in shorthand to produce at the end an accelerated momentum, drawing the reader ineluctably toward a devastating conclusion, is very similar to the strategy we see at work in poems by Damas such as "Limbé," "S.O.S.," and "Nuit blanche." "S.O.S." (or "Save Our Souls," as it appeared originally in *Soutes* in 1936) displays in exemplary form the techniques of accumulation and reduction that also govern "La grasse matinée." When Damas published "S.O.S." a second time, in the "definitive" Présence Africaine version of 1972, he altered the versification so that the word "mais" (but) in the second stanza always stands alone, thereby creating a steady downbeat but also accentuating the action verbs, now isolated and stacked up, forming a single column. Here is the version published in *Soutes* (1936) and *Pigments* (1937):

mais froidement matraquer mais froidement
descendre mais
froidement étendre mais froidement
matraquer descendre étendre
couper leur sexe aux nègres
pour en faire des bougies pour leurs églises

but coldly to bludgeon but coldly
to take down but
coldly to spread out but coldly
to bludgeon take down spread out
to cut the genitals off negros
in order to make candles for their churches

Here is the version published by Présence Africaine in 1972:

mais
froidement matraquer

mais
froidement descendre
mais
froidement étendre
mais froidement
matraquer
descendre
étendre
et couper leur sexe aux nègres
pour en faire des bougies pour leurs églises (51–52)

In this second version, Damas pummels the reader not just with the infinitives, "matraquer / descendre / étendre"—which set loose an abstract and absolute violence—but also with the connective "mais," which he has managed to throw into relief by isolating it each time on its own line. This repeated "mais" does not behave precisely like the "non" of Prévert's "Le temps des noyaux," hammering away at the opposition with a bullhorn. The "mais" here functions more like a stutter, a repeated hesitation—"but," "but," "but"—peculiar to Damas's way of imagining frustration as rhythmic sound. This stuttering advance leads toward its gruesome conclusion, a prescient evocation of the types of atrocities that would be inflicted a few years later on Jews, Communists, and blacks.[85] The anticlerical imagery of the last couplet is fully in keeping with the socialist, populist agenda of *Soutes*, as is the simple, understated vocabulary laced with an occasional swear word or colloquialism. Finally, the biting irony of "S.O.S." seems consistent with the tone of "La grasse matinée"—the beggar's morning is anything but "rich" ("grasse"). Such irony is conveyed in both cases through similar prosodic means.

A final comparison will suffice to make clear that crucial aspects of the way Damas uses language (and that Senghor identifies as "African") might be attributable to a phenomenon of the interwar period: a turn toward more popular—and populist—cultural forms on the part of many poets in Damas's immediate milieu. In the early 1930s Robert Desnos, Damas's closest friend among the surrealist crowd, took his distance from the surrealist movement in order to pursue his interests in journalism, the radio, and the "chanson populaire." It is worth comparing Damas's "Solde," for instance, to Desnos's "Une Ville" of 1930, which contains the same anaphoric structure but in the context of a playful song:

Dans la ville où l'on prend le diable par les cornes
Dans la ville ouverte et fermée
Dans la ville où l'on tient comptoir pour tous les désirs . . .[86]

In the city where one takes the devil by the horns
In the city open and closed
In the city where one bartends for all desires . . .

During the same period Prévert, too, embraced popular music as a formal inspiration; in the early 1930s he was involved in Le Groupe Octobre, a theatrical troupe composed of anarchists, socialists, and workers' groups for whom he composed songs and plays.[87] Many of Prévert's poems of the period play with the sounds of ditties and nursery rhymes (even the opening sequence from "Tentative de dîner" is constructed along these lines). In general, Prévert tends to treat serious matters—such as war, poverty, loss, and malnutrition—in a sing-song way. More complicated than it might at first appear, Prévert's strategy is to make his lyrics accessible while deriding positions taken by the most powerful men of his day. As in the poems of *Pigments*, carefully controlled repetitions lead the reader from the nursery to the battlefield, from dancing to devastation. Damas, like Prévert, also cradles his readers with lines like "Danube blanc / Danube rouge" ("Nuit blanche") only to conclude with references to Gobineau and Adolf Hitler, thereby barely masking the imminence of destruction in the lilt of a childish song. Finally, "La grasse matinée" also contains verses approximating the playful but gothic undertones of the nursery rhyme. In the section already cited, "café arrosé rhum / café-crème / café-crème / café-crime / café-crime arrosé sang," a turn to violence is disguised in something akin to a hopscotch jingle. "La grasse matinée" ends with the same refrain with which it began, employing the circular form so common to Damas's poems. The four lines starting from "Il est terrible" are repeated again, only this time broken up into six lines so as to add emphasis to the word "cassé" [broken], revealing the terrible anger hidden within an experience of "faim" [hunger], the last word of the poem (and a nasal rhyme with "étain").

Although the lines have no metrical consistency, varying between five and eight syllables each, they do suggest in their accumulated force how something so small—a "little noise [petit bruit]"—can gain momentum and become "terrible." Both Prévert and Damas count on this momentum, on the latent but building force of this "little noise"—the beating of the monosyllable, which is indeed a feature of their shared, period-specific "rhetorical rhythm." Both poets work with techniques of recombination and accumulation to build momentum, stoking a fire with small sticks in order to cause, ultimately, a conflagration. Damas's "Un clochard m'a demandé dix sous" [A beggar asked me for a dime], first published in *Esprit* in 1934, is a perfect illustration:

Moi aussi un beau jour j'ai sorti
Mon assortiment[88]
de clochard
moi aussi avec des yeux qui tendent
la main
j'ai soutenu la putain de misère
moi aussi j'ai eu faim dans ce sacré pays
cru pouvoir
demander dix sous
par pitié pour mon ventre creux
moi aussi jusqu'au bout de
l'éternité de leurs boulevards
à flics
combien de nuits ai-je dû
m'en aller aussi
les yeux creux
moi aussi j'ai eu faim les yeux creux
cru pouvoir demander
dix sous
jusqu'au jour où j'en ai eu
marre
de les voir se foutre de mon assortiment
de clochard
et jouir jouir
de voir un nègre les yeux ventre creux

Me too one fine day I took out
my beggar's
display
me too with eyes that hold out
a hand

I supported that whore poverty
me too I was hungry in that damn country
believed I could ask
for a dime
pity for my hollow stomach
me too to the end of
their eternal boulevards
filled with cops
how many nights I too
had to get lost
eyes hollow
me too I was hungry eyes hollow
believed I could ask
for a dime
until the day I was
sick
of seeing them not give a shit about my beggar's
display
and rejoice rejoice
to see a nigger with eyes stomach hollow

Prévert's poems and "Un clochard m'a demandé dix sous" share stylistic and lexical similarities as well as a thematic focus on poverty and class war. To be sure, Damas adds to the mix an overt *prise de position* with respect to the "nègre," who is both like the white "clochard"—"Moi aussi" is repeated five times in the *Esprit* version, eight times in the *Pigments* version—and decidedly different. But herein lies the interest of the comparison. It is clear that Damas was vulnerable to a host of influences, from Aragon to Hughes, from Desnos to Prévert. It is also clear that Damas's verses recall more specifically the musical technique of the "cut," which James Sneed has described in "On Repetition in Black Culture" as an abrupt "skipping . . . back to another beginning which we have already heard."[89] This "cut" interrupts the development of a theme to register the ineluctable circularity of culture; "black music" especially "draws attention to its own repetitions" (151), but all expressive practices, adds Sneed, engage repetition to some extent.

Damas's choice of publication venue—or, alternatively, the editor's decision to publish his poems—proves that his work was consistent with a platform extending beyond that provided by either the surrealists or the reviews grouped around African American, Pan-African, or Caribbean causes. Neither Senghor nor Césaire attempted (as far as we know) to publish poetry in *Soutes*. (Senghor was rather politically conservative at the time, attending mass and keeping company with assimilationists such as Blaise Diagne, whereas Cesaire did not directly become involved in Popular Front politics.[90]) Although criticism has treated Césaire, Senghor, and Damas as largely harmonious members of a single movement, it must be stressed that Negritude was only one of several banners to which Damas pledged allegiance. His early poems indicate that he enjoyed complex and multiple affinities—with his Antillean and African peers at the schools he attended, with the African American writers he read (and sometimes befriended), but also with members of the French Socialist Party and the platform they were advocating throughout the interwar period. This last affiliation would add a significant feature to his rhetorical rhythm, distinguishing him from the other poets of Negritude by aligning him with a socialist period style.

The influence of the French Socialist agenda on Damas's actions—as well as his poetics—was deep and long-lasting. For instance, when Damas compiled a list of poets for his 1947 anthology, *Poètes d'expression française* (published just one year before Senghor's), he used the imperialist category of the "outre-mer" as the criterion of selection, as opposed to the racial category chosen by Senghor for his *Anthologie de la nouvelle poésie nègre et malgache*. This mode of selection was consistent with the approach taken by the SFIO, la Section Française de l'Internationale Ouvrière, the socialist wing of the left that emerged in 1905 (and to which Damas belonged). Conforming to the SFIO's way of mapping the world—along class rather than racial lines—Damas excluded from his anthology poets from Haiti (because they were not part of the French colonies) and instead included poets from Indochina. Damas reveals his debt to the SFIO in his preface to the *Anthologie* where he explains that what draws the poets included in his volume together is their shared struggle "against poverty, illiteracy, the exploitation of man by man"; they are all victims, he states, of "the social and political racism suffered by the man of color, *yellow or black*."[91]

Damas's allegiance to the SFIO would reveal itself in other ways as well. He represented the socialists as a delegate to the French National Assembly from 1948 to 1951 and even entered into conflict with Césaire who, in 1950, deviated from the SFIO platform by attacking a new law put into place by the Socialist majority that suppressed freedom of expression in the colonies.[92] This is not to say that Damas was more invested in being a Socialist than in being a proponent of Negritude but simply to point out that he had commitments to a variety of poetic and political agendas at the same time. A graphic illustration of his participation in the world of French Socialism can be found in a set of photographs preserved in the Schomburg Center for Research in Black Culture documenting the funeral of Leon Blum on April 3, 1950. Here we observe Damas as he serves as a pallbearer along with other delegates from francophone Africa and the Caribbean (see figs. 4.1 and 4.2). These photographs testify to the fact that Damas remained a significant member of the Socialist fold from the time he published in the syndicalist review, *Soutes*, all the way through the postwar period.

Figure 4.1: Photograph by Jean Prével. View of state funeral for French Socialist leader Léon Blum, held in Paris, France, in 1950. Léon-Gontron Damas is shown serving as pallbearer, standing on the left at front of casket. Photographs and Prints Division, Schomburg Center for Research in Black Culture, The New York Public Library, Astor, Lenox, and Tilden Foundations.

We are now in a better position to identify Damas's poetic rhythm as it can be distinguished from both the rhythms of the poet's language as it was spoken by a particular generation (the linguistic rhythm of the *évolué*, or highly educated French speaker) and the "register" of poetic language as it was practiced by a subgroup within that generation (the rhetorical rhythm of the Parisian socialist poets). As we have seen, Damas shares with Prévert, Aragon, and Desnos a tendency to exploit incremental repetition, syntactic segmentation, and anaphora; like them, he transforms lineation into a kind of score that, when realized, recalls an insistent knocking or hammering sound. However, in Damas's case, this hammering sound is often compared to a *tam-tam*, or, on Kotchy's reading, to the recursive patterning of a calypso lyric. The fact that a rhythm of insistence characterized much written poetry at the time should give us pause; perhaps Damas's poetic rhythm

Figure 4.2: Photograph by Jean Prével. View of funeral procession for French Socialist leader Léon Blum, in Paris, 1950. Léon-Gontran Damas is shown near front of procession. Photographs and Prints Division, Schomburg Center for Research in Black Culture, The New York Public Library, Astor, Lenox, and Tilden Foundations.

was informed by his African blood, but it is equally likely that he drew at least some of his rhythmic tendencies from a more local source.

Still, a Damas poem sounds different from a poem by Prévert, Aragon, or Desnos—and this is not simply because he writes about the violence of slavery and colonialism instead of class conflict and social injustice. What is the difference between the "croa-croa" or "non non" of Prévert's verses and the "MOI MOI MOI" or "noires noires noires" of Damas's own? Certainly it matters that Damas is speaking from the position of a diasporic subject, and that his themes as well as the experiences that inform them are different from those of Prévert, Aragon, and Desnos. Furthermore, it would be inaccurate to insist that all Damas poems sound the same way. The love poems in *Névralgies*, for instance, employ techniques of versification and incremental repetition similar to those found in *Pigments* while remaining tonally distinct. Damas's last poem, *Black-Label*, recapitulates the spectrum of tones offered in earlier poems, adding the tones of prayer and invocation to the rhythms of anger and abjection. What we find in the early Damas poems I analyze here, however, is a very particular sonic vibe that the reader picks up in the act of interpreting the marks on the page. Poems like "Fragment," "Limbé," and "Un Clochard m'a demandé dix sous" are notable for their use of the labial nasal consonant /m/ or the alveolar consonant /n/ followed by either an open vowel (as in "mais") or the diphthong /w/ (as in "moi" or "noire"). Even if they are pronounced silently, never brought to full vocalization, this pairing of phonemes, peculiar to Damas's style in *Pigments*, solicits readers to bring their bodies into action, to take the place—to play the role—of the speaker who is not there.

True, a similar solicitation is effected by the letters "croa" in Prévert's poem, letters that evoke an animal register of sonic phenomena rather than a lexical term. But Damas's particular genius is to have discovered *within lexemes* (that is, semantic units) a nonsemantic or animal-like register. He does not have to invent an onomatopoeia like "croa"; instead, he can accentuate the onomatopoeic capacity of phonemes and syllables in general—that is, their capacity to call the body into being. Onomatopoeias do not contain "silent" letters; each letter must be pronounced. To that extent, they suture pronunciation to alphabetic phoneticism more closely than any other type of word. But Damas does not use onomatopoeias, he just draws the sonic potential of the letters of an average lexeme into the foreground, causing us to hear them *as* onomatopoeias—that is, as letteral equivalents of animal sounds. It is by targeting the animal, corporeal sound—not the music, but the sound—in the lexeme that he unearths something like a moan in "rythme en rythme," the "mwa" in "moi," the stutter in "mais . . . mais . . . mais. . . . " It is from these sonic discoveries that he constructs lines such as "le matin mauve / du Mahury mien / à marée montante . . . au miroir déformant où se meut à merveille / ce monde / malgré moi mien" in "Croyez-m'en," or the labial sequence of "Un clochard m'a demandé dix sous": "Mon . . . main . . . moi . . . main . . . misère . . . m'en . . . moi . . . marre. . . . "[93] The mouthy "MOI" of "Fragment" and the noisy "noire" of "Limbé," repeated again and again, may serve as an insistent affirmation of the "me," the speaker of the poem, but they are also vocal gestures that the reader is invited to perform. These rhythmic repetitions of mouthy sounds seem to reach out to the reader to be actualized, to be brought to phenonalization through verbal performance. Through buccal gestures prescribed by the "noire" and the "moi," the virtual vibration of the poem passes from letters to lips, allowing the "current" to "pass" into our throats.

In conclusion, it is worth returning to the definition of "poetic rhythm" offered by Meschonnic, for it allows us to clarify specifically what it is that makes a Damas poem so recognizably his own. Poetic rhythm, for Meschonnic, is less a matter of stresses and beats than it is a total linguistic transmutation affecting every element of the poem: it is "*the passing of the subject into language*, the passing of meaning, or rather, . . . the process of meaning-making as it occurs in every single element of discourse, every single consonant, every single vowel."[94] This is a capacious definition indeed, and one might object that Meschonnic has moved too far from the common understanding of "rhythm" as "the return of the similar," a recurring and recognizable pattern of stresses.[95] In effect, we have moved here from the terrain of "rhythm" per se as a phenomenon of stresses and beats into the terrain of "oversound," the affective tone that emerges "not in the words, not in the melody, not in the dance, not in the meter."[96] To recall, an oversound is a tone associated with the pathos of a human voice heard from another room when the words are not discernible; the poem's oversound derives from "the commitment of feeling to sound."[97] We could think of Damas's poetic rhythm, then, as his way of segmenting words and repeating their phonemes so as to accentuate their potential to produce an affective tone, or oversound. Rhythm and tone both contribute to our sense that a human voice is being overheard. Rhythm and tone are both fabrications of craft, ways in which an author can manipulate the givens of a medium—here, written French—to produce the illusion that one embodied being is being heard by another embodied being, that "human relatedness" (Poirier) is occurring when we read a poem.[98] To return to Adorno's terms, we might say that an "aesthetic subjectivity"—our sense that the poem has a subjectivity, or that we are being addressed—is manifested not only by the presence of a lyric "I," but also in "every single element of discourse, every single consonant, every single vowel" that has been saturated by the labor of the poet's craft (Meschonnic).[99] The "aesthetic subject" is thus not a writer, or an empirical subject, "passing" into words as some kind of authentic, prescribal being. Rather, the aesthetic subject is an irreducible combination of multiple elements: the writer as an individual, factual being; the linguistic and rhetorical tools he or she is given to rework during any given period in history (the linguistic and rhetorical rhythm); and—something Adorno did not count on—the reader's contribution to how the poem will ultimately be performed ("ré-énoncé") as a result of rhythmic features and tonal qualities interpreted each time anew.

The pairing of the labial consonant and the diphthong or open vowel can be—and has been—related to the abject, the infantile, and the aggressive. But to reduce Damas's entire oeuvre to this register of sound (or affect) is to ignore the diversity of his creative production. Damas's readers may find a spectrum of situations and emotional states in his work. What is consistent throughout, however, is the attention he pays to the capacity of phonemes or phonetic clusters to evoke in the reader a particular response. Of course, this response is conditional upon the existence of a shared horizon of expectations. There is nothing to guarantee that we, as readers, will vocalize the "m'en" in "Croyez-*m'en*" or "ryth*me‿en* rythme," or that it will impress all readers as expressing a similar affect. We should recall that the relation of phonemes to affects can be established only because we, as a specific community of writers and readers, recognize such phonetic clusters as evoking such affects. Because the communicative nature of print is predicated on the author's absence, no one can tell us exactly how a poem should be recited—or danced, for that matter. But the reason we can read and "hear" and "dance" a Damas poem at all, the reason we can claim to be susceptible to its rhythms (or its moans), is that we share the same linguistic habitus; our tongues and throats and ears are all trained to interpret and produce the same range of vocal sounds and to attach these sounds to specific alphabetic and diacritical marks. We, like Damas, are readers—and readers of lyrics in particular. (Otherwise, we would be excluded from experiencing the poem entirely.) What Poirier refers to as "human relatedness" thus depends heavily on our apprenticeship in the phonic values of the language concerned as well as our knowledge of the conventions of the lyric tradition.

Ultimately, Rancière may be right. It may be impossible to know precisely what the poem is saying, who is saying it, or how it should be read. But that does not mean that the poem is "mute," that it makes no sound. Making sound is something that Damas's poems compel us, as readers, to do. Developing an eye for the sound of the text might even help us to realize a variety of "politics" à la Rancière. For if politics is a "distribution of the sensible" in which "that which was heard as noise is now heard as speech," then we might think of the politics of Damas's poetry as inhering in his attempt to make speech sound like the noise it always, fundamentally, is.[100] To be political in that sense, it would not be enough for the Negritude poets to enter the field of cultural production on the semantic register alone—that is, to introduce a lyric "I" that represents an explicitly black subject. Something else would have to be revealed about the *means* of representation as well, the way in which noises come to bear semantic weight. Damas manipulates phonemes and their rhythmic patterning in such a way as to turn semes back into sounds, to reveal the acoustic materiality upon which representation depends. That is why he consistently drags the "tone of meaning," or oversound, in the direction of nonmeaning—that is to say, in the direction of the sonic particles that allow meaning to be made.[101] Strategically, he employs the very marks of identity—the semantically loaded "MOI MOI MOI" or "noire noire noire"—to broadcast the /mwa/ /mwa/ mwa/ or the /nwa/ /nwa/ /nwa/ that underlie these marks of identity. He discloses the embodiment of the author through the materiality of the signifier, a materiality that escapes but grounds all attempts to represent identity itself. In this manner, Damas succeeds in bringing together two ways of being political: He speaks for a people, insisting that they take up audible and visible space, and he unmasks the means by which such audibility and visibility are obtained.

5

RED FRONT / BLACK FRONT

Aimé Césaire and the Affaire Aragon

Aimé Césaire's *Cahier d'un retour au pays natal* has now received two generations of readings by Antillean critics, provoking impassioned responses from, among others, Frantz Fanon, Édouard Glissant, Raphaël Confiant, Daniel Maximin, Patrick Chamoiseau, and Dany Laferrière. Fanon was among the first to take Césaire to task for what he considered to be the poet's failure to model the way in which poetry can contribute to the formation of a "national culture." In *The Wretched of the Earth*, he writes that Césaire's language is too "florid," and therefore his poetry is incapable of generating a "literature of combat" calling on "the whole people to fight for their existence as a nation."[1] A generation later, Confiant, in his turn, would attack the language of the *Cahier*, but this time from a different angle: in his controversial *Aimé Césaire: Une traversée paradoxale du siècle*, he excoriates Césaire for neglecting to provide ethnographic descriptions in the Kreyol language of his native land.[2]

How should current scholars evaluate these critiques? Could it be that Fanon and Confiant were blind to the ways in which the *Cahier* actually does shoulder the burden to bear witness? Is it possible that the poem did end up contributing to a "national" or, at least, a regional culture after all? How might new work in postcolonial studies not only revise our reception of the *Cahier* but also change the very way we define the political valence of a poetic text? In order to respond to these questions, this chapter takes a closer look at discourses on the politics of poetry, both those that were extant during the period of Negritude's emergence and those in circulation today. The political conditions and cultural context that initially governed Césaire's reception in the 1940s have evolved such that critical assessments of the first wave differ in important respects from those of later periods. Yet the questions the *Cahier* raised—for poetry and for postcolonial criticism alike—are still highly pertinent and have by no means been resolved.[3] Although postcolonial theory's relationship to poetry has developed over time, poetry remains a controversial genre for postcolonial studies, demanding a constant reevaluation of what it means to represent a self, a people, or a nation in written form. For the most part, postcolonial studies' dominant approach to poetry is still influenced by assumptions that were made during the period when Negritude first emerged, assumptions that Negritude poetry itself should place in question. By returning to the conditions of Negritude's emergence, I hope to unearth the debates responsible for establishing a set of dichotomies that still hold sway in many areas of current scholarship and that hamper poetry's ability to play a significant role in the evolution of postcolonial studies within the academy. My thesis is that although the early reception of Negritude was colored by this set of dichotomies—between poetry and politics, aesthetic autonomy and engagement, lyric subjectivity and historical agency—Negritude holds the key to pushing us beyond them. As I first proposed in the introduction, the poetry of Negritude is not only a product of the European literary tradition; it is also a major intervention into that tradition, one that places pressure on modes of reading that seek to define the politics of poetry in only one way.

The background of contemporary postcolonial studies (or at least one significant background) is composed of several layers or historical phases, each of which contributed to the mapping of the field that scholars of Negritude work in today. The first historical phase—the one that laid the foundation for the dichotomy between poetry and politics—took place at the beginning of the twentieth century in a young Soviet Russia; there a battle was waged between an innovative avant-garde and a suspicious rearguard (promoting socialist realism) over precisely what would constitute engaged art. The second phase began when that battle hit Europe; not incidentally, it coincided with the moment when Césaire and his contemporaries Léopold Sédar Senghor, Léon-Gontran Damas, and Étienne Léro also arrived in France. The Soviet polemic was imported to surrealist Paris in December 1930 via a set of events that have come to be known as the Affaire

Aragon. Finally, the same dichotomies introduced into circulation by the Affaire Aragon (hermetic poetry versus transparently descriptive prose; elite versus proletarian literature; universal versus particular) resurface in the works of Fanon and Jean-Paul Sartre, pivotal figures for the emergence of postcolonial critique. In short, surrealism and the debates it ignited would come to play a large role in the development of postcolonial theory in both French and English traditions. For critics such as Fanon and Sartre (in the mid-twentieth century) and Edward Said and Robin Kelley (at the century's close), surrealism represents the pinnacle of an anti-narrative poetics, a poetics of the nondescriptive, nonmimetic, and non-ethnographic. When Fanon states in *The Wretched of the Earth* that a poetry "full of images" is a "blind alley," and when Said, forty years later, reiterates in *Culture and Imperialism* that poetry wields a nonteleological, "nomadic, migratory, and anti-narrative energy," the type of poetic language being singled out—either to be rejected or celebrated—is one that cannot be "exhausted" by recourse to its "literal meaning."[4] It is a surrealist language that swerves away from what Breton called "the reality of its content."[5]

The consistent question addressed to poetry by engaged critics (whether from Russia, Paris, London, or New York) is whether a language resistant to representation—to "the reality of its content"—can still refer to a singular situation and thereby exert critical force. Crucial to the debate, however, is what one means by the verb "to refer." Césaire's harshest contemporary critics have been those who accuse him of evading transparent reference and practicing "elitism" by refusing to describe concrete solutions or address his compatriots in a language they can understand.[6] In 1948 Sartre had already accused Césaire of obscurity, but he then excused him on the grounds that free association was the only way in which he could identify his "âme noire" (black soul) and overcome the ideology embedded in French.[7] Sartre had just published in book form his influential *Qu'est-ce que la littérature?*, a work that argues against reading poetry as a transparent lens on reality. Prose "refers," Sartre insists, while poetry merely gestures vaguely toward itself.[8] According to Sartre, then, Césaire could only be retrieved for politics if his poetry were read as symptomatic of a collective predicament. For Sartre, the hallucinatory imagery of the *Cahier* indicates a process of introspection that is itself political insofar as the capacity for introspection is precisely what black subjects in general have historically been denied.

What remains unacknowledged in Sartre's readings—as well as those of Fanon—is that the *Cahier* is far from offering a homogeneous surface of dense figuration (the "subtilités" and "raretés" that Fanon derides).[9] It is constructed of more than a fabric of imagery that maintains a consistent distance from topical and political discourses of the period.[10] In fact, if we examine the *Cahier* closely, we find that it appropriates a number of clichéd phrases tightly associated with the interwar discourses of anticolonial struggle and revolutionary combat. These discourses work to situate the poem, allowing it to refer explicitly to a precise time and place, despite the intransigently idiosyncratic nature of some of the imagery. However, at times, the way in which these appropriated discourses re-anchor and resituate the poem is through typographic and phonic means, rather than semantic or lexical means. That is, Césaire does not simply quote the extant discourses of anti-imperialist rhetoric; he also reveals their figurative nature in his own figures; he echoes the rhythm and phonic insistence of overtly political poems that are themselves echoes of specific refrains. Reference, in other words, surfaces in another guise, "turning" words back—to employ Glissant's metaphor of the *détour*—toward a specificity they might otherwise elude.[11]

When used in literary critical discourse, the verb "to refer" is generally understood to consist in an act of pointing: by convention, a written word is related to—and exhausts its meaning in—a clearly identifiable context ("a poetics of the proper name," as I will call it, after Jacques Derrida).[12] Alternatively, however, "to refer" can also be conceived as the rule of synecdoche whereby a written word can stand for the entire people who employ it in speech. (For instance, by writing in Martiniquan Creole, a poet would be referencing the particular culture of the island, a singular history of diaspora and syncretic intermingling.) In each case, what is presupposed is that there is a fixed origin to the inscription in a circumscribed context of usage. The first wave of Césaire criticism (represented by Sartre and Fanon) generally adopts the former understanding of reference and finds Césaire wanting. (He does not use language to describe, proclaim, or state.) The second wave of criticism tends to admonish Césaire for using an erudite vocabulary and a set of rhetorical devices that cannot be traced back to Creole or African traditions. Even the more sympathetic scholars of today rescue Césaire's poem by attempting to demonstrate how its rhythmic cadences reference—by echoing—a Caribbean soundscape.[13]

All sets of critics, from whatever generation, hope to find in the poem an evocation of a specific geopolitical context through signifiers ostensibly attached to precise historical referents. But one of the questions Césaire's work raises is whether this critical focus on content and reference in fact ends up obscuring other ways in which poetic language works, other ways that might at first appear to be irresponsibly playful (or "florid") but that turn out to be, if not referential in the strict sense, at least engaging in referential acts of pointing and naming in ways that only a written poem can.[14] The complexities of the *Cahier* suggest that attending to what a poem's language *does*—not just to what it seems to say—may be an important part of assessing its politics. If we read the *Cahier* solely to learn about conditions in Martinique or to identify a clear directive or political agenda, then we not only risk leaving the specifically poetic dimensions of the poem behind, we also neglect to consider the ways in which those poetic dimensions (the use of typography, syntactic deviations, parallelisms, and extended metaphor) actually develop the signifying force of the words in unexplored ways. While we never want to forget the immediate material conditions out of which the *Cahier* emerged, it is also important to accord the poem the plurality of meanings (or gaps in meaning) that critics celebrate and even politicize in the poetry of other authors, such as Charles Baudelaire and Stéphane Mallarmé.[15] At the same time, though, we should be wary of making the poem say whatever we want it to say, of playing with internal puns and potentially irrelevant etymological roots to the point where all referential gestures—all contexts evoked by proper names or descriptions—are lost. In sum, Césaire's *Cahier* raises a host of questions concerning the appropriate reception conditions for a poem written by an experimental writer self-identified as both politically engaged and militantly black. What hermeneutic limits, we must ask, does a militant politics impose on the interpretation of poetry? Conversely, what pressures does a densely figurative poem place on the content-oriented approaches of identity politics? Do overtly committed works—even highly experimental ones such as the *Cahier*—establish restrictive parameters of analysis? Where do we locate those parameters—within the poetry or beyond it?

THE SCANDAL OF WRITING

Near the beginning of what I consider to be the second movement of the *Cahier*, there appears an extremely curious word: "tourte."[16] Neither translator nor critic has yet been able to satisfy my desire to understand what this word means. Césaire's most recent English translators, Clayton Eshleman, Annette Smith, Mireille Rosello, and Annie Pritchard, render the word as "torte" and do not include it in their glossaries. What a "torte"—in English, a small round tart—is doing in this poem is, according to these translators, self-evident. It is not at all evident to this reader, however. Here is the passage—the only one—in which the word "tourte" appears:

Tourte
ô tourte de l'effroyable automne
où poussent l'acier neuf et le béton vivace
tourte ô tourte
où l'air se rouille en grandes plaques
d'allégresse mauvaise
où l'eau sanieuse balafre les grandes joues solaires
je vous hais[17]

Torte
oh torte of the terrifying autumn
where new steel and perennial concrete
grow
torte oh torte
where the air rusts in great sheets
of evil glee
where sanious water scars the great
solar cheeks
I hate you[18]

The text's grammar suggests that "tourte" is a place—one, in fact, where something grows, something inorganic, of steel and cement: "où poussent l'acier neuf et le béton vivace." However, in most dictionaries—*Le Robert, Harrap's, Larousse*—the "tourte" is defined as a patisserie, a small round bread sometimes stuffed with meat; a diminutive of "tourterelle," or "turtle-dove"; and, in slang, "ninny," or "imbecile." However, "tourte," like the word "pâté," may also be a local term for a grouping of homes, an assemblage of dwellings.[19] When the poet apostrophizes the "tourte," it is hard to believe that he is calling out to a small round tart—"tourte / ô tourte"—or that he would address it at the end of the passage as "vous" ("je vous hais"). Round, flat, and fertile, arriving at harvest time ("l'effroyable automne"), "tourte" is most likely another (feminine) personification of the island of Martinique, or of the "ville plate." Combining the different senses of the word, a reader could imagine "tourte" to be a muse apostrophized, a reminder of the "tourterelles" in the beginning and the "Colombe" at the end, or even a source of nourishment—very rich nourishment indeed—that nonetheless turns out to birth nothing more than modernity, skyscrapers, and parking lots—"le béton vivace."

I have checked multiple annotated scholarly editions and glossaries and have found no reference to the word "tourte." I have, however, found the word in the *Dictionnaire français-créole* by Jules Fairie. Here we are told that "tourte" is synonymous with "gros pâté rond au nânnan là-dans"—or a large round pastry with something yummy inside, a "pie" in English. If we look up "pâté," we also find the definition "block" of houses.[20] So it is likely, as I suggested earlier, that Césaire is playing with at least these two meanings, if not more. The critical silence around the word is surprising, given that "tourte" holds such an important and ambiguous place in the sequence of the poem. At the point when the word appears in the definitive edition, the speaker has just arrested the momentum of the chant "voom rooh oh" and its accompanying figurative evocations of hope with a set of central questions. These questions—and their enigmatic answers—are parsed out dramatically and set off against the white of the page:

> Qu'y puis-je?
>
> Il faut bien commencer.
>
> Commencer quoi?
>
> La seule chose au monde qu'il vaille la peine de commencer:
> La Fin du monde parbleu. (PA, 32)
>
> What can I do?
>
> One must begin somewhere.

Begin what?

The only thing in the world worth beginning:
The End of the world, of course. (22)

Here the beginning of one world and the end of another are linked, presented as simultaneous, colliding apocalyptically. The work of ending the colonial situation, it is implied, must begin, and yet no means of beginning are proposed. As if to further undermine or at least complicate the directive to begin the end of the world ("La Fin du monde"), Césaire adds the antiquated colloquialism "parbleu" (most translators settle for the English "of course").[21] Here, apocalyptic transformation meets subtle self-irony, a combination that is typical of the volume's tonal hybridity as a whole. This same complex of resolve and disillusionment, rendered by means of mixed discursive registers in the section cited above, is reiterated in the following "tourte" passage, but this time through figures of dashed hopes and contaminated renewal. The two passages combined seem to lead ineluctably to the typographically and discursively foregrounded exclamation that ends the sequence:

on voit encore des madras aux reins des femmes des
anneaux à leurs oreilles des sourires a leur bouches
des enfants à leurs mamelles et j'en passe:
ASSEZ DE CE SCANDALE! (PA, 32)

one still sees madras rags around the loins of women rings in
their ears smiles on their lips babies at their nipples, these for starters:
ENOUGH OF THIS OUTRAGE! (22–23)[22]

The brief description of the women and children evokes the island's fertility as well as its seductive (and stereotyped) exoticism. However, the "et j'en passe" cuts short any self-indulgent voyage in the tropical imaginary, indicating that what looks enticing (the seductive women, the dream of apocalyptic renewal, or even description itself) hides something scandalous, outrageous, something no longer to be borne: "ASSEZ DE CE SCANDALE!" Whereas the phrase "Assez de ce scandale" is fully legible, at first glance lacking all ambiguity, the "tourte" passage is highly figurative, even oxymoronic ("le béton vivace," "d'allégresse mauvaise"). "Assez de ce scandale" demands to be read literally, yet, conversely, there is very little to suggest that, as readers, we are intended to interpret the "tourte" as anything but a trope, a stand-in (based on some form of resemblance) for something that is decidedly not just a small round tart or a group of habitations. Similarly, we are not asked to read the lines "l'air se rouille en grandes plaques" and "l'eau sanieuse balafre les grandes joues solaires" as literal descriptions; air cannot rust and water cannot "scar" the cheeks of the sun. These two types of language, the literal and the figurative, stand in tension with one another (although of course the distinction between the two is never absolute, as we shall see). Within a small space, we are offered varieties of discourse that work in two different ways and that call upon us to perform two different hermeneutic operations.

The thematic content of the poem has made exclamation ("ASSEZ DE CE SCANDALE"), as a linguistic resource, seem inevitable, fully consistent with the mounting frustration of a speaker who observes a colonial situation he can neither escape nor rectify. The word "tourte," however, does not seem similarly motivated. To figure the island suddenly—and only once—as a tart, or even as a densely inhabited space, is rather strange. It would be possible to argue that the earlier food imagery (in the passage on Noël, for instance) or the thematics of the "ville plate" justifies the choice of the vehicle. And yet it is not on this level that I would search for the word's motivation. Instead, I believe that the appearance of "tourte" (as a figure for the island) is anticipated phonically by a set of similar-sounding words that Césaire employs before (and after) the passage. If "ASSEZ DE CE SCANDALE" functions perfectly in the register of circumstantial, referential, and therefore critical statement, if it fulfills the *Cahier*'s political mission by announcing dissent, "tourte" is equally motivated by the *Cahier*'s poetic mission and its dedication to the play of sound. And Césaire is always concerned with responding to the exigencies of both.

How does "tourte" function as a phonically and graphemically motivated figure? The various phonemes involved—/t/, /u/, /r/—return repeatedly throughout the poem, embedded in words that both anticipate and perpetuate the sounds of the word "tourte." The noun "tour" contained in "tourte" appears in many guises on the preceding pages, most notably in the verb "tourner." Cesaire's question "Qui tourne ma voix?" (PA, 31) associates "tour" with deviation (Eshleman translates it as "Who misleads my voice?"). A few pages earlier (PA, 24) "tourner" appears to indicate the senseless gyration of the island's inhabitants, their inability to move forward or escape a recursive pattern: "Ce qui est à moi, ces quelques milliers de mortiférés qui tournent en rond dans la calebasse d'une île" (What is mine, these few thousand deathbearers who mill in the calabash of an island [PA, 15]). Again, a few pages later (PA, 35), the action of turning is associated with other forms of pointless movement, the ceaseless rocking back and forth of rocking chairs and the nonadvancing, frustrated circling of a young mare: "autour des rocking-chairs méditant la volupté / des rigoises / je tourne, inapaisée pouliche" (PA, 35) (among rocking chairs contemplating the voluptuousness of quirts / I circle about, an unappeased filly [PA, 25]). Finally, we might add to our list the repetitive turning of the wheel that makes the needle of the mother's Singer sewing machine advance along hem or seam. In the description of the young boy's home, the Poet-as-Singer is ironically personified as a machine that turns round and round without moving and yet simultaneously manages to propel something forward.

On one level, this constant turning of the wheel of language might appear fruitless, misleading. Perhaps the momentum is beyond the poet's control, a force internal to language that "turns" his own voice away from its explicit intention. And perhaps the cry "ASSEZ DE CE SCANDALE" refers as much to the turning of the "tourte"-trope as it does to the colonial fabrication of an exotic isle. In other words, the scandal might be poetic turning itself. However, Césaire intimates that the very existence of a space for the self in language is dependent upon such turning, such force, insofar as "turning" is a rhetorical movement disguised here thematically as a physical action. That is, writing requires a coup de force, an intentional turning of the self toward language and a turning of the reader's attention to that self fabricated *in* language. The new opening Césaire wrote for the 1947 Bordas edition begins with such a gesture of turning on the speaker's part: "Puis je me tournais vers des paradis pour lui et les siens perdus" (PA, 7) (Then I turned toward paradises lost for him and his kin [1]). But toward what, precisely, is the speaker turning? Toward a river of "*tourte*relles," those peace-loving aviary inhabitants (doves) of a poetic imaginary (7). In one sense, then, the speaker begins by turning toward turning; to write poetry is, after all, to turn toward, to subject oneself to words that turn, words that deviate, words that take a detour, words that lead elsewhere than where one thought one would go.

The word or word fragment "tour" appears repeatedly throughout the poem: "voom rooh oh/ à empêcher que ne *tour*ne l'ombre" (PA, 30); "Il *tour*ne, pour tous, les blessures incises / en son tronc" (PA, 50); "le soleil *tour*ne autour de notre terre" (PA, 58); "les *tours* joués à la sottise" (PA, 61). We also find it echoing in "ma mémoire est en*tour*ée de sang" (PA, 35); "Pardon *tour*billon partenaire!" (PA, 39); "ma négritude n'est ni une *tour* ni une cathedrale" (PA, 47); "je te livre l'in*tour*ist du circuit triangulaire" (PA, 64). And of course we should not forget the "re*tour*" of the poem's title itself. I would hazard the guess that words with some form of "tour" in them are the most frequent in the volume, with the sole exception of words containing some form of the word "vers." The final word of the poem, "verrition," is anticipated by "inverse" (PA, 7); "vérole" (PA, 8); "lèvres ouvertes" (PA, 8); "véridiques" (PA, 13); "vernissée" (PA, 14); "vertigineuse" (PA, 14); "déverse" (PA, 19); "vers" (PA, 21, 22, 24, 30, 58); "ouverte" (PA, 23); "épervier" (PA, 25, 45, 62); "perversité" (PA, 29); "verdâtre" (PA, 36); "véritablement" (PA 37, 47); "envergure" (PA, 38); "vermine" (PA, 39); "verni" (PA, 40);"verre" (PA, 46); "vertu" (PA, 48); "vergers" (PA, 51); "cadavérise" (PA, 59); "perverse" (PA, 60); "vérifier" (PA, 60); "grand'verge" (PA, 61); and "traverser" (PA, 63), not to mention all the key words with /v/ in them repeated throughout the poem: "voici," "vent," "ville," and "voix," or the play between "rêvé" (PA, 16, 42–43) and "crevé" (PA, 19), "vriller" (PA, 17, 57); "voom rooh oh" (PA, 30); "virile" (PA, 49, 51); "vire" (PA, 55); "navire" (PA, 62); and so on. It could be argued that the opening verbal construction, "tourner vers," in "Puis je me tournais vers" is the phonic, graphemic, and semantic kernel that rehearses in miniature the largest number of images in the poem.

The final lines of the *Cahier* throw this seminal construction, "tourner vers," into relief. As we know, the last lines of the poem provide an image of a "je," a poetic subject, who searches for the "malevolent tongue" or "language" of the night ("la langue maléfique de la nuit") in this tongue's "verrition." Although "verrition" refers, as I have argued, to many things, it is possible to understand the neologism as a self-reflexive allusion to the condition of being a verse, a "vers." Here the tongue's status as verse would imply both immobility and gyration; "verrition" would evoke a language/tongue that turns toward, that becomes verse ("je me tournais vers") without striking out in any direction in particular. On this reading, what the speaker would be "fishing for" ("pêcher ma langue") would be a language/tongue that tropes, turns, even as it remains fixed in place on the page. Highlighted in the *Cahier*'s enigmatic conclusion, both "tourte" and "vers" are obviously part of a larger network of semantic and phonic interconnections undergirding the entire poem. On the one hand, "tourte" and "vers" are elements of the poem's phonic texture; on the other, they are the poem's thematic kernel, a compressed way of evoking the great problematic of the poem: how is it possible both to trope (turn) and to move forward (make progress in the political struggle) at the same time?

Finally, all this semantic richness is captured in the phonetic and graphemic structure of the word "tourte" itself. The "t" sound at the beginning of "tourte" is repeated in the "t" sound that ends it, suggesting thereby the circularity, the gyrating movement, with which the word is associated in Césaire's imagery. As a marker for that which ceaselessly turns, a kind of round dead end, "tourte" is indeed an ideal choice. Similar to the island, "tourte" always seems to end up where it began but not without making a good deal of noise. After all, the problem, for Césaire, is not that his fellow Martiniquais are silent but rather that they are a people "a côté de son vrai cri" (PA, 9) (detoured from their true cry [2]). They speak like "perroquets babillards" (PA, 8) (babbling parrots [2]); they create nothing but an "inanité" "sonore" (PA, 8), to evoke Mallarmé once again. In the section on Noël, for instance, the city is transformed into a "bouquet de chants" (bouquet of songs) until, that is, the bouquet "se liquefie en sons, voix et rythme" (PA, 16) (liquefies into sounds, voices, and rhythm [8]). Ultimately, this potentially resonant music, a music of words, dissolves into meaningless noise, an "obsession des cloches" (obsession of bells) the repetitive percussion of raindrops "qui tintent, tintent, tintent" (PA, 17) (that tinkle, tinkle, tinkle [9]). In the French original, the thrice repeated letter "t" in "tintent" must catch the eye. The fate of the chant of Noël (the chant of rebirth, of the coming of the Savior) thus threatens to become the fate of Césaire's chant: will the *Cahier*, through the force of its own poetic momentum, liquidate into pure rhythm, the repetition of the letter "t"?

Césaire's major concern is that not only will the voices of his people "tournent en rond," revolve endlessly upon a fixed axis, but also that his own poetry might do nothing but turn round and round within its own hollow, reverberating cavity (or "calebasse"). This fear is justified to the extent that poetry in general resists the form of statement or assertion, and thus ostensibly cannot do the work of logical argument in a public sphere (or the work of incitement in a political one). In the specific case of Césaire, the concern might be even more urgent. How, for instance, can he prevent the passage on the "tourte" from influencing our way of reading the line: "ASSEZ DE CE SCANDALE"? On the one hand, the exclamation clearly refers to the scandal of poverty, abuse, alienation—and their disguise—on the island of Martinique. The demonstrative pronoun "ce" impresses us as referring directly to the description that preceded it. And yet, as is the case with any deictic construction one finds in a poem—"here," "now," "this," "that"—there is more than one referent to be found. "Ce" could, in fact, refer to the act of describing itself. The scandal might be writing, writing of misery instead of taking up arms to eliminate it. As formalist readers, we might pounce on (and get caught up in and derailed by our appreciation of) the alliteration of "ce" and "scandale" and "assez." In other words, Césaire can present us with two different types of discourse, the slogan and the figure, the protest and the pattern, but he cannot prevent one from influencing our reading of the other.

Perhaps it is precisely Césaire's apprehension of the recuperative (and leveling) effects of poetic form that motivates him to isolate "ASSEZ DE CE SCANDALE" as a unit of discourse by placing it in uppercase letters and presenting it as a single line.[23] The effect of the capitalization is to transform the song (or chant) into a shout (an exclamation). But that is to imagine the poem in oral terms. As a unit of text, "ASSEZ DE CE SCANDALE" imitates typographically and evokes visually the newspaper headline (le gros titre); it places the poetic line in the same journalistic context as "Debout les nègres!," the slogan displayed (often in uppercase letters) on the front pages of news organs associated with black anti-imperialist and workers movements of the 1930s such as *La Race Nègre*.[24]

Not incidentally, this slogan, "Debout les nègres!" resounds throughout the *Cahier*, first as the reiterated "Au bout" (of "Au bout du petit matin") and then as the crucial "Debout" of the concluding passages. As a piece of text, the capitalized phrase "ASSEZ DE CE SCANDALE," similar to "Debout á la barre," evokes journalistic discourse. The typography of "ASSEZ DE CE SCANDALE" seems, then, to set up a kind of visual block, as if Césaire wished to create a check on the turning motion of metaphor and the vertiginous detours of paronomasia. Drawn to but also wary of the effects of surrealism, Césaire is imitating in 1947 not only the language of Éluard and le Comte de Lautréamont but also the historical discourse of anti-imperialist, anticapitalist propaganda. A tension is thus revealed within the poem between a language of direct command and a language of detour. Which takes precedence—"Debout les nègres," the headline we find in *La Race Nègre* (see http://faculty.sites.uci.edu/aestheticsubjectivity/), or "Tourte/ ô tourte," the call made by the poet that seems to begin and end with itself?

RED FRONT

How can poetry, Césaire asks, assume the responsibility of contestation, the burden of the constative (of witnessing), and yet keep faith with the poetic function? Or, put differently: how can poetry be "in service" to the teleology of revolution yet remain "in service" to the nonnarrative, troping forces of poetry? These questions enjoy a considerable genealogy, as I have noted, but I will begin my own investigation at a particular point in their elaboration. In the winter of 1931–32 a debate concerning the political valence of poetic language took place as a result of what was to become known as the Affaire Aragon. Arriving in Paris in the fall of 1931, Césaire might very well have heard news of the Affaire. As a reader of *L'Humanité*, and as a schoolmate of Jules Monnerot (who responded to the Affaire at the time), it is unlikely that he would have been ignorant of the debates the Affaire had ignited.[25] The issue of poetry's relation to politics was, to say the least, in the air.[26] I am prone, then, to believe that the Affaire left an imprint on Césaire's poetry and poetics; further through Sartre's investment in the debate, it also left an imprint on postcolonial theory and its broader approach to the cultural politics of literature.

Although familiar to many scholars, the details of the Affaire Aragon are worth repeating. First, in October 1930 Louis Aragon was sent along with Georges Sadoul to Kharkhov, in Soviet Russia, to represent the surrealist movement at the Second International Congress of Revolutionary Writers. Troubled by the French Communist Party's agenda for proletarian literature, an agenda advanced by Henri Barbusse (the literary editor of *L'Humanité*) that appeared to exclude surrealism, Breton had charged Aragon and Sadoul with the mission of arguing against Barbusse's notion of socialist realism in favor of surrealism's doctrine of absolute imaginative freedom. During the course of their stay, Aragon and Sadoul apparently had a change of heart and opted to adhere to the party line. At the beginning of December they signed a letter addressed to the Union internationale des écrivains in which they denounced the petit-bourgeois "idéalisme" and "freudisme" of the surrealist movement and proclaimed their full commitment to "la littérature prolétarienne."[27] In a move that would later seem incomprehensible to Breton, Aragon and Sadoul agreed to submit all their future literary activity to the approval and control of the French Communist Party headquarters in Paris.[28] Meanwhile, however, Aragon continued to write letters to Breton confirming his allegiance to surrealism and celebrating the triumphs he indicated had been enjoyed by the surrealists during the course of the union's proceedings.

As soon as Breton heard about what Aragon and Sadoul had done, he demanded an explanation. Upon his return to Paris in December 1930 Aragon tried to convince Breton that his signature on the letter to the union had been extorted, but he also maintained that the self-criticism imposed by the Communist Party would ultimately not be harmful to the surrealist cause. While steadily growing further apart, Aragon and Breton nonetheless managed to collaborate on a series of non-Communist-Party-affiliated projects, such as the two protest tracts against the Colonial Exposition of 1931 and the third and fourth issues of *Le Surréalisme au Service de la Révolution*, published in November 1931.[29] This uneasy *entente* was not destined to last, however. In this same month of November, all hell broke loose: the French police seized an edition of *Littérature de la Révolution Mondiale* (an organ of the Union international des écrivains) in which Aragon's pro-Soviet poem "Front rouge" (Red front) had appeared at the end of 1930.[30] Written while Aragon was in still Russia and inspired by the work of Mayakovsky, "Front rouge" contained several lines advocating militant aggression against the liberal government of Léon Blum. "Front rouge" clearly echoed the rhetoric and exclamatory tone of Mayakovsky's 1918 "Left March" ("La marche à gauche") in which the Russian poet calls upon his comrades to take up arms, move forward—"Allons, en marche . . . !" (Aragon's translation)—and employs the conventional revolutionary syntagm, "Assez de," as in "Assez de chicane bavarde! . . . Assez de lois, vieilles et fausses . . . !" ("Enough nonsense! . . . Enough laws, old and false"), which, of course, we find again in the *Cahier*.[31] Aragon translates Mayakovsky's revolutionary rhetoric (and imitates the heterogeneity of his discursive styles) by combining direct commands—"Feu sur Léon Blum"—with suggestive images constructed along the lines of Lautréamont's famous extended prepositional phrases, such as "la fleur d'encre de l'infamie" (the ink flower of infamy).[32] Taking the commands "Feu sur Léon Blum" (Shoot Léon Blum) and "Descendez les flics"

(Kill the cops) literally as a call to arms (and extracting them from their poetic context) Blum's department of justice accused Aragon on January 16, 1932, of attempting to incite unrest, an act punishable by a prison sentence of five years.[33]

The second phase of the Affaire then began. Upon hearing the news of the accusation against Aragon, Breton immediately drafted a rebuttal. He circulated this rebuttal as a petition, acquired over three hundred signatures, and published it under the name "Misère de la poésie: 'L'Affaire Aragon' devant 1'opinion publique" (Poverty of Poetry: The Aragon Affair Before Public Opinion).[34] Breton's act of solidarity probably saved Aragon from being brought to trial, for the Blum government, at first incensed by the poem's treasonous call for violent insurrection, felt even more threatened by the negative publicity it would receive as a result of surrealist agitation. The Affaire initially attracted little attention; the only newspaper to contain a report was *Le Populaire* (in January 1932). However, by March, after Breton's petition had been widely circulated, a number of papers—*L'Humanité*, *Paris-Midi*, *Paris-Soir*, any one of which Césaire might have read—contained articles on Aragon's plight. Not wanting to be associated with dictatorial tactics of censorship, Blum's justice department simply dropped the case. Whatever merit Breton's argument might have had for the three hundred signatories of "Misère de la poésie," it does not seem to have impressed Aragon. A few days after "Misère" appeared, *L'Humanité* published the following notice:

> Our comrade Aragon has let us know that he had absolutely nothing to do with [il est absolument etranger à] the publication of the pamphlet entitled "Misère de la poésie" signed by André Breton. He wants it to be clearly understood that he disapproves of everything stated in this pamphlet and rejects the insinuations it makes with respect to his own name. He believes that all communists must interpret the attacks contained in this pamphlet as incompatible with the class struggle and thus objectively counter-revolutionary.[35]

Aragon's affiliation with the surrealists promptly ended there.

However, the Affaire did not. A crucial split had been introduced into the leftist literary and artistic milieux of Paris. Breton's "Misère de la poésie" presented a set of arguments that both reflected and then shaped twentieth-century definitions of poetic language and its relation to political agency. He states, for instance, that "a poem should not be judged according to the successive images it evokes but rather on its power to incarnate an idea; freed from any need for rational sequence, these images are no more than a stepping stone."[36] Yet, as a stepping-stone to further action, the poem is not evacuated of all force. The reference made to realizable action would be only one aspect of a poem's meaning, and, for Breton, a subordinate and even insignificant, rapidly transcended aspect. The greater meaning, he argues, is derived not from the literal sense of individual words or verses but rather from the interplay among all the poem's words and verses: "The poem transcends [dépasse] both in signification and in significance [portée] its immediate content. It escapes, by its very nature, the reality of this content [la réalité même de ce contenu]."[37] "In matters of interpretation," he continues, "the consideration of a poem's literal meaning in no way exhausts its meaning as a poem." It would be pointless, then, to put a poem on trial. Accordingly, "Misère de la poésie" begins by objecting to the very principle of dragging poetry before "la justice": "We rise up against any attempt to interpret a poetic text for judicial ends [Nous nous élévons contre toute tentative d'interprétation d'un texte poètique à des fins judiciaries]."[38]

What Breton objects to most strenuously is the notion that a reader (here, a judge) could dissect a poem, dividing it into, on the one hand, phrases or words that signify in a clearly direct, referential manner (such as "Camarades descendez les flics," or "Assez de ce scandale," for that matter), and, on the other, phrases or words that elude immediate comprehension and can only be read as figurative—such as "Les astres descendent familièrement sur la terre" (The stars descend familiarly to earth), the line that Breton cites from "Front rouge," or "l'air se rouille en grandes plaques / d'allégresse mauvaise," to draw an example from Césaire. These are both figures that distance the poem from any concrete circumstance or empirical phenomenon they might nonetheless be evoking indirectly. According to Breton, no reader, and certainly no judge, would ever be in a position to determine which phrases in a poem are figurative and which are not, for all are part of a network of associations ultimately in the service of "incarnating an idea." Breton is forced to admit that "Front rouge" contains some fairly clear directives (not just "Camarades descendez les flics" but also "Feu sur Léon Blum . . . pour l'anéantissement total de cette bourgeoisie" [Shoot Leon Blum . . . for the total elimination of this bourgeoisie]). He alludes to the poem's radical heterogeneity, the way it juxtaposes densely metaphorical passages ("Les fleurs de ciment et de pierre / les longues lianes du fer / les rubans bleus de l'acier" [Flowers of cement and stone / long creepers of iron/blue ribbons of steel]) with chunks of journalistic prose referring to precise current or historical situations ("L'intervention devait débuter par l'entrée en scène de la Roumanie sous le prétexte . . . d'un incident de frontière" [The intervention must have begun with the entrance of Romania onto the scene with the pretext . . . of an incident at the frontier].

Yet even as Breton identifies generic, tonal, rhetorical, and diacritical inconsistencies within Aragon's poem, he nonetheless reserves for every single word in the poem—in whatever structure it might be imbedded—the right to behave like poetic language, that is, to be meaningful with respect to a set of internal associations based on other words found in the poem (what he calls the "poetic drama") *and* to be meaningful with respect to a set of external associations based on historical references, dates, proper names, and place names (what he calls the "social drama"). Poetry, for Breton, is first and foremost a language that leads away from an initial "point d'appui," a language that steers us away from literal readings, immediate contexts, toward "*autre chose*," as Breton writes in italics.[39] Small wonder, then, that surrealist poetics, posed in these terms, might seem to fail as a resource for a politically engaged, anti-imperialist liberation movement—either in the 1930s or in the academy of today.

BLACK FRONT

Thus began the third and least-studied phase of the Affaire Aragon, the transformation it underwent in the hands of, precisely, an anti-imperialist liberation movement. Despite its avoidance of "the social drama," Breton's surrealism did in fact hold a strong appeal for politically engaged Caribbean poets living in Paris and not simply, as Sartre famously claimed, because it allowed poets (of color) to sound the very depths of their repressed unconscious. Active members of the surrealist avant-garde at the time Breton composed "Misère de la poésie" included Étienne Léro, René Ménil, and Jules Monnerot, Caribbean-born poets who frequented the same cafés as the surrealists and attended their debates on "la liaison entre le politique et l'esthétique, [et] l'anticolonialisme en général" (the link among politics, aesthetics, and anticolonialism in general).[40] As if to cement their bond to the surrealist poetics of the period, Léro, Ménil, and Monnerot chose the name of a 1926 pamphlet by Breton, "Légitime défense," as the title of their own journal, and yet comments interspersed throughout its pages suggest that this repetition of Breton's gesture would not occur without a difference.

The ripples created by the passage of the Affaire through French and Franco-Caribbean cultural life can be felt in the articles and poems of this slim publication, which, however ephemeral, was nonetheless critical in establishing surrealism's use-value for colonial subjects.[41] Critics generally attribute the appropriation of Breton's title to a desire on the part of the Caribbean students to align themselves with surrealism's oneiric poetics. But this hardly explains the careful and nuanced *prise de position* executed in the pages of the review. Critics have failed to elucidate fully the cultural politics inscribed in *Légitime Défense*, and thus have left several of its emphases unexplained. Why, for instance, would the editors of *Légitime Défense* have chosen that title in 1932? Why didn't they borrow a title from a more recent work? What did Breton's "Légitime défense" contain that would have made it attractive to Caribbeans studying in Paris at that time?

Breton's "Légitime défense" is an uncompromising critique of the French Communist Party's aesthetic spokesman, Henri Barbusse, who governed the literary column in *L'Humanité* during the 1920s and against whom Aragon was to argue at the Congress in Kharkov. Breton's short essay contains an unequivocal rejection of the very position Aragon came to assume during the Affaire. By appropriating the title *Légitime Défense* in 1932, Léro and Ménil were situating their argument at the antipodes of Aragon's, tacitly affirming the argument against socialist realism that Breton elaborates in "Misère de la poésie." But the story gets more complicated. Along with the indirect allusion (through the title) to the debate animating the Affaire, Léro adds a concrete reference to Breton's position when he titles his contribution to the issue "Misère d'une poésie," thereby troping on the title of Breton's petition "Misère de la poésie" by changing the definite article to the indefinite "une." Léro's move at once produces a rapprochement between Antillean poetics and surrealist poetics and emphasizes the singularity (and distinction) of the Antillean case. His "Misère d'une poésie" contains no direct allusions to the Affaire Aragon; instead it presents an implicit argument that the "poverty" referred to in the title is not the poverty of a poetry reduced to its literal meaning (a proletarian poetry, as defined by Barbusse) but rather the poverty of a poetry that has no literal meaning whatsoever, a poetry without referents in the real world of actual black experience in the colonies.[42] The poetry of Gilbert Gratiant, Léro writes, "translates neither the social iniquities of his country nor the passions of his race, nor the value of disorder and dream."[43] The twist is significant. Léro is not opposing the deployment of external referents in a poem, nor is he objecting to the reduction of hermeneutics to the work of identifying these referents; instead he is lamenting Antillean poetry's avoidance of such markers of collective memory, experience, and longing. He is execrating the lack of the type of directive and direction Aragon so famously offers in his "Front rouge."

Read as a response to the Affaire Aragon, *Légitime Défense* appears to strike a balance between the two positions represented respectively by Aragon and Breton and seeks to find room within poetry for both metaphorical detour and referential advance. That is why the editors, in their preface, insist upon both the date of their adherence to surrealism and the nature of the surrealism to which they adhere: "nous acceptons également sans réserves le surréalisme auquel—en 1932—nous lions notre devenir. Et nous renvoyons nos lecteurs aux deux 'Manifestes' d'André Breton, à l'oeuvre tout entière d'Aragon" (we also accept, without reservation, the surrealism to which—in 1932—we bind our future. And we refer our readers to the two 'Manifestos' of André Breton, the oeuvre of Aragon in its entirety), and the list goes on.[44] For the editors to state, in 1932, that they support the work of Aragon "in its entirety" was to say a great deal indeed.[45] What they mean, in short, is that they intend to embrace Aragon's call, "Feu sur Léon Blum," and the aesthetics of reception that would allow it to be politically salient while simultaneously supporting Breton's ideal of a revolutionary language capable at any moment of exceeding its "sens littéral."

Many critics have claimed that *Légitime Défense* does no more than promote surrealism as a solution to the poverty of Antillean verse. Anticipating Sartre, Léro and Ménil do indeed locate the resources for constructing a properly representative Antillean poetry in the fragments of repressed experience wrested from the black unconscious by means of automatic writing (and, in Sartre's version, by means of dense metaphor). Much of the poetry included in the volume may very well be, as Ménil later concluded, "anachronique" in the strong sense of the word—that is, disengaged from any reference to a specific historical moment or political struggle. But there is one poem that stands out, not because of its geographical or historical specificities but because of its indirect metaphorical and phonic allusions to the poetics of Aragon's "Front rouge." I am thinking here of Léro's poem "S.O.S."—the international Morse code for "emergency," the eminently decodable signal of distress, a clear call to action if there ever was one. "S.O.S.," I believe, draws from the hybrid poetics of Aragon's "Front rouge" in order to sketch out a new possibility both for the composition of colonial and postcolonial poetry—a possibility realized in Césaire's *Cahier*—and for this poetry's reception and theorization. Léro's "S.O.S." contains no commands to rise up, such as Aragon's "Descendez les flics" or "Sifflez sifflez SSSR SSSR" (Whistle whistle SSSR SSSR). Nor does it advocate insurrection or make reference to military initiatives (as does "Front rouge"). The contents of the poem are simultaneously anodyne and incendiary in that peculiarly surrealist way.[46] "S.O.S." evokes through an almost Pierre Reverdy–like set of "rapprochements" a scene of fire breaking out in a "salle de cinéma"; we never know whether that fire is real or on the screen, a safely confined virtual fire or a spectacle that can at any moment leap off the screen into the real. "Si l'incendie éclate / Il n'y a pas de sortie de secours" (If fire breaks out, there's no exit), the poem warns us. The title, however, explicitly performs the pointing gesture of reference itself: "S.O.S."—Pay attention! Look here! "ASSEZ DE CE SCANDALE!" It enacts in an exemplary manner one of poetry's available verbal gestures: finger-pointing, alerting with concision and diacritical urgency.

At the very same time, however, the title demonstrates the way in which poetry can point not directly through naming or finger-pointing but by means of phonic resonances and metaphorical associations. A reader of the time would have had to have been deaf (or blind) not to recognize in "S.O.S." a phonic and visual echo of the primary leitmotif of Aragon's "Front rouge": "L'U.R.S.S. ou comme ils disent S.S.S.R. . . . SS un air brulant c'est l'es / pérance c'est l'air SSSR . . . Sifflez sifflez SSSR SSSR . . . S R/S S/S R/S S. . . ." (L'U.R.S.S. or as they say S.S.S.R. . . . SS a burning melody it's h/ope it's air SSSR). A call to attention addressed to the French proletariat in Aragon's poem becomes, in Léro's poem, framed by "Misère d'une poésie," a call to attention (S.O.S.) addressed to the Caribbean. The first few lines insist on the letter "s" (as well as the phoneme /s/, as in "sur" and "cinéma") that appears so prominently in the title, drawing a portrait of the dark heart of a theater:

Que le soir meure sur la ville
Et sur l'obscène exploit
Mise en scène du coeur cinéma

Coeur simulacre du voyage
Pour celle qui a peur du paysage
Et que lasse l'exclusive image
Si l'incendie éclate
Il n'y a pas de sortie de secours
. . .
Tourne toujours
Moi seul ne vois point
Assez n'est cécité et cinéma

Let the evening die on the city
And on the obscene exploit
Mise-en-scène of the heart cinema
Heart simulacrum of the voyage
For she who fears the landscape
And is weary of the exclusive image
If the fire breaks out
There is no exit
. . .
Turn always
Me alone sees not at all
Enough is not blindness and cinema

In "S.O.S.," Léro has condensed the immense heteroglossic complexity of "Front rouge" into a single but sharp discursive contrast. Léro combines linguistic registers, as does Aragon, but their sequence is more telling: "S.O.S." or "HELP: URGENT MESSAGE!" is followed not by an account of mishap, as one might expect, or a command to bring reinforcements but rather by a spectacle from which there is no escape. In other words, the message that follows the warning "S.O.S." turns out to be metaphoric and allusive rather than denotative and referential. It is almost as though Léro were saying, just as Césaire does in the final ecstatic image of the *Cahier*: "S.O.S.: Look! Look here! I'm turning! Turning! Spinning away!" And in fact, the only imperative we find in "S.O.S." is not "Feu sur les colons" ("Fire on the colonizers") but—coincidentally?—"Tourne toujours." At the same time, however, the context of the poem "S.O.S." toward which the title points us is not simply an undecodable sequence of surrealist metaphors. The rhetoric of fire or burning is ubiquitous in Marxist and anarchist revolutionary sociolects (which are intensely metaphorical to begin with). *Brûler* and *incendier* (to burn up) are verbs used *au sens figuré* by Aragon in "Front rouge" and by Breton in "Légitime défense" to designate acts of insurrection against an oppressive force. It is difficult, therefore, to determine in Léro's poem where the metaphor ends and where the call to action begins. Imagery, sonic effects, and typographic emphasis—all poetic means—draw Léro's poem into conversation with Aragon's. The word "Assez" in "S.O.S." connects on one level to "cécité" (blindness) and "cinéma" (spectacle) through phonic associations internal to the poem. But on another level, "Assez" leads us out of the poem to militant discourses of the period that stage spectacles (and blindnesses) of a different kind.

WRITING THE SCANDAL

In this final section, I want to propose that Césaire's *Cahier* accomplishes something similar to what Léro accomplishes in "S.O.S.": a destabilization of discursive registers such that we are never sure when a written unit (a word or phrase) will turn toward the "reality of its content" or when that unit will spin away toward other verbal units found either within the poem or beyond it. Both Léro's "S.O.S." and Césaire's *Cahier* suggest that the act of blurring the line separating intra-, inter-, and extratextual associations possesses its own political charge in the realm of interpretation. Such a blurring of registers imposes on us a strategy of reading sensitive to both the historical context of the literary and the literary context of the historical, the metaphoricity of command and description as well as the political and almost physical forcefulness of metaphor, the way it efficiently turns us toward a complex and discursively rich series of historical events. Printed letters themselves, especially when typographically highlighted, can perform the gesture of turning us toward contexts we might not otherwise evoke. Césaire's poetry makes abundant use of all its resources, not just metaphorical indirection but textuality as a medium with a signifying potential all its own.

Given the intensely evocative nature of Césaire's writing, I cannot conclude, as do many of his critics, that he fails to satisfy the demands of an engaged Antillean expressive practice. The fact is, through his juxtaposition of exclamation and metaphor, anaphora and paronomasia, uppercase and lowercase, Césaire manages to put us in a state of constant alert (S.O.S.!). That is, he forces us to attend to the multiple ways in which referential and figurative inscriptions modify and redirect one another. Determining how this poetic operation works (which words turn in which ways and why) within any given social formation or frame of reception is the task of a properly postcolonial poetics. I would like to conclude, then, by suggesting two sources from which we might draw the elements of such a postcolonial poetics. The first is a text by René Ménil, "Sur la préface de Breton au *Cahier d'un retour au pays natal*" (1965), that makes an argument for considering the language of description not as a faithful rendering of what exists but rather as a recreation of what exists by means of a language that may very well take us on detours through unexpected sites.[47] Referring directly to Breton's "Misère de la poésie," Ménil asks "whether a poet can 'treat a subject' (for example, a political subject, as in the *Cahier* where Césaire treats decolonization)."[48] Ménil's answer is that yes, a poet can "treat a subject," but not without recreating that subject: "Reading the *Cahier*, we realize rather quickly that the Antilles as they are 'in reality', 'for everyone,' and 'in real life,' are one thing. Passing into the writing of Césaire, they become something else. Every reader from the Antilles can confirm that after reading the *Cahier*, the Antilles are no longer what they were before."[49] Here Ménil anticipates one of the founding premises of (old) new historical scholarship, namely, that literature does not merely record a pregiven reality but also shapes it, brings it performatively into being for consciousness in a new way. Ménil's comments suggest further that it is not only the ethnographic or the hortatory that can make a claim for political salience, but that certain practices of reading, encouraged by the opacity of poetry, might constitute a politics as well. That is, the discourses of both description and exhortation might, when located in a figurative context, send the reader on a detour, directing her away from the immediacy of reference toward an exploration of where the terms of description and exhortation come from, in what historical discourses they are embedded, and which ideological purposes they formally served. Ménil is not necessarily encouraging a search for origins but rather a sensitivity to the ways in which poetic making, even as it aims to represent a particular reality, nonetheless employs discursive elements with histories, affective valences, internal networks, and evocative potentials not determined by the exigencies of the "subject" being "treated."

The second pertinent text is Kristin Ross's "Metaphors and Slogans," a chapter from *The Emergence of Social Space*, in which she identifies a set of strategies employed by Rimbaud that are displaced and reworked by Césaire. Ross dubs the kinds of figures I've been identifying in Césaire's text (such as "le béton vivace") or Léro's ("si l'incendie éclate") elements of a "metaphorical sociolect"; we know we have encountered such a sociolect when the author deploys a type of metaphor containing social content even as it distorts common usage.[50] Through the metaphorical sociolect, reference to precise conditions is often signaled in an indirect or veiled manner. Ross's example of the sociolect's simultaneous distortion and directness is Césaire's use of the term "marronnage" to designate the resistance and escape of slaves.[51] As Ross points out, some metaphors in the *Cahier* initially marked as "surrealistic" or "nonreferential" (such as "l'arbre tire les marrons du feu" [the tree pulls chestnuts/escaped slaves from the fire] turn out to "represent a higher degree of referential truth" insofar as they belong to and reinvoke the highly metaphorical sociolects of countercultural or politically subversive movements.[52] Metaphor, on this reading, does not function to turn the reader away from ethnographic description but rather to turn her toward a rich and diverse context for deciphering the author's allegiances and the potential meaning of his words. The terms of the figure thus pass through a social reality (and its discursive construction) that may be reached by a detour.

Consider, for instance, Césaire's "ô tourte de l'effroyable automne / on poussent l'acier neuf et le béton vivace," the passage with which we began. The juxtaposition of two contrasting semantic fields—the vegetal ("pousser") and what I will call the industrial ("acier," "béton") is by no means solely surrealist. This juxtaposition is typical of a critical discourse on modernity from Zola onward; it is even utilized by Aragon himself in the verse from "Front rouge" I cited earlier: "les fleurs de ciment et de pierre / les longues lianes de fer / les rubans bleus de l'acier" ("the flowers of cement and stone / the long creepers of iron / the blue ribbons of steel"). When Césaire writes of a "tourte," a village/tart/bird/island/woman from which grows "new steel and lively concrete," he is not being oneiric or florid at all but merely taking a detour through another equally polemical rhetorical tradition—one that metaphorizes history as nature—to make a political critique. Sometimes Césaire uses *détournement* to return us to a historically specific context for meaning-making. He employs imagery typical of the critique of capitalist industrialization, suggesting that without that imagery even the most militant, engaged discourse couldn't function at all. This does not mean that every metaphor in poetry (or in militant rhetoric, for that matter) can be traced back to a countercultural sociolect; further, metaphors do not point unequivocally in one direction even when they do evoke associations with extratextual phenomena. My demonstration is meant to show the many and diverse ways in which words "turn" as well as the innumerable sites toward which they turn by means, for instance, of phonetic association, as in the case of "tourte," a figure that turns us toward the problem of figuration itself.

Ultimately, "tourte," although possessing a set of dictionary definitions, ends up creating a kind of puncture in the semantic fabric of the text, almost as if it were another neologism but even more opaque than those that critics frequently discuss. For none of the dictionary definitions—tart, ninny, species of bird, or even (the most likely) a group of huts—really helps us to make sense of its presence in the poem. To this extent, then, "tourte" is no more than an inscription and, when pronounced, a group of phonemes. Its strange hollowness as a vehicle of sense signals to the reader that it might bear other kinds of relationships, nonsemantic relationships, to words, sounds, and marks within the poem and without.

To return to our earlier questions, Césaire could very well be indicating that, indeed, poetry criticism has an obligation to remain within certain limits, to avoid detaching the poem—and the poet—from the complex set of contexts that should determine its interpretation. But he is also implying, I believe, that postcolonial theory must acknowledge that these contexts are less easy to circumscribe than might at first appear to be the case. As Paul Gilroy has argued persuasively, postcolonial cultural production is in general richly layered, full of latent cross-fertilizations and interconnections. Reference occurs through a variety of appropriations, samplings, and signals that have to be carefully deciphered, one by one. The politicized hermeneutics of Césaire's poetry might thus best be summarized as the charge to postcolonial scholars to regard the contexts for interpreting a poem as multiple but constrained. Stuart Hall is prescient on this point:

> For signification depends upon the endless repositioning of its differential terms; meaning, in any specific instance, depends on the contingent and arbitrary stop—the necessary and temporary "break" in the infinite semiosis of language. This does not detract from the original insight [of Derrida's notion of the "trace" and the supplemental

> structure of signifying play]. It only threatens to do so if we mistake this "cut" of identity—this positioning, which makes meaning possible—as a natural and permanent, rather than an arbitrary and contingent "ending"—whereas I understand every such position as "strategic" and arbitrary, in the sense that there is no permanent equivalence between the particular sentence we close, and its true meaning, as such. Meaning continues to unfold, so to speak, beyond the arbitrary closure which makes it, at any moment, possible.[53]

Figurative language is thus not a code ("S.O.S.") to be reduced to what cryptographers call a plaintext; but neither is it simply an aleatory stream of associations, a form of free play. Marks on a page do not turn away from every "point d'appui," from every link to a referent in the empirical or discursive universe. There is, as Césaire reminds us, a lasso binding us—and our marks—to a whirling center. Specific forces draw us in, a determinable set of interpretive frames within which the "langue maléfique de la nuit" can be heard, or the obscurity of the mark read. The poem itself provides us with these frames if we are willing to engage in intratextual, intertextual, intermedial, historical, and biographical recontextualization. One of Césaire's gifts to poetry theory (as well as postcolonial studies) is his revelation that poetic language may have a concrete history in resistance movements but also that resistance movements may find the force of their rhetoric *in poetry*. Where, then, are we to locate "lyric" language? Where does lyric language end and circumstantial language begin? Who writes "ASSEZ DE CE SCANDALE!"—the lyric subject or the newspaper? Is there a discrete language of the lyric subject, or is that language already shot through with phrases, slogans, and metaphors that have been recycled any number of times in political tracts and rallying cries—and will be recycled yet again in the crucible of craft? Might the aesthetic subjectivity we associate with a "lyric I" be at once the empirical, historical subject as he is transformed through the *techne*, media, and conventions of writing *and* the voice of history, of collective struggles, as that voice enters into the language of lyric? Could this be what Adorno meant when he stated that "the artistic subject is inherently social, not private"?[54]

Ultimately, it is up to us as readers to determine whether something as mobile as a word ("tourte") or as rigid as a phrase ("ASSEZ DE CE SCANDALE!") is or is not "a site of entanglement" (Glissant), a "necessary" or "temporary 'break'" (Hall).[55] Is the highlighted phrase ("ASSEZ DE CE SCANDALE!") a way of returning us to the level of the letter, to its typographic display and the visual echo it sets up with other instances in which letters matter? Does a typographic decision provide us with a context for reading we might not otherwise have had? Consider the journey throughout the *Cahier* of the "S" of "ASSEZ," which I have traced back to the exhortations of black nationalist newspapers of the 1920s and 1930s, Léro's poem, "S.O.S.," and the "Sifflez SSSR" of Aragon's "Front rouge." Traveling from site to site, a grapheme lights up each word in which it appears with a topical charge. On this reading, the repeated grapheme could serve, in the *Cahier*, as an allusion to historical context, a way of referring us back to a frame—one of many—for interpreting its language. Alternatively, the "S" could send us more deeply into the sonic "calebasse" of the written text. So too the insistent return of the word "tour" could indicate either the self-enclosed nature of the poem or, instead, its intertextual commerce with Léro's poem ("Tourne toujours") and the cultural politics of *Légitime Défense*.

The urgency of Césaire's poetic language is indeed haunting. He wants us to wake up, to take note, to ready ourselves for action. But this same urgency does not justify a precipitous reading, one that would pick up only one signal issuing from only one site. Our responsibility to the text is to respond to its call not by determining unilaterally what it means but by patiently taking a fuller inventory of all the ways in which it might achieve meaning and agency in a complex world. The limited role that poetry has played in francophone postcolonial studies is overdetermined by a long tradition that has only barely—and sporadically—been refreshed by deconstructive and Deleuzian modes of linguistic analysis and ideology critique. These modes need to be explored to a far greater extent if francophone postcolonial studies is going to accommodate a poem as hermetic, tropological, and discursively heterogeneous as Aimé Césaire's *Cahier*. At the same time, however, it is important to note that postcolonial poems themselves pose a challenge to these very same deconstructive and Deleuzian modes of analysis. The urgency of the postcolonial condition must also be acknowledged if a truly postcolonial poetics, a mode of reading responsible to both the history of suffering *and* the history of *poiesis*, is to be forged.

6

TO INHABIT A WOUND

A Turn to Language in Martinique

CALENDRIER LAGUNAIRE

j'habite une blessure sacré
j'habite des ancêtres imaginaires
j'habite un vouloir obscur
j'habite un long silence
j'habite une soif irrémédiable
j'habite un voyage de mille ans
j'habite une guerre de trois cents ans
j'habite un culte désaffecté entre bulbe et caïeu
j'habite un espace inexploité
j'habite du basalte non d'une coulée
mais de la lave le mascaret
qui remonte la valleuse à toute allure
et brûle toutes les mosquées
je m'accommode de mon mieux cet avatar
d'une version de paradis absurdement ratée
—c'est bien pire qu'un enfer—

j'habite de temps en temps une de mes plaies
chaque minute je change d'appartement
et toute paix m'effraie

tourbillon de feu
ascidie comme nulle autre pour poussières
de mondes égarés
ayant craché le volcan mes entrailles d'eau vive
je reste avec mes pains de mots et mes minerais secrets

j'habite donc une vaste pensée
mais le plus souvent je préfère me confiner
dans la plus petite de mes idées
ou bien j'habite une formule magique
les seuls premiers mots
tout le reste étant oublié
j'habite l'embâcle
j'habite le débâcle
j'habite le pan d'un grand désastre
j'habite le plus souvent le pis le plus sec
du piton le plus efflanqué—la louve de ses nuages—
j'habite l'auréole des cactacées
j'habite un troupeau de chèvres tirant sur la tétine
de l'arganier le plus désolé
à vrai dire je ne sais plus mon adresse exacte
bathyale ou abyssale
j'habite le trou des poulpes
je me bats avec un poulpe pour le trou de poulpe

frère n'insistez pas
vrac de varech
m'accrochant en cuscute ou me déployant en porana
c'est tout un
et que le flot roule
et que ventouse le soleil
et que flagelle le vent
ronde bosse de mon néant

la pression atmosphérique ou plutôt historique
agrandit démesurément mes maux
même si elle rend somptueux certains de mes mots

—Aimé Césaire[1]

"Calendrier lagunaire," situated above *en exergue*, is—I recently discovered—the poem printed on Aimé Césaire's tomb. This tomb may be found in a small cemetery located in a hilly suburb overlooking Fort-de-France. The words of the poem are engraved in gold onto a slab of grey-blue marble, typographically arranged in two columns with a cameo portrait of Césaire nestled between. The tomb is no bigger than any other in the cemetery, although it does occupy the very first row of tombs to the immediate left of the cemetery gates. If the visitor didn't know the tomb was situated at precisely this site, she might easily walk right past it without stopping. The only element that stands out, the element that marks this tomb as different from all the others, is the long and winding poem presented on the vertical tombstone jutting straight up from the grave. Several other tombstones in the cemetery also bear short lyrics, trite yet appropriate rhymes about the inevitability of death or the permanence of love. But Césaire's is the only one to contain no less than three hundred and six words, eight of which are found almost exclusively in botanical, zoological, or geological treatises.[2] Surrounded by the garden-variety sentiments of mourning in a French that is easily legible to approximately 93 percent of the population, the poem that serves as Césaire's epitaph reads almost like a foreign language, so definitively does it belong to a different register, so clearly does it indicate radical particularity on the level of discourse and form. Césaire's words are "sumptuous," as the poem's last line tells us, but they are also highly specialized, technical, ostentatiously erudite. Some phrases are indeed ambiguous in intention ("[d'un] vouloir obscur"); others belong to a recognizable, almost Baudelairean lyric discourse ("j'habite donc une vaste pensée") or recall a now classic surrealist style ("ayant craché le volcan mes entrailles d'eau vive"). However, certain words are singularly exact in denotation: "s'accrocher en cuscute" and "se déployer en porana," for instance, refer to two different modes of plant existence, ways of inhabiting—or, more precisely, cohabiting—in either a parasitical or symbiotic relation. "Calendrier lagunaire" can be considered daring, even avant-garde, insofar as it takes chances with diction; Césaire's manner of juxtaposing incommensurable registers of discourse is reminiscent to some extent of surrealism, yet ultimately it remains vigorously original and comparable to nothing other than the style he himself develops in the *Cahier d'un retour au pays natal.* Just how an avant-garde epitaph (replete with terms like "en cuscute" and "en porana") might find a home in a discursive site of communal mourning is one of the questions that will occupy me in this final chapter. My goal is to study Césaire's oddly foreign vocabulary, to find a rationale that explains its appeal, and to demonstrate that internal self-difference, or intrinsic non-self-identity, is ultimately the model for the aesthetic subjectivity that Negritude has forged. But first: a reading of "Calendrier lagunaire."[3]

Césaire himself chose this poem as an epitaph—and for reasons we can probably discern.[4] Despite the difficulty of its rhetorical figures, "Calendrier lagunaire" clearly thematizes the dialectic of residence (place) and transcendence (placelessness) appropriate to a meditation on death. It was included in *moi, laminaire*, published in 1982, a set of poems generally considered to constitute his most mature poetic style.[5] Césaire's trademark anaphoric verse structure is here combined with a crafted system of images and an unusually personal first-person tone that may have made it a strong candidate for the status of epitaph. Clayton Eshleman and Annette Smith, Césaire's English translators, observe that "The 'I' [of the poem] . . . is no longer a stylized one, part of the mythopoesis as in previous collections, but a more concrete, human, and real one, reflecting on a full and difficult career."[6]

There are reasons to contrast the earlier heroic voice of the *Cahier* and the less mythically adorned "I" of "Calendrier lagunaire." Césaire's heroic mode relies heavily on active verbs such as "partir," "crier," "refuser," "chercher," and "inventer," whereas "Calendrier lagunaire" associates the speaker with an almost passive verb, "habiter," as though merely continuing to exist in a place, to survive, constituted a heroic act. Paradoxically, however—given the insistent "j'habite" (repeated twenty times)—the speaker does not actually appear to reside, to *be*, in any particular place. That is, he seems to inhabit a spectacular number of places and, at the same time, to fail at being able to inhabit any single one—at least in the root sense of "habiter": to lodge, reside, or occupy "*de façon durable*" (in a permanent way).[7] Of course, not knowing one's exact address ("à vrai dire je ne sais plus mon adresse exacte")—indeed, not *having* an exact address ("chaque minute je change d'appartment")—is a situation congruent with the unearthly status of death. As the dictionary tells us, in its second sense, "habiter" can mean to "animate," "haunt," or "possess." It is likely, then, that "Calendrier lagunaire" was chosen to decorate the tomb because it suggests that the poet, even when deceased, continues to animate the Martiniquan landscape. His spiritual presence can still be felt.

We must not be misled, however, by the funereal and memorial context in which the poem now resides. "Calendrier lagunaire" was composed when the poet was still very much alive, and it is also in this context that the poem must be read. During the decade of the 1960s Césaire was at the height of his efforts as a leader to foster a greater sense of Martiniquan identity. He struggled with the French president, Charles de Gaulle, to establish political and economic autonomy for Martinique, gaining a reputation in Paris for being "un dangereux indépendentiste."[8] He increasingly placed in question the cultural politics of assimilation that he had earlier, in part, embraced by attempting to develop the island's fragile infrastructure according to the rhythms and customs of its citizens. By 1975 he had taken the dramatic step of inaugurating the Service Martiniquais d'Action Culturelle (locally known as "SERMAC"), a state-funded center charged with identifying and protecting what he considered to be the indigenous cultural legacy of Martinique's African descendants.[9] When Césaire wrote "Calendrier lagunaire," then, his major preoccupation was how to inhabit a specifically Martiniquan space, not how to figure the placenessness of death, or how to remain spiritually once gone. The "habitation" Césaire seeks is not a "dernière demeure," a final resting place; nor does he hope to build a "Habitation," with a capital H, the French term for the colonial plantation. Césaire's repeated use of the verb "habiter" evokes obliquely these contexts, but he is clearly gesturing toward a different way of being, a way of inhabiting a particular place that has little to do with either the monocultural cultivation of the Habitation or the perfect homogeneity of transcendent space.

I believe it would be a mistake, then, to interpret the word "paradis" in line 15 as referencing the afterlife to which the poet might have aspired. Instead, it reads as an ironic allusion to the "tropical paradise" that Martinique—at least according to the French imaginary—was supposed to be. The lines "je m'accommode de mon mieux cet avatar / d'une version de paradis absurdement ratée," followed by the parenthetical "c'est bien pire qu'un enfer," can be read in the vein of the *Cahier*, that is, as a lament for the failure of Martinique to realize itself, to be what it could be. The poem tells us that the embodiment of paradise has been so falsified, the "avatar" so tragically degraded, that any comparison of the island with its possibilities is simply "absurd." As in the *Cahier*, the speaker experiences his "native land" not as whole and sheltering but rather as broken and afflicted. Yet, at the same time, the affliction in which he dwells is "sacred," perhaps because it harbors a collective past ("une guerre de trois cents ans"), a history of suffering. To shuffle off that earthly mantle, that shared history of pain, would be to deny the possibility of any consecration whatsoever. "Calendrier lagunaire" is emphatically a poem about dwelling on the physical earth and in the physical body. It is a poem about dwelling in suffering, and suffering, as we learn in the *Cahier*, is the only site upon which brotherhood might be established and unity achieved.

Throughout the course of the poem we learn that habitation can take place not merely in architectural structures but also in a variety of other, more abstract types of shelter. The pairing of "habiter" with an abstract as well as a concrete noun (a "vaste pensée" as well as an "appartement") is actually a fairly common poetic practice and not a jarring agrammaticality. Poets frequently use the verb "habiter" to figure interior states in spatial terms. In fact, the first line of "Calendrier lagunaire" recalls a similar poem by René Char titled "J'habite une douleur" (I inhabit suffering). Although it would be difficult to prove a direct connection between the two poems, it is worth noting that they both employ the verb "habiter" to explore how one might reside—or, to evoke Heidegger more directly, how one might "dwell"—not only in houses and temples but also in moods and metaphysical states: "J'habite une douleur" (Char); "j'habite une soif irrémédiable" (Césaire). In both poems, a metaphysical or affective state—such as being in pain or feeling an unrelieved yearning—is figured in physical, bodily terms: thirst and wounding in Césaire; the weight of the body and its submission to time in Char.[10] Further, "Calendrier lagunaire" implicitly equates habitable spaces, such as the "appartement" of line 18, with physical wounds, of which there are many: "I inhabit from time to time one of my wounds / every moment I change apartment." Curiously, the speaker intimates that agitation is to be preferred to stasis: "all peace scares me," he writes, perhaps because, as in the poem by Char, "il n'y pas de siège pur," there is no place out of time, out of history, out of suffering—except the pure nonspace of death. And yet it is clear that the speaker is seeking some kind of resolution, some way out of the "tourbillon de feu" ("whirlwind of fire") that we also encounter at the end of the *Cahier*. As in the earlier poem, the speaker adopts a restless turning around and around; he accepts residence in a barely tolerable "disaster," gaining meager nourishment from the breast of the hardest, least accommodating landscape: "le pis le plus sec du piton le plus efflanqué"; "la tétine de l'arganier le plus désolé" (the driest udder of the skinniest peak; the tit of the most desolate argan tree).

Finally, in order to achieve even the loneliest shelter, he tells us, he must wage battle: "je me bats avec un poulpe pour le trou de poulpe." This octopus hole, "ronde bosse de mon néant" (the round [hump] of my nothingness), is ultimately the wound where he dwells—alone with his nourishing words and his secrets: "je reste avec mes pains de mots et mes minerais secrets."[11] The poem thus associates the speaker's specific act of dwelling with the possession of words and buried treasure—or with words *as* buried treasure. The image of buried treasure (or "ore") refers us to a local intertext: "Calendrier lagunaire" was published for the first time in the same volume as Césaire's ode to René Depestre, the Haitian author of the 1956 volume *Minerai noir* (Black ore).[12] When Césaire depicts the speaker of "Calendrier lagunaire" as seeking shelter in the greatest depths of the ocean, as constructing his abode with the aid of words and hidden jewels, he is reiterating his pledge in "Le verbe marronner / à René Depestre" to "marronner" (to escape like a slave into the hills), to outwit the colonial power and its "atmospheric or rather historical pressure"—and to do so by using a language as esoteric as it is explosive. Against the critique that his hermetic style serves poorly to found a revolution of the masses (a critique launched first by Frantz Fanon), Césaire defends himself in "Le verbe marronner" by insisting that only a language forged in the depths, a language growing out of pain and emerging from the wounds of loss, can preserve the hope of something new. It is as though he were searching for some "espace inexploité" not only in geographical terms (a "morne" for the "marron" to cultivate beyond the precinct of the Habitation) but also in verbal terms. The speaker seeks the possibility of vocalizing something volcanic that has not erupted into the landscape of language before. This new vocalization would be situated in a very unique space, one "entre bulbe et caïeu," that is, in a space on the stem between the large offshoot and the smaller one. Translating vegetal into verbal terms, one could say that the "unexploited space" between "bulbe" and "caïeu" is situated in the imaginary interval between two alphabetic letters: we have to imagine a site between the "b" and the "c." The words with which the poet "remains" would be miraculous words indeed; they would exist like secrets, the beginning of a magic formula that has not yet produced its miraculous material results ("j'habite une formule magique / les seuls premiers mots . . .")—either as language (possibility of utterance) or as place (possibility of being).

Imaginary as they may be, the speaker nonetheless clings to these words (he is "laminaire"), to inhabit the depths where such words are found, perhaps for the very reason that they are connected to something that has been lost ("tout le reste étant oublié"). Like the remainders of only half-understood African languages, half-heard rhythms, and half-remembered belief systems with which slave-descendants must make a life, these words constitute the holy wound, the "blessure sacrée," that hurts but preserves. The speaker is attempting to inhabit a space that is both there and not there ("entre bulbe et caïeu"), just as one might entertain a memory that recalls only that the memory has been lost. Césaire, like other intellectuals of his generation, believed that large gaps existed in the chronological self-awareness of Caribbeans. The opening line, "j'habite une blessure sacrée," obviously references the Middle Passage and the subsequent impossibility of belonging to a culture anchored in the ecology from which it emerged.

Returning to the title of Césaire's poem, "Calendrier lagunaire," we can begin to understand why a habitation in a "blessure sacrée" would be so traumatic. We can also grasp why such a habitation might accurately be evoked by the image of a constant tossing and turning, a buffeting by waves. A "calendrier lagunaire," or "lagoonal calendar" (as Eshleman and Smith translate it), suggests a register of temporality appropriate to a shallow body of water separated from the sea by sandy dunes. In Martinique, this lagoonal landscape is typically inhabited by the mangrove, a tropical tree growing in clusters in marshes near the sea. A lagoonal calendar would chart the cycles of a marshy landscape rather than the cycles of the moon (a "calendrier *lunaire*"); it would provide an organization of time consistent with the strange temporality associated with living in a region of lagoons—or, to force a word-play, a regions of *lacunes* (gaps). The word-play is not so forced, actually, for the two words, "lagoon" and "lacuna," share a common root in the Latin "*lacuna*." A "calendrier lacunaire" is another name one could give to a temporality rendered spatially as a paper calendar filled with gaps.

The Caribbean archipelago is a lagoonal space consisting of a series of straits that connect a "repeating island" (in the lovely phrase of Antonio Benítez-Rojo).[13] But the Caribbean archipelago is also *lacunaire*: it is filled with absences, forgettings, breaks with the past. Lagoons are associated in the poet's mind with death, with the ghostly presences of slaves who drowned in bodies of water. In the *Cahier*, Césaire alludes to lagoons as tombs filled with blood: "Que de sang dans ma mémoire! Dans ma mémoire sont des lagunes. Elles sont couvertes de têtes de morts" (So much blood in my memory! In my memory there are lagoons. They are covered with the skulls of the dead).[14] No wonder the poet is unsure whether or not he wants to fill in these gaps. To do so would be to cover up the blood, to suture the "blessure sacrée." Accordingly, he contents himself with magical half-formulas, placing faith in just the promise of a more harmonious world: "ou bien j'habite une formule magique/ les seuls premiers mots / tout le reste étant oublié." Césaire chooses to reside, then, *in potentia*, opting to respect rather than repair the loss. His poetry is difficult and resistant to immediate understanding in part because he aims to preserve some mystery, a few "minerais secrets," as an homage to what can never be recuperated, what can never be healed by memory, what can never provide stable ground.

Lines 31–32 provide the sharpest depiction of the poet's ambivalent attitude toward the production of continuities in a landscape and history riddled with holes. He tells us that he resides in both the "embâcle" and the "débâcle," the freezing and the loosening up of the obstructing ice. An "embâcle" obstructs the flow of water, as in the case of ice that blocks the passage of water in a narrow strait. Conversely, a "débâcle" is the rupture of the ice layer caused by a sudden thaw, permitting the water to flow smoothly again. Here, Césaire situates himself in two landscapes at once, an "embâcle" in which connection is prevented and a "débâcle" in which connection is restored. The challenge he confronts is to dwell in the violent space of their irreducible *différend*. If all he has left is words, then these words must allow him to withstand the rough buffeting of the waves ("et que le flot roule"), the aspiration of the sun ("et que ventouse le soleil"), and the erosion by wind ("et que flagelle le vent"). He will cling like a "moi, laminaire"—the algae on the rock—even while spinning round and round on a stalk, a "vrac de varech," a cluster of kelp like a vibrating mess of branches and roots.[15] With this magnificent image of turmoil in splendor, the poem leaves us wondering how a dwelling in such a vertiginous space could possibly be sustained.

What would it mean to dwell in the pregnant abyss, and what kind of language could provide shelter there?

A HOMELESS DWELLING IN LANGUAGE

Before helping us to communicate,
language helps us to live.
—Émile Benveniste[16]

Arguably, the thinker most responsible for associating language with shelter, poetic words with spatial abode, is Martin Heidegger. I have resisted the perhaps inevitable recourse to his poetics as long as possible in order first to explore some of the unique connections between language and shelter established in Césaire's poem. The translators of "Calendrier lagunaire," Eshleman and Smith, also resist the pull toward Heidegger, choosing the word "inhabit" (as opposed to "dwell") to translate the French verb "habiter." Now it is time, however, to examine Heidegger's essays on dwelling a bit more closely and to ask what they might add to our reading (as well as what they might obscure). The evocation of Heidegger is on some level counterintuitive—as Eshleman and Smith must have recognized—given the context, both political and aesthetic, in which he developed his theories. As is well known, between 1935 and 1951, the period during which his essays on "dwelling" were written, Heidegger was concerned with identifying a poetic language capable of building a world for a supposedly unified, or at least a homogeneous people. His vision of poetry as "dwelling"—a dwelling underlying and making possible real shelters—is nothing like Césaire's portrait of life in the depths. Heidegger's vision presupposes a totalizing language, less hermetic than "authentic," a language of "true meanings" that "stays with things," "lets things be" (rather than "enframing" them for exploitation).[17] It also presupposes and is addressed to a totalized population, an autochthonous "*Volk*," in intimate and continuing contact with their own soil.

Nothing, of course, could be further from the Martiniquan truth. Here, as elsewhere in the Caribbean, a group of heterogeneous, displaced peoples, brought together as a result of centuries of forced migration, struggle to find a home in a land they do not own. They speak a language imposed by a colonial power that exists in tandem, and in conflict, with yet another language derived from the colonial situation—Creole (or Kreyol), itself a testimony to the way languages recombine elements rather than spring from one consistent root. Nevertheless, it is worth retaining at least one idea from essays such as "The Origin of the Work of Art," "Building Dwelling Thinking," "Language," and ". . . Poetically Man Dwells . . . ," namely, that dwelling is a metaphysical state. It can be generated by language and therefore does not depend on the construction of actual edifices. Connected to this idea is the notion that dwelling, as a metaphysical state, hinges upon acts of naming. In other words, one can only dwell if one makes a shelter of names that call out, that produce an intimacy between mortals and their surroundings.[18] In "Language," for instance, Heidegger asks: "What is this naming? Does it merely deck out the imaginable familiar objects and events—snow, bell, window, falling, ringing—with words of a language?" He then responds: "No. . . . The naming calls. Calling brings closer what it calls. . . . Thus it brings the presence of what was previously uncalled into a nearness."[19] Language—particularly poetic language, that which is most purified of "foreground meanings"[20]—is thus not mere decoration, but instead a necessary intermediary that listens and waits.

Occasionally in these famous essays Heidegger intimates that the language of naming is not, in fact, a stable one, established by the poet once and for all. In "Building Dwelling Thinking" we read: "The real dwelling plight" is not the lack of adequate homes but rather "that mortals ever search anew for the nature of dwelling, that they *must ever learn to dwell.*"[21] If we are to take Heidegger's emphasis seriously, then the most authentic, the most healing and beneficial act is not to establish an authentic language composed of purified, nontechnical, noninstrumental names; rather, the most healing and beneficial act is to *search for*—rather than to purport to find—the names that listen to the strange and unfamiliar landscape in which we are always, to some extent, "homeless." Heidegger's moment of radical negativity occurs, then, when he suggests that "dwelling" in and through language is more problematic than it at first seems: dwelling might in fact have to do with a "concentrated perception," a "taking-in" that leaves something more to be discovered, something more—and other—to be said.[22] And herein lies an incipient postmodern, even avant-garde Heidegger, the Heidegger whose thinking leads him toward a critique of finality and an embrace of the negativity inherent in the concepts of "listening," remaining "ready for the unforeseen," "the reservoir of the not-yet-uncovered," and "strife."[23]

Surprisingly, however, it is Heidegger's least persuasive propositions that have retained purchase in Martinique's contemporary discourses on the relation of language to place. The legacy of what Philippe Lacoue-Labarthe calls his "nostalgia for presence" has been handed down in some unexpected ways.[24] For instance—and perhaps paradoxically—the movement known as "Créolité" proves a fertile ground for unearthing old Heideggerianisms, albeit in a different guise. Advocates of Créolité such as Raphaël Confiant, Jean Bernabé, and (with more qualifications) Patrick Chamoiseau have stated that French should be eclipsed as a literary language in favor of the indigenous Creole spoken by almost the entirety of the Martiniquan population. Stressing the need to provide a unique language for a unique people, the *créolistes* have insisted on the widespread use of Creole as an academic and diplomatic language, even while celebrating the values of hybridization and *métissage*—the "créolisation" of culture in general—that defines the Caribbean past. As *Éloge de la créolité* demonstrates, the ideology of Créolité contains some unpleasant remainders of Heideggerian thought insofar as it promotes *one* language above all others as singularly capable of preserving the identity of a people (often depicted in barely disguised folkloric terms).[25] To be sure, the analogy is not exact: Heidegger promoted one *kind* of language ("natural" language as opposed to distorted language, for example, or Friedrich Hölderlin's poetry as opposed to "the clever talking" of radio broadcasting), and not a single language *tout court*. However, his belief that there could exist a writing consistent with the history and values of a people—in short, a writing consistent with *and constitutive of* their world—resembles the belief that underlies the *créoliste* project. When *créolistes* argue that Creole takes the adequate measure of Caribbean reality, when they seek to establish it as the national language, and when they excoriate authors who do not write in Creole, they slip into an identity thinking that unintentionally echoes the conceptual errors of Heidegger's language politics.[26] To be sure, Creole is hardly a monoglossic language composed of words boasting etymologies that can be traced back to pure meanings "lost to us" in the present, fallen age.[27] Creole is saturated with a history of oppression and invention peculiar to the lands where it is spoken; its authenticity does not reside in its ability to reveal an a-historical *phusis*, Nature as "the pristine ground, because it is the ground of those beings that we ourselves are."[28] A close examination of Creole—and a close examination of French or High

German, for that matter—unearths the history of the relations between peoples and places, cultures and cultivations, that contribute to making language and nature what they are now.

I do not mean, then, to maintain a neat opposition between the *créoliste*'s position and that of Césaire. Césaire does not represent some absolute alternative to the totalizing moments in either Heidegger or Créolité. His desire to recapture a link with Africa, expressed with periodic urgency in the *Cahier*, recalls in an odd way Heidegger's nostalgic yearning for a former, more authentic world. In addition, Césaire's attraction to archaic terms and his advanced studies in Greek and Latin all point to a tendency to honor what he calls the "primitivism" of ancient systems of thought.[29] In contrast to the theorists of Créolité, who draw attention to the richness of the recent past, Césaire mourns the break with the past, the absence of roots caused by the Middle Passage. He does not reject the culture of the present as irrelevant or superficial, but he does thematize its fragility, its lack of historical depth. The poem renders well the groundless ground of his native Martinique with its juxtaposition of "bathyale" (from the Greek *bathus*, meaning "profound"), and "abyssale" (from the Greek *abyssos*, meaning limitless, or without bottom ["sans fond"], like the "grand trou noir" of the endlessly unknown). To this extent, he shares with Heidegger an understanding of modernity as loss (rather than exultant, compensatory creativity). His desire to forge a poetic language is not so different from Hölderlin's; similar to the German poet (as least in Heidegger's version), Césaire too dreams of repairing the wound inflicted by industrial "Enframing" ("the commandering everything into assumed availability").[30]

However—and this is a crucial difference—Césaire targets a very *particular* instance of "enframing," namely, the reduction of human beings to commodities in a slave economy. Further, he also identifies a very *particular* instance of ungrounding: the temporal and spatial ungrounding of the Middle Passage. Finally, however, it is not clear that repairing the wound (to forge some seamless identity) is really his poetic goal. Césaire can be said to practice a poetics of "dwelling" only insofar as he seeks a language able to name (to draw him closer to his surroundings); yet this language, albeit "sumptuous," is born of—even coincident with—the experience of suffering ("mes maux"). No doubt, Césaire enjoys the "sumptuous" result of historical pressures, the words rendered iridescent, like jewels, by the "historical" burden they bear: "la pression atmosphérique ou plutôt historique / agrandit démesurément mes maux / même si elle rend somptueux certains de mes mots" (The atmospheric or rather historic pressure / even if it makes certain of my words more sumptuous / immeasurably increases my plight). But these words do not point back to some essential, primordial language in which the poet might dwell. Instead, Césaire's words—and, as we shall see, predominately his names—register historical suffering and displacement; they reflect centuries of conquest and thus an intermingling and layering of languages rather than the purity or authenticity of a single one. The last line of "Calendrier lagunaire" suggests, through homophonic play, that the Middle Passage is responsible for creating both the pains the poet feels ("mes maux") and the words the poet makes ("mes mots"). In this way, Césaire intimates that there is ultimately no language he can fabricate that would afford a comfortable abode, a place in which to "dwell." "To inhabit a sacred wound" is to render a tangle of branching seaweed ("vrac de varech") "sumptuous," to cling to the depths of language (like an algae, or verbal "laminaire") because it is only in those linguistic depths ("mes mots") that one finds the history of current pain ("mes maux").[31] And it is only by writing with a language shot through with history that one can "search anew for the nature of dwelling."[32]

CALLING THINGS BY THEIR NAMES

> We translate our Latin texts together. We build the world anew.
> —Aimé Césaire[33]

The first thing one notices when approaching the poetry of Césaire is the immensity of his vocabulary and the diversity of its origins. René Hénane, glossing the *Poésies complètes*, compiles an alphabetical list of no less than 671 terms drawn from the specialized discourses of botany, geology, zoology, pathology, mineralogy, psychiatry, and biology.[34] Much attention has been paid to Césaire's surrealist imagery; indeed, his inventive juxtapositions were the first aspect of his style to receive commentary by Sartre and Breton. But few critics have faced the challenge presented by Césaire's vocabulary, and no one, to my knowledge, has adequately explained either the purpose or the effects of its diversity.

This vocabulary can properly be considered global. It contains words from at least fifteen different languages (thereby linking his poetic language to four continents): Greek; Latin; Arabic; French; Martiniquan Creole, or Kreyol; Arawak; Carib; Portuguese; Spanish; Italian; Egyptian; Celtic; Malaysian; Norman; and Guyanese. Yet, in his interviews, Césaire always claims a regional basis for his word choices, especially for those words designating species of flora and fauna endemic to Martinique. In an interview accorded to Jacqueline Leiner to commemorate the reprinting of his wartime review, *Tropiques*, Césaire explains that the desire to anchor his poetry in a specific place was particularly urgent during the Vichy occupation of Martinique (1939–1943):

> We did not want to put together a journal of *abstract* culture; rather, we wanted as much as possible to apprehend *Martiniquan* reality in its *Martiniquan* context—to situate it precisely. We wanted this journal to be a tool that would help Martinique to re-center itself [*se recentrer*]. We had realized that there was nothing else in this area. Absolutely *nothing*! So, we decided to study, systematically, the flora and fauna and so on. Even a very repressive regime [Vichy] couldn't stop us from doing that![35]

Césaire's wager is that by foregrounding in the pages of *Tropiques* the specific identity of the Caribbean landscape, authors would be able surreptitiously to invoke the unique identity of the people who inhabit it. The flora and fauna (and the unique culture emerging from it) could be better comprehended if they were evoked not through vague allusions to tropical foliage but rather by means of discriminating designations, the exacting scientific lexicon of genii and species. As he suggests in another interview, calling things "by their name" establishes the specific identity of both the place and the person naming:

> I am an Antillean. I want a poetry that is concrete, very Antillean, Martinican. I must name Martinican things, must call them by their names. The *canafistula* [*canéfices*, the botanical term in the French] mentioned in "Spirals" [*Spirales*] is a tree; it is also called the drumstick tree [*cassier* in the colloquial French]. It has large yellow leaves and its fruit are those big purplish bluish black pods, used here also as a purgative. The

> *balisier* [a French term] resembles a plantain, but it has a red heart, a red florescence at its center that is really shaped like a heart. The *cecropias* [the botanical term] are shaped like silvery hands, yes, like the interior of a black's hand. All of these astonishing words are absolutely necessary, they are never gratuitous.[36]

Césaire is making a semiotic rather than a Heideggerian point here. He is insisting on the power of reference, affirming that a class of nouns (the generic and species designations of flora and fauna) can provide an intimate relationship with the Caribbean landscape that they are intended to systematize. In yet another testimonial, this time a letter to Lilyan Kesteloot from the 1970s, Césaire reiterates the same idea: "If I name with precision (what people call my exoticism), it is because by naming with precision I believe I am recovering for the object its singular value."[37] Interestingly, he associates the word "exoticism" with his own writing, not that of a Louis-Antoine de Bougainville, for instance, an explorer describing the fauna of a tropical island. That is, he accepts (but revalues) the charge of "exoticism," acknowledging that to defamiliarize the landscape, to remove it from the discourse of tourist pamphlets and restore it to science, is a way to establish its singularity so that it might be seized and valued anew.[38] The scientific lexicon of botany, although it certainly seizes or "enframes" the plant in a rationalizing system, does not necessarily prepare it for exploitation ("commandeering it into assured availability").[39] In a startling reversal of circumstances, it is the scientific (and, previously, the colonial) discourse that accomplishes this revaluation; the botanical lexicon remains more closely allied to the local or, as we shall see, to the global history hidden beneath the local.

Of course, Césaire cannot be sure that a Martiniquan would recognize the curious botanical terms that he embeds in the poem, such as "en cuscute" or "en porana." Neither is it clear that an inhabitant of Martinique would be able to identify an "arganier." Césaire's explanation of his use of "precise" names is illuminating to a certain extent, but there is difference he does not register between calling a plant a "canéfice" (*canafistula*) and calling it a "cassier" or "casse" (drumstick tree). In the first case, the poet names a "Martiniquan thing" with its generic botanical name; in the second, a more colloquial designation conjures up a history of recent observation and cultural use. Similarly, in "Calendrier lagunaire," Césaire could have employed the local term "bois-fer" or "bois fè" rather than the more technical "arganier," thereby reducing the exoticism of the allusion. But the poet seems purposely to seek out the exotic, "the astonishing." He opts for the term that would be as unfamiliar to Martiniquans as it would be to the French. Therefore, choosing the designation "arganier" can have little to do with a desire to evoke a Martiniquan's intimacy with her own island. The "value" of which Césaire speaks is an equivocal one ("I believe I am recovering for the object its singular value"). What does Césaire mean by "singular value" and what does it have to do with dwelling in a Martiniquan landscape? How do his technical, erudite, and sometimes archaic names bring Martiniquans "nearer" to their environment? How does his poetry help them "listen"? "Listen" to what?

There are at least two ways in which Césaire's allusion to "value" can be interpreted in this context. First, "value" can be understood as the generic value accorded to an element of landscape from the perspective of a botanist. A precise botanical vocabulary determines the "value" of the plant by finding a place for it in a binomial taxonomy of genetic inheritance and relation. "Binomial nomenclature" is a product of the eighteenth-century rationalization of nature, an Ur-case of what Michel Foucault describes in *Les mots et les choses* as a shift from the episteme of "Représenter" to the episteme of "Classer."[40] In this shift, the science of natural history replaces a descriptive language saturated with opinion, anecdote, and observation with designations that have nothing to do with the plant itself and thus are (supposedly) neutral and timeless. In binomial nomenclature, the first term of the name is the generic name of the plant; it names this plant forever, and is forever applicable to it, no matter what new properties—chemical, medicinal, or ritual—are attributed to it over time.[41] Paramount in the classificatory system devised by the Swedish botanist and physician Carl Linnaeus (in *Systema naturae* of 1735) is the attribution to the plant of a class identified by means of visual discrimination.[42] Eschewing the cultural history of plants—at least for the sake of designation—Linnaeus's system imposes a two-word name "consisting of a generic name followed by a one-word specific epithet."[43] In this case, the "singular value" of the plant would be, quite simply, its discovery as a genetic variant, its differentiation as a species to be set aside from any other by an act of trained discrimination.[44] The gaze that discriminates one plant species from another, that classifies it, names it, and enters it into a taxonomy, is one that renders the plant available not for quotidian use but rather for scientific understanding.

Cesaire's fascination with botanical nomenclatures suggests that he privileges the scientific designations of Martiniquan flora and fauna over popular names. In the context of neocolonial Martinique, these designations ("canafistula" and "cecropias," for instance) serve a purpose beyond that of drawing attention to laws of vegetal heredity, for instance. When used in a poem, they lend a particular value to the Martiniquan biosphere by placing it in the larger context of scientific rationalization, which is charged with integrating all systems of life regardless of their geographical or cultural (or "racial") context. Paradoxically, it is only by naming the specific in a universal language that a thing may be celebrated for its unique qualities, its "singular value." The "recentering" Césaire is interested in, then, has to do with the recentering of the island of Martinique in the global imaginary; he wants Martinique to be revealed not as periphery but as center—that is, as the origin of an ecosystem acknowledged throughout the world for its richness and diversity. "Gratitude is due to Henri Stéhlé," writes Césaire in an unpublished homage to the botanist who centered his research on the Caribbean—the botanist he published in *Tropiques*—"for having contributed more than any other scholar to making our small country [*notre très petit pays*] known throughout the entire world"; "We thank him for helping us to take the full measure of our humanity."[45]

Insofar as Césaire intends the botanical terms he employs to evoke in the reader's mind a particular landscape, he can be considered to rely on a traditional poetics of reference. Césaire wants us to see *through* the word to a "Martiniquan thing." However, at other times, he asks us to appreciate names not as referents but rather as clusters of phonemes; he thereby releases them from their referential obligations so they can engender sound patterns in verse (as in "un culte désaffécté entre bulbe et caïeu"). For the most part, though, whether he designates his local surroundings with contemporary French, Creole, or Latin terms, his basic premise is that names remain legible as classifications, not as proper names for singular entities. And this emphasis on generic phenomena in particular—the general class of *Cecropia* not that particular *Cecropia peltata* growing on *that* spot—is important to note. He clearly prefers generic names and therefore could be said to be speaking—despite his assertion to the contrary—in "abstract" terms about a concrete place. ("We did not want to put together a journal of *abstract* culture; rather, we wanted as much as possible to apprehend *Martiniquan* reality in its *Martinique* context—to situate it precisely."[46]) Or, to put it differently, the concretion he seeks is not the concretion of the thing in itself, *that* "arganier," the deictic particular. In fact, Césaire is perhaps the least "deictic" poet of the Caribbean. Even Saint-John Perse hopes we will see in the botanical term "*abutilons*" the decorative plant growing right there beside *his* veranda.[47] Césaire, in contrast, reaches for the *regional*, not the autobiographical. He wishes to employ names—whether descended from *béké* Creole or Linneas's Greek—to refer to species and formations peculiar to the island on which he was born ("the Martiniquan *context*"). What matters first and foremost is that the name, with its specificity, helps to build the sense a Martiniquan might have of being at the center of her own world ("*se recentrer*")—or, quite simply, of *having* a world. In the interview with Jacqueline Leiner, Césaire acknowledges the connection in his mind between the emergence of a Martiniquan self-consciousness and a greater appreciation for the specificity—through naming—of the place where one lives:

> We thought such a program [undertaken by *Tropiques*] might help Martiniquans to acquire a certain consciousness of themselves [*une certaine conscience d'eux-mêmes*]. To produce articles on local flora and fauna we called on people we had close at hand—and they were by no means surrealists. From a noted scholar, Father Pinchon, I requested a study on fauna, and from another, Sthélé [sic], a study of flora.[48]

We have been taught by earlier critics that the early "prise de conscience" promoted by Negritude relied upon the emergence of black internationalism, Pan-African solidarity, and a diasporic sense of displacement that focused entirely on what had been lost (Africa), not on what was already there. But it is clear that in 1941, when *Tropiques* published Stéhlé's "La végétation des Antilles françaises," the poet was already resolved to consider identity intimately intertwined with an ecological as well as a social milieu. If, in the mind of the colonial imaginary, Martinique was associated with monocultural sugarcane or banana production, it would be liberating to contradict that imaginary and to assert the richness and diversity with which the Martiniquan people were already, at least in part, familiar. Poetic naming would be a way to see, to take note of, and to celebrate the immense diversity hidden under the mantle of monocultural production. Moreover, discerning an even greater number of species and learning their generic names would be part of the epistemological and political project of recapturing the lost history of exploration and occupation, displacement and cultivation, singular to the region. Césaire instinctually seized this possibility: that a story of the Martiniquan people and their island was lodged within these names.[49]

A CRITICAL REGIONALISM

There was, in fact, very little in Césaire's literary background—except, perhaps, his knowledge of Lautréamont—that could have inspired his interest in the technical, generic designations of things.[50] Why, then, did he believe that such designations might lead to a greater consciousness, a recentering of the Martiniquan self?

To answer this question it is necessary to consider the context for Césaire's appreciation of Stéhlé's work. Earlier critics have observed Césaire's predilection for complex plant imagery, his mapping of a vegetal order onto the order of the human; however, the presence of Henri Stéhlé in *Tropiques* and the import of ethnobotany elsewhere in his work have largely been ignored. Césaire's exposure to ethnobotany as a potentially subversive discipline began early on, during his years at the Lycée Schoelcher in Fort-de-France. Up until the 1960s Martinique's primary and secondary schools employed textbooks produced exclusively in France for French schoolchildren.[51] As is well known, young blacks in the colonies were required to recite the same absurd platitudes as students in the *métropole* (such as the infamous "Nos ancêtres les gaulois"). Official history books as well as geography and science texts all focused on Europe, thereby limiting the student's awareness of plants and climates to those of different and far-off continents. But Césaire was privileged to have at the Lycée Schoelcher a professor of natural sciences, Eugène Révert, who was at the time compiling evidence for his doctoral thesis on the flora and fauna of the Antilles, *La Martinique: Étude géographique* (published in 1947). As Eshleman and Smith underscore in their introduction, Révert's intervention was crucial: "The abundance of Martinican fauna and flora" appearing in Césaire's poetry "probably has as its first cause" the influence of Révert; "he taught geography and attempted to interest his students in the peculiar geographical characteristics of Martinique at a time when standard examination questions were based on mainland French history and geography."[52]

To teach local geography and regional botany was at the time a revolutionary gesture—and Césaire seized this fact right away. It was a stab in the back of the colonial regime that wished Martinique to exist only in the form in which the rulers had defined it: as a territory to be made, not known. Any reminder of the specificity of the Caribbean ecosystem worked against the policy of "assimilation," which was intended to transform blacks, mulattos, Indians, Chinese, and Syrians into universal Frenchmen, sharing a single culture and, paradoxically, a single geography. The last thing the assimilationist project aimed to provide was an "authentic" language through which to inhabit a specifically Caribbean space. Césaire's interest in botany—introduced first in Révert's classroom—grew from his apprehension that something radical and contestatory was contained in the project of identifying, studying, naming, and classifying the genii and species of Martinique.

When Henri Stéhlé arrived in Guadeloupe from Montpellier in 1934, he immediately established himself as an important successor to Révert, holding a post at the Services Techniques et Scientifiques de l'Agriculture and publishing an exhaustive study of the flora of Guadeloupe two years later. In 1938 he was named the director of the Tivoli Experimental Garden in Fort-de-France, after which he established the first accredited schools of agriculture in the Caribbean (at Tivoli and Pointe-à-Pitre). Between 1939 and 1946 Stéhlé collected samples of over eight thousand regional species, identifying hundreds of new genii of flowering plants. If the editors of *Tropiques* wished to find an expert on the ecology and agricultural history of the archipelago, they could do no better than to invite the participation of Stéhlé, who, like them, continued his meticulous work of consciousness-raising during the war-time years known colloquially as the "temps Robert."[53]

The first article Stéhlé contributed to *Tropiques* is fairly modest in its aspirations. Sandwiched between J. Chambon's essay on the spiritual exercises of the yogi and an announcement of Breton's passage through Fort-de-France, Stéhlé's "La végétation des Antilles françaises" attempts to establish an account of Martinique's multilayered history through a description of "degraded" virgin forests and complexly articulated "jardins créoles."[54] His description reads like a virtual roadmap for the approach to the Caribbean that would soon be favored by advocates of Créolité. He states, for instance, that one must "leave behind the established roads and settlements" in order to discover in the "forest paths" a world of "robust vegetation." Once removed from the domination of a single history, a single road, one would find, he assures his reader, a multiplicity of strata, each one "rich in species of every category."[55] Presaging the interest the *créolistes* would take in individual inventiveness, he notes how the "jardin créole" gathers together a wide variety of heterogeneous plants, "each one as useful as the next for alimentary and medicinal purposes."[56] Stéhlé then makes three further points that were formative for Césaire. First, he underscores the diversity of species that can only be found in the region of Martinique. Next, he acknowledges the degree to which all nature in Martinique is in fact culture, arguing that the only virgin forest remaining on the island extends between the towns of Céron and Grand-Rivière (both on the northern coast). Finally, he asserts what he calls the "liens étroits," or tight bonds, that exist between "man and vegetation," adding that if the latter has a profound influence on the former, the opposite is true as well. The article ends with an equivocal portrait of the "enchanted islands" as an "admirable synthesis of the Metropole's past and that of the most diverse countries found on far-off continents [Africa and India]."[57] But this seemingly forced celebration of colonialism ("admirable synthesis") is countered by frequent allusions to the destruction of "the primitive [virgin] forests of the French Antilles" by the sugar, then banana, then coffee, then coconut plantations. The "admirable synthesis" is the result, as Stéhlé puts it, of "the intensive activity of man."[58]

Whatever Stéhlé's true attitude toward Empire might have been, he provides Césaire with a starting point for seizing the Caribbean landscape as saturated with history and rich with opportunities for the anchoring of local identity not in the far-off land of the Gaules but in the proximate and nourishing diversity of "Martiniquan things." In his next contribution to *Tropiques*, titled "Les dénominations génériques des végétaux aux Antilles françaises: Histoires et légendes qui s'y attachent," Stéhlé presents a convincing case that the generic (and species) names accorded to flora and fauna embed both a folklore and a rich historical narrative of the islands. Published in February of 1944, "Les dénominations génériques" adds to Stéhlé's earlier appreciation of the landscape an account of the process by which this landscape enters (and produces) language. His opening sentence demonstrates an awareness that the signifiers themselves tell a story as complex as the genetic constitution of the plants. "That it is necessary to identify the vegetal kingdom with names . . . was so evident to man from the beginning that plant designations actually meld into the language of peoples: to tell their story [the story of plant designations] is to retrace the folklore of humanity."[59] Stéhlé's understanding of nomenclature is actually in stark conflict with that of Linnaeus, who liked to name plant species after the names of the famous white European males who "discovered" them. In fact, Linnaeus was responsible for banishing from the botanical nomenclature of the Caribbean many plant names derived from what he considered to be "barbarous" Amerindian languages.[60] One might argue that the names of these European males—their botanical work facilitated by the voyages of Empire—constitute a part of the history of the island evoked through plants. But Stéhlé is more interested in the generic designations that encode local history, those few that remain despite Linnaeus's effort to stamp them out. Lamenting that "in general, [the] replacement of [indigenous names] by 'creole' names has been almost complete," he then goes on to enumerate the few cases in which names derived from African languages still designate Caribbean varieties.[61] He also observes cases where Hindu names have inserted themselves into both everyday and taxonomic registers. But "the majority" of names, he insists, reflect "the science of the first European colonists to arrive on the islands." Unfortunately, he observes, "the widespread substitution of creole names for autochthonous or other imported ones is such that the influence of European civilization masks all remainders of African or Asiatic influence."[62]

One might conclude from Stéhlé's remarks that European languages covered over any history of observation and discrimination that might have remained. The unique perspective of those who arguably lived in closest contact with the givens of the island was erased from the face of the planet. But, counter to our expectations, Stéhlé introduces a curious fact. While it is true that Europeans imposed nomenclatures that reflected their own experience of the region (rather than that of the Pre-Colombians), that is not the whole story. The first colonizers included "men of science" (*savants*) whose training taught them both to observe specific differences and to search for names that could capture the circumstances in which they were discovered. By a remarkable "coincidence," as Stéhlé puts it, Linnaeas's somewhat unfaithful follower, Jean-Baptiste Christophore Fusée Aublet, who collected a large number of samples from the Caribbean region, chose to use designations "dominated by Carib names."[63] Thus, some of the words used by Carib and Arawak peoples (and thus their observations) are actually conserved in botanical nomenclatures. Pre-Colombian names for plants of the Caribbean accordingly lend their "native flavor" to generic designations, writes Stéhlé, "infusing the discourse on this vegetation with the perfume of the archaic past."[64]

It turns out, then, that instead of suppressing a pre-Colombian past, botanical designations (in this case) preserved that past more faithfully than did the local Creole names, influenced as they often were by the overlay of the Norman, Celtic, and other dialects that were spoken in the Caribbean at the time.[65] As opposed to Linnaeus, who purposefully divorced plants from their local environment and conditions of use, the botanists of the Caribbean sought to recall an element of the plant's relation to a specific ecosystem or human habitus. Stéhlé notes that "many denominations evoke a habitat or a particular adaptation to a way of life. Plants that thrive in dry regions are represented by *Philoxéros* (to love the dry); the *amarante bord-de-mer* (the amaranth beside the sea), familiar to Caribbean fisherman, as well as the *amies des pierres* (friends of the rock) are both known as *Lithophila* (rock lovers)"; finally, *Philodendron* (Greek for "fond of trees") is the generic domination for plants that "grow beside trees and climb up to their highest branches."[66] Generic designations of a botanical nomenclature sometimes even evoke directly a context of human practice. To cite Stéhlé's example: the tree called the *catalpa*, or the "feuille Haiti" in Creole, is accorded by botanists the designation *Thespesia populnea*, thereby referencing through the Greek "*thespesios*" the fact that in the Hindu culture the Thespesia is a sacred tree. The botanical designation allows Stéhlé to recall that this tree "is always planted around the temples . . . and is the object of the greatest veneration," whereas the Creole name effaces the memory of the Hindu immigrants whose practice gave the tree its scientific name.[67]

The point here is not to determine which terms—Creole or Greek, colloquial or botanical—remain closer to a Caribbean way of being, or which ones safeguard more surely the specificity of a landscape and its relation to the human. No doubt there are ways in which all languages preserve—and betray—the human histories and natural properties that inspired them. Taxonomies, like poetic languages, sometimes function according to rules of relation that have little to do with the need to reference an existential condition.[68] It is possible, then, that no one language has a greater purchase than any other on the lived reality of an island. It is not clear that poetic speech (*pace* Heidegger) helps us "listen" to the "call" of the world any better than the taxonomic, systematizing, and rationalizing lexicons of the Enlightenment pursuit. In "Calendrier lagunaire," Césaire demonstrates his understanding that the project of naming is indeed an ambiguous one, and that "recentering" through naming might be achieved—and frustrated—in a variety of ways. He therefore employs a multiplicity of strategies to direct his readers toward the particularity of Martinique. He evokes elements of the landscape with colloquial terms, such as "piton," for instance. The "pis du piton le plus sec" would conjure forth for an inhabitant of the island its unique geoclimate: after the eruption of Mont Pelée, a rain shadow was formed on the northeastern flank, creating arid conditions on the western side, or a "piton le plus sec." He also mobilizes arcane terms found in botanical treatises, such as the Arab-derived "cuscute" and the Norman-derived "caïeu." He does so not merely to show off his considerable erudition but, more important, to signal an awareness of the complex layering of languages and perspectives that have participated in the making of Martinique.[69] To the extent that Césaire uses names of local plants to evoke global forces—the traversing of Europe by Moors, the presence of Normans in the Caribbean—he practices what I would call, after Michael Davidson, a "critical regionalism." Treating Martinique as center, not periphery, Césaire takes a "microscopic look at the resilient flora and fauna" to offer "not an isolationist's remove from [global] events but a lens to see the impact of those events on a single area."[70] Anticipating the work of Édouard Glissant, Césaire underscores "the inextricable connection between the political and the natural landscape."[71] He exposes the global underpinnings of "local color."

Each word Césaire uses promises either to conjure forth for the reader a precise element of the region's landscape or to provide access to the colonial history of the region's multiple occupations.[72] But who is the ideal reader for Césaire? Who could possibly decipher all the allusions embedded in the names? Whose library would contain the scholarly tomes necessary to track down the meanings and origins of all his words?

In conclusion I would like to propose that decoding the hidden significance of the name is perhaps not the only, or even the most important, way in which that name allows readers to "inhabit" the Caribbean. Perhaps the name, even when the meaning and the context have been forgotten, does another kind of recentering work. If we return to the "Discours d'inauguration de la Rue Henri Stéhlé," a text I have cited several times in passing, we find Césaire's ultimate explanation for his fascination with exotic scientific lexicons and archaic terms. His comments are revealing, for they suggest that an interest in naming may have less to do with aiding our habitation in landscape than in facilitating our habitation in language as a kind of site in itself. In the "Discours d'inauguration," after praising Stéhlé's achievements, Césaire turns to his own personal response to the botanist who "helped us know ourselves better, to take the full measure of our humanity."[73] "I always thought that Stéhlé himself, Stéhlé the great *savant*, invited us to go beyond science," writes Césaire; he had "a gift for being amazed" and was capable of "flights of lyricism."[74] Unable to "resist the pleasure of citing him," Césaire then proceeds to enumerate some of Stéhlé's more remarkable verbal performances:

> . . . l'empâtement anfractueux et cloisonné de l'acomat-boucan . . .
> . . . les contreforts digitiformes du gommier dacryodes . . .
> . . . les racines aériennes (arc, échasses, béquilles) de telle clusiacée:
> la symphonia globulifera . . . [75]

Need I translate these clotted, juicy, tongue-twisting lines? Or are we in contact here with something untranslatable and irreducible, something that has little to do with what these words might denote (the Caribbean flora and fauna) or what they might indirectly recall (the Caribbean past)? Could it be that Césaire is simply pleasuring in the sound of these words, in their percussive patterns rendered even more piquant by an awareness that they do in fact name something empirically real? Here, as elsewhere in his poetry, Césaire is exhibiting his *gourmandise*, his ability to savor the flavor not simply of spoken words but more precisely of the grapholect, words drawn from the repertoire of the written. His global vocabulary can be explained at least in part, then, by his taste for diversity *in writing* as well as diversity in the cultural and ethnic sphere. From this perspective, all terms are "necessary," as Césaire concludes, "not gratuitous" insofar as they produce a soundscape, a verbal "*mascaret*," a rushing roar. At the same time, though, the provenance of the words does matter; not any words, no matter how exotic, will do. They must still name "Martiniquan things" and they must do so with the words of the victims and the conquerors, the invaders and the migrants, following one after the other like waves.

It is this premonition that the poem contains a buried treasure in its soundscape that lends the poem its abyssal depth, its reverberating tone. Ultimately, the ideal reader is precisely the one who cannot fill in all the gaps, the reader for whom some lexical items remain empty strings of consonants and vowels. The title "Calendrier lagunaire" itself names a poem that would preserve an empty space, that would speak for the matter—the verbal matter, or the matter of blood—that can never thoroughly yield sense. Perhaps that is why Césaire thought that "Calendrier lagunaire" would be the appropriate poem to engrave on his tomb. Surrounded by more legible songs of mourning, it provides an appropriate language of absence, of letters and loss. It turns us toward that language of (potentially) empty letters as though toward a "formule magique" or "blessure sacrée."

Césaire is thus succumbing to several impulses at once. He wants his names to be incantatory and indexical; they are meant to anchor his descriptions, to locate the speaker (and reader) at a specific spot on the globe. He also wants his names to be identifiable, even classifiable, *as names*; they should reference, in other words, the naming function, the circumstances of the act of naming. He selects names that tell a story of Empire, that reveal the intrusion of epistemologies, taxonomies, and discriminations coming from other shores. Finally, he multiplies the sites of obscurity in his poem, inviting us in this way to listen to the sound (and observe the shapes) of language in writing. The unyielding substance of his words provides an "espace inexploité" ("unexploited space"), serving as a block to full comprehension, forcing gaps and producing wounds. In the end, it is these wounds in the fabric of meaning that outline a place in which to dwell.

Here, lyric obscurity, as Daniel Tiffany has suggested, prefigures a community yet to come. One of the "manifold tasks of obscurity," Tiffany writes, "is to found a community that recognizes itself in the necessity of creating a secret language."[76] In response to critics of Césaire's hermetic exoticism one might reply: "Obscurity, rather than being the principal impediment to poetry's social relevance, would provide the key to models of community derived specifically from the nature of lyric expression."[77] From this perspective, Césaire's poem can be seen as an example of avant-garde mourning. It resists the temptation to define either the self or the community as linguistically, racially, or even geographically self-identical ("chaque minute je change d'appartement"), offering writing instead as the "espace inexploité" where the treasures of subjectivity may reside.

CONCLUSION

In the previous chapter, I suggested that Césaire was able to find a way to make his poetry matter—both in local and global contexts—despite the complexity of its figures and lexical content. "Calendrier lagunaire," the poem inscribed on Césaire's tomb, clearly has a meaning for the local population of Martinique, many of whose members regularly visit the grave. There exist, however, many interpretative communities for any given poem, each of which is based on a different assumption—for instance, that the poem contains a secret language available only to initiates (as Daniel Tiffany has suggested), or that it establishes an intimate relation between speaker and reader, paradoxically available to all. In the case of "Calendrier lagunaire," the multiplicity of languages evoked and the quantity of connotative networks established seem to serve as solicitations to the reader; it is as though we were being invited to enter the poem to find our own space in which to dwell.

A number of the poem's references may, however, always remain opaque. The language of Césaire's poetry is rich enough to inspire a wide variety of interpretations, leading readers—as I suggested in chapters 5 and 6—toward far-flung contexts by circuitous routes. Some allusions may only be grasped by other inhabitants of the region, those who share Césaire's landscape and who discern the rhythms of their speech in his writing or recognize a Creole proverb beneath (what appears to be) a hermetic metaphor. Yet other references in the poetry will be available uniquely to specialized scholars, those who are interested in tracing the derivations of Césaire's words with etymological dictionaries in hand. When approached from a global perspective, a poem like "Calendrier lagunaire" seems to resonate in limitless ways. Examined through what Jessica Berman calls a "transnational optic," it offers a revelation of the history not only of the Caribbean but also of the connection of non-Caribbeans to that history.[1] In words derived from Arabic or Norman, Greek or Arawak, we find the sedimented traces of multiple migrations, both forced and elective, that contribute to the lexical density of the poem—not to mention the cultural density of our present moment. Both as an inventory of local fauna and flora and as a register of successive invasions, expeditions, and colonial regimes, the poem can serve as the island's memory, a verbal tomb in itself, encapsulating in fifty-four lines innumerable lives.

Literary critics often weight poetry with a mnemonic function, arguing that poetry accomplishes a cultural (even ethical) task when it commemorates important events, recalls through its meter a long national tradition, or draws attention to its language as a palimpsest of vernaculars and roots. Recently Laura Doyle has refreshed our notion of poetry as a form of cultural memory, observing as she presents a new paradigm for modernism studies that literature in general may "*carry the intercultural accretions of empires past.*"[2] Some of these accretions, I have suggested, may be found embedded in lexemes; as "Calendrier lagunaire" makes evident, names ("dénominations"), once treated as historical objects, can index the various events that brought them to the region. Other accretions, it is worth noting, may be embedded in formal features; such is the case in the poems I have studied by Damas, poems like "Solde" or "Fragment" in which multiple traditions of poetic writing (or "rhetorical rhythms") are referenced through prosodic and typographical features. Césaire and Damas make a particularly strong case for considering the poetic text as a heterogeneous surface, the result of accumulating and mutually informing cultural and linguistic elements. Negritude, as a movement born of multiple invasions and imperial histories (the French, British, Dutch) and migrations (Arawak, Carib, Tamil), is an exemplary "geomodernism," Doyle's term for a modern literature that responds to "transperipheral and international exchanges."[3] Negritude poems, like the works Doyle is discussing, may allow us—when viewed in the proper light—to reflect on "the long global history that has prepared their emergence."[4]

Fed by tributaries from African, African American, Caribbean, and French traditions, Negritude authors "*labor in the volatile space between or among contemporaneous empires.*"[5] Thus one of the (many) tasks of the reader of a Negritude poem is to grasp the history of the empire(s) that its languages and modes of fabrication may recall or "carry" (they "carry the intercultural accretions of empires past"[6]). To examine that freight is, on the part of the reader, to engage in a critical archeology, to sift through the author's formal and lexical choices in search of the "long global history" these choices evoke. I would characterize this close attention to the marks on the page—the choice of the word but also its placement—as a variety of political work. If such attention helps to impede the erasure of imperial gestures, then the formal analysis of poetry leads us toward, not away from, the reality of the past.

But who, precisely, embeds the words in the poem that "carry the intercultural accretions of empires past"?[7] Who is responsible for "carrying" that freight? Have we returned here to an account of writing as author-centered, an account in which an empirical subject makes conscious, intentional decisions that determine which words will be used to recall which "transperipheral and international exchanges"?[8] Does the new modernist studies paradigm that Doyle advocates merely redirect the agency of the author from the project of self-expression (identified with the lyric) to the project of rememoration (identified now with the modernist text)?

I think not. The value of Doyle's perspective is that it suggests a way out of the author-centered discourse (emphasizing the author's putative intentions or message) while leaving room for the poem to express something singular about the author in a particular space and time. It is the words in the poem that transmit the "intercultural accretions," and those words and their sequencing emerge in the way they do for a wide variety of reasons. That is, the poem results from a concatenation of forces, forces that interact and join to produce (our sense of) the text. Theodor Adorno calls this concatenation "the genial knot," indicating thereby that "genius" is not so much a person as a function.[9] The empirical subject is the living agent responsible for intercepting during moments of composition and revision the multiple forces operating at any given moment in history. Each element of the poem is capable of embedding an element of the past. Therefore, when Doyle writes that literature carries "intercultural accretions," we may imagine their presence to be due to any one of a number of factors. How could any author be entirely responsible for all the resonances (etymological, connotative, rhythmic, sensual) that her words produce?

The aesthetic subjectivity of the work is thus not equivalent to the "lyric I" who seems to speak in the poem; it is closer to the overall tone the reader thinks she hears when she reads. Aesthetic subjectivity is an entity far more vast than the localized empirical subject or author, who is traversed by forces of which she may be unaware. All writing is to some extent a form of ventriloquism, a lending of one's voice to historical, technological, and psychic forces. To Adorno's eyes, what makes a poem political is not so much its ostensive message, then, but the fact that it embeds deeper agencies in a way that can only be revealed by readers over time.

If we follow Adorno in distinguishing between the empirical person and the aesthetic subject, and between the intention of the author and the labor of craft, then we must be wary of any paradigm that neglects to consider the impact of craft-related decisions strictly internal to textual dynamics. The productive demands of the print media apparatus (the *dispositif* of the typosphere) as well as the sensual potentials of inscription—from graphemic and syllabic patterning to typographic layout, or *mise en page*—all impose their own restrictions and offer their own resources. The responsibility for what we judge to be the sedimented history or "intercultural accretions" embedded in the poem must be shared among three partners: the empirical author and her intentionality; the "ears" and "eyes" of the text, animated by a writer at a particular moment in the history of the genre and the medium; and the contemporary reader who lends the poem her own voice. Without an author there would be no writing, but without generic conventions, medium-specific restrictions, and readers in search of meanings, there would be no aesthetic subjectivity, no trace of history or technology—and thus: no poem at all.

"Although art in its innermost essence is a comportment," writes Adorno, "it cannot be isolated from expression, and there is no expression without a subject."[10] Negritude, to be sure, begins with the subject. The "sphere" of the individual is ultimately the space that must be preserved if any freedom is to be won. As long as the particular individual remains excluded from the "universal"—that is, as long as being black, subaltern, diasporic, queer, or resistant means that one's full rights are denied—then that particular individual becomes the bearer of society's (un)truth: "in this age of universal social repression, the picture of freedom against society lives in the crushed, abused individual's features alone."[11] Or, in the words of *Aesthetic Theory*: "As long as the particular and the universal diverge there is no freedom. Rather, freedom would secure for the subject the right that today manifests itself exclusively in the idiosyncratic compulsions that artists must obey."[12]

What Adorno means to say, I believe, is that writing—and creativity more generally—models a form of comportment that valorizes the "idiosyncratic compulsion," the urge (or motivation) that fails to conform to whatever appears rational, predetermined, and normative in a given case. Recast in Nathaniel Mackey's terms, we might say that writing reveals "the discrepancy between presumed norms and qualities of experience that such norms fail to accommodate."[13] It is these "qualities of experience" that the experimental poem attempts to voice not by describing them but by capturing their rhythm, their tone, with the means—inscriptive, typographic, syllabic, alphabetic—at hand.

The living subject does not have to disappear in this materialist account. Her implication in the aesthetic subjectivity of the artwork can still be assumed: "Whoever resists the overwhelming collective force in order to insist on the passage of art through the subject, need on no account at the same time think underneath the veil of subjectivism," Adorno reassures us.[14] It isn't necessary, in other words, to fall back on the intentional fallacy, on the theory of an expressive lyric subject ("the veil of subjectivism"), to acknowledge that a living subject is indeed the agent that "comports" herself in an aesthetic manner. It is a living agent who passes the materials of art through her very being and thereby redirects them toward new functions. "Aesthetic autonomy"—Adorno might just as well have written "aesthetic subjectivity"—"encompasses what is collectively most advanced, what has escaped the spell."[15] Paradoxically, the poem captures what is most "advanced" or progressive in the collective means and technologies of the time in order to turn those means and technologies against that which is most mystified and regressive in the "overwhelming collective force," the compulsion of the norm.[16]

THE POLITICS OF POETRY

In their own sphere (the sphere of the literary) and in their own way, the poems of Negritude bring to the fore what is most "advanced" about modernist print culture: its potential to articulate difference, to give voice to a "blackness" that is not the norm. Negritude, as Christopher Miller has suggested, may not be political or operational in the same way as overtly political organizations of the time were, but Negritude was political in its own way—a point that may require clarification. The militant syndicalist organizations that Miller champions, such as the Comité de Défense de la Race Nègre (CDRN, founded by Lamine Senghor a few years before Césaire and Damas arrived in Paris), were certainly less poetic and more direct in their anti-imperialist demands.[17] The CDRN may very well have produced more measurable effects during the interwar period than the publications of Negritude writers, no matter how radical they seemed in the literary context. Miller has gone so far as to state that the advent of Negritude spelled "the demise of radicalism," consigning to oblivion "a generation of far more radical thinkers and activists."[18] Certainly, Negritude was not the only black movement in France to advance a protest against imperialism, and authors like Miller and Philippe Dewitte have helped us to situate Negritude's political intervention within the broader spectrum to which the CDRN belonged.[19] Nonetheless, it must be acknowledged that poetry circulates in a realm distinct from that of a newspaper or official party organ. That is, the discursive and mediological register in which activists like Lamine Senghor expressed themselves is quite different from that of Léon Damas's *Pigments*, Aimé Césaire's *Cahier d'un retour au pays natal*, or Léopold Sédar Senghor's *Hostie noire*. As opposed to the protest declared in a news organ, the poetry volume draws attention to its own language and even to the medium (the printed word) in which that language is disseminated.[20] Miller bases his contention that the CDRN was a more radical expression of black revolt on his observation that the discourse of *La Voix des Nègres* is less diluted by complex imagery and intertextual associations. It is the "lack of literary pretension" on the part of Lamine (a distant cousin of Léopold Sédar), Miller contends, that made his "radical critique of France" possible: "writers who were less elite and less aesthetically sophisticated were less indebted to the French system."[21]

Yet, as I have argued, all language—whether poetic or journalistic—relies on metaphors, rhetorical constructions, typographic emphasis, and the force of alliteration. Poetry encourages us to recognize these medialogical crossovers and interpenetrations in a way that an article like "Le mot nègre" (published in *La Voix des Nègres*) does not. Ultimately, the effect a poem has may depend in large part on the way it is read, the context and protocols of its reception. To modify my earlier statement, then, it is not that Negritude poets made a difference only in "their own sphere," namely, the sphere of modernist literary production. Negritude poets made a difference far beyond the sphere of the literary (the borders of which may be highly unstable). It does not seem accurate to claim, as does Peter Hallward (echoing Alain Badiou) that literature and politics function in two utterly discrete ontological and epistemological registers.[22] Rather, the truth of the matter may be that literary works exert a force beyond their own sphere but not in ways we can always anticipate—and they do so because their conditions of reception change.

The year 1998 was a turning point for francophone postcolonial studies: it was the year in which Miller's highly influential *Nationalists and Nomads: Essays on Francophone Literature and Culture* and J. Michael Dash's equally influential *The Other America: Caribbean Literature in a New World Context* both appeared. While it would be an overstatement to say that these two works alone altered our protocols of reading, it is clear that they helped produce a sea change, leading us further away from formalist and deconstructive styles of reading toward what many consider to be more contextualized, historical, and ethnographic modes. One effect of this sea change is that the locus of the political has been situated more frequently in narrative than poetic texts. In this book, I have not tried to turn back the clock, to return to modes of reading that may have tended to neglect historical context; rather, I have sought to question where that historical context should be located. I have developed strategies of reading that combine close analysis of the written text with biographical and historical scholarship. The category of the "aesthetic subject" has been deployed to preserve a distinction between the living author (and the collective he claims to represent) and the lyric "I" who claims responsibility for the language of the poem. I believe this distinction to be fundamental to critical work.

My assertion that the category of the "aesthetic subject" is critical, that it ultimately works in the service of freedom, may result from my own training and background. That is, I believe that Negritude poems are political—that they helped to forge change—because of the context in which I first read them. This reception context was entirely different from the one that holds sway in the academy today. In conclusion, I want to turn to that context not to stage an autobiographical moment but instead to indicate an alternative "positioning that makes meaning possible," to quote Stuart Hall's phrase once again.[23]

The reason I find most current accounts of Negritude (as "universalizing," "elitist," or colonial[24]) to be profoundly inaccurate is that I was first exposed to Negritude at the tail end of the period we call "the '60s," when poetry was the genre most closely associated with the impulse of emancipation. That is, the reception conditions that framed my first reading prepared me to interpret Negritude as a militant movement and the *Cahier* as a militant work. In 1976 my high school English teacher, Frank Banton, presciently assigned the senior class Césaire's *Cahier* in the important—and inflammatory—1969 English translation. The translators, John Berger and Anna Bostock, had rebaptized the volume *Return to My Native Land*, thereby suppressing the vital term "Notebook."[25] This edition contains a fiery preface by Mazisi Kunene, the South African poet who published both in Zulu and English. At the time, Kunene was a representative for the African National Congress, living in exile from South Africa and agitating against apartheid. A preface by Kunene would have placed Césaire squarely at the center of the most militant struggles against colonial oppression abroad and racist discrimination at home. The fact that Kunene makes no allusion to the *Cahier*'s original composition in French shows that it was taken for granted by the 1960s generation that publishing in colonial languages was an astute strategic move, necessary for the global transmission of a local (but shared) message.[26]

I remember that what struck me most about Kunene's preface—and colored my first experience of the poem—was his discussion of Eldridge Cleaver's *Soul on Ice* (published in 1967). Kunene brought Césaire's work into comparison with Cleaver's on the grounds that both were mobilizing violence in a homeopathic manner, attempting to turn the violence of colonialism against the colonizer himself. This was the period when the Black Panthers, inspired in part by that famously faulty 1967 English translation of Frantz Fanon's *Black Skin, White Masks*, were gaining momentum for their overtly combative alternative to the ethos of Martin Luther King Jr. Black Nationalists like Cleaver advocated violence as a privileged means of activism while simultaneously promoting a cultural politics that invested heavily in the poetic genre. In *Soul on Ice*, Cleaver, the "minister of information" for the Black Panthers, speaks admiringly of Césaire as "the big gun from Martinique."[27] Defending the poet against the condescension shown to him by James Baldwin at the Congrès des écrivains et artistes noir (held in Paris in September of 1956), Cleaver writes that Césaire had "penetrated into the heart of the great wilderness which was Europe and stolen the sacred fire . . . that fire . . . *burns*."[28] An ambiguous literary figure, Cleaver had helped organize the Black House in San Francisco with poets Amiri Baraka and Sonia Sanchez during the late 1960s. Baraka, like Césaire and Cleaver, also held poetry in high esteem; experimental writing in general appeared to sustain the negativity of an anger directed against white cultural and political institutions alike. Before his arrest for carrying an illegal weapon in 1968, Baraka (LeRoi Jones until 1968) had formed the Umbra Poets Workshop along with Lorenzo Thomas and Ishmael Reed. Even as he represented one of the most militant strands of Marxist antiracism, Baraka read alongside poets like Larry Neal and Jay Wright at the St. Mark's Church Poetry Project, founded by Paul Blackburn in 1966.

Although I was too young to participate directly in this world, I felt its impact throughout the 1970s. The bookstores on 8th Street were full of slender volumes by Lucille Clifton, Nikki Giovanni, and June Jordan. Ntozake Shange's *For Colored Girls Who Have Considered Suicide When the Rainbow Is Enuf* was enjoying its first production as an off-Broadway play (1975). I learned subsequently that Shange herself had studied Negritude; she even wrote a paper titled "Negritude in Senghor, Césaire, & Damas" while completing her master's degree at the University of Southern California. (It apparently ended up in Damas's own hands.) This unpublished paper, which can be found in the Damas archives of the Schomburg Center for Research in Black Culture, captures the tenor of the time. Shange analyzes the poetry with sensitivity to alliteration and assonance (sometimes quoting the original French—which current scholars rarely do), arguing that Negritude was "essential to the development of black consciousness" because it praised the beauty of African culture while justifying the stirrings of black revolt.[29] When Shange was introduced to Negritude poetry in school, it was considered to be part of a violent yet literate reaction against racism, discrimination, segregation, and white supremacy.

Shange read Damas—and obviously had direct contact with him—during a period when Black Studies and African American studies departments were just beginning to be formed. Materials in the Damas archive suggest that throughout the 1970s the aging paternal figure associated with Pan-African movements in France was active in establishing the academic credentials of the first Africana and Black Studies departments in the United States.[30]

Figure 7.1 Group photo of Léon-Gontran Damas and African American intellectuals (left to right, top to bottom. [Unidentified], Ishmael Reed, Jayne Cortez, Léon-Gontran Damas, Romare Beardon, Larry Neal, Nikki Giovanni, and Evelyn Neal. Photographs and Prints Division, Schomburg Center for Research in Black Culture, The New York Public Library, Astor, Lenox, and Tilden Foundations.

Scholars of African American studies, postcolonial theory, and francophone studies owe a huge debt to the figures of Negritude whose tireless participation in colloquia and other scholarly projects made possible the existence of the very academic venues in which Negritude's putative "universalism" is now regularly attacked. Negritude poetry—as "symbolic capital" but also as a troubling, thought-provoking poetic movement—was central to producing the institutional spaces in which the question of the relation between radical politics and cultural expression can now be discussed.

While arguably not as militant as the members of the CDRN and the journalists of *La Voix des Nègres*, the Negritude poets clearly had a political impact that went well beyond the French readership of the 1930s and well beyond the walls of the academy. The *Cahier* did not on its own incite colonial subjects to revolt (although it was credited with stoking the fires of the African independence movements of the 1960s).[31] In essence, Negritude poetry accomplished that not-so-subtle work we used to call "consciousness raising." Thus, it could be said that Negritude constituted a "politics" in precisely the terms proposed by Jacques Rancière: the poetry of Negritude ushered in a new "distribution of the sensible" insofar as it permitted subaltern subjects, the offspring of slaves, to be "heard as speaking subjects." Negritude made "what was unseen visible" and "what was audible as mere noise heard as speech."[32] In short, Negritude allowed black poets to be full participants in what Rancière has called the "aesthetic regime." This "aesthetic regime" is a lyric regime, and the poetry of Negritude establishes itself solidly as a text-based (rather than oral) movement. Negritude poets not only adopted typographic innovations introduced by other writers; they also developed their own way of harnessing the resistant force that the printed word harbors in its material being. The poets of Negritude in this sense *raced textuality*. They drew on the complex specificities of their racialization under modern capitalism to exert pressure on thematic, lexical prosodic, typographical, and rhetorical norms.[33]

Poetry in print offers a plethora of ways to subvert norms of reading and interpretation. For this reason, it offers a support that is arguably more adequate than traditional narrative genres for engendering multiple enunciations of the "I," instantiations of subjectivity in writing that invite constant *re*-enunciation. Whereas all texts require "positioned" readings (we always read from some site), poems, especially experimental poems, suggest by their very hermeticism, complexity, and exuberant language use that each position we take, each meaning we find, each interpretation we develop is no more than a "contingent 'ending,'" a "temporary 'break,'" "the 'cut' of identity."[34] There is always something left unopened, a gap in our interpretation. "There is always something 'left over,'" as Stuart Hall remarks.[35] If a poem is like a person, then the aesthetic subjectivity of the poem is that person unbound. The "'cut' of identity" is one we make whenever we take a stand or make a reading. However, the richer the language of the poem—the more fully it explores its typographic, lexical, rhetorical, and phonic resources—the more likely it is to ambiguate and thus multiply its meanings and complicate the "identity" suggested by the poem's "I." In this light, the Negritude poem offers the promise of an identity that can be performed but will never resolve into essence, the promise of an identity that acts like a resistant force of "materiality as it plays itself out in/as the work of art."[36]

APPENDIX 1

ENGLISH TRANSLATION OF LÉON-GONTRAN DAMAS'S "HOQUET," BY CARRIE NOLAND

HICCUP

And try as I might to take seven sips of water
three to four times in twenty-four hours
my childhood comes back to me
in a hiccup that shakes up
my instinct
as the cop does the scamp

Disaster
tell me about disaster
tell me about it

My mother, wanting a son with good table manners
    Hands on the table
    bread is not to be cut
    bread is to be broken
    bread is not to be wasted
    the bread of God
    the bread of the sweat on your Father's brow
    the bread of the bread

A bone is eaten discretely and with care
a stomach must be sociable
and a sociable stomach
doesn't burp
a fork is not a toothpick
it is forbidden to wipe your nose
so others can see
so other can know
and sit up straight
a well-brought-up nose
doesn't sweep the plate

And then and then
and then in the name of the Father
of the Son
of the Holy Ghost
at the end of each meal

And then and then
and then disaster

tell me about disaster
tell me about it

My mother, wanting a son memorandum

If you don't know your history lesson
you can't go to church
Sunday
in your Sunday clothes

This child will bring shame to our name
this child will be our name of God

Be quiet
Haven't I told you to speak French?
the French of France

the French of the French
the French French

Disaster
tell me about disaster
tell me about it
My Mother, wanting a son
son of his mother

You haven't greeted the neighbor
your shoes are dirty again
and I have to find you in the street
on the grass or in the Savana
in the shade of a Monument for the Dead
playing
squabbling with some kid
with some kid who hasn't been baptized

Disaster
tell me about disaster
tell me about it
My mother, wanting a son very do
very ré
very mi
very fa
very sol
very la
very si
very do
ré-mi-fa
sol-la-si
do

I remember now you hadn't yet done
your vi-o-lin lesson
A banjo

You say a banjo
how do you say
a banjo
you did say
a banjo
No, sir
            you should know it's not tolerated in our home
neither ban
neither jo
neither gui
neither tar
the **mulattos** don't do that
leave it for the **negros**

APPENDIX 2

ENGLISH TRANSLATION OF AIMÉ CÉSAIRE'S "CALENDRIER LAGUNAIRE," BY CARRIE NOLAND

LAGOONAL CALENDAR

I inhabit a sacred wound
I inhabit imaginary ancestors
I inhabit an obscure desire
I inhabit a long silence
I inhabit an irremediable thirst
I inhabit a one-thousand-year journey
I inhabit a three-hundred-year war
I inhabit an abandoned cult
between bulb and bulbil I inhabit the unexploited space
I inhabit not a vein of the basalt
but the rising tide of lava
which runs at full pitch back up the gulch
to burn all the mosques
I accommodate myself as best I can to this avatar
to an absurdly botched version of paradise
—it is worse than hell—
I inhabit from time to time one of my wounds
each minute I change apartments
and all peace frightens me

whirlwind of fire
ascidium like none other to hold the dust of wandering worlds
having spat out the volcano my fresh-water entrails
I remain with my loaves of words and my secret minerals

I inhabit thus a vast thought
but mostly prefer to confine myself
to the littlest of my ideas
or I inhabit a magic formula
but only the first few words
the rest forgotten
I inhabit the ice jam
I inhabit the thaw
I inhabit the face of a great disaster
I inhabit the driest udder
of the most emanciated flank—the lever of these clouds—
I inhabit the halo of the Cactaceae
I inhabit a herd of goats pulling on the teat
of the most desolate argan tree
to tell you the truth I no longer know my correct address
bathyal or abyssal
I inhabit the hole of an octopus
I fight with the octopus over an octopus hole

brother don't insist
a mess of kelp
clinging like a parasite
or twining porana-like
it's all the same

        and let the wave toss
        and let the sun leech
        and let the wind whip
round hill of my nothingness

the atmospheric, no historic pressure
increases immeasurably my plight.
even as it charges with beauty my words

NOTES

INTRODUCTION

1. See Jean-Pierre Bobillot, "Naissance d'une notion: La médiopoétique," in *Poésies et médias XX–XXIe siècle*, ed. Céline Pardo, Anne Reverseau, Nadja Cohen, and Anneliese Depoux, 155–73 (Paris: Nouveau Monde, 2012). Elaborating on Régis Debray's *Cours de médiologie générale* (Paris: Gallimard, 1991), Bobillot distinguishes a "*médiologie*," a typology of supports (such as paper and pen or typewriter), from a "*médialogie*," a typology of modes of diffusion (such as print publication or the Internet). A "*poésie typosphérique*" is a poetry written to be published in print and read (166). On media specificity and the "alphabetic I" of lyric poetry, see also Brian Rotman, *Becoming Beside Ourselves: The Alphabet, Ghosts, and Distributed Human Being* (Durham, NC: Duke University Press, 2008).
2. See Ronnie Leah Scharfman, *Engagement and the Language of the Subject in the Poetry of Aimé Césaire* (Gainesville: University Presses of Florida, 1980).
3. In the "aesthetic regime," or "*le régime de l'écriture*," the word becomes detached from its context of utterance and addresses an unknown rather than immediate community. The text is "oublieuse de son origine, insouciante à l'égard de son destinataire." Jacques Rancière, *La parole muette: Essai sur les contradictions de la littérature* (Paris: Hachette,

1998), 82. I examine the implications of Rancière's model more fully in chapter 4.

4. On the birth of lyric poetry as "something essentially graphic," not oral, see Giorgio Agamben, "*Corn*: From Anatomy to Poetics," in *The End of the Poem: Studies in Poetics*, trans. Daniel Heller-Roazen (Stanford, CA: Stanford University Press, 1999), 33. Although this is not the place to enter into extended dialogue with Franco Moretti and his model of "distant reading," I would like to situate myself in the growing, neo-Darwinian field of literary studies that approaches the text as resulting from a battle to survive in a field of production that overdetermines its nature. The best riposte to this variety of criticism—which I consider to be an undialectical corrective to theories of authorial intentionality, is provided by Alexander Gil Fuentes in his doctoral dissertation, "Migrant Textuality": "I make the more radical claim that texts adapt by default. Put differently, no text (or literary device) ever *survives* a recontextualization intact, and vice-versa, no context remains intact." Gil Fuentes, "Migrant Textuality: On the Fields of Aimé Césaire's *Et les chiens se taisaient*" (Ph.D. diss., University of Virginia, December 2013), 62, available at *Academic Commons*, http://academiccommons.columbia.edu/catalog/ac:161180. As I will argue further in the following, the advantage of Adorno's notion of "aesthetic subjectivity" is that it offers a recursive, dialectical model of creation that takes into account both the pressure of material, economic forces and the force of the author's unique intervention in the field.

5. See Theodor Adorno, *Aesthetic Theory*, ed., trans. and intro. Robert Hullot-Kentor (Minneapolis: University of Minnesota Press, 1997), 167. Sometimes called an "artistic subject" or an "artistic identity," the "aesthetic subject" is a hybrid entity resulting from the dialectical engagement of a living writer with the demands of artistic production. I flesh out the concept of aesthetic subjectivity in chapter 1.

6. Virginia Jackson, *Dickinson's Misery: A Theory of Lyric Reading* (Princeton, NJ: Princeton University Press, 2005), 90. Jackson argues persuasively that "lyric reading" often neglects the production and reception conditions that shape our interpretation of the "I" in the poem and its relation to history.

7. As Françoise Vergès points out in the context of Frantz Fanon, many Antilleans (including the Negritude writers) are mulattos, or "black métis Creole of the French Antilles." Vergès, "Creole Skin, Black Mask:

Fanon and Disavowal," *Critical Inquiry*, 23, no. 3 (Spring 1997): 511. Damas had the lightest skin and thus was most easily identified as mulatto, not black, but this did not stop him from proclaiming his blackness as a politics and a history he shared with Césaire and Senghor. As many critics have observed, for Césaire, being black ("nègre") was primarily a cultural identity, whereas Senghor tended to associate blackness with racial identity.

8. Quoted in René Depestre, "An Interview with Aimé Césaire," in *Discourse on Colonialism*, trans. Joan Pinkham, ed. Robin Kelley, 79–94 (New York: Monthly Review Press, 2000), 83.
9. I would thus qualify Chris Bongie's contention that Édouard Glissant understands more clearly than Césaire the predicament of the Caribbean poet; both know that the attempt to "speak for" a people is problematized by the recourse to writing and the use of French. Bongie, *Islands and Exiles: The Creole Identities of Post/Colonial Literature* (Stanford, CA: Stanford University Press, 1998), 42–43.
10. Jacques Rancière, *Dissensus: On Politics and Aesthetics*, trans. Steve Corcoran (New York: Continuum, 2010), 137.
11. Ibid. Césaire's written gestures "isolate" him "from exactly that collectivity with which [he] yearns to identify," as Scharfman so precisely puts it. Scharfman, *Engagement*, 94.
12. Rancière is describing varieties of interpreting art, not what the art is in some essential, transhistorical sense.
13. Édouard Glissant, "Une errance enracinée," in *L'intention poétique* (Paris: Gallimard, 1990), 51. All translations are my own unless otherwise indicated. Glissant is writing here about Saint John Perse; he is contrasting the relation the *conteur créole* maintains with a live audience with the relation Perse maintains—or fails to maintain—with a specific community. Although it could be objected that the *conte créole* is a narrative form with more links to epic than lyric, Glissant is making a point about how the "I" form of Perse's poetry (which, like Césaire's *Cahier d'un retour au pays natal*, shares both lyric and epic attributes) abjures communion with a specific audience in order to achieve a greater communion with a universal body, or humanity in general. The case of Perse is not identical to that of Césaire, although both employ effects—an unusual lexicon and dense figuration—that distance them from the Antillean community.

14. Melvin Dixon, introduction to *The Collected Poetry*, by Léopold Sédar Senghor, trans. Melvin Dixon (Charlottesville: University Press of Virginia, 1998): "I am struck by the fact that the principal architects of negritude were primarily from the Western Hemisphere—not only Léon Damas and Aimé Césaire . . . but also Paulette and Jane Nardal and René Maran from the French Antilles and Claude McKay from Jamaica. . . . Perhaps this is one reason why so many African writers from Wole Soyinka of Nigeria to Ezekiel Mphahlele of South Africa have taken issue with Senghor" (xxix); "Senghor's poetic method depends on the otherness of his audience"(xxx).
15. Léopold Sédar Senghor, *Ce que je crois* (Paris: Grasset, 1988), 136.
16. See Susan Stewart, *Poetry and the Fate of the Senses* (Chicago: University of Chicago Press, 2002): "What might seem at first glance to be rule-governed behavior is in fact constantly in tension with the vital and ultimately inarticulate forces of pain and emotion that compel such expression. . . . Aesthetic form constantly is put under pressure to change and renew itself in order to accommodate what time and experience have brought to it" (328). For an equally compelling study, see Mutlu Konuk Blasing, *Lyric Poetry: The Pain and the Pleasure of Words* (Princeton, NJ: Princeton University Press, 2007): although the poem's "I" is, above all, "not to be confused with an extralinguistic entity," it is still the case, as Blasing argues further, that this "I" is one that "must be heard *as choosing words*, intending sounds to make sense. . . . The poem . . . is an act of intending to mean" (27, 29). For an alternative view, see Rei Terada's review, "Poetry and the Fate of the Senses," in *Comparative Literature* 56, no. 3 (2004): 269–74.
17. Stewart, *Poetry and the Fate of the Senses*, 328–29. The reaction against a deconstructive approach was launched by Walter Benn Michaels and Steven Knapp in "Against Theory" *Critical Inquiry* 8, no. 4 (Summer 1982): 723–42. Since then a generation of scholars in the United States—and, interestingly, France as well—has argued for a return if not to the artist's intention as the source of all meaning, then at least to an acknowledgment of the intersubjective (author–reader) relation implicit in reading. On the effacement of physical presence in the lyric, see Jackson, *Dickinson's Misery* and Amy Hungerford, *The Holocaust of Texts: Genocide, Literature, and Personification* (Chicago: University of Chicago Press, 2003). Hungerford argues that, whereas Paul de Man

"sees personhood as the product of rhetoric," personhood should be seen "as the product of rhetoric plus embodiment" (63); "the conflation of texts and persons impoverishes our ideas not only of art . . . but also of persons, since it renders the fact of embodiment irrelevant, when embodiment is exactly what situates us in history and makes us vulnerable to oppression" (21).

18. Jahan Ramazani, *A Transnational Poetics* (Chicago: Chicago University Press, 2009), xiii.
19. Laurent Jenny, "Méthodes et problèmes: La Poésie, 2003" at the Université de Genève website, http://www.unige.ch/lettres/framo/enseignements/methodes/elyrique/index.html. Jenny writes that the most "delicate" question posed to lyric poetry is that of "the exact status of the *lyric subject*. Precisely what value should we accord to the Je who expresses itself in the poems? Must we identify it completely with the poet and treat it as an autobiographical subject?" Author's emphasis.
20. See Dominique Combe, "La référence redoublée," in *Figures du sujet lyrique*, ed. Dominique Rabaté (Paris: Presses Universitaires de France, 1996); Michel Deguy, *La poésie n'est pas seule* (Paris: Seuil, 1987); and Jean-Michel Maulpoix, *Du lyrisme* (Paris: Jose Corti, 2000). For a summary of the debates, see Jean-Michel Maulpoix's website: http://www.maulpoix.net. Other influential movements in poetry and poetry criticism include Jean-Marie Gleize's "littéralité" [see Gleize, *Poésie et figuration* (Paris: Seuil, 1983)]; the "grève lyrique"—or strike against lyricism—conducted in the pages of *La revue de littérature générale* by Olivier Cadiot and Pierre Alféri; the experimental movement, Ouvroir de Littérature Potentielle, or OULIPO; the new multimedia practice (and theory) of poets such as Christophe Hanna, Olivier Quintyn, Franck Leibovici, Suzanne Doppelt, and Emmanuel Hocquard; the exploration, after Wittgenstein, of poetry as a "forme de vie" (see Marielle Macé, *Façons de lire, manières d'être* [Paris: Editions Gallimard, 2011]); and critics grouped around the French sound poets, such as Jean-Pierre Bobillot. For a refreshing view of the contemporary poetry scene in France, see Christophe Wall-Romana, "Dure poésie générale," *Esprit Créateur* 49, no. 2 (2009): 1–8.
21. For an insightful treatment of the representation of race in experimental writing, see Timothy Yu, *Race and the Avant-Garde: Experimental and Asian American Poetry Since 1965* (Stanford, Calif.: Stanford

University Press, 2009). See also two ground-breaking studies in the anglophone context: Aldon Lynn Nielsen's *Black Chant: Languages of African-American Postmodernism* (Cambridge: Cambridge University Press, 1997); and Nathaniel Mackey's *Discrepant Engagement: Dissonance, Cross-Culturality, and Experimental Writing* (Cambridge: Cambridge University Press, 1993).

22. On the notion of "contramodernity," see Simon Gikandi, *Writing in Limbo: Modernism and Caribbean Literature* (Ithaca, NY: Cornell University Press, 1992).
23. Pascale Casanova, *La république mondiale des lettres* (Paris: Seuil, 1999), 65.
24. Ibid.
25. The status of the Antilles and French Guiana (where Césaire and Damas, respectively, were born) was not exactly that of a colony. The population of the French Antilles were accorded citizenship in 1848; yet, as Nick Nesbitt observes, "The citizenship extended to the inhabitants of the vieilles colonies in 1848 had always been, as it remained in 1945, partial and subaltern." Nesbitt, *Caribbean Critique: Antillean Critical Theory from Toussaint to Glissant* (Liverpool: Liverpool University Press, 2013), 88. Martinique, Guadeloupe, French Guiana, and Réunion received the status of French "départements" in 1946, but, despite Césaire's tireless efforts, the citizens of the départements have not obtained full self-determination.
26. See Jacqueline Leiner, "Entretien avec Aimé Césaire par Jacqueline Leiner," in *Tropiques*, vol. 1 (Paris: Jean-Michel Place, 1978), xiv: "What I have tried to do is to inflect the French language, to transform it in order to express, let's say: This me, this nigger-me, this Creole-me, this Martinican-me, this Caribbean-me. That's why I was much more interested in poetry than in prose—precisely because the poet is the one who creates his language, while the writer of prose, in the main, uses language."
27. F. Abiola Irele, "The Harlem Renaissance and the Negritude Movement," in *The Cambridge History of African and Caribbean Literature*, vol. 2 (Cambridge: Cambridge University Press, 2004), 760.
28. On Caribbean creolization as cultural identity, see Wilson Harris, *Tradition, the Writer and Society: Critical Essays* (London: Beacon, 1967); Kamau Brathwaite, Verene Shepherd, and Glen Richards, *Question-*

ing: Creolization Discourses in Caribbean Culture, in Honor of Kamau Brathwaite (Kingston, Jamaica: Ian Randle and Oxford: James Currey, 2002); and Édouard Glissant, *Le discours antillais* (Paris: Seuil, 1981).

29. See these two impressive studies: Brent Hayes Edwards, *The Practice of Diaspora: Literature, Translation, and the Rise of Black Internationalism* (Cambridge, MA: Harvard University Press, 2003); and Gary Wilder, *The French Imperial Nation-State: Negritude and Colonial Humanism Between the Two World Wars* (Chicago: University of Chicago Press, 2005).

30. Charles W. Pollard, *New World Modernism: T. S. Eliot, Derek Walcott, and Kamau Brathwaite* (Charlottesville: University of Virginia Press, 2004): "as Caribbean writers have transformed the methods of modernism, modernism itself has become a more discrepant cosmopolitan literary movement" (9).

31. The place of Jacques Roumain in the story of Negritude is an ambiguous one. Césaire claimed that he had not read Roumain—or known of *La Revue Indigène*—before he composed the *Cahier*, even though Roumain was a Student at the Institut d'Ethnologie in 1938. Damas may have been more familiar with the work of Roumain through his friendship with Langston Hughes. Irele contends that "When Césaire wrote his *Cahier d'un retour au pays natal* and published it in the journal *Volontés* in 1939, he had fully absorbed the lessons of both the Harlem Renaissance and the Haitian Renaissance, which merged with other influences in French literature and the esthetic and social revolutions that marked European culture in the interwar years, in particular Marxism and Surrealism, to produce the great statement of the black condition his long poem has come to represent." Irele, "The Harlem Renaissance," 774. The articles in *Tropiques* reveal the influence of *La Revue Indigène*, but I am not convinced that the first 1939 version of the *Cahier* does.

32. Jean Bernabé, Patrick Chamoiseau, and Raphaël Confiant, *Éloge de la créolité* (Paris: Gallimard, 1989), 45; the authors state that Césaire did not accomplish the "tâche première de construire cette langue écrite." For a contextualization of Césaire's choice and that of the entire équipe of *Tropiques*, see Alex Gil, "The Césaire Gambit: Marking and Re-Making the Present," *@elotroalex*, August 11, 2013, http://elotroalex.webfactional.com/?s=The+C%C3%A9saire+Gambit: "They understood that a cultural, and by extension political, revolution was necessary if they

were to join their imagined global dialogue as equals, and their chosen vehicle was print and French. Given their goals their choice makes sense, a bundle of paper with French markings could travel farther than spoken Creole in the 1940s."

33. See Gilbert Gratiant, preface to *Fab' compè zicaque*, "Le langage créole et ceux qui le parlent," reprinted in *Fables créoles et autres écrits*, preface by Aimé Césaire (Paris: Stock, 1996), 47. Gratiant dates the composition of his first poem in Creole around 1935. Lafcadio Hearn had also attempted to construct a written form for Caribbean Creole as early as 1885. On the adoption of Martiniquan Kreyol by Raphaël Confiant and Patrick Chamoiseau as an exoticizing strategy for attracting French readers, see Maryse Condé's polemical "On the Apparent Carnivalization of Literature from the French Caribbean," in *Representations of Blackness and the Performance of Identities*, ed. Jean Muteba Rahier (Westport, CT: Bergin & Garvey, 1999).
34. Frantz Fanon, *Peau noire, masques blancs* (Paris: Seuil, 1952), 30: "Historiquement, il faut comprendre que le Noir veut parler le français, car c'est la clef susceptible d'ouvrir les portes qui, il y a cinquante ans encore, lui étaient interdites."
35. Senghor, until granted French citizenship around 1935, was officially a colonial subject. The residents of four Senegalese cities—known as the "Quatre Communes," Saint-Louis, Dakar, Gorée, and Rufisque—became citizens of France during the Second Republic, but Senghor was born in Joal, south of Dakar.
36. For a rehearsal of Ngũgĩ's points in the language of sociology, see Pierre Bourdieu, "The Production and Reproduction of Legitimate Language," in *Language and Symbolic Power*, ed. John Thompson, trans. Gino Raymond and Matthew Adamson (Cambridge: Polity Press, 1991), 43–65.
37. Ngũgĩ wa Thiong'o, *Decolonising the Mind: The Politics of Language in African Literature* (Portsmouth, NH: Heinemann, 1986), 3.
38. Influenced by Arthur de Gobineau and Lucien Lévy-Bruhl, Senghor believed that African culture was emotional and intuitive, and thus African languages were less conceptual than European languages. Although, as scholars have argued, he added a dose of Bergsonism and reinterpreted these qualities as positive, the record shows that his attitude toward indigenous languages was not consistent. See Léopold

Sédar Senghor, *Libertés I: Négritude et humanisme* (Paris: Seuil, 1964), 32, originally published in *L'Homme de couleur*, 1939.

39. Léopold Sédar Senghor, "Comme les lamantins vont boire à la source," postface to *Éthiopiques*, reprinted in *Oeuvre poétique* (1954; repr. Paris: Seuil, 1990), 166–67.
40. Senghor, "Le problème culturel en A.O.F," in *Libertés I*, 19. Senghor argues for bilingual education in French West Africa but adds the troubling observation that Africans must be taught to write in their original languages because "notre peuple, dans son ensemble, n'est pas encore à même de goûter toutes les beautés du français" (ibid.).
41. Léopold Sédar Senghor, *The Collected Poetry*, trans. Melvin Dixon (Charlottesville: University Press of Virginia, 1991), 276 (in English, 13).
42. Ibid., 588, (in English, 247).
43. Senghor, *Oeuvre poétique*, 427.
44. Fanon, *Peau noire, masques blancs*, 13.
45. Ibid., 14.
46. Ibid., 22.
47. Over the past two decades, a number of works have sought to correct the assumption that no literary tradition existed in the francophone Caribbean. See, for instance, Jennifer M. Wilks, *Race, Gender, and Comparative Black Modernism: Suzanne Lacascade, Marita Bonner, Suzanne Césaire, Dorothy West* (Baton Rouge: Louisiana State University Press, 2008); Dominique Chancé, *Histoire des littératures antillaises* (Paris: Ellipses, 2005); Patrick Chamoiseau and Raphaël Confiant, *Lettres créoles: Tracées antillaises et continentales de la littérature: Haïti, Guadeloupe, Martinique, Guyane, 1635–1975* (Paris: Hatier, 1991); Jack Corzani, Léon-François Hoffman, and Marie-Lyne Piccione, *Littératures francophones II: Les Amériques: Haiti, Antilles-Guyane, Québec* (Paris: Belin, 1998); Régis Antoine *Les écrivains français et les Antilles: Des premiers pères blancs aux surréalistes noirs* (Paris: Maisonneuve et Larose, 1978); and Jack Corzani, *La littérature des Antilles-Guyane Françaises* (Fort-de-France: Désormeaux, 1978).
48. Fanon, *Peau noire, masques blancs*, 30.
49. Ibid., 29.
50. Ibid., 30.
51. Ngũgĩ provided this narrative to me in response to a question I raised—why did Césaire write in French?—during the Q&A session after his

second René Wellek lecture at the University of California, Irvine, in May of 2010. As ever, I remain grateful to Ngũgĩ for his generous attention.

52. On writing in Gikuyu, see Ann Biersteker, "Gikuyu Literature: Development from Early Christian Writings to Ngũgĩ's Later Novels," in *The Cambridge History of African and Caribbean Literature* (Cambridge: Cambridge University Press, 2004), 306–28. Biersteker indicates that the earliest publications in Gikuyu were early twentieth century vocabulary lists (the work of missionaries) and translations of the New Testament (1926).
53. Leiner, "Entretien avec Aimé Césaire par Jacqueline Leiner," x, xi, xiii; original emphasis.
54. Ngũgĩ, *Decolonising the Mind*, 16.
55. Aimé Césaire, préface to *Fables créoles et autres écrits*, by Gilbert Gratiant (Paris: Stock, 1996), 8. An earlier publication in Martinique is prefaced by Max-Pol Fouchet, who frames the "fables" in a far more conventional, typically exoticizing and infantilizing manner: "Antilles! Les Iles! Comme nous en rêvons. . . . Et comment n'en point rêver dans l'univers dur de l'Europe 'aux anciens parapets.'" Max-Pol Fouchet, préface to *Fables créoles et autres écrits* (Fort-de-France: Désormeaux, 1976), 11.
56. Césaire, preface to *Fables créoles*, 8.
57. Leiner, "Entretien avec Aimé Césaire par Jacqueline Leiner," x, xi, xiii; original emphasis.
58. See Glissant, "Poétique naturelle, poétique forcée," in *Le discours antillais* (Paris: Seuil, 1981), 236–45.
59. Glissant, *Le discours antillais*, 237.
60. Gil, "The Césaire Gambit."
61. Jean Bernabé, Patrick Chamoiseau, and Raphaël Confiant, *Éloge de la créolité* (Paris: Gallimard, 1989): "Césaire, un anticréole? Non point, mais un anté-créole, si, du moins, un tel paradoxe peut être risqué. . . . La Négritude césairienne est un baptême, l'acte primal de notre dignité restituée. Nous sommes à jamais fils d'Aimé Césaire" (18). Compare these words to Confiant's: "On ne peut aujourd'hui être fils authentique de Césaire." Raphaël Confiant, *Aimé Césaire: Une traversée paradoxale du siècle* (Paris: Stock, 1993), 38. To their credit, the authors of *Éloge de la créolité* recognize that writing in Creole in the 1930s was not an option, but that it became so in the 1980s due to a number of factors (including

the attention it attracted in the field of linguistics). For a compelling treatment of Creole language politics, see Pierre Bourdieu, "Price Formation and the Anticipation of Profits," in *Language and Symbolic Power*, ed. John Thompson, trans. Gino Raymond and Matthew Adamson (Cambridge: Polity Press, 1991), 68–69. See also Christopher Miller's compassionate discussion of the dilemma facing African writers in *Nationalists and Nomads: Essays on Francophone African Literature and Culture* (Chicago: University of Chicago Press, 1999); curiously, here, Miller does not extend the same compassion to Césaire (see 118–25).

62. Jean-Michel Djian, "Rencontre avec Aimé Césaire," in *Léopold Sédar Senghor: Génèse de l'imaginaire francophone* (Paris: Gallimard, 2005), 229. On Césaire's childhood, see Patrice Louis, *Aimé Césaire: Rencontre avec un nègre fondamental* (Paris: Aéria, 2004), 20–21.

63. See Jacques Rancière, *Mallarmé: La politique de la sirène* (Paris: Hachette, 1997).

64. An unfortunate consequence of the position advanced by both Ngũgĩ and, in the Caribbean context, the Créolistes is that, although sympathetic in some respects, they tend to be overly prescriptive, limiting authors to one language, one cultural role, and even one subject matter. Ngũgĩ's own account shows that even he could not marry writing and militancy, the narrative subtlety of his earlier fiction and the impact of propaganda. In 1977 he was forced to abandon the text as a material support when he made the decision to write in Gikuyu. For years he wrote plays (rather than novels), dramatizing "the content of our people's anti-imperialist struggles to liberate their productive forces from foreign control" (*Decolonising the Mind*, 29). By his own admission, he placed content above form (ibid., 78), recognizing—like many an engaged realist before him—that the urgency of the situation called for a reprioritizing of values. Césaire, too, turned to writing plays a decade earlier, but these plays remain stubbornly textual, employing the same type of complex imagery and intertextual web of allusions found in his poetry.

65. Patrick Chamoiseau, *Écrire en pays dominé* (Paris: Gallimard, 1997). The "*marqueur de paroles*" is a character (as well as narrator) in *Texaco* and other novels by Chamoiseau. On another note, there are several ways to understand what a tradition of writing might be in the Caribbean islands. See also Chamoiseau and Confiant, *Lettres créoles*.

66. See Patrick Chamoiseau, *Chemin d'école* (Paris: Gallimard, 1994).
67. Aimé Césaire, *Cahier d'un retour au pays natal* (Paris: Présence Africaine, 1983), 11; and Aimé Césaire, *The Collected Poetry*, trans. Clayton Eshleman and Annette Smith (Berkeley: University of California Press, 1983), 37.
68. Chamoiseau, *Écrire en pays dominé*, 21. "Je soupçonnais que toute domination (la silencieuse plus encore) germe et se développe à l'intérieur même de ce que l'on est. Qu'insidieuse, elle neutralise les expressions les plus intimes des peuples dominés. Que toute résistance devait se situer résolument là, en face d'elle, et déserter les illusions des vieux modes de bataille. Il me fallait alors interroger mon écriture, longer ses dynamiques, suspecter les conditions de son jaillissement et déceler l'influence qu' exerce sur elle la domination-qui-ne-se-voit-plus" (21–22). Chamoiseau's imagery of volcanic explosion ("jaillissement") as well as his hyphenations ("la domination-qui-ne-se-voit-plus") are both derived from Césaire's stylistics.
69. For a forceful, Hegelian version of the argument that aesthetic creation can produce substantive transformation, see Nick Nesbitt, *Voicing Memory: History and Subjectivity in French Caribbean Literature* (Charlottesville: University of Virginia Press, 2003), 23.
70. Chamoiseau, *Écrire en pays dominé*, 21.
71. See Edwin C. Hill Jr., *Black Soundscapes White Stages: The Meaning of Francophone Sound in the Black Atlantic* (Baltimore: Johns Hopkins University Press, 2013).
72. See Glissant, *Le discours antillais*; and Glissant, *Pays rêvé, pays réel, suivi de Fastes et de Les Grans Chaos* (Paris: Gallimard Poésie, 2000); and Carrie Noland, "Édouard Glissant: A Poetics of the Entour," in *Poetry After Cultural Studies*, ed. Heidi R. Bean and Mike Chasar (Iowa City: University of Iowa Press, 2011). On Martiniquan toponyms in particular, see Vincent Huyghues-Belrose, "Le nom des lieux à la Martinique: Un patrimoine identitaire menacé," in *Études Caribéennes*, December 11, 2008, http://etudescaribeennes.revues.org/3494?id+3494.
73. For an excellent reply to the accusation of essentialism on Césaire's part, see Richard Price and Sally Price, "Shadowboxing in the Mangrove," *Cultural Anthropology* 12, no. 1 (February 1997): 3–36.

74. J. Michael Dash, *The Other America: Caribbean Literature in a New World Context* (Charlottesville: University of Virginia Press, 1998), 99. Luís Madureira maintains, as I do, that Dash, otherwise a sensitive reader, in this case reads "too hastily." See Luís Madureira, *Cannibal Modernities: Postcoloniality and the Avant-Garde in Caribbean and Brazilian Literature* (Charlottesville: University of Virginia Press, 2005), 5. See also Miller, *Nationalists and Nomads*. Miller concludes that Césaire's *Cahier* is "primitivizing and Romantic" (90). For a contrasting view, similar to my own, see Gil Fuentes, "Migrant Textuality."

1. "SEEING WITH THE EYES OF THE WORK"

1. A. James Arnold, "Césaire's *Notebook* as Palimpsest: The Text Before, During, and After World War II," *Research in African Literatures* 35, no. 3 (Fall 2004): 133–40. See also the more detailed study of the changes the *Cahier* underwent, especially after Césaire's trip to Haiti in 1944, in Lilian Pestre de Almeida's *Aimé Césaire: Une saison en Haïti* (Montreal: Mémoire d'Encrier, 2010). Arnold's position has evolved: he recently coedited and cotranslated with Clayton Eshleman *The Original 1939 Notebook of a Return to the Native Land*, bilingual ed. (Middletown, CT: Wesleyan University Press, 2013).
2. See Thomas A. Hale, "Les écrits d'Aimé Césaire, bibliographie commentée," *Études françaises* 14, no. 3–4 (October 1978). I am counting the 1939 *Volontés* edition as well as the extracts printed in *Tropiques*, no. 5 (1942). For a list of new editions since 1978, see Lilian Pestre de Almeida, "Présentation: Cahier d'un retour au pays natal," in *Aimé Césaire à l'oeuvre*, ed. Marc Cheymol and Philippe Ollé-Laprune, 97–105 (Paris: Éditions des archives contemporaines, 2010). See also Alex Gil, "Bridging the Middle Passage: The Textual (R)evolution of Césaire's Cahier d'un retour au pays natal," *Canadian Review of Comparative Literature* 38, no. 1 (March 2011): 40–56.
3. Arnold, "Césaire's *Notebook*," 133. As Alex Gil points out, the *Cahier* exists in four distinct forms: "The first version could be called spiritual, the second and third surrealist, while the last one, with spirit and sex removed, political. When you speak of the *Cahier d'un retour au pays natal* which one are you talking about?" See Gil, "The Césaire Gambit:

Marking and Re-Making the Present," *@elotroalex*, August 11, 2013, http://elotroalex.webfactional.com/?s=The+C%C3%A9saire+Gambit.

4. Arnold has stressed, for instance, the great degree to which Césaire's style was influenced by the surrealists after he met Breton in 1941; see his annotations in Aimé Césaire, *Poésie, théâtre, essais et discours*, ed. A. James Arnold (Paris: Éditions CNRS, 2013), where he claims that Césaire underwent a "conversion à une écriture surréaliste de 1941 à 1943" (65). During this period, the Chilean review *Leitmotiv* published Césaire's "Colombes bruissement du sang" in 1943 (later titled "Serpent soleil"); "Conquête de l'aube" appeared in the first issue of *VVV*; André Breton introduced Césaire's "Les pur-sang" with "Un grand poète noir" in a 1944 issue of *Hémispheres* (no. 2–3); Roger Caillois (probably under pressure from Breton) published Césaire's "Poème" in *Lettres Françaises* in 1945; immediately after the war Breton saw to it that "Batouque" appeared in *Fontaine* (vol. 35) and "Le Grand-Midi" in *Confluences* (vol. 6).
5. According to Pestre de Almeida, the *Volontés* edition has 7,445 words while the Présence Africaine edition has 9,666; see Pestre de Almeida, *Aimé Césaire: Cahier d'un retour au pays natal* (Paris: L'Harmattan, 2008), 100.
6. A. James Arnold, "Poétique forcée et identité dans la littérature des Antilles francophones," in *L'héritage du Caliban*, ed. Maryse Condé (Paris: Jasor, 1992), 22. Again, when Arnold published the bilingual edition of the *Cahier* in 2013, cotranslated with Clayton Eshleman, he persisted in referring to the work as the "preoriginal" in his introduction—despite the volume's title, *The Original 1939 Notebook of a Return to the Native Land*, xix.
7. Arnold, "Césaire's *Notebook*," 133.
8. By "high modernism," a contested designation indeed, I mean an innovative literature that challenged the habits of most readers. My use of the term corresponds to the definition implicit in Adorno's *Aesthetic Theory*; however, I grant Jessica Berman her point, well supported in *Modernist Commitments: Ethics, Politics, and Transnational Modernism* (New York: Columbia University Press, 2011), that experimental practice goes well beyond the confines of Western Europe, articulating politics with form in a variety of ways: "If we step outside the hypercanon of European modernism . . . into the worldwide sphere of textual activity, we discover a multiplicity of transnational modernisms that

foreground their ethical and political dimensions as essential horizons for modernist experimentation" (28–29). See also Theodor Adorno, *Aesthetic Theory*, trans. Robert Hullot-Kentor (Minneapolis: University of Minnesota Press, 1997).

9. A. James Arnold, *Negritude and Modernism: The Poetry and Poetics of Aimé Césaire* (Cambridge, MA: Harvard University Press, 1981). In particular, Arnold studies the intertextual relation between Césaire and Paul Claudel; Saint-John Perse; Charles Péguy; and Leo Frobenius. More recently, Arnold has provided a useful summary of the contexts of issue number 20 of *Volontés*; see Césaire, *Poésie, théâtre, essais et discours*, 71–73.

10. As Alex Gil has written, "textual transformation [is] a process determined by the adaptation of addressable textual units to different *editorial* and *textual* environments, rather than [. . .] a shift in what we would call a coherent poetics born out of the author's purported artistic integrity or journey of self discovery." "Migrant Textuality: On the Fields of Aimé Césaire's *Et les chiens se taisaient*" (Ph.D. diss., University of Virginia, December 2012), 57, available at *Academic Commons*, http://academiccommons.columbia.edu/catalog/ac:161180.

11. See David Alliot, *Aimé Césaire: Le Nègre fondamental* (Gollion, Switz.: Infolio, 2008), 53. Pelorson (sometimes spelled "Pellorson") was a former ENS student: he changed his name to Georges Belmont after the war (perhaps because of his collaborationist activities under Vichy). See Kora Verón "Césaire at the crossroads in Haiti: Correspondence with Henri Seyrig," *Comparative Literature Studies* 50:3 (2013): 430–44.

12. "In Memorium" was published in *Volontés*, 18 (June 1939); "Héritage" and "Aux tirailleurs Sénégalais morts pour la France" were published in the same issue of *Volontés* as the *Cahier*, that is, no. 20, in August 1939.

13. Miller may be considered to be the strongest link—beside Jolas—between *transition* and *Volontés*. Although he published only once in *transition*, he was part of the anglophone expatriate milieu to which many other *transition* writers belonged.

14. The translation never appeared, but Yale University possesses a typescript dated 1932 of a French version of "Anna Livia Pluribelle" composed by Samuel Beckett and revised by Philippe Soupault and Jolas himself, so that might have been the text *Volontés* intended to publish.

15. According to Alex Gil, Queneau cofounded *Volontés*. Apparently he met Césaire in the editorial office of *Volontés* and later encouraged

Gallimard to publish Césaire's first full volume of poetry, *Armes miraculeuses*, after the war. See Gil, "Breaking News: It Was Queneau!" *@elotroalex*, September 12, 2013, http://elotroalex.webfactional.com/research-sejour-report/.

16. Craig Monk, "Eugène Jolas and the Translation Policies of *transition*," *Mosaic* 32, no. 4 (December 1999): 17–34.
17. See Marjorie Perloff, "Logocinéma of the Frontiersman: Eugène Jolas's Multilingual Poetics and Its Legacies," at http://epc.buffalo.edu/authors/perloff/jolas.html.
18. Eugène Jolas, *Man from Babel* (New Haven, CT: Yale University Press, 1998), 116. The book was posthumously published by Yale University Press in 1998; Jolas died in 1952.
19. Eugène Jolas, "Revolution of the Word," *transition*, 16–17 (June 1929). The manifesto was largely written by Jolas but cosigned by fifteen collaborators, including Kay Boyle, Hart Crane, Elliot Paul, and Caresse Crosby. Céline Mansanti has suggested that the manifesto was written to serve as an alternative to surrealism; in fact, during the period, *transition* welcomed several dissident surrealists, including Robert Desnos (who was friendly with Damas), Roger Vitrac, Tristan Tzara, and Antonin Artaud; see Mansanti, *La revue transition (1927–1938): Le modernisme historique en devenir* (Rennes: Presses Universitaires de Rennes, 2009), 164–77.
20. His *Mots-déluge* of 1933 is, in his own words, "a book of French neologistic poems." Jolas, *Man from Babel*, 112.
21. Jolas, "Revolution of the Word," 16–17.
22. *Charpentes* 6, no. 1 (1939); editors included André Gide, Jean Giorno, and Jules Supervielle. This issue contains Césaire's translation of Sterling Brown, "Les hommes forts," Senghor's "Neige sur Paris," and Damas's "Aux premiers âges." As for "Nigg," I have been unable to discover anything more about this author. The verses published under this pseudonym are fairly conventional except for their subject matter and do not resemble poems by Senghor, Damas, or Césaire.
23. See Perloff, "Logocinéma of the Frontiersman" (np).
24. Eugène Jolas, "Logos," *transition* 16–17 (1929): 28.
25. See Brent Hayes Edwards, "Aimé Césaire and the Syntax of Influence," in *Diasporic Avant-Gardes: Experimental Poetics and Cultural Displacement*, ed. Carrie Noland and Barrett Watten (New York: Palgrave

Macmillan, 2009). The anaphoric verse structure results from Whitman's huge influence and probably reached Césaire's ears through the poets of the Harlem Renaissance (and not Jacques Roumain or Jules Laforgue). Even before his trip to New York, Jolas showed an interest in anglophone black writing: in his *Anthologie de la nouvelle poésie Américaine* of 1928, he published translations of Countee Cullen, Langston Hughes, and Claude McKay.

26. My translations.
27. Eugène Jolas, *Mots-déluge: Hypnologues* (Paris: Éditions des Cahiers Libres, 1933), 12; added emphasis. Jolas was inspired by Joyce, but he has neither the linguistic scope of the Irish author nor his stylistic flair. Jolas's neologisms and portmanteau words pepper an otherwise conventional sentence construction. According to specialists of Martiniquan Creole (Kreyol), word creation in that language does not follow the Latinate form adopted by Jolas and Césaire but instead relies on "agglutination" (adding the initial 'l' of the definite article to the noun); "aphérèse" (shortening a word by cutting off the first syllable); "redoublement" (repeating the same morpheme or word twice, as in "doudou" or Damas's "français français"); and "composition" (joining two words together with a hyphen). Two less common procedures that might have informed Césaire's neologistic practice are the creation of the "mot-valise" or "téléscopage," as in "oraliture" or "Francréole"; and "dérivation," the addition of a suffix, as in "marqueur" from the verb "*marquer*." See Teodor Florin Zanoaga, "Observations sur la formation des mots en français littéraire antillais," in *Le français dans les Antilles: Études linguistiques*, ed. André Thibault, 207–21 (Paris: L'Harmattan, 2012). Christian Filostrat maintains that "negritude" was not, in fact, a neologism of Césaire's but rather a borrowing from a nineteenth-century American dictionary. See Filostrat, *Negritudes Agonistes, Assimilation Against Nationalism in the French-Speaking Caribbean and Guyane* (Cherry Hill, NJ: Americana Homestead Legacy Publishers, 2008), 119. As A. James Arnold points out, however, this thesis has not been verified: "D'ailleurs, selon Filostrat, Césaire aurait pu pêcher le mot *négritude* dans un dictionnaire américain du XIXe siècle, à une époque où il était encore courant en Amérique du Nord. La thèse ne sera sans doute jamais validée de façon concluante, mais elle est

réconfortée par le propos, souvent répété par Césaire, que les nègres des États-Unis eurent inventé la négritude"; Arnold, ed., preface to *Poésie, théâtre, essais et discours* (1295).

28. My translation. Compare these lines to the stream of invective that appears at the opening of the 1956 Présence Africaine edition of the *Cahier*, first added to the Bordas edition of 1947: "Au bout du petit matin . . . / Va-t-en, lui disais-je, gueule de flic, gueule de vache, va-t-en je déteste les larbins de l'ordre et les hannetons de l'espérance. Va-t-en mauvais gris-gris, punaise de moinillon." Aimé Césaire, *Cahier d'un retour au pays natal* (Paris: Présence Africaine, 1983), 7. All further references to this edition will be indicated in the text as PA.
29. Christian Filostrat announced the discovery and reprinted the pertinent pages of this third issue of *L'Étudiant Noir* in *Négritudes agonistes*, 119–33.
30. The three pages of new text begin with "je te livre le chain gang." The letter, which was displayed at the 2011 exhibition "Césaire & Lam," held at the Grand Palais, is reproduced in the exhibition catalog, Daniel Maximin, ed., *Césaire & Lam: Insolites bâtisseurs* (Paris: HC Éditions, 2011), 43.
31. I have tried to imitate the lineation of the handwritten manuscript. Nowhere have I ever seen this lineation imitated in print. The lines appear in the *Volontés* edition on page 51. Further references to this edition will be indicated in the text as V.
32. Aimé Césaire, *The Collected Poetry*, trans. Clayton Eshleman and Annette Smith (Berkeley: University of California Press, 1983), 85. A full reading of these final lines would divert me from my current argument. To pursue such a reading, I would focus on the tension between speaking (suggested by the "tongue") and printing (suggested by the past participle / adjective "*imprimée*" in the line "Je te suis imprimée en mon ancestrale cornée blanche"). For a persuasive reading along these lines, see Nick Nesbitt, *Voicing Memory: History and Subjectivity in French Caribbean Literature* (Charlottesville: University of Virginia Press, 2003), 77–82.
33. Eugène Jolas, *The Language of the Night* (The Hague: Servire Press, 1932), 16. Jolas praises other inventors of neologisms, such as Alfred Jarry and the dadaists.

34. Césaire studied at the Rue d'Ulm from 1935 to 1938; I have checked the library catalog, and the 1937 edition of *Physiologie du goût* is still there. See René Hénane, "Note brève: Soleil cou coupé, verrition: l'énigme dévoilée" (paper presented at the conference "Aimé Césaire: Une Pensée pour le XXIème siècle"), cited in Paul-Christian Lapoussinière, *Au bout du petit matin . . . de Nox à Lux: L'Épopée d'Aimé Césaire et de Victor Hugo* (Ivry-sur-Seine, France: Éditions Panafrika Silex/Nouvelles du Sud, 2007), 92–93.
35. Jean Anthelme Brillat-Savarin, *Physiologie du goût, première édition mise en ordre et annotée avec une lecture de Roland Barthes* (Paris: Hermann, 1975), 55.
36. "*Verrition* (*verro*, lat., je balaye) . . . quand la langue, se recourbant en dessus et au dessous, ramasse les portions qui peuvent rester dans le canal semi-circulaire formé par les lèvres et les gencives" (ibid.); all translations are my own unless otherwise noted.
37. Roland Barthes, "Préface" in *Physiologie du goût*, by Brillat-Savarin, 18. Emphasis original.
38. For an early and influential version of this reading of Césaire as an oral poet, see M. a M. Ngal, *Aimé Césaire: Un homme à la recherche d'une patrie* (Paris: Présence Africaine, 1994).
39. On "subvocalization" in poetry, see Lesley Wheeler, *Voicing American Poetry: Sound and Performance from the 1920s to the Present* (Ithaca, NY: Cornell University Press, 2008). On "virtual hearing," see Jacques Roubaud, "Prelude: Poetry and Orality," in *The Sound of Poetry/The Poetry of Sound*, eds. Marjorie Perloff and Craig Dworkin, trans. Jean-Jacques Poucel (Chicago: Chicago University Press, 2009), 20. I treat the problem of voice in writing more fully in chapters 3 and 4.
40. According to Stanislas Dehaene, "when we encounter a new word" silent reading, or "sounding," "is often the only solution." Dehaene, *Reading in the Brain: The Science and Evolution of a Human Invention* (New York: Viking, 2009), 27. With respect to the neural circuits of audition and the areas of the brain associated with speech, "we still activate their pronunciation [the pronunciation of unfamiliar words] at a nonconscious level" (ibid., 28).
41. See Martin Munro, *Different Drummers: Rhythm and Race in the Americas* (Berkeley: University of California Press, 2010); and Lilian Pestre de

Almeida, *Aimé Césaire: Cahier d'un retour au pays natal*, rev. ed. (Paris: L'Harmattan, 2012).

42. Walter Ong, *Orality and Literacy: The Technologizing of the Word* (New York: Methuen, 1982), 8.
43. René Hénane, *Glossaire des termes rares dans l'oeuvre d'Aimé Césaire* (Paris: Jean-Michel Place, 2004). "*Noctiluque*" is a term meaning an animal, zoophyte, or plancton that shines at night (zoology); a Roman name given to the moon (mythology); a fleur that opens at night (biology). "*Cyathée*" comes from the Greek Kuathos, recipient, cup (botany). "*Érésipèle*" is a skin inflammation, often of the face, related to streptococcus (pathology). "*Squasme*" is a scaley skin disease.
44. See Jacqueline Leiner, "Entretien avec Aimé Césaire par Jacqueline Leiner," in *Tropiques*, vol. 1 (Paris: Jean-Michel Place, 1978), xiv. Critics have forgotten that in these remarks Césaire connects the process of "bending" French with the poetics of Mallarmé: "Ainsi, si j'ai beaucoup aimé Mallarmé, c'est parce qu'il m'a montré, parce que j'ai compris à travers lui, que la langue, au fond, est arbitraire."
45. It was Suzanne Césaire who first stated in 1942 that "la poésie martiniquaise sera cannibale ou ne sera pas" while critiquing the *doudouisme* of Martiniquan poetry; see Suzanne Césaire, "Misère d'une poésie: John Antoine-Nau," *Tropiques*, vol. 4 (January 1942): 50. For an account of the impact of that statement, see Marie-Agnès Sourieau, "Suzanne Césaire et *Tropiques*: De la poésie cannibale à une poétique créole," *French Review* 68, no. 1 (October 1994): 69–78.
46. On the appropriation and redirection of intertexts, see Daniel Delas, *Aimé Césaire* (Paris: Hachette, 1991); Jean-Jacques Thomas, "Aimé Césaire, de la poésie avant toute chose" (forthcoming); and Gil, "The Césaire Gambit."
47. On the inclusion of Martiniquan Creole (or Kreyol) terms and phrases, see Annie Dyck, *Le langage césairien, approche d'une écriture polyglossique* (Mémoire de DEA, Université des Antilles et de la Guyane, 1988); and Lambert-Felix Prudent, "Aimé Césaire: Contribution poétique à la construction de la langue martiniquaise," in *Aimé Césaire à l'oeuvre*, ed. Marc Cheymol and Philippe Ollé-Laprune (Paris: Éditions des archives contemporaines, 2010).
48. See Theodor W. Adorno, *Aesthetic Theory*, trans., ed., and intro. Robert Hullot-Kentor (Minneapolis: Minnesota University Press, 1997),

24: "Construction necessitates solutions that the imagining ear or eye does not immediately encompass or know in full detail. Not only is the unforeseen an effect, it also has an objective dimension, which was transformed into a new quality." The term "construction" comes from Paul Valéry. See "Je disais quelquefois à Stéphane Mallarmé": "Mallarmé a sans doute tenté de conserver ces beautés [the use of syllabic repetition] de la matière littéraire, tout en relevant son art vers la construction." Paul Valéry, *Oeuvres*, ed. Jean Hytier (Paris: Gallimard, Pléiade, 1957), 646.

49. I discovered these "Notes de classe" during a research trip to Fort-de-France in November 2010. They were donated by two of Césaire's Lycée Schoelcher students, Michael Yang-Ting and Raymond Cottrell (Archives Départementales de Fort-de-France, Martinique; 1J257/1–7).

50. "Our meetings," recounts Breton, used to take place in the evening after Césaire had finished "the courses he was giving at the lycée, courses that had as their subject matter the work of Rimbaud." André Breton, "Martinique charmeuse de serpents: Un grand poète noir" in *Tropiques* 11 (May 1944): 80.

51. The notes for the class on Rivière are dated Wednesday, December 16, 1942. Breton was in Fort-de-France from April 24, 1941, until twenty-two days later. Breton's comments make it appear likely that Césaire taught Rimbaud both in 1941 and 1942. During the blockade of Martinique and the installation of a Vichy-type government in Fort-de-France, promising *lycéens* were unable to obtain scholarships to study in France. It is for this reason that Césaire began teaching the materials of *khâgne* and *hypokhâgne* to the privileged few in his classes at the Lycée Schoelcher.

52. See Jacques Rivière, "L'Étude sur Rimbaud," originally published in the *Nouvelle Revue Française* in two installments (July and August 1914), then republished in 1930 by Éditions Kra as a separate book, *Rimbaud*; and finally collected with other writings on Rimbaud by Rivière in *Rimbaud, Dossier 1905–1925*, ed. Roger Lefèvre (Paris: Gallimard, 1977). The passage quoted here is found in "Notes de classe" and on pages 166–67 of the 1977 Gallimard edition.

53. Césaire, *Collected Poetry*, 47.

54. Albert B. Lord argues that the oral poem is organized by means of "formulas" composed of several words, or "repeated phrases." Lord, *The Singer of Tales* (Cambridge: Harvard University Press, 1960), 31.

"Substitution" occurs in the framework of grammar" (ibid., 35) as opposed to circulation and permutation of phonemes or phoneme clusters outside of lexemes or grammar.

55. Rivière, "L'Étude sur Rimbaud," 168–69.
56. Ibid., 169.
57. Ibid., 167.
58. See, on this point, Jean-François Lyotard, *Discours/figure* (Paris: Klincksieck, 1971), 215; and Jean-Pierre Bobillot, *Trois essais sur la poésie littérale* (Paris: Al Dante, 2003), 22–26.
59. See Garrett Stewart, *Reading Voices: Literature and the Phonotext* (Berkeley: University of California Press, 1990), 15; see also Bobillot, *Trois essais*, 135.
60. Roger Dragonetti, "La littérature et la lettre (Introduction au Sonnet en X)" in *Études sur Mallarmé*, ed. Wilfried Smekens (Ghent: Romanica Gandensia, 1992), 49; added emphasis, my translation.
61. "Structure, une autre." Mallarmé, "Crise de vers," *Oeuvres complètes*, vol. 2, ed. Bertrand Marchal (Paris: Gallimard, Pléiade, 2003), 211.
62. Mallarmé, "Crise de vers," 211; Mallarmé, "Crisis of Verse," in *Divigations*, trans. Barbara Johnson (Cambridge, MA: Belknap, Harvard University Press, 2007), 208.
63. Mallarmé, "Crisis of Verse," 208, translation modified; Mallarmé, "Crise de vers," 211. Although Mallarmé is concerned at first with the abandonment of traditional metrical forms (such as the alexandrine twelve syllable line), he proceeds to re-envision the role of the writer as well.
64. Arthur Rimbaud, "Lettre XI à Georges Izambard," May 13, 1871, *Oeuvres complètes* (Paris: Gallimard, Pléiade, 1954), 268.
65. See Césaire, "Introduction à la poésie nègre américaine," *Tropiques* (Paris: Jean Michel Place, 1978; published in the second issue of *Tropiques*, July 1941, and conceivably part of his dissertation): "Car enfin, voilà une poésie qui n'offre pas à l'oreille ou à l'oeil *un corps inattendu et indiscutable de vibrations*. Ni l'éclat des couleurs. Ni la magie du son. Tout au plus du rythme, mais de primitif, de jazz ou de tam-tam c'est-à-dire enfonçant la résistance de l'homme en ce point de plus basse humanité qu'est le système nerveux" (41). In retrospect, Césaire's assessment is troubling, for he fails to recognize the technical solutions arrived at by Johnson, Jean Toomer, and McKay (the poets he introduces). In contrast, throughout the 1960s and 1970s,

Césaire expresses considerable admiration for African American culture: "La culture noire est d'une terrible et extraordinaire vitalité," he states in an interview with L. Altoun in 1970. L. Altoun, "Aimé Césaire et le théâtre nègre," in *Le théâtre* (Paris: Christian Bourgeois, 1970), 112.

66. Césaire, "Introduction à la poésie nègre américaine," 41.
67. Ibid.
68. See, among others, Brent Hayes Edwards, *The Practice of Diaspora: Literature, Translation, and the Rise of Black Internationalism* (Cambridge, MA: Harvard University Press, 2003); Jean-Baptiste Popeau, *Dialogues of Negritude: The Cultural Context of Black Writing* (Durham, NC: Carolina Academic Press, 2003); and Chidi Ikonné, *Links and Bridges: A Comparative Study of the Writings of the New Negro and the Negritude Movements* (Ibadan, Nigeria: University Press PLC, 2005).
69. Lilian Pestre de Almeida offers a scholarly appraisal of the impact on Césaire of Haitian and African religions (and thus their languages, myths, and expressive forms) in *Aimé Césaire: Une saison en Haiti.*
70. Adorno, *Aesthetic Theory*, 267.
71. Jean-Paul Sartre, "Orphée noir," preface to *Anthologie de la nouvelle poésie nègre et malgache de langue française*, ed. Léopold Sédar Senghor (Paris: Presses Universitaires de France, 1969); my translation.
72. For an account of Rimbaud's materialism, his awareness of the economic conditions of poetic production, see Carrie Noland, *Poetry at Stake: Lyric Aesthetics and the Challenge of Technology* (Princeton, NJ: Princeton University Press, 1999).
73. Adorno, *Aesthetic Theory*, 29.
74. Ibid., 267.
75. See William James, *Essays in Radical Empiricism*, intro. Ellen Kappy Suckiel, preface Ralph Barton Perry (1912; repr., Lincoln: University of Nebraska Press, 1996); and Bruno Latour, "How to Talk About the Body: The Normative Dimension of Science Studies," *Body & Society* 10, no. 205 (2004): 205–29.
76. "Je crois d'ailleurs—j'ai subi l'influence de Mallarmé—que le mot a sa musique, sa couleur, sa forme, sa force propre. Mais je crois aussi qu'il est PRÉHENSIBLE. C'est lui qui me permet d'appréhender mon Moi; je ne m'appréhende qu'à travers *un mot*, qu'à travers *le mot*." Leiner, "Entretien avec Aimé Césaire," xii; original emphasis.

77. Adorno, *Aesthetic Theory*, 166. As a variant to "the subject in art" (267), the phrase is also translated as "the aesthetic subject" (29, 221, 356) and "the artistic subject" (231).
78. Emile Littré, *Dictionnaire de la langue française*, vol. 3 (Chicago: Encyclopaedia Britannica, 1982), 4939.
79. On the Afro-Caribbean "soundscape" in Césaire, see Martin Munro, *Different Drummers: Rhythm and Race in the Americas* (Berkeley: University of California Press, 2010).
80. Engaging a different vocabulary, Kelly Oliver, following Freud, characterizes the ability to express subjectivity through a mediating artistic language as "sublimation," which is the sign of a healthy, nonpsychotic self. See Oliver, *The Colonization of Psychic Space: A Psychoanalytic Social Theory of Oppression* (Minneapolis: Minnesota University Press, 2004).
81. See Jean-Paul Sartre, *Qu'est-ce que la littérature?* (Paris: Gallimard, 1948); and Sartre, *What Is Literature?*, trans. Bernard Frechtman (New York: Philosophical Library, 1949): "The words are there like traps to arouse our feelings and to reflect them toward us. Each word is a path of transcendence" (45).
82. On Adorno's conception of the "mediating subject," see David Sherman, *Sartre and Adorno: The Dialectics of Subjectivity* (New York: State University of New York Press, 2007): The "mediating subject" is not something transcendent and sublime but "always already tethered to the social, historical, and psychophysiological grounds that engender it" (177).
83. Adorno, *Aesthetic Theory*, 167.
84. Ibid.; German original quoted from Theodor W. Adorno, *Ästhetische Theorie* (Frankfurt: Suhrkamp, 1970), 250.
85. Adorno, *Aesthetic Theory, 250*. The phrase "durch dem Akt von dessen Sprache" lends to the work's language the agency of a performative speech act. A few lines further Adorno adds: "The intervening individual subject [who writes] is scarcely more than a limiting value, something minimal required by the artwork for its crystallization" (ibid.).
86. Adorno comes out of a German tradition of scholarship on the *lyrisches Ich*; for a succinct account of this critical tradition and the poets who animated it—Johann Goethe, Stefan George, Hugo von Hofmannsthal, and Rainer Maria Rilke—see Dominique Combe, "La référence dédoublée: Le sujet lyrique entre fiction et autobiographie," in *Figures du sujet*

lyrique, ed. Dominique Rabaté (Paris: Presses Universitaires de France, 1996), 39–63.

87. See Deepika Bahri, *Native Intelligence: Aesthetics, Politics, and Postcolonial Literature* (Minneapolis: University of Minnesota Press, 2003): "The postcolonial work, particularly of the cosmopolitan variety, is separated with difficulty from the fate of art as such in the age of advanced monopoly capitalism" (104). On the curious modernist temporality of Martinique, see Richard Price, *The Convict and the Colonel* (Boston: Beacon, 1998).
88. Adorno, *Negative Dialectics*, trans. E. B. Ashton (New York: Continuum, 1992), 265.
89. Theodor W. Adorno, *Minima Moralia*, trans. E. F. N. Jephcott (London: Verso, 1978), 17–18.
90. Adorno, *Aesthetic Theory*, 167.
91. Adorno, *Negative Dialectics*, 265.
92. It could be argued that the "individual," for a Marxist, is inevitably a product of her social conditions; but Adorno is clear here that the very thing that distinguishes one individual from another (despite a shared conditioning) also provides resistance to those conditions.
93. For instance, on Césaire and Claudel, see Arnold, *Negritude and Modernism*; on Victor Hugo, see Lapoussinière, *Au bout du petit matin*; on Lautréamont, see René Hénane, *Césaire et Lautréamont: Bestiaire et métamorphose* (Paris: L'Harmattan, 2006); on Charles Baudelaire, see Mireille Rosello, *Littérature et identité créole aux Antilles* (Paris: Karthala, 1992).
94. See, for instance, Lilyan Kesteloot, *Black Writers in French: A Literary History of Negritude* (Washington, DC: Howard University Press, 1991); Pestre de Almeida, *Aimé Césaire: Une saison en Haiti*; Romuald Fonkoua, *Aimé Césaire* (Paris: Perrin, 2008); and Prudent, "Aimé Césaire."
95. "Whereas the two 1947 editions [of the *Cahier*] were revised exclusively by the addition of new material to the 1939 preoriginal, inflecting and intensifying its effects, the 1956 excised much of that same material and substituted for it blocks of text that would align the poem with Césaire's new political position, which embraced the immediate decolonization of Africa in militant tones." Arnold and Eshleman, *The Original 1939 Notebook*, xix. Arnold and Pestre de Almeida see signs

of Césaire's Catholicism, his exposure to Haitian vaudou, and even his intimate relationships flitting in and out of the editions published between 1947 and 1956.

96. Pestre de Almeida, *Aimé Césaire: Cahier d'un retour au pays natal* (2012), 185; my translation; original emphasis.
97. See Nathaniel Mackey, *Discrepant Engagements: Dissonance, Cross-Culturality, and Experimental Writing* (Cambridge: Cambridge University Press, 1993); and Eric Keenaghan, "Newly Discrepant Engagements: A Review of Three Recent Critical Works in Modernist Postcolonial Studies," *Journal of Modern Literature* 29, no. 3 (Spring 2006): 176–90. See also Timothy Yu, *Race and the Avant-Garde: Experimental and Asian-American Poetry Since 1965* (Stanford, CA: Stanford University Press, 2009): "What is needed is . . . [to acknowledge] the existence of multiple and even competing groups whose practices we might recognize as avant-garde and whose aesthetic programs are inflected by their different social identifications" (4).
98. Mackey, *Discrepant Engagements*, jacket cover.

2. THE EMPIRICAL SUBJECT IN QUESTION

1. Aimé Césaire, *Cahier d'un retour au pays natal* (Paris: Présence Africaine, 1983), 22. All further references will be to this edition, indicated by PA and the page number in the text.
2. Aimé Césaire, *The Collected Poetry*, trans. Clayton Eshlemen and Annette Smith (Berkeley: University of California Press, 1983), 45. I have modified the translation slightly: Eshlemen and Smith translate "un homme qui crie" as "a man screaming." They make the same choice in their translation of *Et les chiens se taisaient*, where they systematically translate "cris" as "screams"; see Aimé Césaire, "And the Dogs Were Silent," in *Aimé Césaire: Lyric and Dramatic Poetry*, trans. Clayton Eshlemen and Annette Smith (Charlottesville: University of Virginia Press, 1990). All further quotations in English will be from this translation, and I will provide the page number in the text.
3. The official "Hommage à Aimé Césaire" website, established around the time of his death on April 17, 2008, presents on its homepage the opening lines of this passage: "Je viendrais à ce pays mien et je lui dirais:

'Embrassez-moi sans crainte . . . Et si je ne sais que parler, c'est pour vous que je parlerai'" (http://www.hommage-cesaire.net/). Lilian Pestre de Almeida also notes the tendency among scholars to ignore the deflating passage that follows: "On oublie la chute terrible dans la réalité la plus mesquine, celle de la strophe 39 ["Et voici que je suis venu!"]. En clair, on lui fait dire le contraire de ce qu'affirme le poème, d'où le danger des morceaux choisis d'une oeuvre beaucoup plus complexe." Aimé Césaire, *Une saison en Haïti* (Montreal: Mémoire d'encrier, 2010), 100.

4. On Césaire's use of triplicates, and, more generally, on his rhetorical style in political discourse, see Serge Gavronsky, "Aimé Césaire and the Language of Politics," *French Review* 56, no. 2 (December 1982): 272–80.
5. Arthur Rimbaud, *Oeuvres complètes*, ed. Rolland Renéville and Jules Mouquet (Paris: Gallimard, Pléiade, 1954), 244; original italics; my translation.
6. For a full account of the genesis of *Et les chiens se taisaient*, see Alex Gil, "Migrant Textuality: On the Fields of Aimé Césaire's *Et les chiens se taisaient*" (Ph.D. diss., University of Virginia, 2012); available at *Academic Commons*, http://academiccommons.columbia.edu/catalog/ac:161180. Gil demonstrates convincingly that the work was first conceived as a stage drama and that the excisions Césaire effected in the later versions transformed what was an originally coherent accompanying commentary (of the Chorus, for instance) into hermetic ecphrastic poetry: "Once you remove the mimetic action on the stage that authorizes and gives meaning to them, lines such as these transform into a peculiar form of detached *ecphrasis*; soon enough, when the geographical and historical references disappear as well, these ostensive lines end up being removed completely or disfigured to refer to a vague archetypal history of the African diaspora and colonialism" (41).
7. Theodor Adorno, *Aesthetic Theory*, trans., ed., intro. Robert Hullot-Kentor (Minneapolis: Minnesota University Press, 1997), 216, 167, 169.
8. Ibid., 231. The mediated/immediate dichotomy, when applied to the subject, is a distortion of Adorno's thought; as he states in his "draft introduction" to *Aesthetic Theory*, "the subject is in itself objectively mediated" (356). "The objectivation of art through its immanent execution requires the historical subject. If the artwork hopes through its objectivation to achieve that truth that is hidden from the subject, then this

is so because the subject is itself not ultimate" (169). Adorno is arguing here with Riegl's "concept of 'artistic volition'"; as I maintained in chapter 1, for Adorno, it is only when the author, as empirical subject, abandons volition that her action becomes creative (169).

9. Peggy Phelan, comment offered at her seminar, "Literature and Performance," held at University of California, Irvine, March 1–3, 2011.
10. Phelan poses the question in these terms: "What is the repertoire of images from which identity is shaped?" (ibid.). See also Judith Butler's probing analysis of subjectivity in *Giving an Account of Oneself* (Amsterdam: Koninklijke van Gorcum, 2003), which is grounded in premises similar to those implicitly at work in what Phelan calls "the performance world view."
11. Léon-Gontran Damas, *Pigments—Névralgies*, ed. and postface Sandrine Poujols (Paris and Dakar: Présence Africaine, 2005), 41; my translation. "Solde"—dedicated, we might note, to Aimé Césaire—expresses the quintessential sensation of falsity that Fanon also associates with "*l'expérience vécue*" of the assimilated colonial subject.
12. See http://faculty.sites.uci.edu/aestheticsubjectivity/.
13. Aimé Césaire, *Poésie, théâtre, essais et discours*, ed. A. James Arnold (Paris: Éditions CNRS, 2013), 1293; my translation. Césaire is inspired here by Claude McKay's *Banjo*, excerpts of which were published in French translation in *La Revue du Monde Noir*. Césaire's relationship to black popular culture (celebrated in *Banjo* as an authentic alternative to white culture) was problematic; he did not easily embrace, as did Damas, either Caribbean or African American popular forms (see chapter 3).
14. Césaire, *Poésie, théâtre, essais et discours*, 1292. The quotation comes from Jules Michelet, *Le peuple*, 1877, xxix ("Lettre-préface à M. Edgar Quinet"). Once again Césaire establishes an intertextual relation with a canonical (white) French author in order to depict a condition that he racializes.
15. In *L'Étudiant Noir* (the title of which was *L'Étudiant Martiniquais* before Césaire became editor), Césaire may have also had African colonials in mind, but "Nègreries" fits into a series of Antillean writings of the period that target the *évolué* of the Antilles in particular (see essays in *Légitime Défense* and *La Revue du Monde Noir*). At the time, Antilleans

were taught that they were superior to Africans; Césaire, in this context, is challenging Antilleans to embrace their African past.

16. Aimé Césaire, *Et les chiens se taisaient: Tragédie (arrangement théâtral)* (Paris: Présence Africaine, 1956), 115. All further references will be to this edition.
17. Nick Nesbitt, *Voicing Memory: History and Subjectivity in the French Caribbean* (Charlottesville: University of Virginia Press, 2003), 22.
18. For a full account, see Alex Gil, "Découverte de l'Ur-texte de *Et les chiens se taisaient*," in *Aimé Césaire à l'oeuvre*, ed. Marc Cheymol and Philippe Ollé-Laprune (Paris: Éditions des archives contemporaines, 2010), 145–56. See also Gil, *Migrant Textuality*: "A dizzying chain of textual events, these four major versions trace a journey from historical particularity to an oneiric universalism and on to what we may be tempted to call a reconciliation of the two in the attempts to stage it at the height of the anti-colonial movement of the 1950s" (2–3).
19. See the "Letter to André Breton," April 4, 1994, quoted in Gil, "Découverte," 147. See also Kora Véron "Césaire at the Crossroads in Haiti: Correspondence with Henri Seyrig," *Comparative Literature Studies* 50:3 (2013): 403–44. The letters Véron discovered reveal that André Gide first intended to publish the play, called *Toussaint Louverture*, in his Algerian review, *L'Arche*, in 1944, but Césaire thought his "tentative" remained "trop historique" (437), so he kept revising it.
20. Rodney E. Harris, *L'humanisme dans le théâtre d'Aimé Césaire* (Ottawa: Naaman, 1973), 56.
21. Yvan Labejof claims in "Autour d'une mise en scène de "Et les chiens se taisaient"" that he heard a French radio production directed by Sylvia Monfort, but he does not provide a date. See *Aimé Césaire: L'homme et l'oeuvre*, ed. Lilyan Kesteloot and Barthélémy Kotchy (Paris: Présence Africaine, 1973), 155. Janis L. Pallister repeates Labejof's claim in *Aimé Césaire* (New York: Twayne, 1991): "A performance of the Césaire's play has been broadcast on French radio by Sylvia Monfort et al., but evidently not successfully so" (48). The radio play in German translation was largely a product of Janheinz Jahn's revisions. Césaire did not want Jahn to stage the radio play, which was an abbreviated version of his 1946 text; but Jahn did so without Césaire's permission, basing the German version on his own 1955–1956 translation for radio. See Gil,

Migrant Textuality, 224. A review of the German version of the radio play, titled *Und die Hunde Schwiegen*, indicates that the long monologues did "not lead to a real plot"; nonetheless, the play appears suited for radio because of its "lyric-rhythmic circular dance." See "'And the Dogs Were Silent': The Rebel Wasn't," *Frankfurt Evening Post*, January 16, 1956, anonymous reviewer, trans. Jonathan Blake Fine.

22. Scholars have not been able to pin down the precise number of times *Et les chiens se taisaient* has been produced on stage. In his annotations to Aimé Césaire, *Poésie, théâtre, essais et discours*, A. James Arnold presents the evidence we have: "À la quatrième de couverture, imprimée après la page de titre dans l'édition Désormeaux de 1976, Césaire ajouta: 'Cette pièce a fait l'objet de tentatives de mise en scène de Sarah Maldo[r]or, d'Yvan Labéjof et du regretté Jean-Marie Serreau.' Or, les archives de Serreau consultées par nous au département des Arts du spectacle de la Bibliothèque nationale de France ne retiennent aucune trace de sa mise en scène, ce qui est regrettable" (783–84). Clément Mbom refers to the 1956 performance of *Et les chiens se taisaient*, performed at the Sorbonne during the Premier Congrès des Écrivains et Artistes Noirs, in "Aimé Césaire: Poète ou dramaturge?" in *Soleil éclaté*, ed. Jacqueline Leiner (Tubingen: Gunter Narr, 1984), 262. The only mention of the Haiti performance I have found is in "Les fondements littéraires de la réception d'Aimé Césaire au Bénin" by Guy Ossito Midihouan in *Aimé Césaire et le monde noir*, ed. Richard Laurent Omgba and André Ntonfo (Paris: L'Harmattan, 2012). In 1978 Sarah Maldoror released an approximately thirteen-minute documentary film (16 mm) titled *Et les chiens se taisaient* comprising a collection of the Rebel's speeches, starting with the "Mort au cri 'Morts aux blancs'" speech that I analyze further in this chapter.

23. Ernstpeter Ruhe, *Aimé Césaire et Janheinz Jahn: Les débuts du théâtre césairien* (Würzburg: Königshawusen and Neumann, 1990), 9. Gil quotes from the stage directions in the "Ur-text" to show that this earliest version was more "theatrical," and potentially easier to stage, than the 1946 rewrite; see *Migrant Textuality*, 29–30.

24. Interview with François Beloux, "Un poète politique: Aimé Césaire" in *Le Magazine Littéraire* 34 (1969): 27–32, at 30, quoted in Gil, *Migrant Textuality*, 155.

25. See letter to Jahn quoted in Ruhe, *Aimé Césaire et Janheinz Jahn*, 8: "piece où j'ai tant mis de moi-même et de mes problèmes."
26. A. James Arnold, introduction in *Aimé Césaire, Lyric and Dramatic Poetry*, xv.
27. Ruhe, *Aimé Césaire et Janheinz Jahn*, 17.
28. On this period, see Pierre Bouvier, *Aimé Césaire et Frantz Fanon: Portraits de décolonisés* (Paris: Les Belles Lettres, 2010), 111–23. See also Aimé Césaire with Françoise Vergès, *Nègre je suis: Nègre je resterai* (Paris: Albin, 2005): "À Haïti, j'ai surtout vu ce qu'il ne fallait pas faire! Un pays qui avait prétendument conquis sa liberté, qui avait conquis son indépendence et que je voyais plus misérable que la Martinique, colonie française!" (56). Immediately after the war, France appeared to be the gold standard of antiracism and tolerance; at the time, the Fourth Republic seemed to promise Martinique greater liberties within the fold of departmentalization. As documentation of Césaire's many interventions in the Assemblée nationale reveal, he regretted supporting departmentalization once he realized that the "territoires d'outre-mer" would not be granted the same rights as those enjoyed by the departments of the "hexagone." See Ernest Moutoussamy, *Aimé Césaire: Député à l'Assemblée nationale 1945–1993* (Paris: L'Harmattan, 1993). Césaire's first known public speaking engagement on political matters (in Haiti he gave nine lectures on literary topics), occurred in late December 1944; in this speech before a Martiniquan audience he referred explicitly to the problem plaguing Haitian self-governance: the distance between the elites and the people; see Thomas A. Hale, who cites an account of Césaire's speech published in *Justice*, the organ of the Martiniquan Communist Party, in "Littérature orale: le discours comme arme de combat chez Aimé Césaire," *Soleil éclaté*, ed. Jacqueline Leiner, 173–186 (Tübingen: Gunter Narr Verlag, l984), 177.
29. On the Prometheus myth, see K. A. Poniewaz, "Les regards des dieux: La vision tragique de *Et les chiens se taisaient*," in *Jeux du Regard* 3 (2007): 129–37; and Alain Moreau, "Eschyle et Césaire: Rencontres et influences dans 'Et les chiens se taisaient,'" in *Soleil éclaté*, ed. Jacqueline Leiner, 285–301 (Tübingen: Gunter Narr Verlag, 1984); on the Oedipus myth, see A. James Arnold, *Modernism and Negritude: The Poetry and Poetics of Aimé Césaire* (Cambridge, MA: Harvard University Press, 1981); on Claudel's theatre as intertext, see Ernstpeter E. Ruhe,

"L'Anticlaudelianus d'Aimé Césaire: Intertextualité dans *Et les chiens se taisaient*," *Oeuvres et Critiques* 19, no. 2 (1994): 231–41; and on the Biblical subtext, see Lilyan Kesteloot and Bartholémy Kotchy, *Aimé Césaire, l'homme et l'oeuvre* (Paris: Présence Africaine, 1973).

30. Harris, *L'humanisme dans le théâtre d'Aimé Césaire*, 49; my translation.
31. See Gil, "Découverte": "Plus encore que la matière historique qui doit passer à la trappe, l'abondante matière qui change de place dans l'économie générale de la pièce retient notre intérêt. A maints endroits la réplique d'un personnage de l'Ur-texte se retrouvera dans la bouche d'un autre personnage, antagoniste parfois! Le fait que les répliques ne correspondent plus à la psychologie de tel ou tel personnage souligne de façon indiscutable la décision d'abandonner le drame historique à la faveur de l'oratorio marqué au coin du surréalisme" (154).
32. Eshleman and Smith translate these lines as "My law is that I should run on an unbroken chain until the fiery joining that volatilizes me purifies me and ignites me with my amalgamated gold prism" (50). The "de" in French is unclear, though; it may be that the "amalgamated gold prism" is not what "ignites" him; it is what is destroyed. He is purified of ("épuré de") the prism.
33. I have modified the Eshleman and Smith translation, which reads: "You gods down there / benevolent gods / I'm carrying off in my broken-down mug / the buzzing of a living flesh/ here I am . . ." (67).
34. Femi Ojo-Ade reads the drums as a positive force (the African convocation to a community) that overpower the negative force of the dogs, but this does not seem to be substantiated by the symbology of the play. See Femi Ojo-Ade, *Aimé Césaire's African Theater: Of Poets, Prophets, and Politicians* (Trenton, NJ: Africa World Press, 2012), 51–59.
35. See Douglas Kahn and Gregory Whitehead, *Wireless Imagination: Sound, Radio, and the Avant-Garde* (Cambridge, MA: MIT Press, 1992).
36. Marianne Wichmann Bailey, *The Ritual Theater of Aimé Césaire: Mythic Structures of the Dramatic Imagination* (Tübingen: Gunter Narr, 1992), 153–54. In "Autour d'une mise en scène," Yvan Labejof explains that in Martinique the "chiens" of the title would evoke both the dogs used to hunt down escaped slaves ("marrons") and reincarnated souls (154).
37. See Ojo-Ade, *Aimé Césaire's African Theater*, 59.
38. Bailey, *The Ritual Theater of Aimé Césaire*, 159.

39. On "fresque historique," see Rodney Harris, *L'humanisme dans le théâtre*, 56.
40. In the *Cahier*, the speaker resists the temptation to be "a man of hate." That colonialism turns the colonizer (and not just the colonized) into a beast is a point Césaire makes clearly in *Discours sur le colonialisme* (and one that he actualizes in *Les chiens* through the figure of the dogs): "La colonisation, je le répète, déshumanise l'homme même le plus civilisé; que l'action coloniale, l'entreprise coloniale, la conquête coloniale, fondée sur le mépris de l'homme indigène et justifiée par ce mépris, tend inévitablement à modifier celui qui l'entreprend; que le colonisateur, qui, pour se donner bonne conscience, s'habitue à voir dans l'autre la bête, s'entraîne à le traiter en bête, tend objectivement à se transformer lui-même en bête" (Césaire, *Poésie, théâtre, essais et discours*, 1453). The *Discours sur le colonialisme* was published in 1948, 1950, and 1955.
41. For the annotated text, see "L'homme de culture et ses responsabilités," in Césaire, *Poésie, théâtre, essais et discours* (1553–1559).
42. Ibid., 1555. For a contrasting view, see Nick Nesbitt, *Caribbean Critique: Antillean Critical Theory from Toussaint to Glissant* (Liverpool: Liverpool University Press, 2013); Nesbitt contends that in Césaire's preface to Guy Fau's *L'abolition de l'esclavage* of 1972, "Césaire explicitly affirms a quasi-Fanonian vision of the necessity and justice of anticolonial violence" (ibid., 112).
43. On the relations between Fanon and Césaire, see Bouvier, *Aimé Césaire et Frantz Fanon*; and André Lucrèce, *Frantz Fanon et les Antilles* (Fort-de-France: Le Teneur, 2011; 71–94), which also contains Césaire's "Hommage à Frantz Fanon," first published by Présence Africaine in 1962. This text also affirms Césaire's conviction that violent revolt is the only way to overthrow a colonial regime. The editors of *Poésie, théâtre, essais et discours* did not include this "Hommage" in their collection.
44. See also the *Cahier*: "ne faites point de moi cet homme de haine pour qui / je n'ai que haine" (PA, 50).
45. For instance, at the end of the second added monologue, the Rebel rejects the "glèbe usée" (or sterile earth) of inaction evoked earlier and states that now he is ready to move forward on more firm and fertile ground: "je suis prêt! / glèbe tassée, je suis prêt."
46. Bailey, *The Ritual Theater*, 112.

47. "Christophe, Lumumba, the Rebelle," Bailey observes, "all draw away from the people in whose name they act" (*The Ritual Theater*, 113). Even the ending of *Une tempête*, which is often read as a victory for the rebel, Caliban, ends with Caliban leaving the stage, his "La liberté ohé, la liberté!" reduced to "les debris du chant." Prospero, the figure of European reason, fares no better; he makes "mechanical" gestures while uttering a "langage appauvri et steréotypé." See Aimé Césaire, *Une tempête* (Paris: Seuil, 1969), 91–92.
48. The Rebel realizes he cannot advance toward his goal without "le cri," this time drawn from a hollow, a "creux boueux," that is strangely reminiscent of the "grand trou noir" at the end of the *Cahier*.
49. An important exception is Rémy Sylvestre Bouelet's reading of the self-reflexive monologue in Césaire's plays in the context of a dialectical unfolding; see Bouelet, *Espace et dialectique du héros césairien* (Paris: L'Harmattan, 1987), 19. Bailey interprets the self-reflexive moment as an instance of "ego-shedding and initiatory descent. His conflict now is with himself" (ibid., 211). For both, the pattern is that of dialectical advance toward synthesis.
50. Staging the self-reflexivity of the Rebel serves an important didactic function as well, for one of the rationales for colonization cited by the "Grand Promoteur" is that slavery is justified because blacks are nothing more than "les Danseurs de l'Humanité" (23), an echo of the Administrator's claim that the white race is the only race of "people qui pense" (11).
51. These are stage directions contained in the 1946 edition, *Les armes miraculeuses*, 123, 139, 145, and 172.
52. I therefore have to differ with Georges Ngal, who opposes "héroisme" to "singerie" in his long list of Césairean dichotomies; see Ngal, "Le théâtre d'Aimé Césaire: Une dramaturgie de la décolonisation," *Revue des Sciences Humaines*, fasc. 40 (October–December 1970): 616.
53. See Aimé Césaire, *La tragédie du Roi Christophe* (Paris: Présence Africaine, 1963), 118 and 110. At the end of the play, Christophe pleads to be relieved of all the trapings of royalty: "Défais-moi de tous ces vêtements, défais-m'en comme, l'aube venue, on se défait des rêves de la nuit. . . . De mes nobles, de ma noblesse, de mon sceptre, de ma couronne. Et lave-moi! Oh lave-moi de leur fard . . ." (147). The Rebel's desire for nudity early on in the play suggests that he hopes to avoid

the fate of the self-aggrandizing King. He does not escape the Lover's accusation nonetheless.

54. The *Cahier* dramatizes this same dilemma by presenting a speaker who vacillates constantly between the gesture of "rising up" ("debout") and the gesture of hurling himself on the ground, both of which are imitated by the Rebel. See the *Cahier*: "Je refuse de me donner mes boursouflures comme d'authentiques gloires. / Et je ris de mes anciennes imaginations puériles" (PA, 38); "Je me cachais derrière une vanité stupide le destin m'appelait j'étais caché derrière et voici l'homme par terre" (PA, 43).
55. This argument is precisely the one made by Judith Butler in *Giving an Account of Oneself*, 40; it is the insight of poststructuralism in general that the "I" is constituted by means of a language, a structure of address, and generic conventions that it does not choose and that shape its self-understanding (and the limits thereof).
56. See Marcel Mauss, "Une catégorie de l'esprit humain: La notion de personne, celle du 'moi'" (a lecture first delivered in 1938), in *Sociologie et anthropologie* (Paris: Presses Universitaires de France, 1950).
57. For an account of "disidentification" as fundamental to identity formation, see José Esteban Muñoz, *Disidentifications: Queers of Color and the Performance of Politics* (Minneapolis: University of Minnesota Press, 5).
58. On the possible influence of Kojève and Hegelian thought on Césaire, see Nesbitt, *Voicing Memory*.
59. Butler, *Giving an Account of Oneself*, 44.
60. "Permanent parabasis" is Paul de Man's term; see de Man, "Rhetoric of Temporality" in *Blindness and Insight: Essays in the Rhetoric of Contemporary Criticism*, 2nd ed., intro. Wlad Godzich (Minneapolis: University of Minnesota Press, 1983). With reference to Schlegel's notion of irony, de Man writes: "The positive name he gives to the infinity of this process is freedom, the unwillingness of the mind to accept any stage in its progression as definitive . . . it designates the fact that irony engenders a temporal sequence of acts of consciousness which is endless" (220); "Irony divides the flow of temporal experience into a past that is pure mystification and a future that remains harassed forever by a relapse within the inauthentic. It can know this inauthenticity but never overcome it" (222).
61. On the persistence of accountability despite the impossibility of complete self-identity, see Butler, *Giving an Account of Oneself*, 44–45. This

is not the place to elaborate on Césaire's position with regard to performance in general; I will simply note that there are real reasons why he would have been wary of any association of blackness with performance. One need only think of Langston Hughes's comments on the pressure he felt to be an entertainer in *The Big Sea*; or Jean Genet's astute grasp of the situation in *Les Nègres*, to understand Césaire's reticence with regard both to popular cultural portrays of blacks (minstrelsy, blacks as natural dancers, etc.) and the deep problematic of colonial mimicry.

62. Roger Toumson and Simonne Henry-Valmore, *Aimé Césaire: Le nègre inconsolé*, (Fort de France, Martinique: Vents d'ailleurs, 2002), 73.
63. Theodor W. Adorno, *Minima Moralia*, trans. E. F. N. Jephcott (London: Verso, 1978), 17–18.

3. POETRY AND THE TYPOSPHERE IN LÉON-GONTRAN DAMAS

1. Aimé Césaire, *Cahier d'un retour au pays natal* (Paris: Présence Africaine, 1983), 44.
2. Aimé Césaire, *The Collected Poetry*, trans. Annette Smith and Clayton Eshleman (Berkeley: University of California Press, 1981), 64–65. The verses are repeated later in the poem.
3. Ibid., 68–69. Negritude poets drew much of their imagination of the African past from the works of Leo Frobenius; see Dominique Combe, *Aimé Césaire: Cahier d'un retour au pays natal* (Paris: Presses Universitaires de France, 1993); Georges Ngal, *Aimé Césaire: Un homme à la recherche d'une patrie* (Paris: Présence Africaine, 1994); and Lilyan Kesteloot, *Black Writers in French: A Literary History of Negritude* (Washington, DC: Howard University Press, 1991).
4. Marcel Cohen is the direct target of Jacques Derrida in *De la grammatologie*. As early as 1927, however, Maurice Delafosse had published *Les nègres* (Paris: F. Rieder), in which he debunks Cohen's scholarship, claiming that it "ne serait pas rigoureusement exact de dire que les nègres ne possèdent qu'une littérature orale et que cette littérature soit nécessairement du genre dit populaire . . . on y [en Afrique noire] observe aussi une littérature orale savante et une littérature écrite" (65). The works of Delafosse had a very strong influence on Damas in particular.

5. According to Joan F. Higbee, Damas became aware of his inferior status even before arriving in France, from the first day he began his studies in Martinique: "To a Guyanese 'WHITE' was not 'BETTER.' His [Damas's] introduction to narratives that asserted European superiority occurred, he told me, when he left Guiana to attend the Lycée Schoelcher in Martinique." Higbee, "Léon-Gontran Damas: My Thesis," in *Léon-Gontran Damas 1912–1978: Founder of Negritude, A Memorial Casebook*, ed. Daniel L. Racine (Washington, DC: University Press of America, 1979), 128.
6. See Raymond F. Betts, *Assimilation and Association in French Colonial Theory 1840–1914* (New York: Columbia University Press, 1961).
7. For an account of the paradoxes of this period, see Petrine Archer-Straw, *Negrophilia: Avant-Garde Paris and Black Culture in the 1920s* (London: Thames and Hudson, 2000).
8. Étienne Léro, "Misère d'une poésie," *Légitime Défense*, 1 (1932), 10; my translation.
9. Benedict Anderson, *Imagined Communities: Reflections on the Origin and Spread of Nationalism*, rev. ed. (London: Verso, 2006): "Print-capitalism," writes Anderson, "made it possible for rapidly growing numbers of people to think about themselves, and to relate themselves to others, in profoundly new ways" (36).
10. Brent Hayes Edwards, *The Practice of Diaspora: Literature, Translation, and the Rise of Black Internationalism* (Cambridge, MA: Harvard University Press, 2003), 8. See also Gary Wilder, *The French Imperial Nation-State: Negritude and Colonial Humanism Between the Two World Wars* (Chicago: University of Chicago Press, 2005).
11. Jacqueline Leiner, "Entretien avec Aimé Césaire par Jacqueline Leiner," in *Tropiques* (Paris: Jean-Michel Place, 1978), xiv.
12. I speak here of the "black *man*" (as opposed to the "black person") and I refer to the black subject as "he" or "him" (instead of "she" and "her") primarily in the interest of concision. However, I am also registering the fact that most theorists of colonial subjection (including Fanon) distinguish between gendered positions in the colonial racial economy. For a sensitive account of how assimilation impacted Caribbean women, see Shireen K. Lewis, "Gendering Négritude: Paulette Nardal's Contribution to the Birth of Modern Francophone Literature," in *Race, Culture, and Identity: Francophone West African and Caribbean Literature and*

Theory from Négritude to Créolité, 55–69 (Lanham, MD: Rowman & Littlefield, 2006).

13. For both Fanon and Damas, "no ontology of the black man can be realized in a colonized society"; see Frantz Fanon, *Peau noire masques blancs* (Paris: Seuil, 1952), 88; my translation.
14. There were, of course, hybrid works: Senghor wrote a poem about Harlem titled "New York" with the intention of reciting it to the accompaniment of a jazz orchestra and solo trumpet. His "Élégies majeures" indicate the instruments with which they are to be accompanied. In 2006 Daniel Delas released a CD and book titled *Senghor et la musique* (Paris: OIF and Le Français dans le Monde, 2006) that displays the efforts of three groups of students (in Dakar, Toulouse, and Tunis) to set his poems to music. To my ear, at least, what emerges from the exercise is further proof that poetic language exists on a different plane from musical rhythm; only one "cut" ("Prière aux masques") convincingly brings out the repetitive, drum-like meter of the poem.
15. Léon-Gontran Damas, ed. *Poèmes nègres sur des airs africains* (Paris: GLM, 1948).
16. See, in particular, "Comme les Lamantins vont boire à la source," the postface to *Éthiopiques*, reprinted in Léopold Sédar Senghor, *Oeuvre poétique* (Paris: Seuil, 1990), 155–68. Senghor explains that his poems should be able to be *recited*—not just "sung"—in the French style (167). "Mais on me posera la question: 'Pourquoi, dès lors, écrivez-vous en français?' Parce que nous sommes des métis culturels, parce que, si nous sentons en nègres, nous nous exprimons en français" (ibid., 166).
17. On the phenomenon of subvocalization, see Lesley Wheeler, *Voicing American Poetry: Sound and Performance from the 1920s to the Present* (Ithaca, NY: Cornell University Press, 2008).
18. Henri Meschonnic, *Critique du rythme: Anthropologie historique du langage* (Lagrasse: Verdier, 1982).
19. According to Alexandre M'Boukou, "Mr. Damas was the bond of continuity between *Légitime Défense* and *L'Etudiant Noir*." M'Boukou, "Léon-Gontran Damas on Race, African-Afro-American Relations, Africa, and Négritude," in *Léon-Gontran Damas 1912–1978: Founder of Negritude, A Memorial Casebook*, ed. Daniel L. Racine (Washington, DC: University Press of America, 1979), 166. Damas was the cofounder de *L'Étudiant Noir*, the goal of which was to end the "tribalization" of

the Latin Quarter (see Racine, *Introduction à Léon-Gontran Damas*, in ibid., 3). On this period and on the importance of the *Revue du Monde Noir* for Damas's poetics in particular, see Michel Fabre, "René Maran: Trait d'union entre deux négritudes," in *Négritude africaine: Négritude caraibe* (Paris: Université de Paris XIII, 1973).

20. Damas became aware of Hughes's literary presence around 1931, when his poems appeared in *La Revue du Monde Noir*. Later Damas tried his own hand at translating Hughes, and apparently he was in the process of writing Hughes's biography when he died in 1978. (I found no trace of this biography in the Damas archive at the Schomburg Center for Research in Black Culture.) Although Damas could not have seen *The Weary Blues* when he began writing in 1926, he would have had access to the text by the time some of the poems were printed in *Esprit* in 1934. The *mise en page* of Hughes's "Poem" is too similar to that of Damas's "Ils sont venus ce soir" to be pure coincidence. For a treatment of the relationship between Jacques Roumain and Langston Hughes that also sheds light on Roumain's relationship to Damas, see Anita Patterson, *Race, American Literature and Transnational Modernism* (Cambridge: Cambridge University Press, 2008).
21. Présence Africaine republished the "definitive" version of *Pigments* with *Névralgies* in 1972; in the meantime, *Graffiti* appeared in 1952; *Black Label* in 1956; and a first edition of *Névralgies* in 1966.
22. Antoine Coron, "Artisans de belles vraies oeuvres," in *Les Éditions GLM 1923–74: Bibliographie* (Paris: Bibliothèque Nationale, 1981), xiii. *Pigments* bears a preface penned by Robert Desnos and an engraving by Frans Masereel. Lévis Mano used two fonts for *Pigments*, Série 18 romain c.12 and Ronaldson old style romain c.9 (31), the same ones he used for many of the surrealist works he published that year: Tristan Tzara's *Vigies*; Henri Michaux's *La ralentie*; Georges Hugnet's *L'Apocalypse*; Georges Bataille's review *Acéphale: Religion, Socologie, Philosophie*; Valentine Penrose's *Sorts de la lueur*; Man Ray's *La photographie n'est pas l'art*; André Breton's *Exposition internationale Paris 1937* and *De l'humour noir*; René Char's *Placard pour un chemin des écoliers*; and Paul Eluard's *Quelques-uns des mots qui jusqu'ici m'étaient mystérieusement interdits*. See also the postface by Sandrine Poujols to the 2005 edition of *Pigments/Névralgies* (Paris: Présence Africaine, 2005), 157–66.

23. Cunard's publishing house, the Hours Press, took part in the renaissance of the book that characterized the French, British, and American avant-gardes. Cunard published surrealists and black writers and was the editor of *Negro: An Anthology* in 1934.
24. Jerome McGann, *Black Riders: The Visible Language of Modernism* (Princeton, NJ: Princeton University Press, 1993), 7.
25. *Esprit* (September 1934), 707. During the era of the Popular Front, Emmanuel Mounier's review carved out a space in both the political and the cultural fields by supporting neither fascism nor communism. Mounier was closely tied to the Catholic metaphysics of Jacques Maritain; they cofounded *Esprit* in October 1932. The editorial decision to include Damas in the pages of the review was probably based on a combination of paternalism and Mounier's doctrine of "personalism," which advanced the idea that every human being has the right (and obligation) to develop his potential as fully as possible. See Bernard E. Doering, *Jacques Maritain and the French Catholic Intellectuals* (Notre Dame, IN: University of Notre Dame Press, 1983), 60–75.
26. My translation.
27. On ethnographic surrealism, see James Clifford, *The Predicament of Culture: Twentieth-Century Ethnography, Literature, and Art* (Cambridge, MA: Harvard University Press, 1988).
28. Marcel Moré, "Poèmes de Léon Damas," *Esprit* (September 1934), 705.
29. Senghor: "Des poètes nègres francophones de ma génération, Damas est, sans conteste, celui qui a le mieux illustré le rythme nègre." Léopold Sédar Senghor, preface to *Léon-Gontran Damas: L'homme et l'œuvre*, by Daniel Racine (Paris: Présence Africaine, 1983), 12. See also Keith L. Walker, *The Game of Slipknot: Countermodernism and Francophone Literary Culture* (Durham, NC: Duke University Press, 1999): "From his poems (which typographically meander across, up, and down the page, resembling musical scores at times) rise pianistic melodies, the hammering cadences of African and Harlem drums, and the stammerings, stutterings, and moans of a Louis Armstrong muted trumpet" (74). Richard Serrano is the only critic I know who has fruitfully questioned this stereotype; see Serrano, *Against the Postcolonial: 'Francophone' Writers at the Ends of French Empire* (Lanham, MD: Lexington Books, 2005).
30. Moré, "Poèmes de Léon Damas," *Esprit* (September 1934), 705.

31. Another poem published in the same issue, "Solde," indicates that the plight of the *assimilé* involves an alienation from the self, an alienation from one's own body.
32. "Cubes" was published in *New Masses* 10 (March 13, 1934). See Seth Moglen, "Modernism in the Black Diaspora: Langston Hughes and the Broken Cubes of Picasso," *Callaloo* 25, no. 4 (Autumn 2002): 1188–1205 and Ryan James Kerman "The *Coup* of Langston Hughes's Picasso Period: Excavating Mayakovsky in Langston Hughes's verse," *Compartive Literature* 66:2 (2014): 227–46. The "Vers en escalier" also appears in Mayakovsky's poetry as the Russian *Lestnitsa*. On the typographic and design features of *New Masses*, published from 1926–1948, see Cary Nelson, *Repression and Recovery: Modern American Poetry and the Politics of Cultural Memory, 1910–1945* (Madison: Wisconsin University Press, 1989), 226–31 and Aldon Lynn Nielsen, *Black Chant: Languages of African-American Postmodernism* (Cambridge: Cambridge University Press, 1997).
33. For a scholarly elaboration of this argument, see Simon Gikandi, "Picasso, Africa, and the Schemata of Difference," *Modernism/Modernity* 10, no. 3 (2003): 455–80.
34. See Wheeler, *Voicing American Poetry*, 75.
35. Richard Burton, "My Mother Who Fathered Me: 'Hoquet' by Léon Damas," *Journal of West Indian Literature* 4, no. 1 (January 1990): 14–27.
36. Originally transported from Senegal to the Caribbean by slaves, the banjo became a popular instrument in jazz bands and music halls and was featured in Claude McKay's novel of the same name (*Banjo*, 1929). The original word for "banjo" is *bagnan*, which is translated into French as a "violon fait d'un gourd." On the wordplay at the end of "Hoquet"—especially the creation of "ban" (or exile) out of "ban / jo"—see "Le vocabulaire de Damas: Entre anti-académisme et modernité" by Gervais Chirhalwirwa and Biringanine Ndagano in *Léon-Gontran Damas, poète moderne*, ed. Chirhalwirwa and Ndagano (Matoury, Guyane: Ibis Rouge, 20009), 41.
37. See Jean-Pierre Bobillot, *Trois essais sur la poésie littérale* (Paris: Al Dante, 2003), 126.
38. Gilles Deleuze, *Critique et clinique* (Paris: Minuit, 1993), 139.
39. Ibid., 141.
40. Ibid., 139.

41. Ibid., 142; Deleuze's analysis anticipates to some extent Jacques Derrida's in *Le monolinguisme de l'autre: Ou la prothèse d'origine* (Paris: Galilée, 1996); Deleuze associates such aggressive stylistics with avant-garde writers like Luca and Beckett, or with "minor literatures," not with writing in general.
42. Bobillot, *Trois essais*, 134. Bobillot writes: "And what if all poetry, from the most classic to the most modern . . . beyond what it seems explicitly to say, consisted in an effort to find spaces within language where it might be possible to stage a return of the repressed—orgasmic and intense? If repression is the very condition of language and meaning, might the return of the repressed be the source of *jouissance*, of pleasure in language? Is this, then, the role of *negativity* in poetry?" (126); my translation.
43. Deleuze, *Critique et clinique*, 142.
44. Fred Moten, *In the Break: The Aesthetics of the Black Radical Tradition* (Minneapolis: University of Minnesota Press, 2003), 94.
45. Glossing the two types of alienation treated by Fanon—the fundamental, universal alienation of the subject at the hands of the Symbolic and the specialized variety of alienation that results from colonial subjectivation—Moten writes: "'Continuous and distinct' seems right to me [as a way of understanding the relation between the two types of alienation] but what is required is that analytic attention of the highest order be given to the range of those continuities and distinctions. In the end, what's important is, I think, the modes of life that emerge from the experience of those whose subjectivity has been interdicted and who operate, at the same time, within a refusal of what has been refused to them" (email communication with the author, November 13, 2012).
46. Édouard Glissant, *Caribbean Discourse: Selected Essays*, trans. J. Michael Dash (Charlottesville: Caraf Books/University Press of Virginia, 1989), 123; see also Moten, *In the Break*: "The illusion of any immediacy of sound is re/written and the overdetermined and deferred fixity of writing is un/written by the material and transformative present of sound" (60). Kamau Brathwaite makes a similar point in *History of the Voice: The Development of Nation Language in Anglophone Caribbean Poetry* (London: New Beacon, 1984).

47. Glissant, *Caribbean Discourse*, 123. See also Houston A. Baker, *Blues, Ideology, and Afro-American Literature: A Vernacular Theory* (Chicago: University of Chicago Press, 1984); and Lindon Barrett, *Blackness and Value: Seeing Double* (Cambridge: Cambridge University Press, 1999).
48. Burton, "My Mother Who Fathered Me": "This fettering of the authentic voice of the Afro-Caribbean within the notational straight-jacket of Europe is, Damas implies, as much an act of violence or rape of innocence as the other enslavements of West Indian history" (25).
49. Brent Hayes Edwards, "The Literary Ellington," *Representations* 77 (Winter 2002): 1.
50. Ibid., 2.
51. Aimé Césaire, "Léon-Gontran Damas: A Man of Considerable Stature," in *Léon-Gontran Damas . . . A Memorial Casebook*, 95.

4. LÉON-GONTRAN DAMAS

1. Henri Meschonnic, *Critique du rythme: Anthropologie historique du langage* (Lagrasse: Verdier, 1982), 72; translations are my own.
2. Walter J. Ong, *Orality and Literacy: The Technologizing of the Word* (London: Methuen, 1982), 7.
3. Susan Howe, "Writing *Articulation of Sound Forms in Time*," in *The Sound of Poetry / The Poetry of Sound*, ed. Marjorie Perloff and Craig Dworkin (Chicago: University of Chicago Press, 2009): "Font-voices summon a reader into visible earshot" (200).
4. Meschonnic, *Critique du rythme*, 72.
5. Jacques Rancière, *Dissensus: On Politics and Aesthetics*, trans. Steve Corcoran (New York: Continuum, 2010), 137.
6. Importantly, this event is not necessarily experienced as "art" per se. For Rancière, the category "art" is a product of a discourse named "aesthetics" that emerges in the eighteenth century.
7. Rancière, *Dissensus*, 137. Emphasis in original.
8. Ibid.
9. Free and obligatory primary education was instituted in the French colonies the same day that slavery was abolished (for the first time) on April 27, 1848. The first Antillean *agrégé* was Louis Achille, in 1915. See MADRAS, *Dictionnaire encyclopédique et pratique de la Martinique:*

Les hommes, les faits, les chiffres (Fort-de-France: Éditions Exbrayat, 1996).

10. Rancière, *Dissensus*, 116.
11. Aimé Césaire, *Cahier d'un retour au pays natal* (Paris: Présence Africaine, 1983), 22; my translation.
12. In *La parole muette: Essai sur les contradictions de la littérature* (Paris: Hachette, 1998), Rancière alludes to the myth of Theuth (also treated in Derrida's *Disseminations*) to underscore his point. Theuth was the inventor of writing and despised foe of the Platonic Republic. As recounted by Socrates in the *Phaedrus*, the invention of writing brings about the end of the author's ethical responsibility to an audience of fellow citizens: "No longer guided by a father . . . the written word spins off in all directions [*s'en va rouler au hasard, de droite et de gauche*]," lending itself to "n'importe qui" (81–82), "the undetermined mass of possible readers [*la masse indéterminée des lecteurs possible*]"(169); my translation.
13. Jacques Rancière, *Mallarmé: La politique de la sirène* (Paris: Hachette, 1996), 86.
14. Ibid., 89.
15. Ibid.; and Stéphane Mallarmé, "Bucolique," in *Oeuvres complètes*, vol. 2, ed. Bertrand Marchal (Paris: Gallimard, Pléiade, 2003), 252.
16. Garrett Stewart, *Reading Voices: Literature and the Phonotext* (Berkeley: University of California Press, 1990), 3. Stewart argues that there is "a veritable deaf spot in the tenets of even the most sophisticated reception theories." See also Adalaide Morris's introduction to *Sound States: Innovative Poetics and Acoustical Technologies* (Chapel Hill: University of North Carolina Press, 1997).
17. See Jed Rasula, "Poetry's Voice-Over," in *Sound States: Innovative Poetics and Acoustical Technologies*, ed. Adalaide Morris, 274–316 (Chapel Hill: University of North Carolina Press, 1997).
18. Michael Golston, *Rhythm and Race in Modernist Poetry and Science: Pound, Yeats, Williams, and Modern Sciences of Rhythm* (New York: Columbia University Press, 2008), 11–12. Comte de Gobineau, the father of modern racism, also believed that each race had a pulse that beat to a different rhythm.
19. Fahamisha Patricia Brown, *Performing the Word: African American Poetry as Vernacular Culture* (New Brunswick, NJ: Rutgers University Press, 1999), 2.

20. It should be noted that Bernard Zadi Zaourou claims to have discerned traces of "négro-africaine" oral forms in Césaire's use of anaphora and other forms of repetition; see Zaourou, *Césaire entre deux cultures: Problèmes théoriques de la littérature négro-africaines aujourd'hui* (Dakar: Nouvelles Éditions Africaines, 1978), 169–75. Other scholars, including A. James Arnold, attribute Césaire's incantatory style to the influence of Charles Péguy, to whom Césaire dedicated an essay in *Tropiques*.
21. Édouard Glissant, *Poétique de la relation* (Paris: Gallimard, 1990), 51; my translation. "Ces enfants ne comprennent pas les formules, ne saisissent pas les allusions, mais c'est à eux que l'homme des contes d'abord s'adresse" (51).
22. Senghor's theory of rhythm owes a good deal to vitalist philosophy, as Donna V. Jones argues in *The Racial Discourses of Life Philosophy: Negritude, Vitalism, and Modernity* (New York: Columbia University Press, 2010).
23. Léopold Sédar Senghor, *Liberté I: Négritude et humanisme* (Paris: Seuil, 1964), 20; also see Senghor, postface in *Ethiopiques*, reprinted in *Oeuvre poétique* (Paris: Seuil, 1990), 164.
24. Léopold Sédar Senghor, *Anthologie de la nouvelle poésie nègre et malgache de langue française*, preface by Jean-Paul Sartre (Paris: Presses Universitaires de France, 1969), 5.
25. Senghor, postface in *Éthiopiques*, 161; interestingly, Senghor is speaking here about Césaire's "Batouque," which follows patterns of lineation similar to Damas's.
26. A third and compelling argument about race-identified rhythm is offered by Brent Hayes Edwards in *The Practice of Diaspora: Literature, Translation, and the Rise of Black Internationalism* (Cambridge, MA: Harvard University Press, 2003). He argues that African rhythm cannot be conveyed directly but instead haunts the text, coming "to mark a certain inaccessibility, a certain part of an 'African' heritage that remains elusive and unconquered" (55).
27. Martin Munro, *Different Drummers: Rhythm & Race in the Americas* (Berkeley: University of California Press, 2010), 139. While Munro is to be commended for reintroducing the question of "rhythm and its relationship to race and culture in the Americas" (4), it is a pity that he does not attend to poetic rhythm more closely. In his twelve pages devoted to Negritude poetry, not once does Munro cite the poems in the original

French. While he purports to analyze the rhythm of the poetry, what he is really talking about is the theme or "figure" of rhythm. "Rhythm does indeed figure constantly in Césaire's poems, and it is often explicitly linked to his idea of black culture." Ibid., 139. The same goes for his discussion of Césaire in "Listening to Aimé Césaire," *Francophone Postcolonial Studies*, 7, no. 1 (2009): 44–60. When Munro does refer to the actual rhythm of the poem, he reduces this rhythm to repetition, as if Caribbean poets were the only ones to employ repetition as a technique. See also Edwin C. Hill Jr., *Black Soundscapes White Stages: The Meaning of Francophone Sound in the Black Atlantic* (Baltimore: Johns Hopkins University Press, 2013). Hill's reading of Damas's last poem, *Black-Label*, contains many fine insights, but he falls into the same trap as Munro, quoting the poetry exclusively in English while asserting that he is discussing "rhythm"; "Damas's aggressive enumeration, forming its own rhythm and beat, creates not only a corpus of self-loathing and self-negation but also a path." Ibid., 115. It is startling—and of deep concern—that some American presses have become oblivious to the difference a foreign language makes. A French original does not have a rhythm identical to that of an English translation.

28. Peggy Phelan, "'Just Want to Say': Performance and Literature, Jackson and Poirier," in *PMLA* 125, no. 4 (October 2010): 942–47, 946.
29. Tom Vander Ven, "Robert Frost's Dramatic Principle of 'Oversound,'" *American Literature* 45, no. 2 (May 1973): 241.
30. Ibid., 243–44.
31. Phelan, "'Just Want to Say,'" 946.
32. Vander Ven, "Robert Frost's Dramatic Principle," 246.
33. Senghor, *Anthologie de la nouvelle poésie nègre*, 5.
34. See, for instance, the definition of "rhythm" provided by Victor Zuckerkandl in *Sound and Symbol: Music and the External World*, trans. Willard R. Trask (New York: Pantheon, 1956), 169–70. For Zuckerkandl, "rhythm" is the "return of the similar," while meter is "the return of the same"; "rhythm" is a recurring and thus recognizable pattern of stresses, with each unit potentially containing a different number of syllables (as opposed to the metrical unit of the alexandrine, which must always have twelve).
35. Phelan, "'Just Want to Say,'" 946.
36. Ibid. Phelan's evocation of Frost—and, later, Richard Poirier—is her way of indicating that the current devotion to the representation of

"subjectivity" ignores two important axioms of poststructuralist performance theory: that authentic subjectivity cannot be so clearly distinguished from performance; and that the self may be performative, a product of its reiterated enunciation.

37. See Richard Poirier, "The Performing Self," in *The Performing Self*, foreword by Edward W. Said (New Brunswick, NJ: Rutgers University Press, 1992), 100. Phelan leans on this essay to establish performance as a constitutive function of subjectivity; see ibid., 88.
38. Poirier, *The Performing Self*, 100.
39. Susan Stewart, *Poetry and the Fate of the Senses* (Chicago: University of Chicago Press, 2002), 63.
40. "Every act is compromised by the medium of its enactment." Rasula, "Poetry's Voice-Over," 278.
41. Stewart, *Poetry and the Fate of the Senses*: "I propose that the sound of poetry is heard in the way a promise is heard. . . . Voice takes place not merely as a presence but as the condition under which the person appears. The realization of expression depends on the bind, the implicit tie of intelligibility between speaker and listener that links their efforts toward closure. Through lyric we return literally to the breath and pulse of speech rhythm in tension with those formal structures we have available to us for making time manifest. In this way, lyric, no matter how joyous or comic, expresses that seriousness, the good faith in intelligibility, under which language proceeds and by means of which we recognize each other as speaking persons. The object of that recognition is a sound that becomes a human voice" (105).
42. Jacqueline Leiner, "Entretien avec Aimé Césaire par Jacqueline Leiner," in *Tropiques*, vol. 1 (Paris: Jean-Michel Place, 1978), xxii.
43. On performance as disappearance, see Peggy Phelan, *Unmarked: The Politics of Performance* (London: Routledge, 1993): "Performance occurs over a time which will not be repeated. It can be performed again, but this repetition itself marks it as 'different.' The document of a performance then is only a spur to memory, an encouragement of memory to become present" (146).
44. "Grapholect" is Walter Ong's term for designating the repertoire of words available through writing as opposed to speech; see Ong, *Orality and Literacy*, 8.
45. Phelan, "'Just Want to Say,'" 946.

46. See, for instance, Senghor, "Poésie française et poésie négro-africaine," in *Liberté III: Négritude et civilisation de l'universel* (Paris: Seuil, 1977), 23–26; and the postface to *Éthiopiques*, reprinted in *Oeuvre poétique* (Paris: Seuil, 1990).
47. *Négritude & poésie: Les grandes voix du sud*, vol. 1: *Léopold Sédar Senghor, Jacques Rabamananjara, Tchicaya U Tam'si* (Vincennes: Frémeaux, 2008; RFI Cultures France, 2007).
48. Senghor is responding to Henri Hell's complaint that the *Cahier* is nothing but a "papillotement incessant des images." Senghor, postface to *Éthiopiques, Oeuvre poétique*, 162.
49. Ibid.
50. Ibid., 165.
51. Senghor, introduction to *Anthologie de la nouvelle poésie nègre et malgache*, 5 and 2.
52. See Lilyan Kesteloot, *Les écrivains noirs de langue française: naissance d'une littérature* (Brussels: Université Libre de Bruxelles, 1963); Hubert de Leusse, *Léopold Sédar Senghor l'Africain* (Paris: Hatier, 1967); and Janheinz Jahn, *A History of Neo-African Literature* (London: Faber and Faber, 1968). For a refreshing alternative, see Paul Ansah, "Senghor's Poetic Method," *Critical Perspectives on Léopold Sédar Senghor*, ed. Janice Spleth (Colorado Springs: Three Continents Press, 1993). Ansah writes: "It is difficult to see how effectively African rhythms can be conveyed in French" (48); "While it is true that Senghor has a great sense of rhythm in his poetry and conveys very pleasant sound effects, there is nothing in this to suggest that he is any more African than Claudel or Saint-John Perse, the two French poets who are closest to Senghor in poetic techniques, or even Victor Hugo whom Senghor himself describes variously as 'Maître du tam-tam' and 'Maître du rythme.'" (49).
53. Meschonnic, *Critique du rythme*, 72; added emphasis.
54. Ibid., 280.
55. Ibid.
56. Ibid.
57. Ibid.
58. See Michael North, *The Dialect of Modernism: Race, Language, and Twentieth-Century Literature* (New York: Oxford University Press, 1994).
59. Meschonnic, *Critique du rythme*, 290.

60. Ibid., 217. "Signifiance" is another term Meschonnic employs to evoke "the organization of the marks by which the signifiers . . . produce a specific semantics, *distinct from the lexical sense*" (ibid., 217; emphasis original)—or, in short, rhythm. The term "signifiance" is also used by Julia Kristeva in *Révolution du langage poétique* (Paris: Seuil, 1974). Meschonnic is not interested, as is Kristeva, in a psychoanalytic interpretation of the semiotic register of language in terms of anal and oral drives.
61. Meschonnic, *Critique du rythme*, 223.
62. One could argue that Damas was exposed early on to French Guyanese Creole and that the African "drumbeat" could have been conveyed to him through that language. However, it is just as likely that the inflections of Portuguese or Amerindian were impressed upon him in that way. We will return to the question of Damas's French presently.
63. Meschonnic, *Critique du rythme*, 223.
64. Ibid.
65. Ibid.
66. Senghor, "Le Problème culturel an A.O.F.," in *Liberté I*, 20; originally presented as a paper at the Dakar Chamber of Commerce for the Foyer-France-Sénégal on September 10, 1937.
67. Léopold Sédar Senghor, *Oeuvre poétique* (Paris: Seuil, 1990), 23.
68. Fred Moten, *In the Break: The Aesthetics of the Black Radical Tradition* (Minneapolis: Minnesota University Press, 2003), 49. Moten retrieves the term "interinanimation" from John Donne; see also Rebecca Schneider, *Performing Remains: Art and War in Times of Theatrical Reenactment* (New York: Routledge, 2011): with reference to the same Donne poem, "The Exstasie" (1633), she notes "a constant (re)turn of, to, from, and between states of animation" (7). In "The Exstasie" we read of "lovers lying still as stone. . . . Here, the live and the stone are inter(in)animate and the liveness of one or deadness of the other is ultimately neither decidable nor relevant." On diasporic reenactments or the bringing back to life of the dead, see Joseph Roach, *Cities of the Dead: Circum-Atlantic Performance* (New York: Columbia University Press, 1996).
69. "Limbé" is sometimes translated as "Dance," but it may also be a Creole term derived from Bantu, meaning "chagrin amoureux." In *Pigments* Damas adds a definition in a footnote: " . . . Aux Antilles, nostalgie

de l'être que l'on a perdu. Par extension, spleen, cafard" (Paris: GLM, 1937), np.

70. Césaire, *Cahier d'un retour au pays natal*, 36.
71. See Hill, *Black Soundscapes White Stages*, 120. Hill also provides a history of the "tam tam" as both an instrument and an idea; it is the latter, I would contend, that plays a greater role in the poetry of Negritude; see 102–5.
72. Bridget Jones, "Léon Damas," in *Critical Perspectives on Léon-Gontran Damas*, ed. Keith Q. Warner (Washington, DC: Three Continents, 1988), 36. Jones suggests that phonetic studies would reveal "the persistence of African speech rhythms in Creolized French"; "Though he writes in a relaxed standard French, Damas often seems as close to Creole as to Mallarmé" (36). See, also, Keith Q. Warner's "New Perspective on Léon-Gontran Damas" in the same volume, 97.
73. Barthélémy Kotchy, "L'expression poétique chez Damas," *Présence Africaine* 112, no. 4, Special issue: "Hommage posthume à Léon Gontran Damas" (1979).
74. Léon-Gontran Damas, *Poésie de la Négritude: Léon Damas Reads Selected Poems from Pigments, Graffiti, Black Label, and Nevralgies* (Folkways Records, FW09924 / FL 9924), available at *Smithsonian Folkways*, http://www.folkways.si.edu/albumdetails.aspx?itemid=1788.
75. On reciting by heart as implicated in the typosphere, see Jacques Roubaud, *La vieillesse d'Alexandre: Essai sur quelques états récents du vers français* (Paris: Maspero, 1978), 120.
76. Janis L. Pallister, *Aimé Césaire* (New York: Twayne, 1991), 44.
77. On Damas's politics during this period, see also Philippe Dewitte, *Les mouvements nègres en France 1919–1939* (Paris: L'Harmattan, 1985), 371–72.
78. See the cover of *Soutes* at http://faculty.sites.uci.edu/aesthetic subjectivity/.
79. Quoted in Sandrine Poujols, postface to *Pigments/Névralgies*, Léon-Gontran Damas (Paris: Présence Africaine, 2005), 161–62.
80. *Soutes*, 2 (February 1936); republished in Jacques Prévert, *Oeuvres complètes*, ed. Danièle Gasiglia-Laster and Arnaud Laster (Paris: Gallimard, Pléiade, 1992).
81. I borrow the term "incremental repetition" from Fahamisha Patricia Brown, who does a fine job of analyzing the marks of oral genres (especially the sermon) in African American poetry; see Brown, *Performing the Word*, 30.

82. "Tentative de description" was originally published in *Commerce* (Aragon's journal) in 1931.
83. *Esprit* 2, no. 23–24 (September 1934), 706. Aragon, too, relied on this period style, obtaining in "Le Songe d'une nuit d'été" (*Soutes* 2, February 1936) an effect similar to Damas's. See also poems published by Robert Desnos in the mid 1930s, for example, "No pasaran" written in 1934 as a protest against the fascists in Spain and circulated as a song. During this period Desnos joined the radical antifascist group Front Commun, and his poems were heavily influenced by popular cabaret music. Damas attended Desnos's Saturday night parties, as did Langston Hughes when he was in Paris. See Katharine Conley, *Robert Desnos, Surrealism, and the Marvelous in Everyday Life* (Lincoln: University of Nebraska, 2003).
84. An "oeuf dur" is really a hard-boiled egg, but I have chosen to translate the expression as "hard egg" in order to approximate the sharp, monosyllabic rhythms of Prévert's poem.
85. Léon-Gontran Damas, *Pigments/Névralgies* (Paris: Présence Africaine, 2005), 52.
86. Robert Desnos, *Oeuvres*, ed. Marie Claire Dumas (Paris: Gallimard, 1999), 647. My translation.
87. See Madeleine Rebérioux, "Le théâtre d'agitation: Le Groupe Octobre," in *Le Mouvement Social* 91 (April–June 1975): 109–99.
88. I am quoting here from the original *Esprit* publication; the version found in *Pigments* is quite different. Damas changes the versification in many places and replaces "mon assortiment" with "mes hardes"; "se foutre de mon assortiment" becomes "se gausser de mes hardes." In the 1972 Presence Africaine version, "se régaler" is replaced by "jouir jouir"; "ce sacré pays" is "ce sacré foutu pays"; and other small changes (39).
89. See James Sneed, "On Repetition in Black Culture," *Black American Literature Forum* 15:4 (Winter, 1981): 146–54, 150.
90. See Janet G. Vaillant, *Black, French, and African: A Life of Leopold Sedar Senghor* (Cambridge, MA: Harvard University Press, 1990), 47 and 70–71.
91. Léon-Gontran Damas, *Poésie d'expression française d'Afrique noire, Madagascar, Réunion, Guadeloupe, Martinique, Indochine, et Guyane 1900–1945* (Paris: Seuil, 1947), 10; my translation; emphasis added. See also Anthony Mangeon, "Miroirs des littératures nègres: D'une anthologie l'autre, revues," *Gradiva* 10 (2009). Damas's anthology, Mangeon remarks,

"attempts of course to get beyond the colonial relation," yet it conceives of itself "in an imperial context," the same context employed by the SFIO at the time (52; my translation). Mangeon sees Damas's approach as consistent with that taken by the signatories of the 2007 manifeste "Pour une littérature-monde en français." Indeed, the turn away from "race" as an organizing category also characterizes the work of Françoise Lionnet and Shu-mei Shih and makes these authors vulnerable to the accusation of trading one limiting framework for another, one based on an imperial paradigm; see Lionnet and Shih, eds. *Minor Transnationalisms* (Durham, NC: Duke University Press, 2005).

92. See Roger Toumson and Simone Henry-Valmore, *Aimé Césaire: Le nègre inconsolé* (Fort-de-France: Vent des Îles and Paris; Syros, 1993), 111–12.
93. Damas, *Pigments/Névralgies*, 85, 39–40.
94. Meschonnic, *Critique du rythme*, 225. Emphasis original.
95. Zuckerkandl, *Sound and Symbol*, 169.
96. Phelan, "'Just Want to Say,'" 946.
97. Vander Ven, "Robert Frost's Dramatic Principle," 246.
98. Poirier, *The Performing Self*, 100.
99. Theodor Adorno, *Aesthetic Theory*, ed., trans. and intro. Robert Hullot-Kentor (Minneapolis: University of Minnesota Press, 1997), 167; and Meschonnic, *Critique du rythme*, 225.
100. See Jacques Rancière, "Politics of Aesthetics," in *Aesthetics and Its Discontents*, trans. Steven Corcoran (Cambridge: Polity, 2009), 24
101. If "speech is the coordination of noise into articulate utterance," and if poetic language is a challenge to this coordination, an attempt to recover the "acoustic aspect" embedded in—and repressed by—sense, then poetry constitutes a constant "dragging of meaning back toward its source in a dispersion of phonetic material awaiting articulation." Stewart, *Reading Voices*, 24–25.

5. RED FRONT / BLACK FRONT

1. Frantz Fanon, *The Wretched of the Earth*, preface by Jean-Paul Sartre, trans. Constance Farrington (New York: Grove, 1968), 239–40.
2. See Raphaël Confiant, *Aimé Césaire: Une traversée paradoxale du siècle* (Paris: Stock, 1993). According to Confiant, Césaire wrote in a language uninflected by Martiniquan Creole (or Kreyol) with few allusions to

customs familiar to the lower class of indigenous Martiniquans to which he belonged.

3. Beyond the Caribbean, debates concerning the pertinence of poetry to political change have also been lively. While at one extreme Victor Hountondji attributes to Césaire's poetry the ability to incite "a cultural revolution first, a political one next," Robert C. Young maintains that literature is largely an irrelevant epiphenomenon. Hountondji, *Le Cahier d'Aimé Césaire: Évènement littéraire et facteur de révolution* (Paris: L'Harmattan, 1993), 63; and Young, *Postcolonialism: A Historical Introduction* (Oxford: Blackwell, 2001).
4. Fanon, *Wretched of the Earth*, 220. Fanon prefers the poetry of René Depestre, which he characterizes as "descriptive and analytical poetry" (226). Strangely, however, René Char's wartime writings are exemplary for Fanon of a properly engaged poetry. Edward Said, *Culture and Imperialism* (New York: Knopf, 1993), 279.
5. André Breton, "Misère de la poésie: 'L'Affaire Aragon' devant l'opinion publique," in *Tracts surréalistes et déclarations collectives*, vol. 1, ed. José Pierre (Paris: Terrain Vague, 1980), 213.
6. Mireille Rosello, introduction to *Notebook of a Return to My Native Land*, trans. Mireille Rosello and Annie Pritchard (Newcastle Upon Tyne: Bloodax Books, 1995), 111. See also Confiant, *Aimé Césaire*.
7. Jean-Paul Sartre, "Orphée noir," in *Anthologie de la nouvelle poésie nègre et malgache de langue française*, ed. Léopold Sédar Senghor (Paris: Presses Universitaires de France, 1948).
8. Jean-Paul Sartre, *Qu'est-ce que la littérature?* (Paris: Gallimard, 1948). The chapters of the book were published serially during 1946 in Sartre's journal, *Les Temps Modernes*.
9. Frantz Fanon, *Peau noire, masques blancs* (Paris: Seuil, 1952), 30.
10. Ibid.
11. See Édouard Glissant, *Le discours antillais* (Paris: Seuil, 1981): "la parole poétique de Césaire, l'acte politique de Fanon nous ont menés *quelque part*, autorisant par détour que nous revenions au seul lieu où nos problèmes nous guettent" (36).
12. See, in particular, Jacques Derrida, *Signéponge/Signsponge*, trans. Richard Rand (New York: Columbia University Press, 1984).
13. See, for instance, the efforts of Lambert-Félix Prudent, "Aimé Césaire: Contribution poétique à la construction de la langue martiniquaise";

and André Thibault, "L'oeuvre d'Aimé Césaire et le 'français régional antillais," both in *Aimé Césaire à l'oeuvre*, ed. Marc Cheymol and Philippe Ollé-Laprune (Paris: Éditions des Archives Contemporaines, 2010).

14. Such a set of assumptions has recently been taken to task by Jahan Ramazani in *The Hybrid Muse: Postcolonial Poetry* (Chicago: University of Chicago Press, 2001). Through studies of anglophone rather than francophone poets (Derek Walcott, A. K. Ramanujan, Louise Bennett, Okot p'Bitek), Ramazani questions the treatment poetry has received at the hands of postcolonial theory, asserting that the "relative metaphoric density of poetry, which helps make it less ethnographically transparent than other genres, has contributed to its marginalization in postcolonial studies" (72). In terms that apply equally well to works in French, Ramazani laments that too often political and sociological analysis of poems "overshadows the figurative dimension of postcolonial aesthetics" (75). For further meditations on the limits placed on expression by postcolonial critics, see Paul Gilroy, *The Black Atlantic: Modernity and Double Consciousness* (New York: Verso, 1993); Eric Luis Prieto, "The Poetics of Place, the Rhetoric of Authenticity, and Aimé Césaire's *Cahier d'un retour au pays natal*," *Dalhousie French Studies* 55 (2001): 142–51; and Brent Hayes Edwards, "Introduction: The Genres of Postcolonialism" in *Social Text* 22, no. 1 (Spring 2004): 1–15.
15. See, for instance, E. S. Burt, *Poetry's Appeal: Nineteenth-Century French Lyric and the Political Space* (Stanford, CA: Stanford University Press, 1999).
16. This passage first appeared in *Tropiques* 5 (April 1942) under the title "En guise de manifeste littéraire." It was written after the meeting with Breton in May of 1941 and dedicated to him. The passage (along with the others) was folded into the Brentano's edition of 1947 and appears on page 32 of the Présence Africaine edition.
17. Aimé Césaire, *Cahier d'un retour au pays natal* (Paris: Présence Africaine, 1983), 32. All subsequent citations from this edition will be noted in the text as PA followed by page number.
18. Aimé Césaire, *Notebook of a Return to the Native Land*, trans. and ed. Clayton Eshleman and Annette Smith (Middletown, CT: Wesleyan University Press, 2001), 22. All further English translations will be drawn from this volume unless otherwise noted.

19. For the suggestion that "tourte" is like a "pâté," I am indebted to Dominique Jullien. A "tourte" may also be a kind of pigeon; in any case, it would make sense for "tourte" to refer to a bird, given the rich network of bird imagery that is threaded throughout the poem.
20. Jules Fairie, *Dictionnaire français-créole* (Ottawa: Leméac, 1974), 449 and 334.
21. "Parbleu," the *Petit Robert* tells us, is a euphemism for "Pardieu," itself already a distortion of "Par Dieu."
22. The Rosello and Pritchard translation reads: "there are still madras cloths around women's loins rings in their ears smiles on their faces babies at their breasts and I will spare you the rest: ENOUGH OF THIS OUTRAGE!" (99). Eshleman and Smith arguably fail to catch Césaire's sarcastic allusion to the stereotypical figure of the *doudous*, a mulatto woman (in one popular version) abandoned by her white male lover who is often seen wearing a "madras." The immediate "scandal" to which Césaire is referring is that of the exoticizing (and eroticizing) of the desperately poor island.
23. There are four other cases in the *Cahier* of such typographical emphasis: "TOUSSAINT, TOUSSAINT L'OUVERTURE"; the chamber pot marked "MERCI"; the twice-repeated "COMIQUE ET LAID"; and the pronoun "NOUS" in the conclusion. In the *Volontés* version, the hymn, "KYRIE ELEISON," is also capitalized. There is far more to say about Césaire's use of typographical emphasis. For brevity's sake, I will merely point out that in every case the capitalized words indicate the relation of the *Cahier* to another text.
24. See also the January 1927 issue of *La Voix des Nègres*, which displays prominently a number of slogans: "Nègres, en garde!"; "À TOUS LES NÈGRES DU MONDE!" The command "Debout," followed by a substantive, is highly typical of French protest discourse.
25. Michael Richardson writes that Césaire "may or may not" have read *Légitime Défense*, the review in which a response to the Affaire appears. Richardson, *Refusal of the Shadow: Surrealism and the Caribbean*, ed. Michael Richardson, trans. Michael Richardson and Kryzysztof Fijalkowski (London: Verso, 1996), 5. A. James Arnold argues that Césaire did not "participate" in *Légitime Défense* and did not "share its Marxist conviction that culture renewal must be preceded by political revolution." Arnold, *Modernism and Negritude: The Poetry and Poetics of Aimé Césaire* (Cambridge, MA:

Harvard University Press, 1981), 9. However, Lilyan Kesteloot is adamant that Césaire was very taken with the manifesto: "then a 'Khâgne' student at the lycée Louis-le-Grand, [Césaire] was the first to hear it and listen to it." Kesteloot, *Black Writers in French: A Literary History of Negritude*, trans. Ellen Conroy Kennedy (Philadelphia: Temple University Press, 1974), 17. Carole Sweeney supplies a probing analysis of the review and its place in the life of Caribbean students in Paris in *From Fetish to Subject: Race, Modernism, and Primitivism 1919–1935* (Westport, CT: Praeger, 2004); she maintains that the link between surrealism, communism, and antiimperialism forged in *Légitime Défense* had a decisive influence on the politics/poetics of *L'Étudiant Noir* (134). See also Philippe Dewitte, *Les mouvements nègres en France 1919–1939* (Paris: L'Harmattan, 1985), 267–75. The fact that Suzanne Cesaire titled her essay in *Tropiques* 4 (January 1942) "Misère d'une poésie" indicates that the Césaires knew about Breton's intervention in the Affaire Aragon at least by the 1940s. Césaire later argued with René Depestre over the role of socialist realism as promulgated by Aragon. Apparently Aragon consistently refused to publish Césaire's work when in charge of organs like *Commune*.

26. That Césaire had been struggling for a while with the nature of poetic language—its political efficacy or lack thereof—is suggested in a letter he wrote to Breton in 1944 (April 4). The letter, which can be found in the Fond Jacques Doucet of the Bibliothèque Sainte Geneviève in Paris, is quoted by Alex Gil in *Migrant Textuality: On the Fields of Aimé Césaire's* Et les chiens se taisient (Ph.D. diss., University of Virginia, 2012), available at *Academic Commons*, http://academiccommons.columbia.edu/catalog/ac:161180. Gil explains that "before he met him, Césaire tells Breton he was a prisoner of reality, of the *Cahier*, of his "*thème*." Now Césaire thanks Breton for the solution, "Se laisser parler. Se laisser envahir par ses rêves. Se laisser dominer par ses images. Il n'était plus question de "thèse," ni de "thème." Il s'agissait tout simplement d'oser la vie, toute la vie" (122). Gil cites the letter in order to advance his argument that Césaire "adapted" his style to Breton's surrealist understanding of poetry's function; however, I would submit instead that Breton merely confirmed a tendency already present in Césaire to let himself be "dominated" by the force of his own imagery ("se laisser dominer par ses images").

27. See André Thirion, *Révolutionnaires sans révolution* (Paris: Robert Laffont, 1972), 296.
28. See ibid., 294–349; and Maurice Nadeau, *Histoire du surréalisme* (Paris: Seuil, 1964), 142.
29. See Louis Aragon's remarks on revolutionary literature in "Le surréalisme et le devenir révolutionnaire," *Le Surréalisme au Service de la Révolution* 3 (November 1913).
30. For an account of the events leading up to the publication of "Front rouge," see Svetlana Boym's *Death in Quotation Marks* (Cambridge, MA: Harvard University Press, 1991); she claims that the poem was written in homage to Vladimir Mayakovsky, who committed suicide in 1930, and she traces the influence on "Front rouge" of Mayakovsky's 1918 "Levyj marsh" (Left march) (174–79).
31. Aragon translated and published Mayakovsky's "Levyj marsh" (Left march) as "La marche à gauche" in *Littératures Soviétiques* in 1955.
32. On the "nontotalizable heterogeneity" of Mayakovsky's poetry, "its combination of poetic and antipoetic elements," see Boym, *Death in Quotation Marks*, 150.
33. The precise charge was: "excitation de militaires à la désobéissance et de provocation au meurtre dans un but de propagande anarchiste" (incitement of the military to disobedience and provocation to kill as a goal of anarchist propaganda). See Thirion, *Révolutionnaires*, 329.
34. The list of signatories included, among others, Bertolt Brecht, Walter Benjamin, Federico Garcia Lorca, and Amedée Ozenfant. Breton probably borrowed the name from Karl Marx's *Misère de la philosophie*, a rebuttal of the works of Pierre-Joseph Proudhon.
35. Quoted in Thirion, *Révolutionnaires*; my translation.
36. Breton, "Misère de la poésie," 213; all translations of this work are my own.
37. Ibid.
38. Ibid., 206. For an account of the issues treated in the trial, see James Petterson, *Poetry Proscribed: Twentieth-Century (Re)visions of the Trials of Poetry in France* (Lewisburg, PA: Bucknell University Press, 2008).
39. Breton, "Misère de la poésie," 213.
40. See Régis Antoine's account in *Les écrivains français et les Antilles: Des premiers pères blancs aux surréalistes noirs* (Paris: Maisonneuve et Larose, 1978), 363. Given the apparently frequent exchanges between

students from the French colonies and surrealist writers, one cannot help wondering why their names do not appear on the petition. Breton, "Misère de la poésie."

41. In the introduction to *Refusal of the Shadow*, Michael Richardson describes *Légitime Défense* as "the first publication in which colonized blacks collectively sought to speak with their own authentic voices" (4). In contrast, in *Les écrivains français et les Antilles*, Régis Antoine questions the originality of the publication (364) and explains why the editors sought to align themselves with the surrealists' oneirism (336).
42. Anticipating Sartre, Léro proposes that surrealist automatic writing provides a means for rediscovering an authentic voice. Léro, "Misère d'une poésie," *Légitime Défense*, 10–11. See also Ménil's article, "Généralités sur 'l'écrivain' de couleur antillais," in the same volume (*Légitime Défense*, 7–9). A further allusion to the Affaire appears in the preface to the issue: "As for Freud [Quant à Freud]," the editors proclaim, "we are ready to use the immense machine for dissolving the bourgeois family that he put in gear." Defending Freud at this point in time would have appeared to be a direct assault on the platform that emerged from the Union des intellectuals: in Kharkov, "freudisme" was condemned as a complacent bourgeois invention. Surrealism had been chastised specifically for promoting the works of Freud. On the attitude of *Légitime Défense* toward Léon Blum's Popular Front, see Antoine, *Les écrivains français et les Antilles*, 366.
43. Léro, "Misère d'une poésie," 11.
44. *Légitime Défense*, 1.
45. It is worth noting that the phrase "in its entirety" is not translated in the English version available in Kesteloot's *Black Writers in French* (37).
46. The title "S.O.S." is reiterated in the title of a poem by Léon-Gontron Damas published in *Pigments* (1937), and in the title of a poem by Amiri Baraka (LeRoi Jones), published in *Black Magic* (1968). It serves as a rallying cry for black liberation movements across time.
47. René Ménil, "Sur la préface de Breton au *Cahier d'un retour au pays natal*," in *Tracées: Identité, négritude, esthétique aux Antilles* (Paris: Robert Laffont, 1981), 204; my translation.
48. Ibid; my translation.
49. Ibid., 207.

50. Kristin Ross, *The Emergence of Social Space: Rimbaud and the Paris Commune* (Minneapolis: Minnesota University Press, 1988), 129.
51. There is a great deal to say about the figure of "marronage" as an indigenous poetics of detour. See, especially, Glissant's *Le discours antillais* and Césaire's poem "Le verbe marronner / à René Depestre," in Aimé Césaire, *The Collected Poetry*, trans. Clayton Eshleman and Annette Smith (Berkeley: University of California Press, 1983).
52. Ross, *The Emergence of Social Space*, 129.
53. Stuart Hall, "Cultural Identity and Diaspora," in *Identity, Community, Culture, Difference*, ed. Jonathan Rutherford (London: Lawrence & Wishart, 1990), 229–30.
54. Theodor Adorno, *Aesthetic Theory*, ed., trans. and intro. Robert Hullot-Kentor (Minneapolis: University of Minnesota Press, 1997), 231.
55. The expression "site of entanglement" is the translation of Glissant's "point d'intrication"; "Il faut revenir au lieu," he writes; " . . . non pas retour au rêve d'origine, à l'Un immobile de l'Être, mais retour au point d'intrication, dont on s'était détourné par force." Glissant, *Le discours antillais*, 36.

6. TO INHABIT A WOUND

1. Césaire, "Calendrier lagunaire," in *moi, laminaire* . . . (Paris: Seuil, 1982). See appendix 2 for the English translation.
2. "Caïeu" (line 8) is a botanical term derived from the Norman "*cael*," from the Latin *catellus*, little dog (a runt, or *rejeton*), signifying a small bulb on the side of the main bulb of a plant. "Valleuse" (line 12, derived from *avaler*) designates a particular geological formation; a small valley abuts the ocean and forms a sort of incision, or "valleuse," in a cliff. "Ascidie" is both a zoological and botanical term, from the Greek *askidion*, meaning a small sack, a recipient for liquids, made of an animal stomach; it is the technical name given to a tiny mollusk in the form of a sack with two openings for taking in and expulsing water and it also designates a pitcher-shaped part of a plant. The "arganier" (line 38), or *argania spinosa*, is the botanical name for a species of tropical tree with very hard wood, known colloquially in the Caribbean as a "*bois-fè*." "Bathyale" (line 40) comes from the Greek *bathus* and refers to a great

depth, at the level of the continental plates in the sea. "Abyssale" has, of course, many familiar connotations, but it is also a technical term for sea-depths beyond the level of the "bathyale" (2,000 meters deep), from 2,000 to 5,000 deep, and thus unfathomable. "En cuscute" (line 45) is a botanical expression derived from the Arabic *kachut*, which means "to attach." Plants "en cuscute" do not have chlorophyll; they wrap their red vines around the living branch and parasitically suck out its green tissue. And "en porana" (line 45) describes in botanical terms a kind of climbing, twining bush, a member of the morning glory family (*convolvulus*) found in the Antilles.

3. Please see appendix 2 for the English translation.
4. For a lovely reading, see Lilian Pestre de Almeida, "En visitant la tombe de Césaire ou Lecture du poème 'Calendrier lagunaire,'" *Présence Africaine* 178 (2008): 148–57: "Plusieurs se sont étonnés que Césaire n'ait point choisi un autre poème, les mots du Rebelle, par exemple. En fait, Césaire n'a jamais vacillé et avait décidé depuis un moment que ce 'Calendrier lagunaire' serait le texte final" (148–49). See also Michèle Constans, "'Essentiel paysage': L'herbier imaginaire d'Aimé Césaire," *Environnement, nature, paysage* 645 (2013), http://cybergeo.revues.org/25910#quotation; M. Souley Ba, René Hénane, and Lilyan Kesteloot, *Introduction à moi, laminaire d'Aimé Césaire* (Paris: L'Harmattan, 2011); Roger Toumson, "Situation de *moi, laminaire . . .* " in *Césaire 70*, ed. Georges Ngal and Stein (Ivry-sur-Seine: Silex/Nouvelles du Sud, 2004); Clarisse Zimra, "La dernière transhumance du rebelle," in *Oeuvres et critiques, Aimé Césaire du singulier à l'universel* (Tubingen: Gunter Narr, 1994); and Bernadette Cailler, "Crevasse, métaphore vive du texte: Réflexions sur un poème de *moi, laminaire . . .*" in *Aimé Césaire, ou, l'athanor d'un alchimiste: Actes du premier colloque international sur l'œuvre littéraire d'Aimé Césaire, Paris, 21–23 novembre 1985*, by Aimé Césaire, ed. Jacqueline Leiner (Paris: Éditions Caribéennes, 1987).
5. "Calendrier lagunaire" was first published in a section titled *Noria* of the *Oeuvres complètes* (Fort-de-France: Désormeaux, 1976). A "noria" is a hydraulic machine for raising water from the oceanic depths. In an interview with Jacqueline Leiner, Césaire recalls: "'Noria,' effectivement, c'est assez juste, dans la mesure où, pour moi, le mot est une sorte de *noria* qui permet de râcler les profondeurs et de les faire remonter

au jour." Leiner, "Entretien avec Aimé Césaire par Jacqueline Leiner," *Tropiques*, reprint (Paris: Jean-Michel Place, 1978), xii. "Calendrier lagunaire" was later reproduced as the first poem in Césaire's penultimate volume, *moi, laminaire* . . . .

6. Clayton Eshleman and Annette Smith, introduction to *The Collected Poetry*, by Aimé Césaire, trans. Clayton Eshleman and Annette Smith (Berkeley: University of California Press, 1983), 24. On the tombstone, all appearances of the first person "je" begin with a lower case "j"; in Eshleman and Smith's version, the "j" is frequently but unsystematically capitalized. Pestre de Almeida believes there is a strong mythic subtext that links the speaker to Protée ("En visitant la tombe," 156). See also A. James Arnold's preface to *Poésie, théâtre, essais et discours*, by Aimé Césaire (Paris: Éditions CNRS, 2013): "À des degrés divers, chaque ouvrage poétique de Césaire depuis 1939 met en scène le Moi et se livre à des variations sur le Moi, mais jamais auparavant le Moi n'avait été de la part de Césaire l'objet explicite d'un recueil. Le pronom de la première personne, pour la seule et unique fois dans son œuvre, est dans le titre d'un recueil. Or cette présence du Moi est problématique au plus haut point: *moi, laminaire* . . . , et ceci dès le titre, procède à l'effacement de ce Moi, non seulement en le privant, dans l'édition originale, d'une majuscule, mais en procédant à sa constante mise en question: il est une laminaire, une grande algue qui, fixée à un rocher, se déploie, pour se rétracter, avant de se redéployer, et ainsi de suite" (60).
7. *Le Nouveau Petit Robert: Dictionnaire de la langue française* (Paris: Dicorobert, 1994).
8. For details on this period, see David Alliot, *Aimé Césaire: Le nègre universel* (Paris: Infolio, 2008), 162–77. Césaire was elected mayor of Fort-de-France in 1945; a few months later he was elected as deputy to the National Assembly for the French Communist Party. In 1956 he resigned from the Communist Party and established his own, Le Parti progressiste martiniquais, in 1957.
9. On the racial politics of SERMAC, see Julian Gerstin, "Musical Revivals and Social Movements in Contemporary Martinique: Ideology, Identity, Ambivalence," in *The African Diaspora: A Musical Perspective*, ed. Ingrid Monson (New York: Garland, 2000). For an account of the so-called preservation of an official Martinican culture, administered through

SERMAC, see David A. B. Murray, *Opacity: Gender, Sexuality, Race, and the 'Problem' of Identity in Martinique* (New York: Peter Lang, 2002).

10. In Char's "J'habite une douleur," bearing the weight of the mortal body ("un fardeau," "le poids") is identified with aging and the suffering that comes from leading an existence governed by time.
11. We should hear in the poet's struggle with a "poulpe" an echo of Lautréamont's *Les Chants de Maldoror*, the hero's epic duel with Maldoror transformed into an octopus in "Chant Two."
12. The "frère" of line 43 might very well refer to Depestre, with whom Césaire was actively debating the value of Communism and of a revolution for Martinique defined in Communist terms. Césaire left the Communist Party in 1956 but Depestre remained a militant. In "Le verbe marronner / à René Depestre," Césaire defends the radical nature of his poetic form by opposing it to an easily digestible colonial discourse: "Depestre le poème n'est pas un moulin à/passer de la canne à sucre. . . ." He also aligns his approach ("j'aime mieux regarder le printemps") with the real revolution: "Justement / c'est la révolution," the coming of spring. Césaire, *The Collected Poetry*, 368–69.
13. See Antonio Benítez-Rojo, *The Repeating Island: The Caribbean and the Postmodern Perspective*, 2nd ed., trans. James E. Maraniss (Durham, NC: Duke University Press, 1996): "The Caribbean is . . . a cultural meta-archipelago without center and without limits, a chaos within which there is an island that proliferates constantly" (9).
14. Césaire, *The Collected Poetry*, 35.
15. The "vr-" combination, as in "*vr*ac de *var*ech" and the "immobile *verri*tion" with which the *Cahier* ends, is often indicative of generative but incipient movement, change, revolution.
16. Émile Benveniste, *Problèmes de linguistique générale*, vol. 2 (Paris: Gallimard, 1974): "Bien avant de servir à communiquer, le langage sert à vivre" (217). My translation.
17. Quotations are from Martin Heidegger, *Poetry, Language, Thought*, trans. Albert Hofstadter (New York: Harper & Row, 1971): " . . . Poetically Man Dwells . . . ," 228; "Building Dwelling Thinking," 148 and 151; and from Martin Heidegger, *Basic Writings*, trans. David Farrell Krell (New York: Harper & Row, 1977), "The Question Concerning Technology," 301–2.

18. In "Building Dwelling Thinking," Heidegger traces the etymology of *buan* (the High German word for "building") to show that it initially referred to "the manner in which we humans *are* on the earth," the way in which we "*Wohnen*" (translated into English as "dwell" and into French as "habiter") (146–47). See also "Bâtir Habiter Penser," in Martin Heidegger, *Essais et conférénces*, trans. André Préau, preface by Jean Beaufret (Paris: Gallimard, 1958), 172–73.
19. Heidegger, "Language," in *Poetry, Language, Thought*, 198.
20. Heidegger, "Building Dwelling Thinking," in *Poetry, Language, Thought*, 148.
21. Ibid., 161; original emphasis.
22. Heidegger, " . . . Poetically Man Dwells . . . ," in *Poetry, Language, Thought*, 223.
23. Ibid., 216; and Heidegger, "The Origin of the Work of Art," in *Basic Writings*, 60, 63.
24. Philippe Lacoue-Labarthe, *Heidegger, Art and Politics*, trans. Chris Turner (Oxford: Basil Blackwell, 1990).
25. See Jean Bernabé, Raphaël Confiant, and Patrick Chamoiseau, *Éloge de le créolité* (Paris: Gallimard, 1989). Richard Price provides a scathing critique of the folkloric, folklorizing tendencies of Créolité in *The Convict and the Colonel: A Story of Colonialism and Resistance in the Caribbean*, 2nd ed. (Durham, NC: Duke University Press, 2006): "An imagined *diversalité* or *métissage* can be packaged as a consumable cultural product" (175). A cautionary note is also offered by Édouard Glissant in *Poétique de la relation* (Paris: Gallimard, 1990), 103.
26. See Raphaël Confiant's strenuous attack on Césaire in *Aimé Césaire: Une traversée paradoxale du siècle* (Paris: Stock, 1993).
27. Heidegger, "Building Dwelling Thinking," in *Poetry, Language, Thought*, 146.
28. Heidegger, "What Are Poets For?" in *Poetry, Language, Thought*, 101.
29. See Jacqueline Leiner, "Entretien avec Aimé Césaire par Jacqueline Leiner," in *Tropiques*, reprint (Paris: Jean Michel Place, 1978), xix.
30. Heidegger, "The Origin of the Work of Art," in *Poetry, Language, Thought*, 84.
31. On the title of the volume, *moi laminaire*, in which "Calendrier lagunaire" was published (after its initial inclusion in the 1976 *Oeuvres*

poétiques published by Éditions Désormeaux), Césaire stated: "Je n'ai jamais séparé mon destin personnel du destin collectif: un vieux reste d'esprit tribal sans doute! Qui à l'inverse m'a préservé de l'engagement littéraire, comme on pouvait l'entendre à une certaine époque. Je suis engagé comme l'algue est accrochée à son rocher." Jean-Pierre Salgas, "Interview with Jean-Pierre Salgas," *Jeune Afrique*, no. 1142 (Paris, Novembre 24, 1982), 73. See also the lovely analysis offered by A. James Arnold in Césaire, *Poésie*.

32. Heidegger, "Building Dwelling Thinking," in *Poetry, Language, Thought*, 161; original emphasis.
33. This is Césaire describing his relationship with Léopold-Sédar Senghor during their years together at the Rue d'Ulm; see Charles H. Rowell, "It Is Through Poetry that One Copes with Solitude: An Interview with Aimé Césaire," *Callaloo* 31, no. 4 (2008): 990.
34. See René Hénane, *Glossaire des termes rares dans l'oeuvre d'Aimé Césaire* (Paris: Jean Michel Place, 2004). See also Pierre Vilar's sensitive treatment of Césaire's lexicon in *Les armes miraculeuses d'Aimé Césaire* (Geneva: Éditions Zoe, 2008) and Papa Samba Diop, *La Poésie d'Aimé Césaire: propositions de lecture accompagnées d'un Lexique de l'œuvre* (Paris: Honoré Champion, 2010).
35. Leiner, "Entretien avec Aimé Césaire par Jacqueline Leiner," ix; emphasis in the original.
36. "Aimé Césaire et les nègres sauvages: Interview par Jeanine Cahen," in *Afrique Action*, November 21, 1960, 23, cited in Thomas A. Hale, *Les Écrits d'Aimé Césaire: Bibliographie commentée* (Montreal: Presses de l'Université de Montréal, 1978), 406.
37. "Si je nomme avec précision (ce qui fait parler de mon exotisme), c'est qu'en nommant avec précision, je crois que l'on restitue à l'objet sa valeur personnelle." Lilyan Kesteloot, *Aimé Césaire* (Paris: Seghers, 1979), 188; quoted in Hénane, *Glossaire des termes rares*, 8.
38. On Césaire's allergy to "exoticism" as a form of colonial subjection, his reaction against *doudouisme* and the tourist vision of his island, see the account of his rediscovery (and revalorization) of the tropical landscape after his meeting with Wifredo Lam in May 1941 in Daniel Maximin, *Césaire & Lam: Insolites bâtisseurs* (Paris: HC Editions, 2011).
39. Heidegger, "The Origin of the Work of Art," in *Poetry, Language, Thought*, 84.

40. Michel Foucault, *Les mots et les choses: Une archéologie des sciences humaines* (Paris: Gallimard, 1966).
41. See Foucault, *Les mots et les choses*, 140–44.
42. Carl Linneaus, *Philosophie botanique*, quoted in ibid., 258, 145.
43. Londa Schiebinger, *Plants and Empire: Colonial Bioprospecting in the Atlantic World* (Cambridge, MA: Harvard University Press, 2004), 198.
44. To recall, Césaire is concerned with the "singular value" that is manifested through the precise naming of each plant; see Hénane, *Glossaire des termes rares*, 8.
45. Aimé Césaire, "Discours d'inauguration de la Rue Henri Stéhlé," unpublished essay written for the dedication of the Rue Henri Stéhlé in Fort-de France, Saturday, April 1, 1982 (Archives Départementales de la Martinique, Fort-de-France), 7.
46. Leiner, "Entretien avec Aimé Césaire par Jacqueline Leiner," ix.
47. Saint-John Perse, *Eloges*, vol. 4 (Paris: Gallimard, 1960), 31.
48. Leiner, "Entretien avec Aimé Césaire par Jacqueline Leiner," ix; original emphasis. Césaire is responding to Leiner's question: "Les articles consacrés à la flore, au folklore antillais ont-ils permis une prise de conscience plus grande de la réalité martiniquaise?" See also Christina Kullberg, *The Poetics of Ethnography in Martiniquan Narratives: Exploring the Self and the Environment* (Charlottesville: University of Virginia Press, 2013, 33–36.
49. On the history embedded in Martiniquan toponomyms, see Vincent Huyghes-Belrose, "Le nom des lieux à la Martinique: Un patrimoine identitaire menacé," in *Études Caribéennes*, December 11, 2008, http://etudescaribeennes.revues.org/3494; and Vincent Huyghes-Belrose, "Le paysage martiniquais entre archéologie et atlas," in *Études Caribéennes*, July 4, 2006, http://etudescaribeennes.revues.org/763.
50. See René Hénane, *Césaire et Lautréamont: Bestiaire et métamorphose* (Paris: L'Harmattan, 2006).
51. See Sylvère Garraudière, *L'École aux Antilles Françaises: Le rendez-vous manqué de la démocratie* (Paris: L'Harmattan, 2007); and Roland Jean-Baptiste Édouard, ed. *40 Ans de lectures sous les Tropiques* (Antilles, Guyare: Bibliothèque Pédagogique de la Circonscription du Marin, 1989).
52. Eshleman and Smith, introduction to *The Collected Poetry*, 1. They continue: "It was also Révert who identified Césaire as a candidate for

France's highest liberal arts institution, the École Normale Supérieure in Paris, and recommended him as well for the Parisian Lycée Louis-le Grand, at which, in September, 1931, he began to prepare for entrance to 'Normale'" (ibid., 1–2).

53. This sobriquet refers to the Amiral Georges Robert, the administrator Vichy placed in charge of Martinique during World War II.
54. Henri Stéhlé, "La végétation des Antilles françaises," *Tropiques* 1, no. 2 (July 1941): 71–75. The article is extracted from the *Bulletin Agricole* of March 1940; all translations are my own.
55. Ibid., 73.
56. Ibid.
57. Ibid., 75.
58. Ibid., 74.
59. Henri Stéhlé, "Les dénominations génériques des végétaux aux Antilles françaises: Histoires et légendes qui s'y attachent," *Tropiques* 2, no. 10 (February 1944): 53.
60. See Schiebinger, *Plants and Empire*, 200. Linnaeus "banished many things: European languages except Greek or Latin; religious names (though he allowed names derived from European mythology); foreign names (meaning foreign to European sensibilities); names invoking the uses of plants" and so on. "What Linnaeus proposed was a naming system abstract in relation to the properties of plants but concrete in relation to the history of botany in Europe" (ibid., 201).
61. Stéhlé, "Les dénominations," 53–54.
62. Ibid., 54.
63. Ibid., 62.
64. Ibid., 63.
65. On the dialects spoken in Martinique, see Patrick Chamoiseau and Raphael Confiant, *Les lettres créoles* (Paris: Hatier, 1991).
66. Stéhlé, "Les dénominations," 65.
67. Ibid., 69–70. In his glossary, René Hénane lists "catalpa" as a "botanical term," but he does not provide an etymology or any other explanation (*Glossaire des termes rares*, 35). This just goes to show how in one generation the local origin of a name can be forgotten, then consecrated as scientific. What, exactly, constitutes the "Creole" language, and what, exactly, constitutes a botanical discourse, changes over time.
68. In this regard, it is worth noting that Linnaeus's nomenclature was standardized and universalized by "the American Code incorporated

after the Congress of 1930"; the terms of this nomenclature potentially betray the "folklore" they contain under the pressure to follow "laws of priority and of phenotype universally recognized." Stéhlé, "Les dénominations," 62.

69. Pestre de Almeida notes that Césaire was "enchanted" by dictionaries: "grand lecteur d'encyclopédies, amoureux des mots, s'intéressant toujours aux cartes géographiques et astronomiques." Pestre de Almeida, "En visitant la tombe de Césaire," 150–51.
70. Michael Davidson, "Life by Water: Lorine Niedecker and Critical Regionalism," in *Radical Vernacular: Lorine Niedecker and the Poetics of Place*, ed. Elizabeth Willis (Iowa City: University of Iowa Press, 208), 18. For Davidson, critical regionalism is "a use of locale to comment on global forces, placing indigenous peoples, local economies, and nonmetropolitan spaces within the orbit of capitalist production worldwide" (ibid.).
71. Ibid., 10.
72. Césaire may have taken his cue from Stéhlé in more ways than we recognize. For Stéhlé, every name, whether from a colloquial or technical lexicon, possesses a significance that can, in theory, be retrieved. Other possible influences of Stéhlé on Césaire can be found in "Calendrier lagunaire," for instance, the choice between two vegetal modes, "s'accrochant en cuscute" or "se déployant en porana," might have been inspired by Stéhlé's first article in *Tropiques*, which discusses at length the difference between the two types of vine (73).
73. Césaire, "Discours d'inauguration de Stéhlé," 7; all translations are my own.
74. Ibid., 5.
75. Ibid.
76. Daniel Tiffany, *Infidel Poetics: Riddles, Nightlife, Substance* (Chicago: Chicago University Press, 2009), 6.
77. Ibid., 4.

CONCLUSION

1. Jessica Berman, *Modernist Commitments: Ethics, Politics, and Transnational Modernism* (New York: Columbia University Press, 2011), 284.
2. Laura Doyle, "Modernist Studies and Inter-Imperiality in the Long Durée," in *The Oxford Handbook of Global Modernisms*, ed. Mark

Wollaeger with Matt Eatough (New York: Oxford University Press, 2012), 685; original emphasis.

3. Ibid.
4. Ibid.
5. Ibid.; original emphasis.
6. Ibid.
7. Ibid.
8. Ibid.
9. Theodor W. Adorno, *Aesthetic Theory*, ed., trans. and intro. Robert Hullot-Kentor (Minneapolis: Minnesota University Press, 1997): "The genial [genius] is a dialectical knot: It is what has not been copied or repeated, it is free, yet at the same time bears the feeling of necessity; it is art's paradoxical sleight of hand and one of its most dependable criteria. To be genial means to hit upon a constellation, subjectively to achieve the objective" (171).
10. Theodor W. Adorno, *Negative Dialectics*, trans. E. B. Ashton (New York: Continuum, 1992), 262.
11. Ibid., 265.
12. Adorno, *Aesthetic Theory*, 42.
13. Nathaniel Mackey, *Discrepant Engagement: Dissonance, Cross-Culturality, and Experimental Writing* (Cambridge: Cambridge University Press, 1993), back cover jacket.
14. Adorno, *Aesthetic Theory*, 42.
15. Ibid.
16. Ibid.
17. See Christopher Miller, *Nationalists and Nomads: Essays on Francophone African Literature and Culture* (Chicago: University of Chicago Press, 1998).
18. Ibid., 2, 40. Miller's contention is that unionist and communist associations for black workers were more critical of the colonial system than the poets of Negritude.
19. Ibid., 42. The CDRN was founded in 1926. See Philippe Dewitte, *Les mouvements nègres en France, 1919–1939* (Paris: L'Harmattan, 1985).
20. It is not clear to me that attacks against white rule are any less virulent in the *Cahier*, Damas's "S.O.S." or even Senghor's "Neige sur Paris" ("I'll never release this reserve of hatred") than in an article such as "Le mot nègre," published by the editors of *La Voix des Nègres* in 1927. "Le mot

nègre," signed "Le Comité," in *La Voix des Nègres* (January 1927), 1: "C'est le gros mot du jour, c'est le mot que certains de nos frères de race ne veulent plus être appelés ainsi." The editors refuse the titles "noir" and "hommes de couleur" because they believe such distinctions support the hierarchy of skin color imposed on the peoples of Africa and the Caribbean; they chose to assume the pejorative "nègre": "Non, messieurs les diviseurs pour régner! . . . Ce nom est celui de notre race."

21. Miller, *Nationalists and Nomads*, 10.
22. See Theodor W. Adorno, "Lyric Poetry & Society," *Telos* 20 (1974); first published in German in 1957.
23. Stuart Hall, "Cultural Identity and Diaspora," in *Identity, Community, Culture, Difference*, ed. Jonathan Rutherford (London: Lawrence & Wishart, 1990), 230.
24. On "universalizing," see J. Michael Dash, *The Other America: Caribbean Literature in a New World Context* (Charlottesville: University of Virginia Press, 1998); on "elitist," see Bongie, *Friends and Enemies*; and on "colonial," see Raphaël Confiant, *Aimé Césaire: Une traversée paradoxale du siècle* (Paris: Stock, 1993).
25. Aimé Césaire, *Return to My Native Land*, trans. John Berger and Anna Bostock, intro. by Mazisi Kunene (Middlesex, England: Penguin, 1969).
26. During that period the goal of black writing was, in so many cases, to confirm international black solidarity, not to circumscribe Creole identity. The regionalism of today's Créolistes might have been received in that environment as something akin to tourist art, or kitsch. For a contemporary, critical view of the Créolistes that shows the extent to which they fall into the trap of tourist art, see Richard Price, *The Convict and the Colonel: A Story of Colonialism and Resistance in the Caribbean*, 2nd ed. (Durham, NC: Duke University Press, 2006).
27. Eldridge Cleaver, *Soul on Ice*, intro. by Maxwell Geismar (New York: McGraw-Hill, 1967), 99.
28. Ibid., 105.
29. Unpublished manuscript in the Léon-Gontran Damas archives at the Schomburg Center for Black Culture, Box #3/Folder: "Critical Studies." The manuscript is not dated but was probably written in the late 1960s.
30. The first African studies program was established at Howard University in 1954; Damas taught at Howard from 1973 to 1978. On this period, see also Richard Serrano, *Against the Postcolonial: 'Francophone' Writers at*

the Ends of French Empire (Lanham, MD: Rowman & Littlefield, 2005), 144–45.

31. The list of scholars who have sought to prove that Negritude inspired independence movements throughout the world is very long. Most recently, Nick Nesbitt reminds us that the works of Negritude had a "preeminent role in the awakening of black diasporic consciousness of this century"; see his account in Nesbitt, *Voicing Memory: History and Subjectivity in French Caribbean Literature* (Charlottesville: University of Virginia Press, 2003), 77.
32. Jacques Rancière, "Ten Theses on Politics," in *Dissensus: On Politics and Aesthetics*, trans. Steve Corcoran (New York: Continuum, 2010), 38. See also "The Paradoxes of Political Art": "Politics breaks with the sensory self-evidence of the 'natural' order that destines specific individuals and groups to occupy positions of rule or of being ruled, assigning them to private or public lives, pinning them down to a certain time and space, to specific 'bodies', that is to specific ways of being, seeing and saying. This 'natural' logic, a distribution of the invisible and visible, of speech and noise, pins bodies to 'their' places and allocates the private and the public to distinct 'parts'—this is the order of the police" (*Dissensus*, 139).
33. Jean-Paul Sartre, *Being and Nothingness*, trans. Hazel E. Barnes (New York: Washington Square Press, 1984), 432.
34. Hall, "Cultural Identity and Diaspora," 230.
35. Ibid.
36. Fred Moten, *In the Break: The Aesthetics of the Black Radical Tradition* (Minneapolis: University of Minnesota Press, 2003), 263.

INDEX

GPSR Authorized Representative: Easy Access System Europe, Mustamäe tee 50, 10621 Tallinn, Estonia, gpsr.requests@easproject.com

www.ingramcontent.com/pod-product-compliance
Lightning Source LLC
Chambersburg PA
CBHW020914310726
48980CB00011B/885/J

* 9 7 8 0 2 3 1 1 6 7 0 4 8 *